THE ARTS OF MANKIND

EDITED BY ANDRÉ MALRAUX
AND GEORGES SALLES

ANCIENT IRAN

ROMAN GHIRSHMAN

The Arts of
ANCIENT IRAN

*From its Origins
to the Time of Alexander the Great*

*Translated by Stuart Gilbert
and James Emmons*

GOLDEN PRESS NEW YORK

49 545

Library of Congress Catalog Card Number: 64-13072
Printed in France

CONTENTS

Preface
by Georges Salles

WHEN a student of the histories of Greece and of Persia compares their respective positions on the map, he may well wonder why and how it was that the destinies of two nations topographically so remote should have, in their greatest periods, so persistently intermingled.

Their physical aspects, too, are totally dissimilar. Greece may be described as a scatter of islands and ragged-edged peninsulas. From the shores of Ionia to the coast of Magna Graecia, from those of Africa to Pontus, the Hellenic world of the fifth century B.C. was composed of free cities loosely grouped in archipelagos, whose busy fleets criss-crossed incessantly an inner sea in which three continents were mirrored. 'Greece,' as a poet said, 'is a huge hand spread masterfully upon the waves.'

Unlike Greece, open on three sides to the sea, Persia is landlocked, a 'middle empire' as René Grousset has aptly described her. This is true not only geographically, but also for her population. Iran may have access, North and South, to the Caspian, the Aral Sea, the Black Sea and the Persian Gulf, but these act less as outlets than as barriers, and all commerce follows overland routes.

Though the centre of the Iranian Plateau, from East to West, is largely a desert region, its southern frontier served not only as a 'land-bridge' linking the Mesopotamian plain to the Indus-Ganges area, but also as a line of communication between the civilizations of Hither Asia and those of the Sino-Indian world. And on its northern boundary the Plateau joins up with the vast world of the Steppes, through gaps in the mountain ranges of Khorasan, Bactria and the Caucasus.

It is generally agreed today that it was through the passes of the Caucasus that the Aryans poured down into Iran in the course (or perhaps towards the close) of the last half of the second millennium B.C. One group settled on the Plateau, while another pressed forward through Afghanistan into the Indus and Ganges valleys.

But even though, because of its shape and geographical position, Iran acted as a 'land-bridge' between East and West, it was also the homeland of a culture of a high order when the Achaemenian empire supplanted the Assyro-Babylonian. Like the latter, and like all the Mesopotamian kingdoms which had followed one another in unbroken succession, Achaemenian Persia faced towards the West. The cradles of our civilization—the valley of the two rivers, the Tigris and the Euphrates, and the valley of the Nile—had from time immemorial been linked to each other by the 'fertile crescent' which runs first across the inland region, then along the Mediterranean coast, its contours defined by the courses of the Euphrates, the Orontes and the Jordan. Three millennia later Greece took over the torch of culture from Egypt, and Persia stepped into the place of Nineveh and Babylon. Thus the civilized world, half Hellenic and half Persian, formed, like the East-West civilization of the past, a diptych, whose hinge ran sometimes west and sometimes east of the Syro-Egyptian coastline.

It was here that during the fifth and fourth centuries B.C. the scenes of a new Iliad were enacted. Athens and Sparta successfully withstood the onslaughts of Darius and Xerxes who in attacking Greece aimed at establishing nothing short of a worldwide empire. A hundred years later the tables were turned. For the first and only time in her history Greece, united under Macedonian hegemony, turned her back on the sea and thrust forward into the East, taking over the imperial ambitions of the Achaemenids.

Alexander's prodigious adventure did not have the results he had counted on. At the close of his victorious campaign he sought to bring about the fusion of two worlds—not merely of two cultures, two States, two forms of government, but also of two races. This fusion was symbolized and consecrated by his marriage to the daughter of Darius III (Codomannus) and the union of 10,000 Greek soldiers with Iranian girls at the festivities accompanying the ceremony.

But his successors, the Seleucids, took little interest in Iran. The true heir of Alexander's grandiose conception was not Greece but Rome, whose fluctuating eastern frontier sometimes touched the Euphrates, but was never to cross it.

As Grousset has rightly pointed out, the Iranians became, in the heyday of the Achaemenids, the imperial race of Asia. Greece, so far as her political conceptions were concerned, never rose above the notion of the *polis*; the 'State' meant simply the 'City.' The Persians, however, built up an empire that was an organic whole, comprising many different races and languages, held together by an efficient central administration and protected by a well-equipped army against foreign invasions, in particular the constant menace of the bellicose nomads on their northern and eastern frontiers. The language Darius employs in the foundation charters of the palaces of Susa and Persepolis, and the message implicit in the mighty terraces and staircases, the pillars and reliefs in these great edifices erected for the annual celebration of the glories of the far-flung empire, set the tone of this 'benevolent despotism' and aimed at promoting a spirit of association rather than one of mere subservience.

During the ten centuries following Alexander's death at Babylon and ending with the Islamic invasion, two great imperial powers contended for worldwide dominion. In the Introduction to our volume dealing with Parthian and Sassanian art attention was drawn to the effects of this rivalry of Rome and Iran, extending to the world of forms and leading to the co–existence of a Greco-Iranian and a Greco-Roman art.

All was cast into the melting-pot by the Moslem invasion and conquest of the country in the seventh century A.D. Once more Semites dominated this part of the Near East, from which they had been ousted by Indo-Europeans in the period of the Achaemenian hegemony. In a forthcoming volume dealing with the arts of Islam it will be shown how the spirit of Iranian creative genius held its own despite the loss of temporal power. Here we will briefly indicate some of the formative elements which went to the shaping of that genius.

Differing in this from the Mesopotamian valley, where traces of the earliest organized human societies dating back to the fourth millennium B.C. have been discovered, the near-by Iranian plateau has not yielded any evidence of communal life previous to the relatively late period when Persia supplanted Nineveh and Babylon.

The proto-Iranian era may be said to have lasted until the rise to power of the Achaemenids, for it is only then that documentary evidence relating to the history of the period becomes available. True, mention was made in records of the ninth century B.C. of the presence of 'Medes and Persians.' But a form of writing peculiar to the dwellers on the Plateau and adapted to the language they spoke did not emerge until three centuries later.

This delay was due presumably to the material difficulties with which the early settlers had to contend. Even today half the area is a salt desert and the other is made productive only by artificial irrigation, an elaborate network of canals.

Trapezoidal in form, this gigantic Plateau, situated between the valleys of the Tigris and Euphrates on the West and that of the Indus on the East, is encircled by great mountain ranges, only parts of which are included in present-day Iran. Persia proper may be said to begin at an altitude of over 3000 feet and its chief towns are at an even greater height: Teheran at 3800 feet, Meshed at 3300, Shiraz at 5200, Tabriz at 4400 and Isfahan at nearly 5400 feet. In the centre of the Plateau lies a great depression, 1800 feet above sea level at its lowest point. As for the climate, Clément Huart has summed it up succinctly: 'Persia is the driest place on earth.'

How singular was the lot of this land so poverty-stricken yet so near a valley which for three or four millennia served as a sort of Royal Road by which man made his gradual ascent to a high state of civilization! Near though it was, the Plateau was little affected by what was taking place in the Mesopotamian plain. When the dwellers in the Tigris and Euphrates valleys began to take an interest in their neighbours, it was towards the West that they turned, and there they came in contact with peoples who, like themselves, were developing an organized society. Distance notwithstanding, they entered into relations with the populations of the Mediterranean coast and Egypt. The only exception was Elam, which at the beginning of the third millennium brought to Sialk, on the edge of the great central desert, certain elements of the Mesopotamian way of life, notably a system of writing. 'But with the abandonment of this trading station,' writes Dr Ghirshman, 'the proto-Elamite script went out of use.' Even the use of writing was forgotten—surprising as this may seem, considering its practical advantages—and not resumed until the Achaemenian period.

The great originality of Dr Ghirshman's work lies in the fact that in his close analysis of the foreign influences which contributed to the evolution of life and art on the Plateau he does not look to the West but locates them, rather, on its northern fringe, in Trans-caucasia and Transoxiana. As a result of its constant intercourse with the nomadic peoples of the Steppes, Iran took over from them, *inter alia*, many elements of the animal art which was their 'speciality.'

The oldest settlement so far known on the Plateau was at Sialk near Kashan in Central Media. The excavation of this site has been carried out by Dr Ghirshman, who dates the first traces of human occupation to the fifth millennium B.C. However, what he names the art of Sialk did not develop until some three thousand years later, at the end of the second and the beginning of the first millennium B.C., when Aryan tribes made their appearance on the Plateau to which they gave their name.

Then, there took place in Eurasia one of those great upheavals which, setting up a chain reaction, profoundly modify the maps of continents. We have a modern equivalent in the wave of 'decolonization' which has brought independence to so many countries hitherto under foreign rule. But for the period and places we are concerned with here, it was not a 'liberation' but the sudden peopling of a region until then but sparsely inhabited. Along with gradual infiltration there also came, it seems, a mass migration into Iran. In any case this was certainly the time when the forbears of the present inhabitants established themselves in the region. Sedentaries are always more or less direct descendants of former nomads. From now on the Plateau was permanently occupied by a racial group that carried its civilization to a height equalling, to say the least, that of the dwellers in the Mesopotamian plain.

'The art of Sialk and its successors—at Khurvin, Hasanlu, Amlash and in Luristan—was an integral part of this new culture,' writes Dr Ghirshman. And he goes on to say that 'it is in the art of Sialk that we glimpse the beginnings of what was to be the art of the Medes and Persians, in other words all the artistic aptitudes that the Aryan tribes recently settled on the Plateau had brought with them to their new home.'

In what respect did the art of Sialk prefigure that of the Medes? Up to what point was Achaemenian art to draw on the heritage of its nomad past? To what extent did the 'sedentary' Achaemenian art join forces with the art of its still nomadic neighbours and kinsmen, the Scythians? We can see that the author is haunted by these questions all through this volume; again and again he bids us turn our eyes towards the northern frontier, to the regions around Lake Urmia and Lake Van, the kingdoms of Mannai and Urartu. Elsewhere he draws our attention to the south-east corner of the Caspian where Soviet archaeologists have brought to light a civilization in every way similar to that of Sialk. Such, in brief, is the angle from which Dr Ghirshman examines the slow, belated growth of an authentically Iranian art.

There is another aspect of the author's approach to which we would direct the reader's attention. The second part of this volume is devoted to a study of the repercussions of Proto-Iranian and Iranian art outside the frontiers of Iran. Of particular interest is the penultimate chapter, dealing with 'The Irano-Urartian *Koine* and the West.' 'It was,' Dr Ghirshman tells us, 'at the time when the kingdom of Urartu was taking form that the Greeks were gradually implanting colonies on the coasts of Asia Minor.' And, at a later page, he points out that, given the fact that Greek art from the third quarter of the eighth century B.C. on was no longer inaccessible to Oriental influences, Iranian art must certainly be included among the art currents that were finding their way to Greece.

This is followed by a succinct account of the changes that took place in the eighth century, both in the Geometric art of Greece and in the art of Sialk. New rhythms were systematized and, at the same time, attempts were made to render plastic values. 'This applies equally to Greek and to Iranian art.'

In examining the factors that went to the shaping of Iranian art we must not overlook the well-nigh unique quality of the light on the Plateau, due both to altitude and to the absence of moisture in the air. The centre of the Plateau is not only 'the driest place on earth'; it is also bathed in a light of a purity unequalled in any other part of the world. A traveller who enters Iran by the southern approaches, starting from the Persian Gulf, and passes through Kazerun, Shiraz, Persepolis, Isfahan and Qum on his way to Teheran, cannot fail to be struck by the progressive changes in the landscape. Everything around him seems to be losing solidity, weight and density, and being transmuted more and more into a world of light, a haze of broken gleams, rose-red, white and azure blue. So much so that the mountains seem to float in air and one almost fancies one could thrust one's hand through them without encountering the least resistance.

Here there is nothing 'picturesque.' Details are merged into an all-pervasive radiance, over which the gaze roves freely and whose colours seem as insubstantial as a sunbeam. Nowhere else does one get so potent a sensation of being transported into an ethereal world, a realm of flawless purity.

How natural, then, that this should have been the homeland of Zoroastrianism, which saw in Ahuramazda the greatest of the gods! Lord of the sky and light, he is symbolized by fire. But 'he may not have images.'

And thus one realizes the aptness of the words used by Masson-Oursel when he speaks of Amitabha, Infinite Light, as being 'that *diaphanous luminosity* worshipped by the Iranians.'

TABLE OF ARCHAEOLOGICAL SITES

I - PERSIA *(Protohistoric, Median and Achaemenian Periods)*

CHRONOLOGY OF DISCOVERIES AND EXCAVATIONS

1836 - Bisutun
1851 - Susa
1878 - Persepolis
1884 - Susa
1897 - Susa
    Excavations resumed
1902 - Tepe Musiyan
1905 - Anau
1905 - Pasargadae
1909 - Rayy
1913 - Hamadan
1913 - Bushire
1928 - Pasargadae
    Excavations resumed
1928 - Discovery of
    the Luristan Bronzes
1931 - Persepolis
    Excavations resumed
1931 - Tepe Giyan
1931 - Turang Tepe
1931 - Tepe Hissar
1932 - Tal-i-Bakun
1932 - Kasr-i-Abu Nasr
1932 - Tal-i-Iblis
1933 - Shah Tepe Buzurg
1933 - Tepe Jamshidi

1933 - Tepe Bad Hora
1933 - Tepe Sialk
1934 - Chashmeh-Ali
1934 - Surkh Dum
1935 - Istakhr
1935 - Naqsh-i-Rustam
1936 - Nad-i-Ali
1936 - Choga Zambil
1936 - Hasanlu
1940 - Persepolis
    Excavations resumed
1946 - Susa
    Excavations resumed
1947 - Hasanlu
    Excavations resumed
1947 - Ziwiyeh Treasure
1948 - Masjid-i-Sulaiman
1948 - Tal-i-Ghazir
1948 - Geoy Tepe
1948 - Bisutun
1949 - Tang-i-Pabda
1949 - Pasargadae
    Excavations resumed
1949 - Gar-i-Kamarband
1950 - Khurvin

1951 - Tal-i-Jari
1951 - Gar-i-Hutu
1951 - Pasargadae-Perse-
    polis-Shiraz Region
1951 - Choga Zambil
    Excavations resumed
1954 - Khurvin
    Excavations resumed
1956 - Tal-i-Bakun
    Excavations resumed
1957 - Hasanlu
    Excavations resumed
1958 - Island of Kharg
1958 - Tal-i-Jari
1959 - Takht-i-Sulaiman
1959 - Kermanshah Region
1959 - Turang Tepe
    Excavations resumed
1959 - Esmailabad
1960 - Yarim Tepe
1960 - Yanik Tepe
1961 - Choga Mish
1961 - Pasargadae
    Excavations resumed
1961 - Rudbar and Marlik

COUNTRIES SPONSORING THE EXPEDITIONS

B. = Belgium - F. = France - G. = Germany - G.B. = Great Britain - Ir. = Iran
J. = Japan - S. = Sweden - U.S. = United States

Dates for each site indicate when excavations began and when they came to an end.
Dates followed by a dash indicate that excavations are still in progress.

Anau: 1905. U.S.
Bisutun: 1836-41. G.B.
    1948-49. U.S.
Bushire: 1913. F.
Chashmeh-Ali: 1934-36.
    U.S.
Choga Mish: 1961-. U.S.
Choga Zambil: 1936. F.
    1951-62. F.
Esmailabad: 1959. Ir.
Gar-i-Hutu: 1951. U.S.

Gar-i-Kamarband: 1949-
    51. U.S.
Geoy Tepe: 1948. G.B.
Hamadan: 1913. F.
Hasanlu: 1936. G.B.
    1947. Ir.
Hasanlu: 1957-. U.S.
Istakhr: 1935. U.S.
Kasr-i-Abu Nasr: 1932-34.
    U.S.
Kharg: 1958-60. F.

Kermanshah Region:
    1959-60. U.S.
Khurvin: 1950. Ir.
    1954. B.
Marlik: 1961-. Ir.
Masjid-i-Sulaiman: 1948. F.
Nad-i-Ali: 1936. F.
Naqsh-i-Rustam: 1935-39.
    U.S.
Pasargadae: 1905. U.S.
    1928. U.S.
    1949. Ir.
    1961-. G.B.

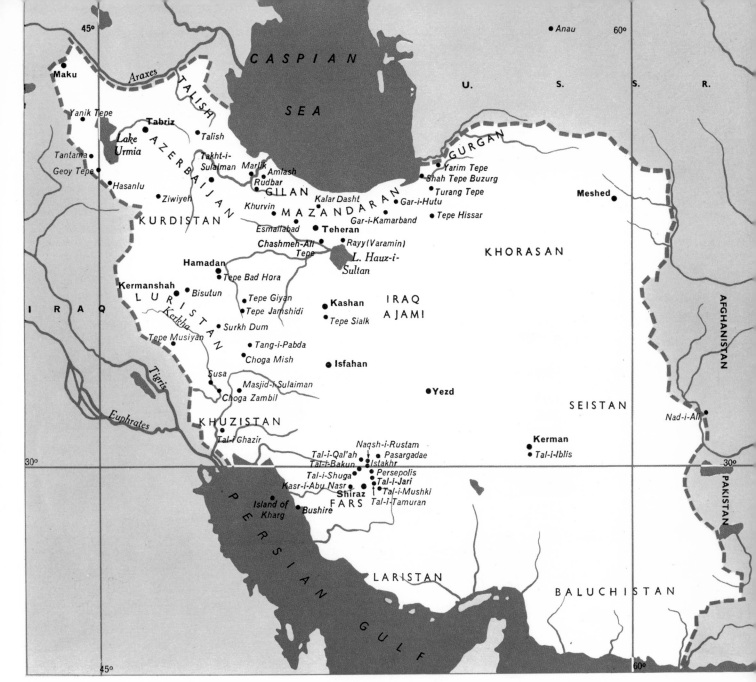

MAP OF DISCOVERIES: PROTO-IRANIAN, MEDIAN AND ACHAEMENID PERSIA

Persepolis: 1878. G.
    1931-39. U.S.
    1940-. Ir.
Rayy: 1909. F.
Rudbar: 1961-. Ir.
Shah Tepe Buzurg: 1933. S.
Surkh Dum: 1934-38. U.S.
Susa: 1851-53. G.B.
   1884-86. F.
   1897-. F.

Takht-i-Sulaiman: 1959. G.
Tal-i-Bakun: 1932. U.S.
    1956. J.
Tal-i-Ghazir: 1948. U.S.
Tal-i-Iblis: 1932-33. G.B.
Tal-i-Jari: 1951-55. B.
   1958. J.
Tal-i-Mushki: 1951-55. B.
Tal-i-Qal'ah: 1951-55. B.
Tal-i-Shuga: 1951-55. B.
Tal-i-Tamuran: 1951-55. B.

Tang-i-Pabda: 1949. F.
Tepe Bad Hora: 1933. F.
Tepe Giyan: 1931-32. F.
Tepe Hissar: 1931-32. U.S.
Tepe Jamshidi: 1933. F.
Tepe Musiyan: 1902-03. F.
Tepe Sialk: 1933-37. F.
Turang Tepe: 1931. U.S
    1959-. F.
Yanik Tepe: 1960-. G.B.
Yarim Tepe: 1960-. G.B.
Ziwiyeh (chance find): 1947.

MAP OF DISCOVERIES: PARTHIAN AND SASSANIAN IRAN

TABLE OF DISCOVERIES

II - IRAN *(Parthian and Sassanian Periods)*

CHRONOLOGY OF DISCOVERIES AND EXCAVATIONS

1673 - Bisutun	1840 - Taq-i-Bustan	1896 - Kasr-i-Shirin
1811 - Naqsh-i-Rajab	1841 - Tang-i-Sarwak	1896 - Sar-i-Pul
1811 - Naqsh-i-Rustam	1851 - Sarvistan	1896 - Taq-i-Bustan
1840 - Kasr-i-Shirin	1877 - Barm-i-Dilak	1900 - Jiruft
1840 - Sar-i-Pul	1880 - Nurabad	1910 - Kasr-i-Shirin

1910 - Sar-i-Pul
1910 - Taq-i-Bustan
1924 - Firuzabad
1925 - Karku
1925 - Kuh-i-Khwaja
1926 - Qal'a-i-Dukhtar
1929 - Sar Meshed
1931 - Tepe Hissar
1931 - Narishan
1932 - Kasr-i-Abu Nasr
1933 - Tang-i-Karam

1933 - Darabgerd
1933 - Naqsh-i-Rustam
    Excavations resumed
1933 - Sarvistan
1933 - Firuzabad
1934 - Nishapur
1935 - Istakhr
1935 - Bishapur
1935 - Shami
1935 - Tang-i-Sarwak
1939 - Kazvin

1942 - Nurabad
1946 - Susa
    Excavations resumed
1948 - Bard-i-Nishandah
1950 - Eiwan-i-Kerkha
1952 - Tang-i-Sarwak
1956 - Khurkha
1957 - Tang-i-Chak-Chak
1959 - Takht-i-Sulaiman
1960 - Kuh-i-Khwaja
    Excavations resumed

COUNTRIES SPONSORING THE EXPEDITIONS

B. = Belgium - F. = France - G. = Germany - G.B. = Great Britain - Ir. = Iran
It. = Italy - U.S. = United States

Dates for each site indicate when excavations began and when they came to an end.
Dates followed by a dash indicate that excavations are still in progress.

Bard-i-Nishandah: 1949. F.
Barm-i-Dilak: 1877. G.
Bishapur: 1935-41. F.
Bisutun: 1913. F.
Darabgerd: 1933-34. G.B.
Eiwan-i-Kerkha: 1950. F.
Firuzabad: 1924. G. and F.
    1933-34. G.B.
Istakhr: 1935. U.S.
Jiruft: 1900. U.S.
Karku: 1925. G.
Kasr-i-Abu Nasr: 1932-34.
    U.S.
Kasr-i-Shirin: 1840-41. F.
    1896. F.
    1910-20. G.
Khurkha: 1956. Ir.

Kuh-i-Khwaja: 1925. G.
    1960-. It.
Naqsh-i-Rajab: 1811-12.
    G.B.
Naqsh-i-Rustam: 1811-18.
    G.B.
    1933-39.
    U.S.
Narishan: 1931-33. U.S.
Nishapur: 1934-36. U.S.
Nurabad: 1880. G.B.
    1942. G. and F.
Sar-i-Pul: 1840-41. F.
    1896. F.
    1910-20. G.
Sar Meshed: 1929. G.
Sarvistan: 1851. F.

Sarvistan: 1933-34. G.B.
Shami: 1935-36. G.B.
Susa: 1897-. F.
Takht-i-Sulaiman: 1959. G.
Tang-i-Chak-Chak: 1957.
    B.
Tang-i-Karam: 1933-34.
    G.B.
Tang-i-Sarwak: 1841. F.
    1935-36.
    G.B.
    1952. G.B.
Taq-i-Bustan: 1840-41. F.
    1896. F.
    1910-20. G.
Tepe Hissar: 1931-33. U.S.

A mon maître et Ami,
le Docteur Georges CONTENAU

« *I wish to extend my very sincere thanks to
Madame Clemence DUPRAT, whose collaboration was
all the more precious as I was away from Paris when
this book was in the making.* »

« *And my affectionate gratitude to my wife, whose
devotion was only measured in terms of long days and
weeks of relentless work.* »

R.G.

2 - SIALK. FRAGMENT OF PAINTED POTTERY: HUMAN FACE (10th-9th CENTURIES B.C.) — TEHERAN MUSEUM

INTRODUCTION

FROM the fifth millennium B.C. on, we can trace a steady progress in material culture on the Iranian Plateau. This progress, however, was not uniform but subject to local conditions, differences of climate and the lie of the land, contacts with neighbouring peoples, migrations and invasions.

It is at Sialk, south of Teheran, in central Media, on the edge of the great desert, that the earliest traces of human settlement in the plain have been uncovered.

The first dwelling-places were mere huts made of branches or in pisé, but very soon a new type of building material was used: first crude lumps of mud dried in the sun, then flat, rectangular mud-bricks shaped in moulds. The inner walls of these houses were coated with red paint. The dead were buried in a contracted position under the floor of beaten earth, along with more or less elaborate grave goods.

The basic elements of human economy were already in existence, and with them the beginnings of trade. To ensure safe delivery of merchandise, or to indicate ownership, seals impressed on wads of clay were brought into use. These seals served as stoppers of jars or were attached by cords to bales of goods. Geometric decoration was the general rule in this early phase of the craft of seal-engraving.

←— 1 - TURANG TEPE (GURGAN). NUDE GODDESS WEARING JEWELLERY
(2nd MILLENNIUM B.C.) — UNIVERSITY MUSEUM, PHILADELPHIA

Tools were mostly of stone; metal tools came only gradually into use. Meanwhile craftsmen took to making toilet articles such as mirrors and large pins with hemispherical heads, while more costly materials were employed for jewellery.

It is in bone-carvings and pottery that we find the earliest manifestations of artistic taste. Pottery long continued to be made by hand and this industry was carried on at home by the woman of the house, 'guardian of the hearth.' This is the explanation usually given for the belated appearance of the potter's wheel—no earlier than the fourth millennium B.C. With the invention of the wheel there was a marked advance in the quality and variety of the pottery, which provides the archaeologist with the most rewarding source of information about the beginnings of Iranian art.

Thanks to these manifold activities, the material culture of Iran, in its prehistoric phase, achieved and maintained for many centuries a remarkably advanced domestic economy, though we find no sign as yet of the emergence of large communities. It was in that natural extension of Mesopotamia, the Susiana plain, that in the early third millennium B.C. the first fully organized state, Elam, made its appearance. The abrupt incursion of an essentially Mesopotamian culture on the Iranian Plateau, following on an enlargement of the sphere of Elamite influence after a political conquest (effected, doubtless, for economic reasons), led to the introduction of writing and the use of clay tablets and cylinder seals. Sialk is the only site on the Plateau that has yielded written records previous to the Achaemenian period. But with the abandonment of this trading station the proto-Elamite script went out of use.

Encouraged by the success of the national Elamite revolt against the Akkadian dynasty, two neighbouring hill peoples, the Lullubi and the Guti, swept down from the high valleys and invaded Babylonia. Holding the main roads into Western Iran, these mountaineers controlled the movements of trading caravans. They came as enemies but established themselves as middlemen, and in their dealings with the Babylonians came under the civilizing influence of the peoples of the plain. This is proved by the bas-reliefs carved by two of their kings on rocks in the Sar-i-Pul-i-Zohab region, one of which (Stele of Huren-Sheikh-Khan) is clearly inspired by the Stele of Naram-Sin. More important for our present purpose, however, is the bas-relief commemorating the victory of Annubanini, King of the Lullubi, to whom the goddess Ninni is leading a string of captives. Despite obvious resemblances to Mesopotamian art, the spirit of this work is definitely Iranian; many generations of princes, in the long course of the history of Iran, copied this prototype in all parts of the Plateau. The idea of the Iranian rock-cut relief was thus launched by the pictorial record of a brilliant feat of arms, placed high on the mountain-side in full view of the caravans that passed below.

Very different was the slow, peaceful penetration in the north-east of the Plateau, evidenced at Hissar, near Damghan. When we see how at one settlement after another the number of painted vases diminished, to be replaced by a black or dark grey pottery completely alien to the Plateau, and if we interpret this change in human terms, it seems clear that a new culture, coming from abroad, must have modified the age-old structure of the indigenous population. As to the origins of this new culture and the people who brought it to Iran, we suggested some ten years ago (*Iran*, p. 46) that 'it seemed to have come from the plains of Russian Turkestan or perhaps from even further afield, near the heart of Central Asia.' This theory has been corroborated recently by the discovery at Zamin Baba, in the Bukhara oasis, of a settlement having much in common with that at Hissar.

During the latter half of the second millennium all trace of human activity disappears on several prehistoric sites in the north-east and western regions of the Plateau. At Giyan, however, the Asianic painted-pottery culture seems to have continued. But there were some notable changes throwing light on the new streams of influence traversing Iran at the time: western influences associated with the migrations of Hurrians, Kassites and Mitannians in the area between the Mediterranean and the Zagros mountains; and others coming from the East, at the beginning of the rivalry between Babylon and Assur—which, it seems, severed all contacts between the Zagros and the West.

It was from the 'mountain crescent,' which hitherto had acted as a shield protecting the dwellers on the Plateau from the mobile peoples of the north and north-east, that the tribes of the outlying areas started their advance, under pressure from peoples in their rear. These invaders overran Sialk, where the almost exclusively grey-black pottery found in Cemetery A testifies to their presence. At Giyan, though retaining its characteristic shapes and texture, this pottery was more or less submerged by survivals of the previous period.

Shortly afterwards, another wave of immigrants replaced the grey-black pottery civilization with a new, highly distinctive culture, that of Cemetery B at Sialk. This culture, we believe, was that of the first Iranian tribes to penetrate (about 1000 B.C.) the western districts of Iran.

There is no means of knowing the exact date of the arrival of the Iranians on the Plateau now named after them. Our view that it took place round about the year 1000 B.C. is borne out by the fact that the first mention of 'Medes and Persians' as forming part of the population of north-western Iran occurs in the second half of the ninth century B.C., in the annals of the Assyrian kings.

Several ways of access were open to invaders of the Plateau. The gap in the mountains near Lake Urmia is assumed to have been one of the main routes taken by invasions coming from the east and north-east. But recent Soviet excavations have brought to light a civilization, closely resembling that of Sialk, which flourished in the flat country near the south-east corner of the Caspian Sea, north of the river Atrek; and this plain, according to geographers, may well have served as a second way of access to the Plateau.

What, then, was the route taken by the Iranians? According to al-Biruni, Siyavush, the legendary king glorified by Firdausi in his *Book of Kings*, came from Iran and founded the first dynasty of the kingdom of Chorasmia. This suggests that the Iranians crossed the Caucasus by the same route as that followed by the Scythians and Cimmerians in their invasions two or three centuries later. Against this view, endorsed by some authorities, others maintain that the Iranians entered the country by the north-east, in the neighbourhood of the Aral Sea. The same route, it is thought, was taken by the Indo-Aryans whose migration into India has been proved by recent discoveries not to antedate the period 1200-1000 B.C., and whose most ancient remains show marked affinities with the material culture of the earliest Iranian settlers on the Plateau. In view of these facts a third hypothesis has been advanced: that the Iranians used *both* the routes encircling the Caspian Sea.

The eclipse of Sialk for nearly two thousand years and the total extinction of Hissar point to a widespread upheaval, towards the end of the second millennium B.C., in which the age-old conflict between the nomadic or semi-nomadic world and the sedentary peoples must certainly have played a part.

Roving tribes of warrior-horsemen, accompanied by their women, children and flocks, forced their way into regions whose fertile or cultivable tracts were already occupied by an indigenous population. Their task was made easier by the division of the country into many petty states. We may surmise that the new arrivals enlisted as mercenaries in the service of local chieftains and were rewarded by grants of small domains, in return for military service rendered in times of war. Then, little by little, they ousted the chieftains they had served. There was now no question—as there had been in earlier times, in the case of the Hurrians, Mitannians and Kassites—of their being absorbed into the autochthonous Asianic population. By dint of slow but steady infiltration they established themselves as masters, to a greater or lesser extent, in various parts of the Plateau. Prehistoric villages were gradually transformed into fortified towns, and the transition from an agricultural, peasant way of life to residence in *oikoi* under the domination of a chieftain or prince, consummated the Iranization of the occupied areas.

The significance of the contacts of this new, progressive civilization with the lands of the Ancient East—Elam, Babylonia, Assyria, Urartu—whose cultures were superior to those of the native populations of the Plateau, can be fully appreciated when we observe the considerable part these contacts played in the formation of the first Iranian State.

Repeated occupations of their country by the Assyrians, as well as Urartian pressure, led the Median peoples, hitherto split up among dozens of tribal chiefs, to unite under Deioces (Daiukku) and his descendants, thereby founding at the end of the eighth century B.C. a kingdom with which that of the Persians was later to be incorporated.

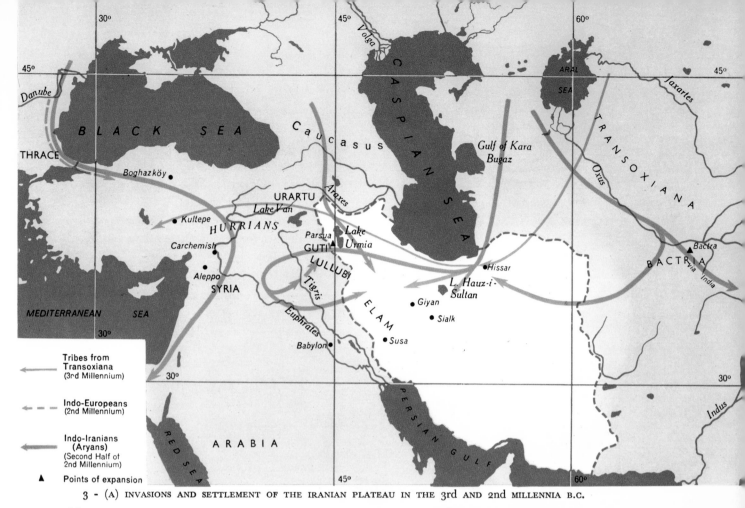

3 - (A) INVASIONS AND SETTLEMENT OF THE IRANIAN PLATEAU IN THE 3RD AND 2ND MILLENNIA B.C.

3 - (B) INVASIONS AND SETTLEMENT OF THE IRANIAN PLATEAU IN THE LATE 2ND AND EARLY 1st MILLENNIUM B.C.

5

The art of Sialk and its successors—at Khurvin, Hasanlu, Amlash and in Luristan—was an integral part of this new culture, which introduced a new system of town-planning as well as previously unknown funerary customs. Indeed the ideas it sponsored were as foreign to the country's past as they were rich in intimations of the future of Iranian art. For it is in the art of Sialk that we glimpse the beginnings of what was to be the art of the Medes and Persians, in other words all the artistic skills that the Aryan tribes recently settled on the Plateau had brought with them to their new home. These early artists had an innate feeling for decorative effect, especially for animal forms, which from the very outset were a fertile source of inspiration for the ceramist, suggesting both the shapes and the plastic ornamentation of his main product and also giving ideas for its painted decoration.

Roman GHIRSHMAN, 1963.

PART ONE

5 - SIALK. TERRACE OF UNBAKED BRICKS AND STONE (10th-9th CENTURIES B.C.)

I

PROTOHISTORIC IRANIAN ART

CEMETERY B AT SIALK

AT the southernmost point of the prehistoric mound of Sialk, whose summit had been levelled in order to increase the area available for building, was constructed a massive polygonal terrace covering some 3,000 square yards. Standing about 65 feet above the plain, this terrace served, presumably, as the site of the ruler's abode (no trace of which has survived). The use of alternating courses of unbaked brick and dry stone to ensure the stability of a mass of masonry anchored on the debris of earlier dwellings was unknown on the Plateau before the first millennium B.C. Another innovation was the division of the area into an upper town where the nobility resided and a lower town for the populace.

This conception of a special residence assigned to the chieftain, and of his relations with his subjects, anticipated the idea of royalty, a later development. It was to leave its mark on the growth of urban life, when fortified towns of this kind became seats of principalities and capitals of kingdoms, even of empires.

At the same time there was a marked change in the method of burial—generally regarded as evidence of the replacement of an earlier population by a new one. Graves were no longer dug under the floors of houses. Instead, down in the plain, west of the hill on which stood the lower and upper towns, both surrounded by ring walls with towers and redans, there now developed a 'city of the dead,' a vast necropolis in which over two hundred tombs were dug.

← 4 - SIALK. CEMETERY B. 'GABLE-ROOF' TOMBS
(10th-9th CENTURIES B.C.) — IN SITU

The graves of the wealthy class and members of the nobility were mere trenches cut in the soil, but over them, once the body had been buried along with a more or less large quantity of grave furniture, mounds were built up, protected by heavy stone or terracotta slabs placed in such a way as to form a gable-roof, giving the grave the shape of a North European house. This idea of providing the dead man (or his ashes) with a resting place resembling the house he had lived in was totally at variance with the burial practices of the dwellers in prehistoric Iran. Moreover, the shape given the tomb, which must have come as a surprise in a land where roofs had always been flat, may well provide a clue to the regions from which the new inhabitants of the Plateau had emigrated. We shall have occasion to recur to this point when, in discussing the Irano-Urartian *koine*, the common cultural heritage of Iranians and Urartians, the similarity of the methods of town-planning in the two countries will be pointed out. Suffice it to note here the survival of the roof with a double slope in the tomb of Cyrus at Pasargadae, whose similarities with the temple of Musasir point clearly to an Urartian origin.

As for the few surviving vestiges of architectural decoration, there is no knowing just where they figured or the purpose they served. All are in terracotta and were found, not in the cemetery, but on the great terrace, where they were brought to light when its surface was being cleared. Some of these fragments consist of fantastic animals, modelled in the round; though the style is highly simplified and primitive, they do not lack expressive power. Also found here were a number of thin plaques whose decorative motifs reproduce those on the painted vases and those engraved on stone. All these pieces evidence a taste for lavish ornamentation, amounting to a *horror vacui*.

Cemetery B at Sialk, with its graves of rich as well as poor folk, shows that the social system was already fully organized, with a sharp differentiation between classes. The iconographical and other characteristics of the objects found there not only give us an idea of the way of life prevailing in this fortified town, but also show that the early centuries of the first millennium were a transitional period; though iron had come into general use, objects in copper and bronze were still being produced in large quantities. The personal weapons and trappings owned by the horsemen in the prince's suite were made indifferently of iron or bronze. Gold seems to have been unknown to the townsfolk of Sialk, even the richest. The jewellery, mostly in silver and occasionally in bronze, was always very thin and simply decorated, often with granulations. The men wore torques and leather helmets with wrought silver plaques sewn on as decoration; the women, braided hair ornaments. A special type of ear-drop in metal or terracotta seems to imitate a bunch of grapes, and the pins almost always end in a gazelle's or a lion's head.

But the objects found in greatest numbers, and the most revealing ones, come from the potters' workshops. There are no indications that this pottery derived from the ancient traditions which presumably survived on the Plateau—save for the use of the oven and the potter's wheel. For everything is new: the consistency of the paste, the method of firing, the special colour of the glaze, the nature of the painted or modelled decoration, the compositional schemes, the way in which themes having a symbolic or funerary significance are treated.

The most characteristic piece is a large terracotta jug, probably copied from a metal prototype [479]*. This is a fully plastic work, for the craftsman's chief concern was to give the jug the aspect of a bird. Made to contain a liquid leaving a deposit, it is fitted with a 'pocket' like a bird's crop at the beginning of the spout. Skilfully adapted to the form of the container, the painted ornamentation in purplish red around the spout and the 'pocket' consists of a sort of collarette of triangles, producing the effect of a feathered ruff or a pair of wings. To stress the resemblance to

6 - SIALK. PAINTED VASE (10th-9th CENT. B.C.) — TEHERAN MUSEUM

the bird he used as his model, the potter has left, just under the beak-like spout, two pale patches on which, with two circular brushstrokes, he indicated a pair of eyes. We cannot say what precisely was the role assigned the bird in the funerary rites of Sialk, but there can be no question of the symbolic purpose of its figuration on so many of the libation vases found on this site.

The purely decorative elements are placed on the otherwise empty surface of the belly of the vase. Geometric motifs (chequer patterns, sun-wheels, circles containing crosses, rayed rosettes) are set out on contrasted planes, almost always in conjunction with forms of wild or domestic, sometimes fabulous animals (bulls, horses, ibexes, some of which are winged). Vegetation was not, it seems, included in the decorative repertoire, and the human figure is—to the best of our knowledge—found on three vases only, of two of which only sherds have survived.

* Numbers thus indicated refer to the illustrations grouped together in the Appendix (p. 374).

11

The lay-out of the decorations is strictly regulated. Animals are painted at the bottom of the belly, near the base of the vase, which hitherto had always been left plain. The reason for this is evident. Bound up with the shape and usage of the vase, the decoration had to display its most ornate portion when the vessel was tilted and its contents slowly poured out; then the animals circling the under-belly and the base itself could be seen to full advantage. The geometric patterns tend to cluster round the neck. Though the linear design tallies with the essentially static conception of space characteristic of Oriental art, the rhythms of the figuration do not always keep to the Oriental tradition of employing a continuous, 'endless' motif. Figures are placed in open spaces, separated by empty passages and the artist, exploiting the freedom of expression these permit, introduces images deriving from a new source of inspiration, the art of the indigenous textiles. Though this 'textile' mode of presentation tells against verisimilitude and stresses the unrealistic nature of the themes employed, it also demonstrates the freshness and spontaneity of this art, so rich in promise for the future.

A close examination of the vase in the Kofler-Truniger Collection, Lucerne, may help to an understanding of the general ideas governing the painted decorations of Sialk pottery. The range of geometric forms is somewhat restricted. Apart from a double collarette of 'feathers' intersected by a row of hatched rectangles and triangles linked together at their tips, the belly of the vase has no ornaments other than two eight-petalled rosettes, separating a man from a lion, and a cross in a painted square. The man is posed with his head and limbs in side view, turned to the right, while his waist and torso are shown in front view. He has an aquiline profile and a long beard, the place for an eye and an ear are left unpainted, as is that of the neck, crossed by two horizontal lines. His plaited hair, loosely floating in the air, forms a hooked curl. His close-fitting upper garment is indicated by six vertical stripes, the trousers and boots

7 - SIALK. PAINTED VASE: WARRIOR-HUNTER (10th-9th CENT. B.C.) — PRIVATE COLLECTION, LUCERNE

being merely outlined. The shoulders are broad and stalwart, and the arms disproportionately short. With his left hand he grips a spear and with his right a big rectangular shield with a chequerwork decoration. Such a shield was obviously *de rigueur* when hunting lions on foot, as is evidenced both by Assyrian monumental sculpture and by the Ziwiyeh ivories. The man wears in his belt a short sword with a round pommel; the scabbard, surprisingly wide at the level of the hilt, shows that this weapon was probably an *akinakes*.

The nearly cylindrical body of the lion is essentially schematic. The eye, jaws, nostrils and ear, however, are more realistically treated, and add to the impression of ferocity conveyed by the gaping mouth. Nor does the unnatural leanness of the legs diminish the sense of feral power conveyed by a 'gesture' that was destined to be widely adopted in the ancient world, notably by the Greeks, who always represented an attacking lion raising one of its forelegs and brandishing it at its foe. In the present case the painter has emphasized the ferocity of the animal by clearly delineating the claws.

The most original feature of this technique is the skill with which the artist has adjusted the design to the shape of the vase. But he has not succeeded in imparting to the composition the sense of movement essential to a hunting scene intended to be lifelike, and he obviously felt qualms about depicting an actual combat between man and beast. True, he evokes a lion-hunt, but he visualizes it in general terms; action is excluded and symbols—abstractions—do duty for reality. Does the scene depict some mythical hero, an Iranian Heracles, slaying lions? We question this, and favour a more realistic interpretation. A funerary vase, used for libations at the burial of some warrior who was also a mighty hunter, might well commemorate one of his exploits. In that case we have here the first of those Iranian funerary memorials which, whether in the form of wall paintings or carved in stone, served to immortalize the memory of the dead.

8 - SIALK. PAINTED VASE: ROARING LION (10th-9th CENT. B.C.) — PRIVATE COLLECTION, LUCERNE

Another scene of the life of a Sialk warrior figures on a potsherd found in the course of our excavations; it represents a war-dance rather like the Greek Pyrrhic dances and conveys a sense of movement associated with the shape of the vase itself and the figures adjusted to it. Here nothing can be isolated without impairing the organic unity of the whole. The same is true of the image of a man riding a winged horse, symbol of Death carrying the deceased to his last abode.

Doubtless there was likewise a precise significance in the motifs used for decorating a group of jugs: horses' protomes[480] bending over the orifice or placed erect at the beginning of the spout. There are also human heads moulded in relief, 'cut short at the chin,' and presented frontally, with staring eyes. All are guardians of the holy water contained in the bird-vase.

In some of these symbolic effigies the figuration is explicit enough to suggest a possible interpretation. Thus on a woman's head found in the course of our excavations at Sialk and skilfully combined with the bird figure embodied in the vase itself, the painter was evidently at pains to depict exactly the oval of the face, the eyes, mouth, nose, a line of hair between the eyebrows and the adornments of the coiffure. Whom, one wonders, does this woman represent? Can it be that some notion of 'Harpies' preying on the dead was already haunting the imagination of the Iranians of the protohistoric period? True, no specific mention of such beings can be found in the written records of the ancient religion

SIALK. PAINTED VASE, DETAIL: LONG BEAK-SPOUT (10th-9th CENT. B.C.) — TEHERAN MUSEUM

of Iran that have come down to us. Nevertheless we must not overlook the handles of Urartian funerary urns with figures of winged women, which clearly have a symbolic function.

There is no need to linger on the small painted pots [481-482], shaped somewhat like *aryballoi*, found in the cemetery, among which are bowls and vases with vertical spouts of a type peculiar to Iran. We would, however, draw attention to the fact that their decoration constantly reverts to the formula habitually employed by the Sialk painters for the vessels with long beak-spouts.

The notion of the animal handle can be observed (in embryonic form) in that of a large jug, the greater part of whose body is painted in plain red. Around the neck, however, are two superimposed bands with criss-cross linear patterns. On the upper band are alternating red and white triangles; the lower one is divided into metopes containing triangles joining at their apexes.

A motif of particular interest for the student of the beginnings of Iranian art is the motif of paired lions on the final metope beside the handle. The animals' manes are indicated, their bodies shown in side-view, and they are represented sitting face to face, fighting or playing in antithetical heraldic attitudes. This motif of confronted lions was diffused far beyond the limits of the Plateau.

Rhytons were included in the Sialk potter's repertory. In the one we show [483], he has had recourse to that favourite motif, the bird. Also, an

11 - SIALK. JUG: WOMAN'S FACE (10th-9th CENT. B.C.) — LOS ANGELES

12 - SIALK. PAINTED VASE: IBEX (10th-9th CENT. B.C.) — BRITISH MUSEUM

13 - SIALK. VASE: HORSE (10th-9th CENTURIES B.C.) — LOS ANGELES

15

askos[484] makes its first appearance at Sialk, here with a discreetly painted decoration. Monochrome pottery imitates the shapes of the costlier ware which only the rich could afford.

As a rule the glyptic art of the dwellers on the Plateau kept in line with that of the contemporary sculptors in Egypt and the Mesopotamian bronze-smiths. During the protohistoric period, however, the Sialk craftsmen seem to have been unaware of—or at any rate unaffected by—the metal-work and sculpture of these highly evolved civilizations. Thus the stone-cutter was inspired or influenced by the art of the potter, who also was a painter, while the subjects of the cylinder seals[485-486]—hunting scenes and animals fighting— are clearly affiliated to the paintings on contemporary vases.

In point of fact only one major art existed on the Plateau during the first two centuries of the first millennium B.C.: that of the painted pottery. Shortly thereafter, with a change in material conditions and under the influence of neighbouring lands, the art of the bronze-smith tended to replace that of the potter-painter and eventually extinguished it completely.

14 - SIALK. PAINTED JUG, DETAIL: ANIMAL HANDLE AND DECORATED NECK (10th-9th CENT. B.C.) — LOUVRE

15 - KHURVIN. VASE WITH LONG BEAK-SPOUT (9th-8th CENT. B.C.) — PRIVATE COLLECTION, TEHERAN

KHURVIN

SIALK lies on the southern edge of central Media and the northern boundary of Media Paretacene. Its art and indeed its culture as a whole suggest that the population was exceptionally homogeneous and that this uniformity was due to the influx of a group of Median tribes. But it can also be interpreted as an outcome of the special conditions the newcomers found on this site, where there seems to have been a break of continuity in its occupation before the coming of the Iranians.

So far as we can judge, the position was somewhat different at Khurvin, a village in central Media some fifty miles north-west of Teheran, on the high-road linking Mesopotamia with Central Asia. While displaying many of the characteristics of the homogeneous civilization of Sialk as regards its Iranian elements, the art of Khurvin has particularities that can only be interpreted as survivals of an earlier age. This, we believe, was due to the fact that a certain part of the population, presumably of non-Iranian stock, held tenaciously to its indigenous traditions.

Another factor that may account in part for the differences in the arts and culture of these two almost contemporaneous sites—Sialk in our opinion may be dated to the tenth and ninth centuries and Khurvin to the ninth and eighth centuries B.C.—is that the occupations of their inhabitants do not seem to have been the same. In the foothills of the Elburz chain beside which Khurvin lies, we have a region that must have always favoured agriculture, since, before artificial irrigation came into general use, it was copiously watered by a number of small streams coming down from the mountains. The population seems to have contained more peasants than that of Sialk where, if we are to judge by the number of tombs in which weapons and harness have been found, the majority of the inhabitants belonged to the ruling class of warriors and horsemen.

Chance finds revealed the existence of the Khurvin cemetery. Here the

tombs were of a simple kind, dug in the earth, and the grave furniture found beside the skeletons, though abundant, has very little artistic merit. But only a few tombs could be excavated scientifically since the majority had already been looted by the local peasants who kept only such articles as could be converted into money—mostly pottery, of which many hundreds of specimens have found their way to the Teheran market in the last ten years. This means that our knowledge of the culture prevailing at Khurvin is imperfect owing to the absence of the objects regarded as worthless by the clandestine diggers, to begin with iron objects which, we have reason to believe, were more numerous here than in the Sialk graves.

The Khurvin pottery is monochrome, black or grey-black, occasionally red, and clearly took its lead from Sialk. Here, again, the type form is the ritual bird-vase with a long beak-spout. In the absence of any painted decoration its interest lies in its plastic structure, which shows that the cultic and practical uses of the vase were inseparable. At Sialk the man making libation held the vase by the handle and tilted it in such a way as to exhibit to the spectators its painted decoration. At Khurvin he gripped the holy vessel with both hands placing his thumbs on concave lugs made for this purpose on both sides of the belly, half way up, and the handle was a mere adjunct, giving balance to the form of the vessel but serving no useful purpose. Thanks to the long spout and the animal's head above it, the black vase we illustrate seems endowed with a curious life, as if it were gazing at us through the animal's disproportionately large eyes and even 'speaking'—since its long beak announces the ritual act which will cause the holy liquid to issue from it.

Improvements in metal-working techniques led, it seems, to a tendency for the potter to join forces with the metal-founder. This resulted in hybrid products like the vase we illustrate. It is made of black terracotta, and has a graceful shape; the large belly is gadrooned all over, a ring replaces the neck, and it is balanced by a small round base. There is an aperture in the belly and to this is fixed with tiny rivets a long bronze spout, with a 'crop' like that of the metal vases found in the Sialk cemetery. Among the latter we dug up one with a lead body and a bronze spout. The practice of making vases of two different materials, the general rule at Khurvin, was, then, not unknown at Sialk. Its origin cannot be traced, but the combination of two metals seems more logical than that of earthenware with bronze.

So far as its forms are concerned, most of the pottery produced at Khurvin closely resembles that of Sialk. The almost spherical type of jug is as frequent as the *aryballos* type or that, peculiar to Iran, of the jug with an upright cylindrical spout. Though no two-handled goblets have been found in Cemetery B at Sialk, these jugs appear to be a local survival of the type of pottery we brought to light at Sialk Cemetery A; and this also applies to a goblet in black earthenware like the others, but with only one handle. Oftener perhaps than at Sialk, small vases found at Khurvin have three feet; some are looped, while others have the highly characteristic form of the shoes with turned-up tips worn by the mounted huntsmen on a Sialk cylinder seal.

It is chiefly the small vases that at Sialk have a tripod form. Those found at Khurvin, with multiple cups attached, came into use on the Plateau in the third millennium B.C. and were being produced everywhere during the early centuries of the first The *kernos*, however, composed of a hollow ring with a small vase above it (through which it was filled) and a bird with a split beak (through which the liquid was poured out), is unique of its kind.

17 - KHURVIN. TERRACOTTA KERNOS (9th-8th CENTURIES B.C.) — PRIVATE COLLECTION, TEHERAN

18 - KHURVIN. TERRACOTTA KERNOS 19 - TERRACOTTA FIGURINE (9th-8th CENT. B.C.) — PRIVATE COLL., TEHERAN

The potters also made square or triangular vessels, whose surfaces were decorated with incised lines and in some cases adorned with the heads of rams or ibexes. In another piece the potter has placed a spouted cup on a support shaped like an inverted trumpet and added on the edges a cup and a small vase; then, as if still further to complicate this curious object, he has added to it a woman's bust in the round with large protruding eyes, her hair being rendered by scratching the clay with a pointed reed.

Most remarkable of the objects made by the artisans of Khurvin is an *askos* shaped like a shoe[487] with a turned-up tip and buttons, resembling the footgear of the Persians on the reliefs at Susa and Persepolis. Do these vases illustrate the type of shoe worn by the villagers at Khurvin? It must not be forgotten that in some Greek tombs terracotta shoes were provided for pedestrians, as well as terracotta horses for the use of riders making their last journey.

Following an age-old tradition, terracotta makers on the Plateau usually contented themselves with rudimentary modelling. Metal-founders, however, produced figurines which show progressive technical improvements. The metal-worker constantly tried to liberate the limbs from the compact mass of the trunk and torso and, though these attempts were often clumsy, they show a new sense of the dynamism latent in a human body. An example is the bronze statuette of a warrior which, judging by the ring behind the head, must have been worn, like the Sialk statuettes, as a pendant. The back is hollow and the back of the legs flat. The warrior's pose is that of a worshipper; this is stressed by the size of the hands, rendered with special care. As in Luristan the face is bisected by a prominent, sword-blade nose and the eye-sockets must originally have been inlaid. The mouth is not indicated and there is no trace of a moustache, though a short beard is rendered by small incisions. The lower part of the body is naked and the penis visible. The man's equipment is of special interest since it comprises all the elements of the battle dress described by Homer. The helmet (presumably in leather) has a semicircular crest and there are no ear-guards. The warrior wears a *mitra*, a large leather belt to which eight plaques, undoubtedly in bronze, were fastened. The breastplate matches the *mitra* and, slung on the right shoulder, covers the man's chest.

This work falls into the class of two-dimensional effigies, though some details indicate an improved technique, for example an attempt at modelling in the limbs and at giving a natural posture to the bent legs. The art of the Plateau was getting into its stride and another forward step was to be taken by the Luristan bronze-smiths.

Weapons, swords, daggers, spears and harness ornaments, though having

20 - KHURVIN. BRONZE WARRIOR FIGURINE (9th-8th CENT. B.C.) — PRIVATE COLL., TEHERAN

21 - KHURVIN. PENDANTS (9th-8th CENT. B.C.) — PRIVATE COLL., TEHERAN

many points in common with those of Sialk, are executed with greater proficiency, and in this respect, too, invite comparison with those of Luristan.

Jewellery bulks large in the group of objects found in the Khurvin cemetery. All these pieces have a core of bitumen covered with gold foil, on which it was easy to punch a simple design of points or of double volutes in repoussé work. Crescent-shaped ear-rings[488] with a ball attached to one of the tips were already being worn on the Plateau in the late second millennium B.C. In replacing the ball with a human head the Khurvin goldsmith introduced a new motif, which was to persist in Iranian jewellery; we find a head, for instance, in the centre of a gold clip of the Achaemenian period.

To the best of our knowledge the type of pin having both a stem and sheath in bronze was peculiar to Sialk. A bronze pin[489] found at Khurvin is fitted with a head and sheath of gold repoussé work adorned with geometric patterns. The reason why a precious metal was employed for the sheath is that this was always open at both ends and intended to be seen when the pin was being worn.

The bronze ornaments—torques, pins, bracelets and pendants—reproduce *ad infinitum* familiar animal motifs; some of the pendants, simply and often carelessly executed, represent human feet. Noteworthy among the current types of ear-rings are those in the form of clusters, like the ones from Sialk, but in terracotta. The trinkets given a double-axe form had a symbolic value. It would seem that this ritual emblem, stemming from certain regions of Asia Minor (Lydia, Phrygia, Caria), was transmitted to the Plateau at the beginning of the first millennium B.C. Examples of it on the Plateau have so far been found only at Sialk and Khurvin. Of interest in this context is the stone mould, probably used in a jeweller's workshop, which was discovered during the clearance of the terrace contemporary with Cemetery B at Sialk. This was used for casting pendants in the form of the double axe (*labrys*). It is further evidence of the affinities between the Sialk and Khurvin cultures.

22 - KHURVIN. BRONZE BELT (9th-8th CENT. B.C.) — PRIVATE COLLECTION, TEHERAN

Among miscellaneous objects used in daily life the mirrors form a class apart and testify to a higher artistic standard. Vast numbers of mirrors with handles were produced; of particular interest is the one consisting of a disk upheld by a figurine acting as a caryatid. In this creation of a Khurvin bronzesmith we have, to the best of our belief, one of the earliest examples of this architectonic theme which was to enjoy an ever-increasing vogue in the art of Luristan, before being taken over by the arts of the West.

23 - KHURVIN. MIRROR WITH CARYATID HANDLE (9th-8th CENT. B.C.) — PRIVATE COLLECTION, TEHERAN

23

24 - HASANLU. MULTIPLE VASE (KERNOS) WITH BIRD AND FIGURE (9th-8th CENT. B.C.) — TEHERAN MUSEUM

HASANLU

THE site of Hasanlu, in the vicinity of Solduz, a small town near the south-western shore of Lake Urmia, lies in a region which in the early first millennium B.C. was included in the kingdom of Mannai, and it has much to tell us of the civilization that flourished in the western part of the Plateau at the time when the Iranians reached the borders of their future kingdom.

The cemetery lies in the plain, near the mound covering the site of the ancient town. The most noteworthy tomb (still unpublished) was found at a depth of thirteen feet, over nine of which were filled with very hard earth mixed with lime. The body was laid directly in the ground, in a crouching position, and with it was not only the usual grave furniture but also the skeletons of a team of four horses offered in sacrifice. The funerary chariot itself, however, does not seem to have been included; the dimensions of the tomb and its contents made this impracticable.

The nature of its art, the shapes of the red and black pottery and the gold jewels found at Hasanlu make it clear that the local culture linked up with the proto-Iranian civilization which we have already spoken of, especially with that of Khurvin. The objects in bronze testify to the homogeneity of this cultural group, whose metal-work gives the impression of being more sophisticated than that of the sites described above, and indicates, moreover, an acquaintance with the arts of Luristan. All the pottery found on this site,

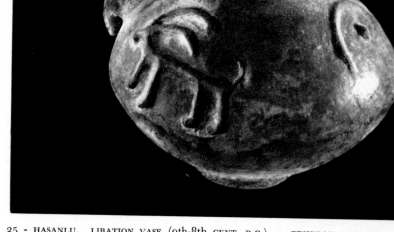

25 - HASANLU. LIBATION VASE (9th-8th CENT. B.C.) — TEHERAN MUSEUM

mostly black (the few red pieces are exceptional), consists of funerary ware. Animals or human figures, all directly associated with the rite of libation in which they act as participants or guardians, are rendered in a distinctive, fully plastic technique, either in relief or in the round. The influence of the bronze-ware can be seen in a black jug (like 'bucchero nero' ware) on which an animal in the round is placed above the spout, as if to watch the liquid flowing through it, and the belly is adorned with a quadruped rendered in relief. Real tripods in the same material rest on supports given the form of shod human feet, as at Khurvin. In a red vase ornamented with three cups and two birds, the spout of which is upheld by a half-length human figure, we have further evidence of the affinities between Khurvin and Hasanlu. But the chief interest of this piece lies in the fact that it shows the way in which ritual vessels were held. In a common earthenware vase from Luristan representing a figure holding a spouted vase in exactly the same manner, we have another instance of the influence of ritual usage on the development of forms. Also in the art of Luristan, we can observe the persistence of a tradition demonstrating a real kinship between the two cultural centres.

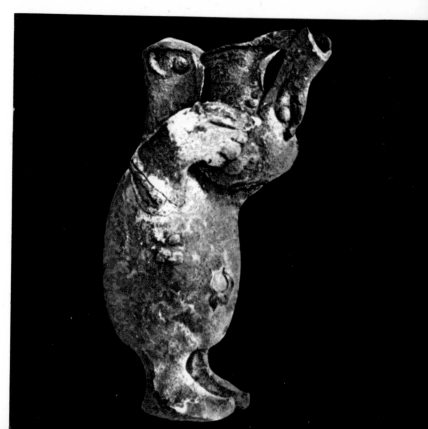

26 - LURISTAN. VASE IN THE FORM OF A HUMAN FIGURE (8th-7th CENT. B.C.) — PRIVATE COLL.

27 - HASANLU. (A) EAR-RING (B & C) NECKLACES (9th-8th CENTURIES B.C.) — TEHERAN MUSEUM

Hasanlu jewellery tends to be larger and more sumptuous than that of Khurvin and Sialk. Yet, despite their size and the precious metal they are made of, the ear-rings in 'clusters' clearly belong to the same family as those of Khurvin and Sialk. The necklaces consist of round gold beads, tubes adorned with soldered double spirals, also in gold, and white stones, either cylindrical or cask-shaped, while the two half circles of a pendant have granulated edges.

The bronze tripods for cauldrons are given the form of men's legs or animals' paws. The bronze-smith also made animal figures in the round; for example a lion couchant, executed in an unusual technique: muscles are schematically rendered by flat planes in relief, fur is suggested by parallel stripes filled alternately with dots and chevrons, and in the treatment of the eye as a small boss with a circular rim in relief we see the beginnings of a stylization that was generally adopted by the metal-workers. A peculiar feature of a series of very similar lions is that their bodies (in bronze) end in a long iron rod. There is no knowing what their function was, but the menacing jaws with enormous fangs assimilate them to 'guardian' animals.

We are unable to agree with those who assign the very fine lion in the Louvre (J. Coiffard Collection) to Luristan. Its geometrically treated limbs, adorned with incised chevrons and rectangles, its mane with a double ruff, its eye with a rim in relief and the four meticulously rendered fangs incline us to attribute it, if not to Hasanlu itself, at least to one of the art centres in the same region which had a tradition and technique of animal art resembling those of Hasanlu.

But the most striking feature of the Hasanlu cemetery is that it contains the earliest Iranian tomb discovered so far in which evidence of the

26

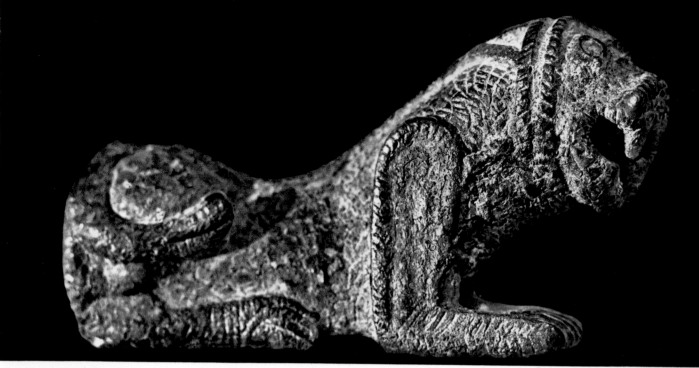

28 - HASANLU (?). CROUCHING LION IN BRONZE (9th-8th CENTURIES B.C.) — LOUVRE

sacrifice of horses—a traditional practice of peoples of Scythian origin—has been found. Thus the hypothesis of a Scythian infiltration into Transcaucasia and north-western Iran in the eighth century B.C. (or even as early as the ninth) seems to be confirmed. Moreover, there is no question of the close intercourse between Scythians and Medians in the region south of Lake Urmia (where Urartian influence played so large a part) at the time of the building of the Hasanlu cemetery, which lay within the territory of the kingdom of Mannai, and the Mannaians are known to have been in direct contact with the Scythians. These facts, which will be discussed in more detail when we come to deal with the relations between Scythian art and the Irano-Urartian *koine*, point to the existence of an ethnical kinship between the arts of all these peoples.

29 - HASANLU. CROUCHING LION IN BRONZE (9th-8th CENTURIES B.C.) — TEHERAN MUSEUM

27

30 - HASANLU. GOLD BOWL WITH RELIGIOUS SCENES (9th-8th CENTURIES B.C.) — TEHERAN MUSEUM

Data in support of our belief that Scythian influences can be discerned in the grave goods of the Hasanlu tomb are also provided by the pieces of harness. Among these we would draw attention to a link-bit in twisted bronze to which, at the point where *psalia* and reins were fixed, flat clips were fastened, giving them a stirrup-like aspect.

This peculiar type of bit has also been found in Scythian tombs, dating to the first quarter of the sixth century B.C., at Kelermes in the Kuban. Yessen believes that it was brought there by the Scythians after their sojourn in Transcaucasia and Iran. Also the use of boars' teeth as ornaments of horse-gear, evidenced at Hasanlu, was specifically Scythian.

Urartian domination of the region is attested by an inscription of King Menuas (late ninth century B.C.), carved in the rock at Tash Tepe, south-east of Lake Urmia, near the modern town of Miyanduab, which is not far from Hasanlu. Equally significant is the presence in the Hasanlu grave of a bronze plaque decorated with a stag's head, the stag being a distinctive emblem of the Scythians. This form of plaque—evidently a pectoral—was an adornment peculiar to the Urartians and it was taken over by the Scythian settlers in Iran.

28

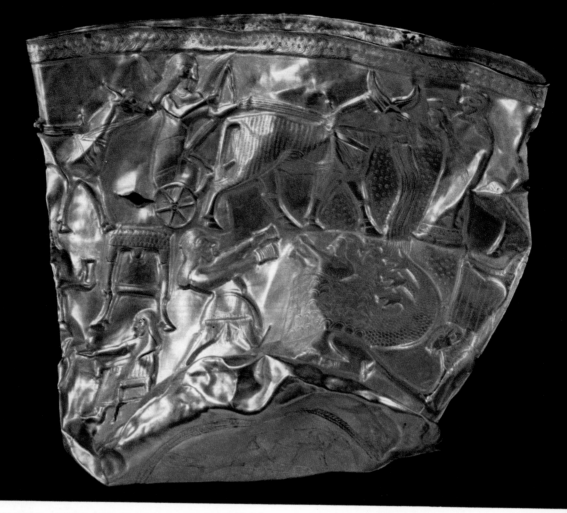

31 - HASANLU. OTHER SIDE OF THE GOLD BOWL (9th-8th CENTURIES B.C.) — TEHERAN MUSEUM

(This is proved, as we shall see, by the gold pectorals in the Ziwiyeh Treasure.)

We have grounds, then, for thinking that the man interred in the Hasanlu tomb was a Scythian. The special, laurel leaf-shaped type of arrows found in it helps us to date the tomb; it cannot be later than the mid-eighth century B.C. Finally, we may be sure that the resumption of the Hasanlu excavations by the University Museum of Philadelphia will throw new light on this highly complex phase of Iranian art and civilization.

These excavations promise to be particularly rewarding. Suffice it here to call attention to the discovery of a large vase of solid gold, found in what was apparently a palace at the top of the mound. This magnificent cult object, decorated with religious and mythological scenes, is iconographically related to many other works found in the regions extending from eastern Anatolia and northern Syria to the Zagros mountains, and dating from the late second and early first millennium B.C. Very different from all that we know of Iranian art in its early, formative phase, this large bowl appears to be the product of local artists working for the ruler of some outlying kingdom, perhaps that of Mannai.

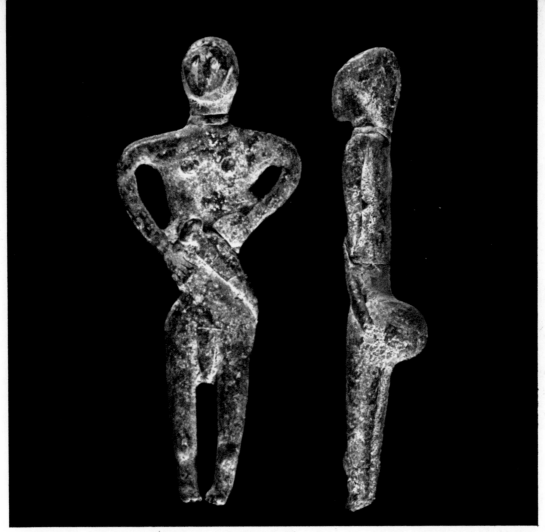

33 - AMLASH. WARRIOR STATUETTE IN BRONZE (9th-8th CENT. B.C.) — PRIVATE COLLECTION, TEHERAN

AMLASH

THE art of Amlash, which we believe to date to the ninth-eighth centuries B.C., has come to light only within the last three or four years. Our knowledge of this phase of proto-Iranian civilization is based entirely on grave furniture from megalithic tombs, accidentally discovered by peasants in the mountainous region south-west of the Caspian Sea. Amlash is a provincial centre whose productions, while keeping within the main art currents of the period, have distinctive features whose originality testifies to an exceptionally fine artistic sense.

This is particularly true of the Amlash potter, and also of the modeller; both have a distinctive touch not to be found elsewhere. Their handling of the human figure and their admirable interpretations of animals, especially the humped ox, have an immediate appeal for the twentieth-century connoisseur, whose tastes and sensibility, conditioned by modern art, predispose him to appreciate just such a synthesis of forms as we find in the art of Amlash.

← 32 - AMLASH. STATUETTE OF THE STEATOPYGOUS TYPE
(9th-8th CENTURIES B.C.) — PRIVATE COLL., PARIS

34 - AMLASH. HUMPED-OX RHYTON (9th-8th CENTURIES B.C.) — PRIVATE COLLECTION, TEHERAN

In this small Iranian community of farmers and stock-breeders, potter and modeller were one and the same artist—an artist gifted with inventive powers of a very high order. Painted decoration has entirely disappeared and the most favoured object is the rhyton, which is given the form of animals familiar to the artist, such as the horse and the stag. Animal-shaped vases of this kind were of course nothing new; always popular with the Eurasian nomads, they were to be constantly employed by the Iranian peoples for centuries to come.

35 - AMLASH. HORSE RHYTON (9th-8th CENTURIES B.C.) — PRIVATE COLLECTION, TEHERAN

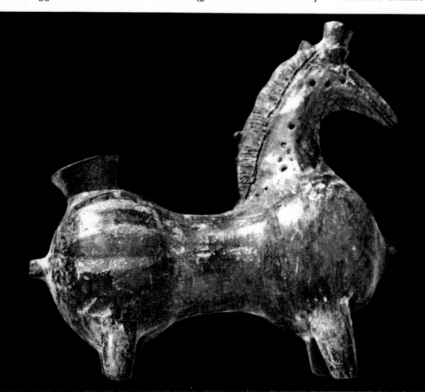

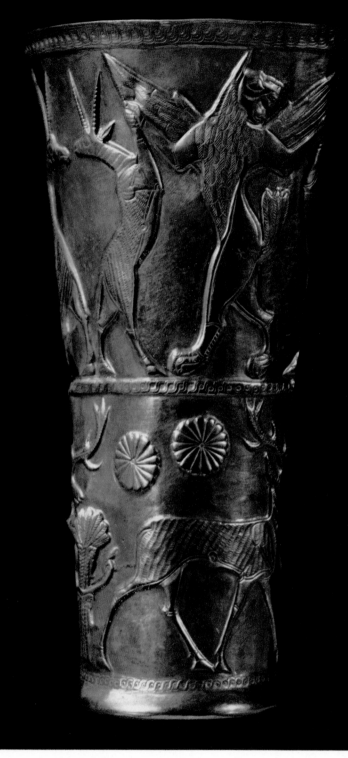

36 - AMLASH. LARGE GOLD GOBLET (9th-8th CENTURIES B.C.) — PRIVATE COLLECTION, NEW YORK

The goldsmith and the metal-worker seem to follow in the footsteps of the modeller. Obviously familiar with certain subjects of Mesopotamian art, the former shows a predilection for tall goblets of gold or silver.

37 - AMLASH.   SILVER CUP WITH RAMS (9th-8th CENT. B.C.) — PRIVATE COLLECTION, TEHERAN

Also made of silver are the cups adorned with scenes of daily life, hunting scenes for example, whose intricate composition called for considerable artistic skill.   The necklaces strung with gold beads carved in the form of birds' and animals' heads suggest that the inhabitants of Amlash were relatively wealthy

38 - AMLASH.   SILVER CUP WITH HUNTING SCENE (9th-8th CENT). — B.C. PRIVATE COLLECTION, NEW YORK

34

39 - AMLASH. HORSEMAN. BRONZE STATUETTE (9th-8th CENT. B.C.) — PRIVATE COLLECTION, TEHERAN

folk, and this is borne out by the productions of the metal-workers. The latter take inspiration from the creations of the modellers in their renderings of the human figure, which is represented either alone (in which case we find pronounced steatopygia) or else on horseback.

40 - AMLASH. HUMPED OX. BRONZE STATUETTE (9th-8th CENT. B.C.) — PRIVATE COLLECTION, TEHERAN

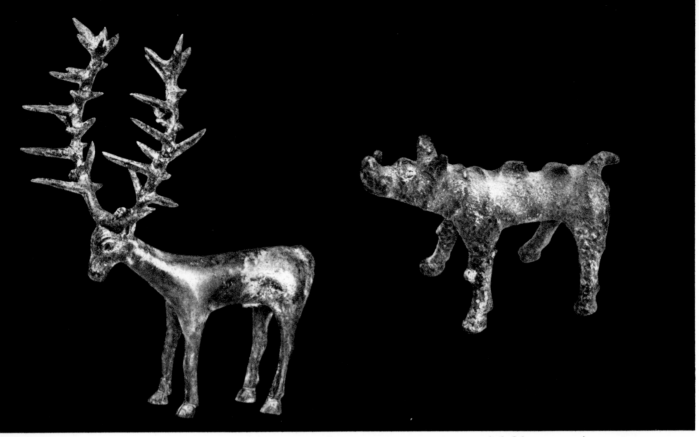

41 - AMLASH. STAG (9th-8th CENT. B.C.) — KANSAS CITY 42 - BOAR (9th-8th CENT. B.C.) — TEHERAN

The metal-workers also produced a great variety of small animal figures, among which the humped ox and the stag predominate, along with effigies of the wild boar and the unicorn.

A bronze plaque representing a recumbent ibex is a work of particular

43 - AMLASH. UNICORN (9th-8th CENT. B.C.) 44 - RECUMBENT IBEX (9th-8th CENT. B.C.) — TEHERAN

36

interest. The animal's horns, curving over its back, and its legs drawn up in such a way that the hooves rest one against the other, are features that were to characterize Scythian art, as we find it a few decades after the date assignable to the Amlash culture.

Among other finds are weapons typical of the fighting gear of these mountaineers, such as a bronze sword with a hilt given the shape of the 'naked goddess' and a pommel in the form of two confronted horses' heads; also a bronze mace-head decorated with three human faces.

Little trace of any Mesopotamian art currents is to be found in the work of the Amlash artists. The reason for this is that a high mountain barrier cut them off from Mesopotamia. But their work reflects some of the distinctive features of the arts which flourished in the Caucasus in the early Iron Age. The bronze figurines in particular point to the north—that is to say the regions traversed by the Iranians in the course of their migration to the Plateau—as the source from which the Amlash artists drew inspiration.

Though in the Amlash phase clay remained the basic medium of artistic expression, progress was now being made in the craft of metal-working. Expressing his lively feeling for form in a more difficult technique, the metal-worker invented and made good a new imagery which had a brilliant culmination in the next phase of Iranian culture: that of the famous 'Luristan bronzes.' This culmination was accompanied by a corresponding decline in the potter's craft.

45 - AMLASH. SWORD HILT: NUDE GODDESS
46 - MACE-HEAD (9th-8th CENTURIES B.C.)
PRIVATE COLL. AND TEHERAN MUSEUM

37

47 - AMLASH. STAG RHYTON IN TERRACOTTA (9th-8th CENTURIES B.C.) — PRIVATE COLLECTION, TEHERAN

Our knowledge of this phase of protohistoric Iranian civilization, the so-called Amlash culture, has been enriched and extended by recent discoveries made at Marlik, not far from the town of Rudbar, in the province of Gilan, by the Iranian Expedition sponsored by the Teheran Museum.

The megalithic tombs at Marlik yielded several gold vases, a number of objects in bronze and silver, and a great many terracotta statuettes. The dating proposed by the present writer was confirmed by the discovery, made by peasants, of two horse's blinkers, in bronze, inscribed in cuneiform characters with the names of King Menuas (810-781 B.C.) and King Argistis (781-760 B.C.).

48 - AMLASH. FEMALE STATUETTE (9th-8th CENT. B.C.) — PRIVATE COLLECTION, TEHERAN →

50 - LURISTAN. IDOL: THE GOD SRAOSHA (?) (8th-7th CENT. B.C.) — PRIVATE COLLECTION, NEW YORK

II

THE CIMMERIANS
AND THE ART OF LURISTAN

WE have drawn attention to the affinities between the civilizations of Sialk, Khurvin, Hasanlu and Amlash, while stressing the fact that the last three were somewhat later in date. There is no denying, however, that the similarity between them was far from total; just as each region of the Greek world displayed local idioms in its contributions to the complex of Hellenic culture, so, from the ninth to the seventh centuries B.C., each region of the Plateau developed an art peculiar to itself in some respects, though keeping by and large to the general trends of the place and period. This phase of the incipient Iranian culture, which might be described as Proto-Median, is given a still more vigorous expression in the art of Luristan.

In the upper valleys of the Zagros range, south of Kermanshah and of the small, ancient kingdom of Ellipi, several groups of tombs of the megalithic type, containing quantities of bronze and iron objects, have been discovered during the last thirty-five years. These cemeteries lay at a certain distance from the contemporary towns or villages, which were not necessarily built on the hills or mounds that had been occupied by the prehistoric dwellers in this region (before the first millennium B.C.), and are often situated in the plains. It would seem that, as at Sialk, the nomad tribesmen of Luristan buried their dead at a certain distance from the inhabited sites.

They had, however, religious centres and one of them, at Surkh Dum, has been scientifically excavated. These sanctuaries give the impression that the newcomers practised a sort of 'amphictyony,' i.e. that a whole group of people observing the same cults had the habit of meeting at a specific holy place. Even today the Lurs, nomads like their ancestors, forgather periodically at certain Islamic places of pilgrimage, whose origins can often be traced to very early times. The Medes seem to have developed a similar tradition, for their capital, present-day Hamadan, before becoming a royal city, bore the name of Hagmatana, meaning 'place of assembly.'

Our proposed identification of these nomad tribes of Luristan with the Cimmerians is supported by the recent researches of Piotrovsky, Melikishvili and Diakonov, and fresh evidence is constantly being advanced. In the first decades of the eighth century B.C. we hear of Cimmerians acting as allies of Urartu, Cimmerian mercenaries serving in the Assyrian army, and others co-operating in the Median revolt. It seems clear that this people split up into two groups, one of which moved westwards towards Asia Minor, and the other east of Assyria into a country which was still named after the Kassites, and which is the present-day province of Luristan. They firmly established themselves in this region, which was admirably suited to a race of mounted nomads and horse-breeders. The conformation of the Zagros range, with its narrow, isolated valleys, facilitated their advance. This involved forcing their way through the territories of various kingdoms, such as those of Mannai and Ellipi, with which, however, the Cimmerians could, when it served their interests, come to terms. We have no knowledge of what they brought with them, but vestiges of their presence can perhaps be detected in the cemeteries of Transcaucasia, where great quantities of weapons, ornaments and horse-gear have been discovered. But though there are similarities between these objects and those of Luristan, the absence of figurative compositions with mythological or religious themes sets the historian another problem when he tries to elucidate the relations between the Medes and the Cimmerians. Their ethnic kinship, their worship of the same gods—the oldest in the Iranian pantheon—and their close collaboration in the fight for political independence (which suggests that the great Median revolt led by Kashtariti may well have had its starting point in Luristan or on its frontier) cannot have failed to promote the fusion of these two Iranian peoples having the same customs and cultivating the same type of art.

A collation of the data elicited by scientific research work with the information given by the depictions of themselves that the men of Luristan have bequeathed to us reveals an intriguing world of which the art historian had but an inkling until quite recently.

Our purpose here is not to make a detailed study of the thousands of objects found in the tombs and shrines of Luristan. A series of illustrations of each category of the funerary and votive ware will suffice to convey both its great diversity and its characteristics. Our aim is primarily to give a more concrete, more vivid idea of the ways of living and thinking of the people of Luristan than was hitherto available because of the lack of any written records.

To begin with, attention must be drawn to a negative factor: not a single human dwelling has so far been discovered in the regions inhabited by the mountaineers of Luristan. Our knowledge of these men and their everyday life is necessarily incomplete, since no direct information is available. None the less the copious offerings of domestic utensils, weapons and personal adornments found in the graves have much to tell us of the manner of men they were, and our understanding of these offerings is supplemented by a study of their iconography. It is clear that these people were much concerned with the after-life and convinced of the perennity, in the land of shades, of the objects that had served them in their life on earth. This may be the reason why the art of Luristan centres on a glorification of the powers presiding over the life and death of every individual:

51 - LURISTAN. IDOL: THE GOD SRAOSHA (?)
(8th-7th CENTURIES B.C.) — BRUSSELS

43

powers engaged in an endless struggle in which not only the man himself and those around him, but a host of weird demonic beings are involved.

The so-called idol embodying the concept of a 'superman' is particularly revealing. The most typical of the open-work bronzes were obviously inspired by the old heraldic Mesopotamian motif of a 'hero' fighting with two beasts. They represent a two-sided half-length figure, both arms outstretched, strangling two monsters with gaping jaws. Round the hero's waist is a wide girdle usually flanked by two cocks' heads and his lower limbs are replaced by the legs and rumps of the monsters he is grappling with. A pin passing through the figure fastens it to a support.

Here, it would seem, we have an effigy of Sraosha, god of justice, whose many-headed, composite image is basic to a whole series of elaborately planned metamorphoses. The polycephaly of this god, all the more striking since each head has two sides facing in opposite directions, his enormous eyes and the projecting ears rendered in the round, symbolize the god's omnipotence and conjure up the idea of Mithras, described in the Avesta as having a thousand ears and myriads of eyes.

For Sraosha personified 'the Mithraic commonalty' and his cult was closely connected with that of Mithras. He is armed with the club which he wields to good effect in his combats with the demons, enemies of Ahuramazda, and the support on which the bronze is always mounted symbolizes this weapon. His animal attribute is the cock, whose function was to awaken the

52 - LURISTAN. VOTIVE IDOL, DETAIL
(8th-7th CENT. B.C.) — BOSTON

44

community and summon them to perform their religious duties. His name seems to derive from *sros* (punishment) and, as a god of justice, he co-operated with Mithras and Rashnu in judging the souls of the dead when they crossed the bridge of Cinvat. Sraosha was not a vanquisher of wild beasts or 'master of animals,' but a high-ranking member of the pantheon of ancient Mazdaean Iran.

There is no hint of any Shamanic cult in these bronzes, and in our opinion they represent the most ancient images of the Iranian religion as it existed in the period when the oral version of the Yashts (the oldest part of the Avesta, the sacred book of the Iranians) was taking form. We believe that the identification suggested here throws light on the true significance of the multifarious objects placed in the tombs as last offerings to the deceased, most, if not all, of which are conceived in terms of a funerary symbolism.

Thus art was put to the service of religious imagery and the rich diversity of the age-old mythology was condensed, epitomized by the artist in a single work of art. What we have here is not a series of episodes nor the climactic scene of a legend but a symbolism rich in intimations that was to permeate Iranian art throughout its long history. By the same token there is no question of a narrative, religious or secular, such as we find in Mesopotamian art, where gods are given a human form. True, this anthropomorphic conception certainly exists, but it is not given expression, for all the art of Luristan is basically symbolic.

The peculiarity of this iconography is even more apparent when the human figure, too, is interpreted on abstract lines and the bronze-worker's vivid imagination is given free rein in a style whose fantastic forms have a baroque intricacy. It is in these works that, with its recourse to the zoomorphic juncture so frequent in Scythian art, the animal style of Luristan attains its singular perfection.

53 - LURISTAN. IDOL: CONFRONTED ANIMALS, DETAIL (8th-7th CENTURIES B.C.) — LOUVRE

45

54 - LURISTAN. VOTIVE PIN 55 - IDOL (8th-7th CENT. B.C.) — PRIVATE COLLECTIONS, TEHERAN AND PARIS

Sraosha is not the only deity figuring on the Luristan bronzes. With his cult was associated that of his sister Ashi, 'the good' (Yasht 17), goddess of fecundity, whom we are inclined to recognize in the winged genius who seems to be protecting two pairs of ibexes and gazelles.

Of a more unusual type is the god seated between the foreparts of two horses; his attitude lends an unwonted sensitivity to the paired, sometimes winged animals over whom he is keeping guard. Have we not here the god Mithras, 'the all-glorious with the collar of gold whom broad-hooved horses carry forward to confront the raging hordes' (Yasht 10), and who, together with Sraosha and Rashnu, judges the souls of the dead?

We have another illustration of the bronze-smiths' skill in devising new methods of representing gods in a long series of pins treated in the openwork technique. These were usually made in two parts, the head and the stem, which then were soldered together. Sometimes an iron tip was attached to the bronze head. Most of the pins appear to have been cast in univalvular moulds and bear the image only on one side. All, it seems, were votive objects and, as such, were deposited in tombs beside the dead. Occasionally the god (recognizable by his horns) was replaced by a tree.

One of the most remarkable pieces of this group represents an androgynous deity standing on a support composed of the protomes of two cocks and holding vanquished animals by their hind legs. Here we have an effigy of the *potnia theron*, mistress of wild beasts, and sometimes a god replaces the goddess: an illustration of a theme which originated in Mesopotamia, was taken over and utilized for several millennia in the arts of Western Asia, and transmitted by them to the Greeks.

Next, we may draw attention to another bronze with a representation of Sraosha in which the god's figure is curiously distorted and stretched to match

46

the flexions of the animals accompanying him. None the less he retains a distinctively human form, and is wearing the fringed garment and the mitre that reappear on the bas-reliefs of Persepolis (for this form of headdress was subsequently adopted by the Persians). Finally we have a god with an animal's head—oddly reminiscent of the Egyptian Hathor—in an equally strange setting, in which a gazelle's head, clamped as it were in a vice, becomes a seat.

The significance of a series of pins, whose themes and technique differ widely from the group described above, is problematic. Within a massive square frame, formed of tresses or fishbone patterns in relief, heads of ibexes, coupled or confronted, are disposed on one or several axes.

Of greater interest perhaps are the many statuettes which, though retaining some of the characteristics of deities found elsewhere, are treated in a new way, indicating presumably that their functions were different. They are given a cylindrical form with a hollow core, and no longer have the double face of the Iranian Janus. Despite the fact that they wear the same costume as Sraosha and have cocks' heads sprouting from their shoulders, these are not gods but goddesses holding up their bare breasts. When completely naked they make the gesture of the Venus Pudica. Sometimes, however, they are shown wearing a curious conical hat, and we cannot help feeling that this concession to a picturesque realism detracts from their hieratic dignity.

56 - LURISTAN. GODDESS STATUETTE (8th-7th CENTURIES B.C.) — PRIVATE COLLECTION, PARIS

Special mention must be made of the pins with large, flat, disk-shaped heads bearing a human face in relief in the centre. They were wedged into crevices in the stone walls of the temple at Surkh Dum, or sometimes placed actually inside the walls. We agree with the view that these pins with round heads were, like the quivers and bucklers, deposited in the temple by individual worshippers as votive objects.

In his account of the discovery of the temple of Surkh Dum or Dumb (meaning 'the red tail') by the expedition led by Dr Erich Schmidt, Godard writes as follows: 'A temple was brought to light at this spot, whose walls were made of undressed stones and in which, lying on the ground or stuck between the stones, or even inside the walls were a great many objects, some of known types, but others unfamiliar, among which were a quantity of pins adorned with religious scenes, male and female figurines, bronze mirrors, cylinders and so forth—but nothing representing a horse or relating to it.' There was a good reason for this; the horse and everything concerned with it was charged with funerary symbolism and was reserved to graves.

The objects found in the temple were votive offerings made by persons soliciting the favour of their gods for purely personal reasons. None the less it is quite possible that among the objects discussed in the following pages some came from tombs, and also that, among the bronzes described as grave goods, some were unearthed at the temple of Surkh Dum by clandestine diggers operating before the arrival of the American expedition. All the pieces we now shall discuss have come to us by way of dealers, and the results of the scientific excavation of the site are as yet unpublished. These and these alone will provide a solution, if only a partial one, of the problem.

The face in the centre of the pinheads may be assumed to be that of the mother-goddess of the Asianic peoples, who was worshipped everywhere from Asia Minor to Susa. It is quite possible that in course of time this ancient goddess, symbol of fecundity and procreation, developed, by syncretism, into the goddess Ashi, sister of Sraosha, whom we have identified among the 'idols' in the tombs. Support is lent to this view by the fact that the borders of some pinheads are decorated with fish and pomegranates, both of which are symbols of Ashi. Often the goddess is flanked by lions or ibexes, presumably her animal attributes. Every woman who desired to have a child applied to her for aid and, in recourse to a sort of sympathetic magic, deposited in the temple the image of a woman in the act of childbirth. Here we may note that the woman's squatting posture recalls a very ancient obstetric tradition, still current in some primitive tribes.

Of particular interest is another pinhead[490] on the lower part of which a man is represented holding on a leash a cow suckling her calf and ridden by a figure carrying a palm branch. Dussaud saw in this branch a *barsom* and thought that the scene illustrated some specific theme of Iranian mythology, perhaps related

49

59 - LURISTAN. RECTANGULAR PINHEAD (8th-7th CENT. B.C.)

60 - LURISTAN. ROUND PINHEAD (8th-7th CENT. B.C.)

to a blood sacrifice. For our part, we are more inclined to think it signifies a prayer to the goddess Ashi, beseeching her to fecundate the flocks during the rutting season. The branch the man is holding may be accounted for by a passage in Yasht 17: 'We offer to Ashi Vanuhi the *haoma*, the milk, the *baresman*, the wisdom of the tongue...' And in another passage in Yasht 18 we read: 'The great Ashi Vanuhi sets foot within the house, the glorious royal house. And the horses are multiplied a thousandfold, and a thousandfold the flocks and herds and their well-liking progeny.'

The treatment of the goddess's face on the various objects associated with her shows steady improvement in the technique of rendering her features and expressing plastic values. But these changes in the figuration are not solely a matter of technical refinements; they also indicate a definite trend towards a greater, ever more intense spirituality.

Noteworthy also in the group of objects dedicated to the goddess Ashi is the appearance of a somewhat peculiar motif, two lions with a single head; a motif which remained in favour for many centuries in the Ancient East and even found its way into medieval European art. Its origin can probably be traced to the structure of an axe, whose blade, shaped like a halberd, issues from a lion's open jaw, the lion's body being split in two parts protruding on both sides, so as to accommodate the socket.

The pinhead on to which the Luristan bronze-smith transposed this

61 - LURISTAN. ROUND PINHEAD (8th-7th CENTURIES B.C.) — BRUSSELS

motif is the oldest known Iranian object of this type, and it is of exceptional interest for the researcher into the origins of Iranian forms. Moreover we find on this same pinhead the first attempt, in Iranian art, to depict a mountain landscape.

On another pinhead we have a truncated version of this theme, in which only the single head of the two lions is represented.

In this stylized motif Dussaud proposed to see 'the nest of serpents symbolizing the earth to which the Great Serpent is seeking to return.' On the other hand, the presence of this creature, thought to be an attribute of Mithras, on the disk, has been taken to equate a representation of the god. However, the way in which the figure holds the chthonian reptile does not seem to bear this out, for grasping a snake by the tail means putting it out of action. More convincing are the interpretations of the two stars (the sun and Venus) above the central head, and two priests wielding the *barsom*.

Most striking here are the chinless faces of the two figures, their barely indicated mouths and big noses curling like elephants' trunks at their extremities[491]. In these faces there are particularities we have already noted in the art of Sialk.

The concept of dualism, resulting from the conflict between Ahuramazda and Ahriman (Good and Evil), pervaded the cult of Zurvan, god of destiny and the firmament. (It was paralleled in China in the age of the Contending States, contemporary with the Luristan

62 - LURISTAN. ROUND PINHEAD (8th-7th CENT. B.C.)

63 - LURISTAN. ROUND PINHEAD (8th-7th CENTURIES B.C.) — PRIVATE COLLECTION, NEW YORK

51

civilization.)   Hence the importance to be assigned to 'Zurvanism,' which was evidently basic to the archaic Iranian religion and preceded Zoroastrianism. It provided Iranian iconography with new themes, marking another phase in the evolution of decorative art.   Thus on a silver plate from Luristan (now in the Cincinnati Art Museum) the composition, though centred on the andro-gynous figure of the god Zurvan, is dominated by a complementary scene showing the presentation of *barsoms* to Ahuramazda and Ahriman, the twin sons of the primaeval god.

According to the literary sources Zurvan was a multiform being and incarnat-ed the three ages of terrestrial life.   His presence is again apparent in the three groups of figures—young, adult and old—who are bringing and handing over branches of palms, emblems of the god's power over the universe.

Effigies of Zurvan and his two sons, treated on a smaller scale, figure on a circular pinhead found in the Surkh Dum temple; presumably this pin was a votive offering on behalf of a dead man, for, like Sraosha, Zurvan presided over the path leading to the bridge of Cinvat on which the souls of the dead were judged.

After the divine effigies we may turn to those of men in the presence of their gods.   These human figures were usually depicted by the Luristan bronze-smiths in attitudes of prayer and adoration—which tends to suggest that each dead man was escorted by his 'double,' whose function it was to hear the decision of his stern Judge, in this case Sraosha.

The action here is taking place in a supramundane atmosphere in which the artist gives free course to his creative fantasy. Hence the peculiar nature of these scenes in which 'barbarian' figurations are handled with a total disregard of balanced proportions and natural volumes.

There was evidently a mass production of such works, made ready in advance in workshops catering for the cemeteries, in which no real likeness to the human figure was insisted upon. The only thing that counted in these funerary images was the gesture, that of a suppliant in prayer, with both arms raised and the palms of the hands turned forward, or that of the man making an offering to the god—in other words positions of the arms expressing more or less elevated forms of religious emotion.

Men and women are usually naked, though equipped with their weapons and jewellery. Special attention is given to the varying coiffures, which consist of one or more upstanding tufts of hair looking like crests. The curious effect produced by most of these heads is due to the unnaturally prominent nose affixed to a face whose erratic features depart widely from the normal.

65 - LURISTAN. WORSHIPPER STATUETTE (8th-7th CENTURIES B.C.) — PRIVATE COLLECTION, NEW YORK

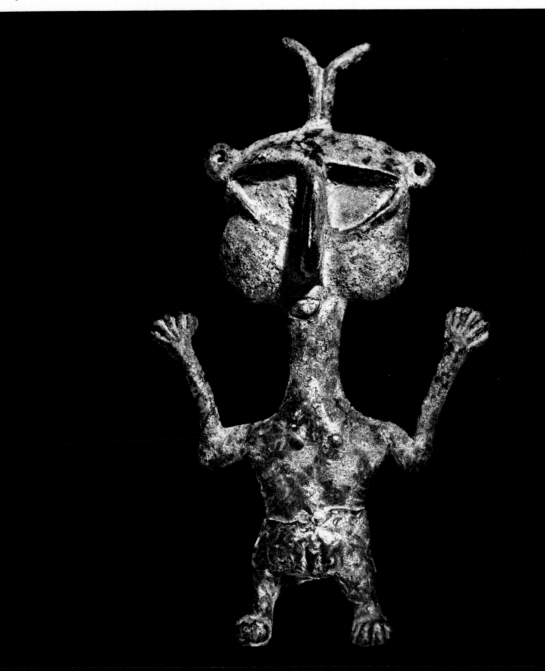

In some of the women's faces, however, the craftsman seems to aim at a special type of beauty characterized by amply rounded cheeks. This is a technical advance and suggests that the Luristan artists were making some attempt to improve on earlier renderings of the human face by stressing its plastic qualities.

But these attempts at modelling were rudimentary at best, except in the case of a small bronze head detached from a statuette which cannot have been more than four inches high. Here, presumably, we have an effigy done from the life, the likeness of a nomad of a distinctive type; in any case this work is an exception to the frankly unrealistic art that was the rule. It also goes to show that the Luristan bronze-smiths were quite capable, on occasion, of modelling in the round.

Among the objects in a tomb we found a seal engraved with the effigy of a horse above which is a figure in a convincingly lifelike posture, that of a seated man with his knees drawn up towards his chin[492].

However, the ancient, well-established tradition of very low relief discouraged figurations in the round, and there was still much to learn of the technique of working in three dimensions.

The one and only figurine of any considerable size (now in the Teheran Museum) bequeathed to us by the art of Luristan bears out this view. It was found in Pusht-i-Kuh, in the foothills of the Zagros mountains, where they abut on the Mesopotamian plain, that is to say at the western

← 66 - LURISTAN. WORSHIPPER STATUETTE (8th-7th CENT. B.C.) — PRIVATE COLL., NEW YORK
67 - LURISTAN. WORSHIPPER STATUETTE (8th-7th CENT. B.C.) — PRIVATE COLL., TEHERAN

extremity of Luristan. A five-line cuneiform inscription, engraved on the figure's garment and beneath the pendants, records both the name of the god represented and the story of this statuette.

The inscription has been translated by Dr Contenau as follows: 'The god of the town of Du-su-tir-ga-zi, of the temple of Tu-ma-ina in the town of Bur-se-se-su. To his temple Marduk, son of Sulman-asridu, governor of Tu-mil, has brought him back and caused him to dwell in his due place.' (No sites having the names mentioned in the text are known to us.) Here we have a small-scale illustration of what was a common practice in the course of the wars between petty chieftains, no less than in those between great powers such as Assyria and Urartu: that of carrying off the gods of the vanquished and transferring them to the conqueror's capital or to one of the towns in his dominion.

What interests us in this figurine is not its points in common with the traditional art of the Luristan bronze-workers, but the fact that an attempt has been made here to give a certain volume to the head and arms. This was something of an innovation, but the artist evidently lacked courage to see it through and, by limiting the three-dimensional effect, betrayed his incomprehension of the organic structure of the body. This is plain to see in the flat, disjointed, unconvincing way in which he handles the torso and lower limbs. Moreover he was hampered by an adherence to the 'law of frontality' (illustrated in the Luristan

68 - LURISTAN. BRONZE STATUETTE (8th-7th CENTURIES B.C.) — TEHERAN MUSEUM

plaques), which made it difficult, not to say impossible, to render forms in terms of visual actuality. The disproportionate smallness of the head is a result of 'verticalism,' evidenced also by the diminutive cap, the unnaturally long nose and by the chin with a pointed beard. Neither the protruding eyeballs, nor the belt, nor the pendants, which might well have tended to attenuate the overall effect of verticality, succeed in doing so.

As was to be expected of an artist working for a warrior clan, the weapons carried by the god were rendered with extreme care. Apart from the sword (in a scabbard fitted with a chape), only the quiver remains. But since this quiver was slung on the god's back, we are justified in assuming that the god held in his hands the bow and three arrows, which were symbols of royalty and power throughout the Iranian world. The way the quiver was hung on the back, by means of leather straps crossed on the chest, resembles that in which we shall see the Median horsemen carrying their swords in the bas-reliefs at Persepolis, and this form of equipment was customary among the peoples of the Eurasian steppes, whose menfolk 'lived on horseback.' Indeed it was adopted as far afield as China.

Another bronze statuette of about the same size was a 'reject'; that is to say the metal-worker laid it aside with a view to recasting it, but never did so. None the less it throws light on certain points of interest. For one thing, it proves that blood sacrifices were practised in Luristan, for the figure is shown holding a sacrificial animal in his arms. The cap with three folds, which the Medes are likewise shown wearing on the Persepolis reliefs, raises a problem of an ethnological order. Was this Median headdress borrowed from the peoples of Luristan, or—as seems more likely—were the inhabitants of Luristan a mixture of Medes and Cimmerians?

Among the many votive objects having a religious or ritual significance there are some which strike a new note. We have, for example, the naïve representation of a rider, weary and wayworn, accomplishing his last journey. Then, again, there is the poignant evocation of a family on the road along which Death is riding. No less touching is the image of an artisan[493] who, humbly kneeling, renders an account of his life; he is naked but has his tools with him: an awl and a cold chisel.

Evidently there were women whose function it was to act as mourners at funeral ceremonies; this would explain two statuettes of women[494-495] from a Luristan tomb, raising their arms in token of despair.

In all these works of 'folk art' the poor quality and inaccuracy of the modelling are compensated for by the eloquence of the gesture.

69 - LURISTAN. COUPLE ON HORSEBACK (8th-7th CENTURIES B.C.) — PRIVATE COLL., TEHERAN

70 - LURISTAN. CAST BRONZE IBEX 71 - HAMMERED BRONZE GAZELLE (8th-7th CENTURIES B.C.) — NEW YORK, BRUSSELS

Among the smaller pieces, representations of animals were even more frequent in the art of Luristan than those of human figures. They are of many kinds and we find great variations in the art and techniques of the bronze-workers. There are, however, no solid grounds for attributing one animal or another to a specific period, to an earlier or later phase of the art of Luristan—which would throw light on its progress or decline—nor have we any means of establishing even a roughly approximate chronology.

The Khurvin tombs yielded, as we have seen, a whole series of small animals which served as trinkets fastened to a necklet, a bangle or a belt. In Luristan, too, hundreds, indeed thousands, of similar pieces have been discovered, and among them quadrupeds are as numerous as birds. Were these, one wonders, animal attributes of the gods and, as such, serving their wearers as magic charms against evil? Or did they represent game animals and promote, by a sort of sympathetic magic, success in hunting? Presumably one of these explanations of their function applies in the majority of cases. Among them figure the domestic animals bred by the nomads of Luristan; their effigies were presumably intended to invoke divine protection of the flocks and herds. Finally, we may note that animal effigies were also used for decorating objects of daily use: seals, tools, chariots and furniture.

From the technical viewpoint one of these objects, a bronze gazelle, is exceptional; contrary to the usual practice, it was not cast in a mould but simply hammered out and fitted together with rivets. This two-dimensional plasticity has a certain power, and indeed the simplified, geometric structure reminds us of the work of some modern animal sculptors.

The mountain ibex was a frequent quarry of the Luristan hunter, and the artists, keen observers, sought to render above all the prompt reflexes of this exceptionally timid animal in moments of peril. It is possible, and of no little interest, to follow the long series of technical experiments made with a view to representing the ibex with its four hoofs bunched together, about to make a sudden leap, on a support of small dimensions. This goes far to rebut the theory, advanced by some, that this method of presentation derived from the steppes of the north-east. It seems, rather, to have been a wholly original invention of the artists of Luristan, for two reasons; one technical, the other that these animal figurines were quite obviously done from life.

On the other hand, the conception of hybrid creatures composed of the foreparts of two animals[496] may not have originated in the mountains of Luristan, since composite animals of this type have been found in Europe, in the Caucasus, and as far east as Mohenjo-Daro in India. Still, it is quite possible that these objects made in the workshops of the Luristan smiths lay at the origin of the famous Achaemenian capitals composed of two animal protomes, which after being used in Iran for royal edifices, made their way eastward to India and westward to the Aegean. In which case the theory that the capital as we find it in the palaces of Susa and Persepolis originally derived from Proto-Elamite seals calls for reconsideration.

Moreover a close study of the small Luristan bronzes makes it clear that the craftsmen of the Cimmerian and Median nomad settlements in the mountains drew inspiration from common sources. Influences of Elam, Babylonia, Assyria and above all Urartu are unmistakable. Meanwhile, however, we will confine ourselves to drawing attention to a new technique: the division of the animal's eye into two parts by a cleft in the eyeball. This was not a local procedure; it had a Urartian origin.

72 - LURISTAN. BIT WITH HORSE PROTOMES (8th-7th CENTURIES B.C.) — BRUSSELS

59

73 - LURISTAN. BIT (8th-7th CENTURIES B.C.) — LOUVRE

74 - LURISTAN. BIT (8th-7th CENT. B.C.) — BRITISH MUSEUM

Many of the weapons and horse trappings found in the cemeteries and shrines of Luristan had never been used. Differing from the votive offerings placed in temples, most of them were merely symbolic objects which the dead man took with him to the Other World for his personal use.

Most frequent in this funerary symbolism is the horse, by itself or with a rider; sometimes, too, there is a pair of horses (recalling those which drew the dead man's chariot). As in the protohistoric civilization of Sialk, it incarnates Death, or Death's emissary, whose task it was to carry the dead man to his last abode.

We have pointed out that the Scythians and all the peoples akin to them buried the dead with their horses. This is evidenced by the Hasanlu tomb, the only one of this type so far discovered in Iran—but there must be others. In Luristan the horse was replaced by horse-bits, called by the peasants who found them *zir-sar* ('under-heads'). A bit placed below the dead man's head acted as a substitute for the horse ridden by him in his lifetime, and symbolically ensured his transit to eternity.

Of the dozens of such objects we have examined not one bore any sign of having been used, or any trace of horses' teeth. One, in fact, adorned with a beribboned stag, weighs over four pounds. These bits, with a rigid cross-bar, are of the same type as the *psalia* with three eyelets which were found in the tombs of Sialk and Hasanlu. (They were being employed by the Assyrians as early as the ninth century B.C.)

When we examine the styles and iconography of the plaques with animal figures we can see how foreign influences were integrated into age-old local traditions. Thus the X-shaped structure characteristic of certain objects was taken over from an imported piece such as the one with a Scythian horse's head in the Godard Collection.

A characteristic instance of a metamorphosis on distinctively Scythian lines is the 'zoomorphic juncture' which so frequently occurs in animal figurations. Moreover ancient themes were given new interpretations and associated with the religious beliefs, mythology and the orally transmitted epic lore of the race of newcomers, having no ethnic affinities with their predecessors in the region, who had established themselves in Luristan.

Despite an admixture of extraneous elements, the Luristan horse bits bear the unmistakable imprint of a nomad mentality. In this context we would draw attention to the practice of attaching wings to creatures[497-498-499] hailing from an imaginary world; also to a type of bit with two recumbent animal protomes in which we have an anticipation of Achaemenian art[500].

75 - LURISTAN. BIT WITH WINGED DOE SUCKLING A FAWN (8th-7th CENT. B.C.) — PRIVATE COLLECTION, TEHERAN

76 - LURISTAN. CLAPPER-HANGER (8th-7th CENT. B.C.)

77 - LURISTAN. REIN-RING (8th-7th CENT. B.C.) — TEHERAN

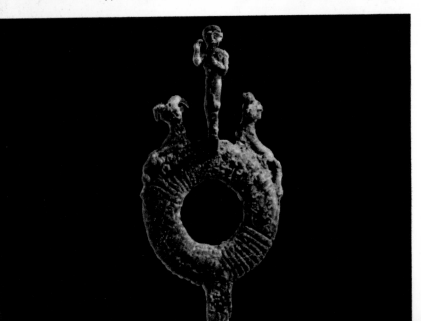

Typical also are the small bells[501] hung on horses' necks (they had had precedents in Sialk) and given the shape of animals or of some nutritive fruit symbolizing fecundity.

Chariots were still used in warfare and to their shafts were added ornamental terminals bearing heads of monsters which were intended to strike terror into the enemy; alongside them figures a bird deriving from the repertory of the Sialk potters. The decorations of the rein-rings were inspired by Mesopotamian and Assyrian themes; here motifs of a rigidly hieratic symmetry strike a contrast with livelier scenes of investiture or of enemies surrendering to the victor. This persistent striving for decorative effects charged with barbaric power makes itself felt also in the rings holding the crossed straps together under the horses' bellies. The purpose served by a piece unique of its kind, bearing a lavish ornamentation that presumably illustrates some epic theme, cannot be determined; it may have formed part of the equipment of a chariot. Here we see a bobbin enclosed in a frame above which is a scene in which various exotic animals are taking part. This is one of the most elaborate compositions in the round produced by the Luristan bronze-smiths[502].

A great many axes have been discovered in the tombs. They are indeed so numerous that they can hardly fall into the class of the ceremonial axes which, judging by the ones figuring on Achaemenian monuments, were real weapons. Here again we have symbolic objects made for the use of the

78 - LURISTAN. REIN-RING (8th-7th CENTURIES B.C.) — TEHERAN

dead man in the Other World. Their shape is not peculiar to Luristan; weapons of this type had been in common use in Hither Asia, some since the third millennium, and the others—notably those with the blades emerging from the open maw of a beast —in the second half of the second millennium B.C. But, on to these basic forms, the nomad bronze-smith grafted a host of curious motifs having a symbolic significance, perhaps religious, perhaps charged with a numinous power operative in the after-life.

Usually the sockets of the axe-heads are open at both ends. We only know of one in which it is closed—in this case with a boldly modelled lion's head. Attempts were made, it seems, to strike a balance between the decorations of the blade and the haft, the latter being more elaborately ornamented when the former is less so. Thus, when the blade has a purely geometric decoration, the tips of the haft are given the form of animals' heads[503], or sometimes of human heads having the Median type of coiffure[504].

One of the most striking of the axes with richly decorated blades is the one representing an archer about to let fly an arrow. Though the rows of spikes projecting from the socket heighten the spectacular effect of the weapon, they serve no practical purpose. The cutting edge placed at a right angle to the handle demonstrates the purely symbolic function of this axe. An embryonic notion of the *gryllus* can be seen in an axe on which two lions' jaws are 'spitting out' the blade as well as the handle. The vein of fantasy is even

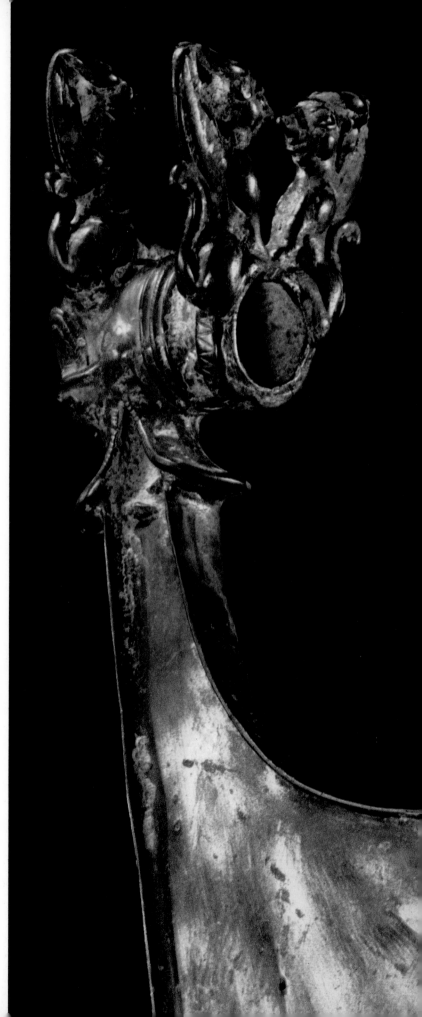

79 - LURISTAN. BRONZE AXE (8th-7th CENTURIES B.C.) — PRIVATE COLLECTION, TEHERAN

80-81 - LURISTAN. BRONZE AXE BLADES (8th-7th CENTURIES B.C.) — PRIVATE COLLECTIONS, NEW YORK AND PARIS

82 - LURISTAN. BRONZE AXE BLADE (8th-7th CENTURIES B.C.) — TEHERAN MUSEUM

83 - LURISTAN. DAGGER HILT (8th-7th CENTURIES B.C.)

more pronounced in various pieces executed in the round, combining several motifs with a view to making clear the symbolism of the object, e. g. the horse with a bird's tail and a rider on its back; or else to making the effigy more convincing by introducing realistic touches.

Typical insignia of power are the halberd[505] having a bearded head in the socket joining the blade to the haft, and an axe of the fenestrate (so-called 'Syrian') type[506].

Unlike the axes, most of which are merely simulacra, the swords and daggers are evidently real weapons. Commonest of these is the dagger with an openwork hilt, inlaid with ivory, bone or wood, the blade embellished with an incised decoration. Often the hilt is fitted with a semicircular pommel having the form of a statuette, or with reliefs illustrating the warrior's religious tenets. To this latter type belongs a sword which must have been owned by a chieftain of considerable importance, since it has an elaborately carved silver hilt. Though executed in a less valuable metal, a sword[507] entirely in iron has a hammered blade and finely decorated haft, and the pommel is adorned with two human heads[508] and two small lions[509] treated in a geometric style and serving as the hilt-guard.

The war mace ceased to consist of a plain round head with a tubular handle and developed an over-all tubular form, giving the craftsman a large surface on which to exercise his skill.

The bronze handles of whetstones (so essential to the warrior's equipment) provided the Luristan smiths with other opportunities for animal figurations. However, the extreme fragility of some of these objects, for example those including representations of antlers, arching above the animal's head, ruled out the possibility of making any practical use of them.

Most of the votive shields from Luristan are alleged to have been found in the temple of Surkh Dum; whether this was so or not, there is no question that it was customary in the kingdom of Urartu to hang shields on the walls of

84-85-86 - LURISTAN.   HANDLES   OF   WHETSTONES
(8th-7th CENT. B.C.) — BRUSSELS, PARIS, SEATTLE   →

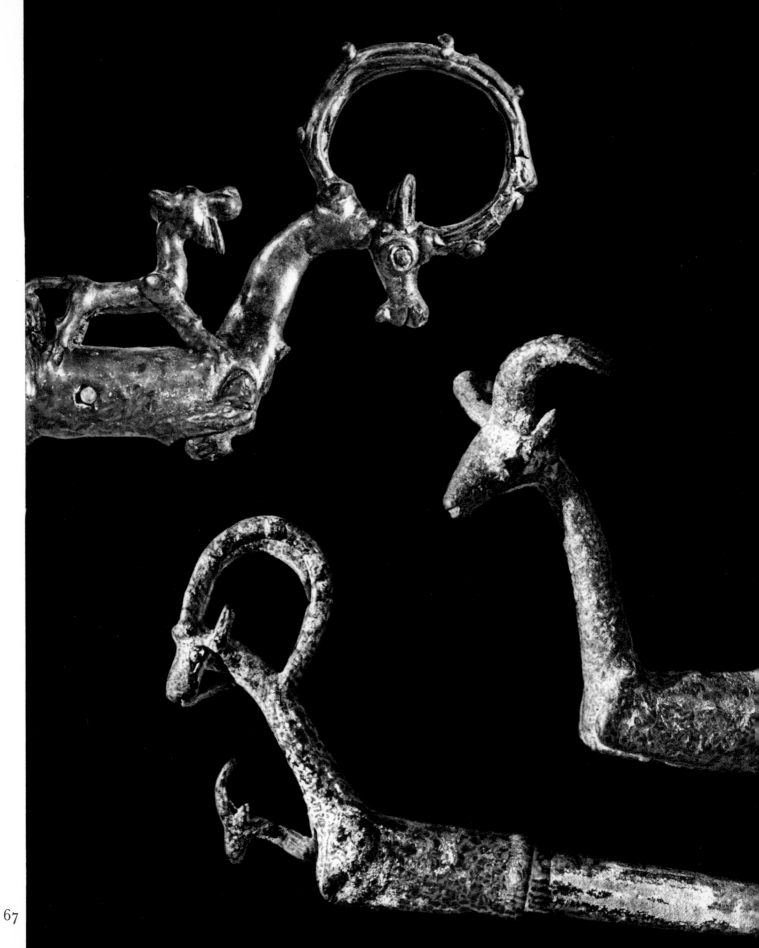

temples. A bas-relief from Nineveh shows a large number of shields fixed to the façade of the temple of Musasir, an important religious centre west of Lake Urmia, where there was a local cult of the god Haldis. This temple was looted by the army of the Assyrian king Sargon II in 714 B.C. In their descriptions of this incident the Assyrian chroniclers speak of 'six golden bucklers and twelve stout silver bucklers' which hung on either side of the dwelling of the god Haldis, 'all exceedingly resplendent' and adorned with 'disks bearing heads of snarling dogs, dragons, lions and aurochs.'

No zoomorphic *umbones* have been positively traced to Luristan. There are, however, small round shields with an *umbo* consisting of a human face cut short at the chin, having perhaps an apotropaic function. An Iranian origin of this type of object seems all the more likely since the iconography of the pins with large round heads described above seems basic to its general design.

Here we have, then, still further evidence of the important part played by the Irano-Urartian *koine* in the origins of the arts of the West. For the round buckler with a figurative *umbo (omphalos)* was not a Greek invention, and was already in use in the East at the time it made its appearance on Greek painted pottery (late eighth century B.C.). We have found it with a zoomorphic *umbo* in Urartu. But the only land to adorn these votive objects with a central boss in the likeness of a *human* head was Iran; this practice originated in the workshops of the Luristan smiths long before it was adopted by Greek and Etruscan armourers.

The faces on the round shields have many striking similarities amongst themselves : the double curve of the eyebrows meeting above the bridge of a projecting nose, cheeks in relief, thin lips. Two of these faces, however, without being portraits in the exact sense, have a less archaic appearance. Thus in a V-shaped head the carefully groomed hair is bunched over the ears in two thick, heavy tufts; this is exactly the type of coiffure we shall find in Achaemenian figurations at Persepolis. Here, for the first time, the eye-sockets were filled with black and white enamel pastes adding lustre to the eye. Another face, with modelling in high relief, shows greater technical proficiency, the general effect being modified by the craftsman's predilection for dark lines. Sometimes the faces did not cover the whole surface of the disk; in such cases a decoration in repoussé, worked over with a graving tool, was added.

87-88-89 - LURISTAN. SHIELD ORNAMENTS: UMBONES AND HANDLE (8th-7th CENT. B.C.) — BRUSSELS, PARIS, BRUSSELS

90 - LURISTAN. CENTREPIECE (UMBO) OF A SHIELD (8th-7th CENT. B.C.) — PRIVATE COLLECTION, BASEL

We can only guess at the purpose served by a small group of bronzes consisting of curved strips of metal pierced at the ends with holes to fix them to some other object. Quite possibly they were riveted to the inner surface of the shield, providing loops through which the forearm could be passed, since a mere handle could not ensure a firm grip of it. (Similar pieces have been discovered at Olympia, the oldest of which cannot, it seems, be dated earlier than the last third of the seventh century B.C.) They are decorated with motifs of a familiar type.

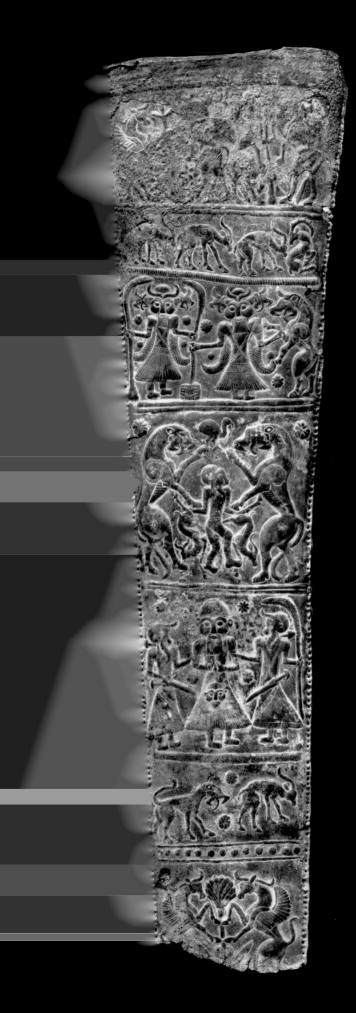

The highly elaborate ornamentation of the bronze plaques embellishing the wood and leather quivers found in the Surkh Dum temple, justifies us in regarding them as votive weapons, and it is on this assumption that we shall base a tentative interpretation of the subjects represented. The scenes on these plaques are arranged in registers and include such motifs as winged bulls recumbent on the Seven Spheres, animals on each side of a Sacred Tree, a god overcoming two lions or fighting with two enemies, and figurations of the palm-tree which were to inspire the Achaemenian artists when they designed the capitals of columns at Susa and Persepolis.

The theme on a quiver in the Metropolitan Museum, New York, is somewhat puzzling. Agreeing with Dussaud, we are inclined to relate the iconographic motif to pre-Zoroastrian eschatology. Dumézil, however (whose views are endorsed by several scholars who attribute the Luristan bronzes to the Kassites, worshippers of the Aryan gods of India, Suryas and Marutas), thinks that we should look not to the religious beliefs of the Iranians but to those of their neighbours and kinsfolk in India. In this case the theme should be interpreted in terms of Vedic theology, the deities on the third register being identified with Varuna and Mithras, those on the fourth with Indra, Rudra and Parjyana (storm gods), and on the last register with the Nasatya twins performing 'the rejuvenation of the decrepit ancient, Cyavana.' Every interpretation needs a factual basis and since we

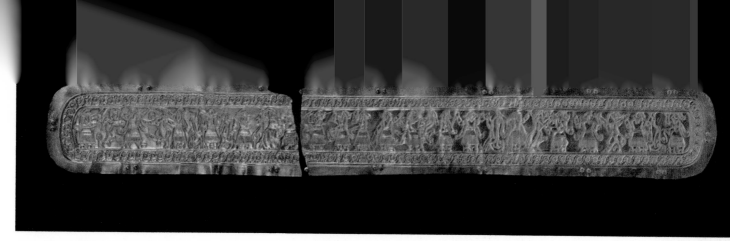

have none to offer in place of those set forth above, we will confine ourselves to saying that in our opinion the date of the Luristan bronzes precludes their attribution to the Kassites and, this being so, we cannot readily accept an hypothesis purporting to explain the theology of the Iranians (now partially reconstituted) in terms of that incorporated in the sacred book of the Aryans of India. It seems quite possible that the figure on the fifth register is the god Zurvan, since it bears a woman's face on its lower body, a feature observed on other monuments. If so, why not identify the figures on the third register as Zurvan's two sons Ahuramazda and Ahriman, the powers of Good and Evil?

The decoration on another quiver is in a more narrative vein and apparently illustrates incidents of its owner's life. There are realistic scenes of hunting and of ritual games, both evoking favourite activities and recreations which the man in question (who already has the aspect and bearing of a Persian nobleman) hopes to continue indulging in after death.

Few articles of jewellery in precious metal are extant, most probably because the peasants who unearthed them thought it best to melt them down to avoid trouble with the authorities.

Belts were an important item in the equipment of these warrior horsemen, and the arrangement of the thematic material figuring on them was strictly regulated. The strap itself was always decorated in the episodic, 'continuous' style, whereas the 'animal style' was given free expression on the buckle. In the former the composition, at once elaborate and condensed, is pervaded with a religious and funerary symbolism governed by laws of its own. But folk art insists on lifelike imagery, and in the scenes of the chase and warfare the artist is only superficially subservient to conventions that might 'cramp his style.' As for the buckles, the bronze-smith enlarges his repertory only under Scythian or Caucasian influences. On a bronze clasp where almost the whole surface is occupied by a 'running dog,'

93 - LURISTAN. GOLD BELT, DETAIL

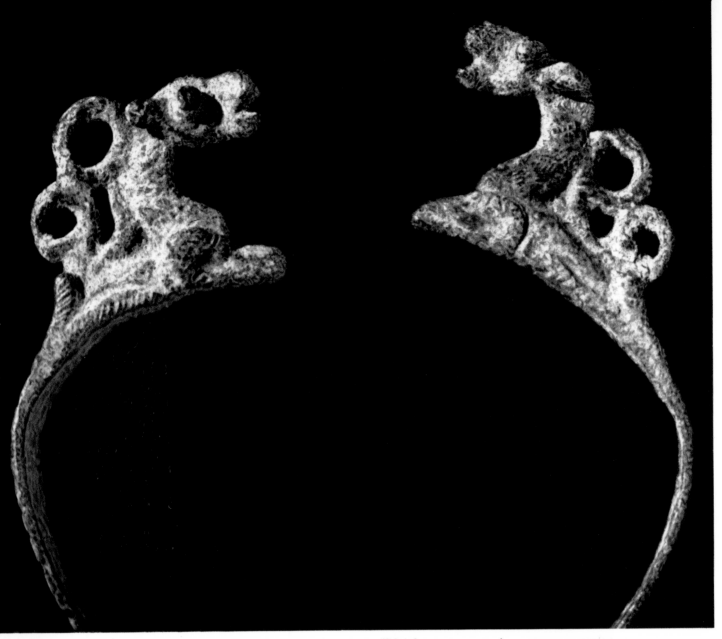

94 - LURISTAN. BRONZE BRACELET (8th-7th CENTURIES B.C.) — TEHERAN MUSEUM

only a small place is left free, in the centre, for the incrustation of a long snake (in iron)[510]. Imported from Koban and unique in Luristan, this object is of special interest since it confirms the theory advanced by Soviet experts who attribute the Koban culture to the Cimmerians. Some equally significant pieces of the same kind have been found near Sinope in Asia Minor which, according to ancient historians, was the Cimmerian capital. The Cernuschi Museum in Paris has a bronze buckle in two parts, male and female, each consisting of an almost rectangular frame with a thick round metal tongue. To the frames are soldered on one side three hooks, on the other three rings, ending in animals' heads. This type of buckle was much used by the Etruscans.

The Luristan craftsmen also made gold, bronze and iron bracelets, some having animal motifs at their extremities, while others opened to admit the wrist and, when closed, were secured with a pin. On the end of one of these is a human head.

Of the articles of personal adornment, the most attractive perhaps are those shaped like frontlets worn on the forehead. They consist of thin strips of gold or silver leaf decorated with hunting scenes. A bronze diadem[511] with its decorative scheme of birds' heads with preternaturally long necks brings us back once again to the world of Scythian art. Here the craftsman's technical skill and the extreme care he has devoted to rendering a protome in full face compel our admiration, and whether the idea of it originated in the Zagros region or elsewhere, it is yet another instance of the singular genius of the metal-workers of Luristan in their handling of animal figurations.

Our discoveries in the Sialk cemetery showed that torques were already being worn by men. This practice continued at Khurvin and in Luristan, where the men wore heavy twisted coils of metal round their necks. This tends to prove the intimate relations between the newcomers on the Plateau and the peoples of the North.

Greece perhaps excepted, no other known Iron Age civilization has yielded so many pins as protohistoric Iran and no other art has furnished so many pins in such a variety of shapes as that of Luristan. There is a rich field for investigation in the mass of objects used for personal adornment and those endowed with a religious function. Much importance was attached to the latter, judging by the number found in tombs, and especially in the temple of Surkh Dum. Characteristic of the first class of objects—those for everyday wear—is the persistence of the familiar animal motifs; in the second class we find an iconography centring on specific themes in which the protagonist is a god or a tutelary genius. In these objects the recourse to demonology, fundamental to Median religious practice, is particularly marked.

Here, too, we find representations of the human figure in profile, equipped with wings. Dating as they do to the sixth century B.C., they evidence a new strain in Iranian art which, as we shall see, comes into prominence under the

95 - LURISTAN.   SILVER FRONTLET (8th-7th CENTURIES B.C.) — PRIVATE COLLECTION, NEW YORK

73

Achaemenians and may perhaps already have existed in Median monumental art. They also add to our scanty knowledge of the type of costume worn by the nomads roaming the Plateau. This consisted of a short tunic stopping above the knee or a long robe with a fringe at the bottom, a bell-shaped cloak open on one side, a coiffure including two tufts of hair above the forehead, a Median mitre (subsequently imitated by the Persians) and a sort of Greek *polos;* this last, however, is somewhat exceptional. This wealth of images shows, moreover, the multiplicity of influences intermingling on the Plateau. Here, for instance, we have a genius seated on what seems to be a panther, clearly of Mesopotamian inspiration, and its posture, shortly after, gave rise to the idea of thrones and chairs flanked by animals, their paws incorporated in the feet of the throne or chair. Elsewhere we see Assyrian influences, as when the artist represents a real tree and groups the seven planets (ranked by Iranians among the demons) above sphinxes' heads. There are also themes deriving from the most ancient arts of Western Asia (these are of particular interest) and others from archaic Greek art. Most typical is the head of a pin on whose field are dispersed, around an undecorated *omphalos,* the *membra disjecta* of animals torn to pieces[512]. In approximately the same periods both Greeks and Iranians had the idea of representing mythological themes in their arts. In Greece these figurations, which took first the form of engravings on fibulae and were then adopted by the potters, were soon abandoned. It was otherwise in Iran, where no sooner were these mythological and legendary themes employed on pottery than they were taken over by the metal-workers who, as is demonstrated by the art of Luristan, continued using them for at least two centuries. How is one to account for the fact that the art of Luristan (most of whose idioms we are still unable to elucidate) died out almost entirely, leaving only some faint vestiges in the Iranian arts succeeding it? It seems possible that the sudden eclipse of Elam and above all the decline of Urartu, coupled with the rise to power of the Median kingdom, may have contributed to slowing down the activity of this Iranian metal-working centre and led to the absorption of its provincial art by one that was already by way of becoming the art of a Great Power.

Some silver pins (none such had been found before 1957) show analogies with the earliest Greek fibulae, not only by reason of the precious metal employed for them but also in their forms, their engraved designs, and their function. They throw further light on the direct or indirect relations existing between Iran and the western world in the eighth and seventh centuries B.C.

We would draw particular attention to the pins employed in pairs, each with a ring to which was fastened a small chain linking them together. These were worn at the level of the shoulders, as was the custom in archaic Greece. On the heads of the current types of pins we find a great variety of finely executed decorations; the one representing a Bactrian camel provides one of the few

98 - LURISTAN. FRAGMENT OF A PIN WITH BIRDS   99 - PINHEAD WITH CAMEL (8th-7th CENT. B.C.) — TEHERAN

75

100-101 - LURISTAN.   MIRRORS WITH LION-HANDLE AND CARYATID-HANDLE (8th-7th CENT. B.C.) — BRUSSELS AND LOUVRE

clues to the dating of the Luristan bronzes. For it was not until the ninth century B.C., in the course of their campaigns on the Iranian plateau, that the Assyrians encountered the camel, to which they gave the name of 'dromedary with two backs.' It may be noted in this context that in the lists of booty, these animals are mentioned only in single units, and we know that it was only in the eighth century that they became widely used in the kingdom of Urartu. But the Medes kept in close touch with their Iranian forbears of Central Asia, particularly with those in the region of Badakhshan, skirting the Pamirs, where lapis lazuli, a precious stone in great demand with the Assyrians, who traded in it, was mined. Finally mention may be made of an iron pin whose head, given the form of a monster, is so disposed that the legs of this fantastic creature fold up under its body like those of the animals on Scythian artefacts[513].

The three varieties of fibula have been found in Luristan. The first is the type most common in Iran from the late eighth or early seventh century on[514]. The second has no spring and its pin is fastened to the arc by a small ring, turning on a stud. This type is rare in Hither Asia (we shall find it again among the objects in the Ziwiyeh Treasure) but seems to have been in general use in the Caucasus. The presence of the third among the objects from Luristan has a certain significance since fibulae given the shape of animals[515] were a speciality of the Cimmerians. They have been discovered in eastern Europe in places where Cimmerian settlements are known to have existed.

The affinity between the Luristan and Khurvin cultures is borne out also by their common usage of pendants in the form of shod feet. The type of shoe with an upcurved tip, common to all the regions we have been dealing with, is embellished and so to say enlivened in Luristan by the addition of a human head. But this element may not be merely decorative; an isolated foot when it has a god's head above, can to symbolize the god in question.

That the two cultures were contemporaneous is also evidenced by a bronze mirror whose handle has the shape of a naked woman in the pose of a caryatid. Unique among the Luristan bronzes is another mirror, of special interest for the light it throws on the relations between the Luristan civilization and that of the Eurasian steppe. It consists of a flat disk having on its back a handle whose extremities represent lions with their heads slewed round, gazing at each other. This type of mirror was not used in Hither Asia and was equally foreign to the Greek world. None the less its sphere of distribution was a vast one, extending from China, across the Altai range in Siberia, to the region of European Scythia. A silver mirror in the same style, decorated with thin gold plaques and scenes incised with a graving tool, was found in a Scythian grave at Kelermes. It is discussed at length by Maximova, who dates it to the first quarter of the sixth century B.C. We discovered a similar object in a Parthian tomb at Susa. It may be assigned to the culture, later by four or five centuries, of an Iranian people who came from the same region as the Cimmerians of Luristan and had kept in touch with them.

Our knowledge of the pottery in the graves of Luristan is somewhat limited, because the peasants who opened them up were looking for objects in bronze, which were easiest to sell, and saw no point in preserving the ritual or domestic utensils. Enough remains, however, to show their marked affinities with the ones found at Sialk. For, unlike the Khurvin, Hasanlu and Amlash potters, those of Luristan made use of painting. But it is to be noted that they made improvements in the form of their vases at the expense of the painted decoration, which gradually dwindled. The potter imitated the bronze-worker and took over from the metal vessels their new elements[516].

Chief among these were, first, the basket-handle placed above the mouth of the vases with long beak-spouts and, secondly, the lugs on the sides, which are given somewhat larger dimensions than before. Copied by the potter from a bronze equivalent, the most distinctive specimen of this type of vessel at once throws new light on the civilization of Luristan and on its relations with foreign centres, and confirms the validity of its attribution to a specific people. Note, for example, the winged figure on the lug riveted to the belly of the vase. Though known for years, it has never been closely studied; attention has been directed almost exclusively to the handles, given the form of bearded personages, on cauldrons

102 - LURISTAN. BASKET-HANDLE VASE (8th-7th CENTURIES B.C.) — PRIVATE COLLECTION

of Urartian origin. Yet a comparative study of these ornamental adjuncts is rewarding and we shall revert at a later page to the subject of the Luristan vases and the Urartian cauldrons, which reveal a constant give-and-take of ideas in the *koine* of Irano-Urartian metallurgy. Meanwhile we confine ourselves to pointing out the fact that the kingdom of Urartu was the home of a flourishing metal-working industry in which the artisans most in favour with the Assyrians and the mercenaries who had acquired wealth in their service, took part. One of their tasks was to train artists hailing from other countries, among whom the Medes, if we are to trust Darius, were highly thought of. As it so happens, the Luristan vase we have been discussing is an exact replica of one of the few vases definitely assignable to Median art.

On the handle of a round vase illustrated here the Luristan bronze-smith created a new motif that subsequently an Achaemenian goldsmith was to copy when he adorned the handles of a vessel in precious metal with two standing ibexes in an heraldic pose.

Among the smaller receptacles, so many of which have been found, drinking cups and dishes, plain in form but richly decorated with repoussé and incised work, have pride of place. Notable is the taste for complex imagery in which, amid real or imaginary animals, man is shown in constant conflict with the powers of hostile nature. This iconographic theme is not distinctively Iranian, and seems to have appealed to peoples in many parts of the world. We find

103 - LURISTAN VASE HANDLE (8th-7th C. B.C.) — CINCINNATI 104 - ACHAEMENIAN VASE HANDLE (4th C. B.C.) — BERLIN

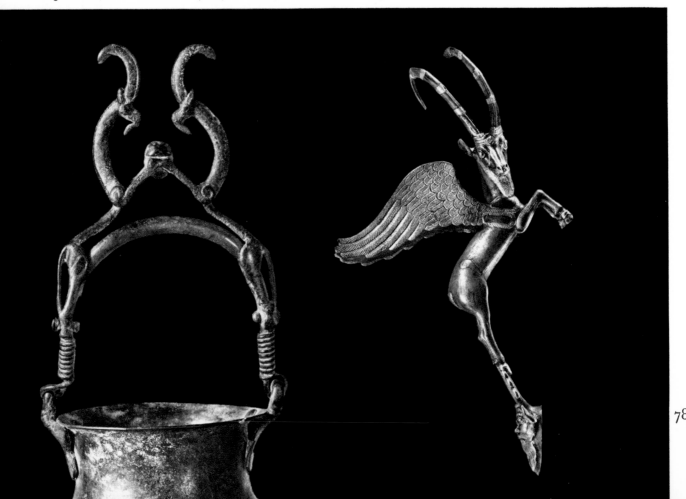

it on Chinese bronzes of the period of the Contending States. But nothing is known of where it originated or how it was transmitted. On the other hand the tutelary animals keeping guard over the liquid in the vase strike a familiar note; from Sialk to Luristan they have retained, intact, their occult significance. A small vase in solid bronze whose neck is divided into metopes embellished with animal motifs in cast bronze is said to have been found on the same site as a rhyton, also in bronze, having the shape of a boar's head. Extremely realistic, this head bears no trace of the traditions of the Luristan bronze-smiths and may well be of Assyrian provenance, for rhytons of this kind were widely used in Assyria in the eighth and seventh centuries B.C.

As at Khurvin and Hasanlu, tripods were in favour in Luristan. Here, too, we find bronze tripods whose legs, copied from terracotta models, have the form of human legs in the high boots worn by the nomad horsemen.

Some of the situlae with embossed decorations discovered in graves in Luristan are clearly influenced by Assyrian art. But though the themes are often Assyrian the spirit in which they are treated is sometimes different. It is known that the Assyrians recruited their artisans, metal-workers especially, in outlying lands, and it seems very probable that a fair number of the bronze-smiths in the Luristan workshops had already worked for the Assyrians. This would account for the purely Assyrian nature of the themes on the situlae found in Luristan and

105-106 - LURISTAN. RHYTON AND VASE
(8th-7th C. B.C.) — TEHERAN

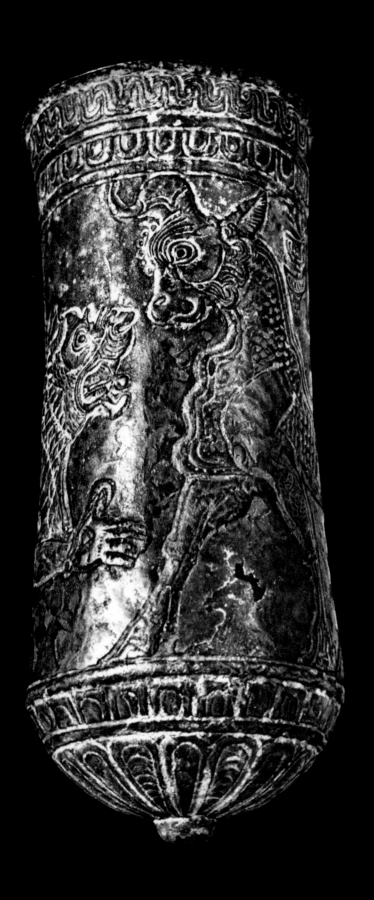

also for the modifications introduced by the local craftsmen, who both changed the ethnic types represented and made characteristic alterations in garments and weapons. We must also remember that, outside Luristan, most of these sacred vessels (now dispersed) were unearthed at Zalu Ab on the main road from Kermanshah to Hamadan, that is to say in a region which must have been included in the kingdom of Ellipi and situated on the frontier of that of Mannai.

Another type of situla (resembling the small Assyrian pails) has lugs that are probably of Urartian inspiration. It has points in common with a cauldron fastening recently acquired by the Teheran Museum; shaped like a bird, with a ring and a loose clasp (now lost), it seems to belong to a group of similar objects whose area of distribution ranged from Urartu, by way of Greece, to Etruria. The first cauldron fastening of the kind discovered in Iran, it suggests that this type of applique had an Oriental origin.

Only one vase in glass paste is known to us[517]. Found in a tomb in Luristan, it was recently added to the Foroughi Collection. Of a nacreous yellow hue, and decorated with black festoons, it is assignable to a well-known family of glassware, generally believed to have originated in Egypt, whose proliferation in the lands along the Mediterranean coast may be dated, according to the best authorities, to the late eighth century B.C. The shapes of these glass-paste vases derived from those in pottery or stone. Vases having the same form as the

107 - LURISTAN. SITULA WITH ANIMAL RELIEFS
(8th CENTURY B.C.) — TEHERAN MUSEUM

one found in the Luristan tomb were made in Elam from the latter half of the second millennium B.C. on. They were produced in large numbers at Susa in the late eighth century B.C. The only difference is that the Luristan vase has two small lugs, never found on the vases in ordinary terracotta. It can safely be dated to about the seventh century B.C. As to the place where it was made, we would suggest an Elamite centre; perhaps even, on the strength of our recent discoveries, Susa itself. Indeed the glass industry seems to have reached a fairly high standard of perfection in Elam, as early as the second millennium B.C. A wooden door which we found in Temple B of Inshushinak, a temple actually built *inside* the Choga Zambil ziggurat, near Susa, about 1250 B.C., was adorned with hundreds of long rods in white glass paste decorated with entwined ribbons of black glass paste, and this may well have given the Luristan glass-worker the idea of the vase in question.

A general survey of protohistoric Iranian art such as that on the preceding pages can but briefly touch on many of the problems it sets the student of the period. For example, how explain the extraordinary growth of the Iranian metal industry in the eighth and seventh centuries B.C.? No other civilization, except perhaps that of the Etruscans, has yielded such a wealth of metal objects, with so great a diversity of forms, so wide a range of subjects and techniques, as those of the metal-workers of Luristan. Yet this art arose in a region where nothing, it seems, had prepared the way for it or even suggested the possibility of its emergence. Luristan, moreover, was a land difficult of access and, so far as is known, played no important part in the political, artistic or economic life of the Plateau. The reasons suggested for the sudden flowering of this highly imaginative and novel art are purely conjectural. True, the incursion of a new ethnic element cannot be ruled out, but even so we must also assume that the invaders found already existent conditions favouring this remarkable artistic development.

Can it have been that some change in the political situation led to a deviation of the trade route between Elam and the North, causing it to pass through the Iranian highland and promoting closer contacts between Luristan and the Median and Elamite cultures? Yet at this time Elam was already losing its ascendancy and, soon after, disappeared for good; also, no very marked traces of the impact of its art on that of Luristan can be detected. To speak of Assyro-Babylonian strains in the arts now coming to birth in Iran does not take us far. That such existed is undeniable, but by and large the art of the Iranian metal-workers has a cachet peculiar to itself. And the same reservations must be made regarding the influence of Mesopotamian art.

Should we assume, then, that a Hurrian substratum in the arts of Western Asia during the first millennium B.C. accounts for these art trends, which, moving eastward from the Hurrian centres in northern Mesopotamia, impinged on the Plateau? This theory seems to be borne out by the fact that the painted pottery of Level I at Tepe Giyan belongs to the family of vases of the Nuzi type found throughout Western Asia. Its proliferation as far as the Zagros range may well have been due to the wide diffusion of Hurrian elements. And 'Hurrian' means, in effect, Urartian.

We have spoken several times of the relations prevailing between the Iranians and the kingdom of Urartu, of which they were subjects to begin with, then the allies, and finally the conquerors. Hence our view that it was in conjunction with Urartu that western Iran constituted a *koine* as regards the metal industry, in which it played a brilliant if subordinate role, or else (as some believe) that of an equally skilled successor. But there is also the possibility that Urartu and Iran competed on an equal footing in their relations with the western world.

The formation and activity of the Irano-Urartian *koine* date to the period when Greece was casting off the thrall of Geometric art and assimilating the more advanced procedures of the East—that is to say, roughly, to the eighth century B.C. It is generally agreed that in this early phase of its evolution Greek art was affected not only by Phoenician and Syrian influences but also by that of Hurrian art (whose traditions went back to the second millennium B.C.) and, lastly, by that of Urartu, which was, geographically speaking, the remotest country. How could the art of the Iranian Plateau, closely tied up as it was with the art of Urartu, have failed to follow likewise the path that now lay open to it, taking advantage of political and economic conditions that favoured the diffusion of Urartian art?

Practically nothing is known of the art of the Lake Van region in the period before the establishment of the kingdom of Urartu. A few fragments of pottery seem to indicate that painted pottery was in use there. But the chief centre of its production, so far as we know today, was Sialk. It is above all in the works of the Sialk potters and in those of the Luristan bronze-smiths (of a later date) that we find analogies with works of the early phase of the 'Orientalization' of the Greek Geometric style, which followed them by some decades. This point will be discussed in a later chapter dealing with the Irano-Urartian *koine* and its relations with the West.

108 - LURISTAN. VASE IN THE FORM OF A FIGURE HOLDING A GOBLET (8th-7th CENTURIES B.C.) — PRIVATE COLLECTION, ROME →

110 - THE MEDIAN TOWN OF KISHESIM AFTER AN ASSYRIAN BAS-RELIEF (8th CENTURY B.C.)

III

IRANIAN ART IN THE SEVENTH CENTURY B. C.

THE revolt against Assyria led by the Median chieftain Kashtariti broke out in 673 B.C. and the Medes were backed by powerful allies: the kingdom of Mannai, the Scythians and the Cimmerians. Esarhaddon, King of Assyria, attempted to sow discord among the rebels. He began by seeking to win over to his cause the Median tribes which had not taken part in the rebellion. One of the longest Assyrian texts so far discovered (by Mallowan at Nimrud), a treaty between the king of Assyria and the Median prince Ramataia, bears this out. The allegiance of several Median chiefs having been secured, it was confirmed by payment of tribute to the king —an event commemorated in an ivory carving found at Nimrud in the throne room of the Temple of Nabu (where the above-mentioned text was also found).

But the crowning success of Assyrian diplomacy was to wean the Scythians from their Median allies and persuade them to join forces with the Assyrians. This new alliance appears to have been sealed by the marriage of the Scythian chief Partatua with an Assyrian princess. Kashtariti, who has been identified as the Phraortes mentioned by Herodotus (i. 102), succeeded nevertheless in setting up a more or less independent state, only to be defeated and killed in 653. His defeat was followed by a twenty-eight-year occupation of Media by the Scythians. He was succeeded by his son Cyaxares, whose long reign (forty years according to Herodotus) was a brilliant period in the history of Media. Allying himself with Babylon, he broke the power of the Assyrians and extended the frontiers of his kingdom as far as Asia Minor. His capital was Ecbatana (present-day Hamadan), whose acropolis, as yet unexplored, is bound to conceal extensive remains of Median, Achaemenian and Parthian times. Excavations there may be expected to yield new information on the principles of town-planning followed by the Iranians, principles identified by us at Sialk and discernible in Assyrian bas-reliefs representing Median towns.

← 109 - OXUS TREASURE. MAN HOLDING A BARSOM (7th-6th CENT. B.C.) — BRITISH MUSEUM

In founding Ecbatana (i.e. 'place of assembly'), on the invasion route of the Assyrian armies, Deioces (according to Herodotus, i. 98-100) or Cyaxares (according to Diakonov) intended it to serve as a defensive outpost against invaders. Although Cyaxares unified Media and reorganized the army and administration, his reign was by no means as peaceful as Herodotus would have us believe. When Babylonian records make mention of the Medes (from 615 on), the name of their king Cyaxares is often coupled with the term *umman-manda*, which cannot refer either to the Medes or the Scythians alone, but suggests a mixed army of Medes and Scythians, perhaps Cimmerians as well. True, the Medes formed in themselves an effective striking force, but they had to reckon not only with external adversaries but also with the unreliability of the petty princes who rallied (or were forced to rally) round them. Moreover, the assimilation of the (presumably indigenous) Asianics needed time. So that, in addition to the complex of peoples of Elamite-Caspian stock already in occupation of the region, the conjunction of Median, Scythian and Cimmerian elements strongly affected the intellectual and artistic culture of the Medes.

III - DUKKAN-I-DAUD. ROCK TOMB   112 - DETAIL   (7th-6th CENTURIES B.C.) — IN SITU

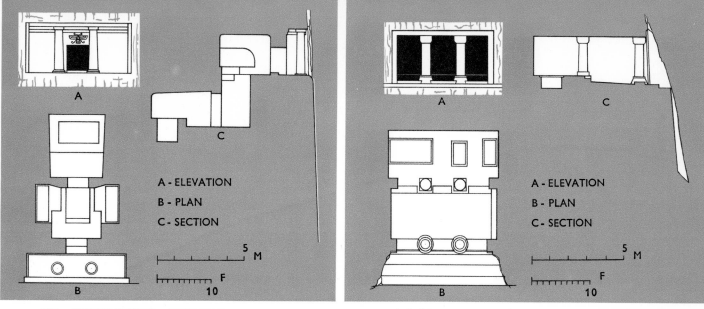

MEDIAN ART

WE know next to nothing about Median architecture. Only a few rock tombs throw any light on the nature of the dwellings of this period. Their most characteristic feature was a porch roof resting on columns in front of the entrance. It is easy to perceive the function of such a roof in civil architecture; it protected the house from direct rays of the sun in summer, while permitting light to enter in winter when the sun was lower in the sky. The same structural device was employed in the palaces of Persepolis, and it is still found in present-day Iranian buildings.

The tombs comprise an entrance hall, one or two funerary chambers, either one above the other (as at Farhad-u-Shirin) or side by side, separated by columns (as at Fakhrika). The graves were intended for one, two or three bodies, and some funerary chambers, like that at Dukkan-i-Daud, included niches in which offerings were placed. The columns are round, resting on plinths or on circular bases or on bases shaped like an inverted ninepin. Certain columns include a listel. The capitals were square slabs or, imitating wood-work, were given the shape of a four-petalled palmette. When the column stands flush with the wall and becomes a pilaster, capitals are replaced by impost-blocks which project right and left, forming two large volutes of the Ionic type and decorated in the centre with an archaic palmette.

The bas-reliefs on these tombs are of an interesting and unusual kind. On the smoothed rock-face of the Dukkan-i-Daud tomb stands the figure of a man conforming to the ethnic type of ancient Media. In his left hand he holds the *barsom*, his right is raised in a gesture of adoration. Is this a priest or the occupant of the tomb? Probably the latter, in our opinion. The winged disk surmounts the entrance to the 'Tomb of Farhad and Shirin' (as it is popularly called) near the village of Sehna, between Kermanshah and Hamadan.

115 - KIZKAPAN. ROCK TOMB, FAÇADE (7th-6th CENTURIES B.C.)

A comparative study of the tombs of Kizkapan and Sakavand raises two problems, that of Scythian participation and that of the influence of Luristan. By and large, the Kizkapan (or 'Abductor's') Tomb, located in the mountains of Iraqi Kurdistan, near the village of Surdash, belongs to the group of Median rock tombs. One feature, however, sets it apart: the entire ceiling, hewn in the rock, is carved in imitation of timberwork[518]. This hypogeum may be assumed to be an imitation of one of the Scythian timberwork barrows recorded from South Russia to Transcaucasia; in which case the Scythian chieftain for whom the tomb was intended was anxious to preserve his ancestral traditions. The decoration reveals an intermixture of Median and Scythian elements. Above the engaged columns supporting the porch roof are three disks in rather low relief, presumably the symbols of Ahuramazda, Mithras and Anahita, or Ahuramazda, Mah and Anahita. The scene over the entrance represents two men standing on either side of a fire altar, each holding a bow of the Scythian type. According to Herodotus (i. 73), it was the Scythians who introduced the use of the bow into Media. Both men have the same type of headdress, but the one on the left wears, over a short garment, a long cloak with drooping sleeves. In view of the fact that for the Iranians the bow symbolized the royal power, it may well be that this commemorative relief represents not a priest but a monarch with his successor.

116 - KIZKAPAN. ROCK TOMB, ENTRANCE
(7th-6th CENTURIES B.C.) — IN SITU

117 - SAKAVAND. ROCK TOMBS OR OSSUARIES (7th-6th CENTURIES B.C.) — IN SITU

Two other tombs are located at Sakavand, south of Bisutun, on the road which, after crossing Luristan, abuts on the plain of Susiana. Simpler in form, they seem to be ossuaries, rather than ordinary tombs. Above one of them is a bas-relief executed in a rather provincial style. The attitude of its main figure is that of the Luristan worshippers; the smaller figure, standing on the other side of the two fire altars, is making the gesture of lamentation which we also find in Luristan statuettes. At Sakavand, then, we are already in Luristan and there is here a fusion of Median and Cimmerian elements.

It is practically certain that these were the tombs of Median kings. The attribution, however, of a given tomb to any one of the kings whose names are recorded in the historical sources remains highly conjectural. The dates of the tombs probably range over the second half of the eighth and the first half of the seventh century B.C. The theory that their prototype is to be sought for in Asia Minor or rather in Urartu has much to commend it. In any case, no rock tomb anterior to the arrival of the Medians on the Iranian Plateau has ever been discovered. The importance of these monuments must not be underrated, for here we find the basic elements that were to characterize the tombs of Darius and his successors. Seen from the outside, the tomb itself looks much like the façade of a private house; the prince is shown standing before a fire altar, in an attitude of worship, with a bow in his hand, symbol of the royal power. Above him is the winged disk, in the centre of which was added, under the Achaemenians, the bust of Ahuramazda (which we identified in one of the disks of the Kizkapan tomb).

The victory of the Medes over the Assyrians and the extension of the frontiers of their state into the heart of Asia Minor brought an influx of wealth into the country, hitherto rather poor. The rise of a luxury-loving Median aristocracy may be taken for granted; this would explain the formation of that corps of goldsmiths whose reputation was so great that Darius called them in to embellish his new palace at Susa. These craftsmen must have been trained by Assyrian goldsmiths, and above all by the Mannaian and Urartian craftsmen imported by the Assyrian kings for service in the royal workshops. Though it had been assumed that Median craftsmen were familiar with iron-working, bronze-founding and pottery-making, and though Median weaving was famous in antiquity, no first-hand evidence of Median art had been available until recently. But it is evident now that its products had been widely diffused beyond the frontiers of the country. That they were much appreciated by the Slavs is indicated by the fact that the Russian word for copper is *med;* whereas the Romans, who got their copper from Cyprus, called it *cuprum.*

THE OXUS TREASURE

The objects found in the Oxus Treasure give us some idea of Median art, to which, until now, only a single work has been (tentatively) attributed: the gold scabbard from this treasure in the British Museum.

The scene represented on this scabbard, of two royal horsemen hunting lions with spear and bow and arrow, together with the decorative setting of wrought gold, vouches for a highly evolved and complex culture. Elements of various origins—Assyrian (the royal headdress), Scythian (the *akinakes* decorated with birds' heads running along the edge) and Urartian (animal-headed volutes)—are incorporated in a composition whose ethnic frame of reference is indicated by the costumes, the horses' trappings and the riders' posture on their mounts. This goes to show how deeply Median art was permeated by a wide variety of influences.

A more exhaustive study of the Oxus Treasure would surely throw new light on Iranian art of the pre-Achaemenian period. Here, however, we must confine ourselves to one part of the treasure, which seems to go back to the seventh or early sixth century, though it also includes works datable as late as the fourth century B.C.

The place where it was discovered has now been identified as the hill known today as Takht-i-Kobad ('Throne of Kavad') in Bactria, on the right bank of the Oxus (today the Amu Darya). The Oxus Treasure contained several dozen gold plaques engraved with figures, most of them holding a *barsom,* sometimes a flower, a spear or a vase as well.

What we have here is a group of objects deposited in a temple by worshippers, each of whom was petitioning the god for some particular favour. Women asked for children, shepherds for the increase of their flocks; the potter or goldsmith donated a vase with an eye to prospering in his craft, the soldier besought a blessing on his arms. The artistic merits of these small 'votive portraits' mattered little to the donor; what counted in his eyes was the value of the metal.

Workshops adjoining the temple, or in its immediate neighbourhood, no doubt manufactured these objects, large and small, on the spot, catering for rich and poor alike. The customer paid for the gold that went into the object, not for the labour. That there were workshops of this kind in the vicinity of the temple of Surkh Dum, in Luristan, is proved by the fact that all its furnishings without exception had a votive or religious function. Quite recently, moreover, there appeared on the Teheran art market some small plaques in bronze and gold, all from Luristan, engraved with figures in exactly the same attitude as those on objects from the Oxus Treasure: worshippers raising their arms or proffering a vase[519-520-521].

The gesture of the man holding the *barsom* in his right hand and supporting it with his left is exactly the same as that of the tribute-bearers offering vases on the Persepolis bas-reliefs. Also, this gesture is repeated by a figure whose headdress is identical with that of the bronze statuette of a god from Luristan.

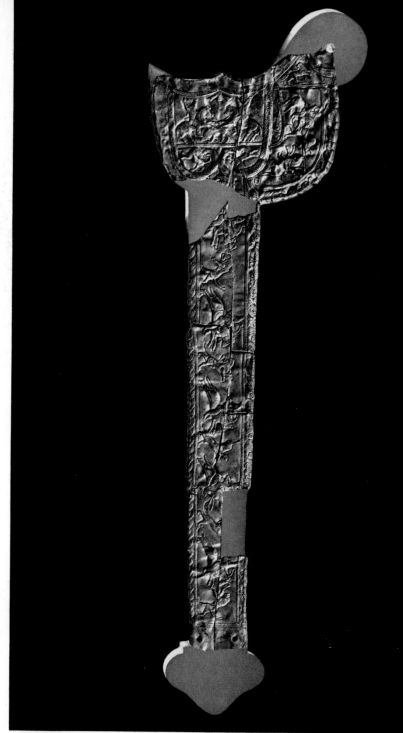

118 - OXUS TREASURE. GOLD SCABBARD (7th-6th CENT. B.C.) — BRITISH MUSEUM

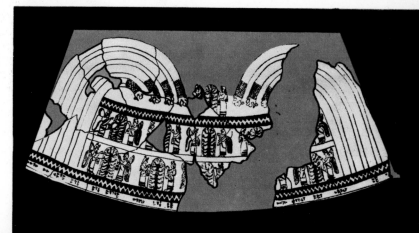

119 - KARMIR BLUR. HELMET OF KING SARDURIS (8th CENTURY B.C.) — ERIVAN MUSEUM

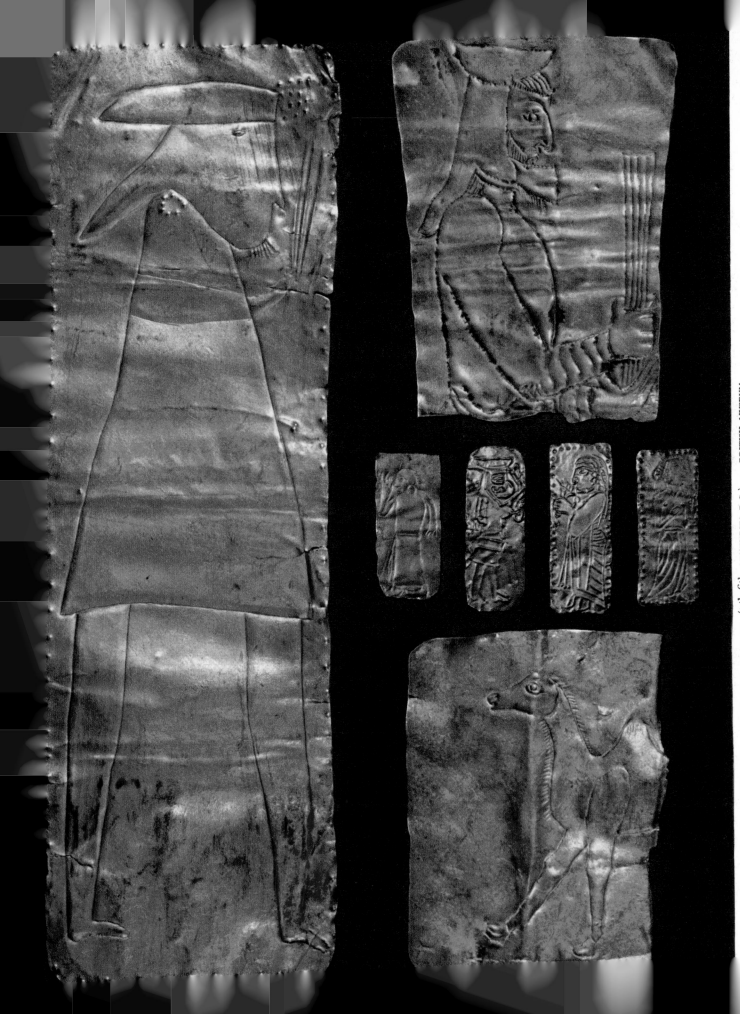

121 - OXUS TREASURE. GOLD VOTIVE PLAQUES (7th-6th CENTURIES B.C.) — BRITISH MUSEUM

The differences observable in clothing and headdress are not without interest; they indicate not only a man's rank in society but the special tribe to which he belongs. The only piece of repoussé work to be found among the gold plaques of the Oxus Treasure seems to represent a personage of high rank. Dressed in the Median fashion, with a jacket drawn in tightly by a belt from which dangles a short Scythian sword, he has a *bashlyk* on his head and wears high boots. On other, more roughly executed plaques, the garment resembles a coat of mail or a pelisse. The headdress is either the Median 'tiara' mentioned by Herodotus (i. 135, vii. 62), who regarded it as being of Persian origin; or the triple tiara which we have identified on the unfinished bronze statuette from Luristan. Elsewhere we find this headdress worn by the tribute-bearers on a relief of King Esarhaddon.

The representation of a horse may probably be associated with a prayer to the goddess of flocks and herds, perhaps the goddess Ashi, of whom the Avesta (Yasht 17, 12) says: 'Those with whom you go . . . have fearsome horses, swiftly moving in free space.' It should be noted, too, that a similar invocation applies to the camel, for the same Yasht (17, 13) says: 'For those with whom you go, O Ashi Vanuhi, have fearsome camels, with pointed humps, full of mettle, sumpter-camels . . .' We must remember that the Oxus Treasure was found in Bactria, a land famed in antiquity for its horses and camels.

There is one reservation to be made, however: in the present state of our knowledge, we have no means of fixing an exact chronological dividing line between objects of the Median period and those which are already Achaemenian. May it not be that some clue to this is given by the change that took place in the usage of the *barsom*, when it became the exclusive apanage of priests? But this is pure conjecture. The problem is further complicated by the fact that the Oxus Treasure comes from Outer Iran, where it is hard to distinguish the Medes from the Eastern Iranians whose art traditions can be perceived in other objects.

Of much interest for the history of Median art is the small group of objects found at Ecbatana (Hamadan) by the French expedition led by Virolleaud and Fossey during brief excavations carried out in 1913. The most important find was a jug, unfortunately in very bad condition, whose design, however, was reconstructed by the late Louis Le Breton. Classical in shape, it has a long spout fastened to the body by seven big, more or less spherical rivets, and a stirrup handle. On the other side of the jug is an applied ornament representing a winged human figure. Both in shape and ornamentation, this jug is identical with one from Luristan (also in the Louvre)[522-523], except for the fact that the head of the winged figure on the Ecbatana jug seems to be that of a younger man. That this latter is a Median work is proved by a relief of the Achaemenian period, from the Apadana of Persepolis, showing a Median tribute-bearer carrying a similar metal vase. True, the shape of the vase has

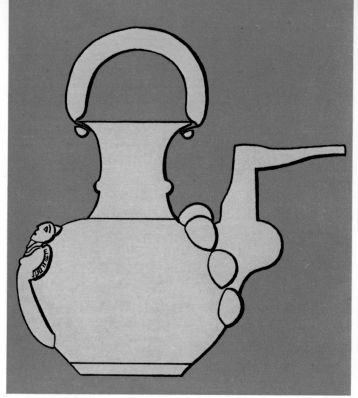

122 - HAMADAN. BRONZE JUG (8th-7th C. B.C.) — LOUVRE   123 - PERSEPOLIS. MEDIAN CARRYING A VASE (5th C. B.C.)

changed slightly in the two centuries (more or less) separating the two objects. Still recognizable, however, is the basket handle which has remained unchanged and was a distinctive feature of Median vases. The vase contemporary with Xerxes has the same sort of spout but the characteristic bulge is replaced by a plain tube linking the spout to the belly.

A bronze bowl mounted on a base has parallels among the vases found in Luristan tombs. The very close kinship between Luristan bronzes and Median metal-work is further confirmed by seven small ibexes from Ecbatana, particularly those with all four legs set close together.

124 - HAMADAN. BRONZE IBEX STATUETTES (8th-7th CENT. B.C.) — BIBLIOTHÈQUE NATIONALE, PARIS

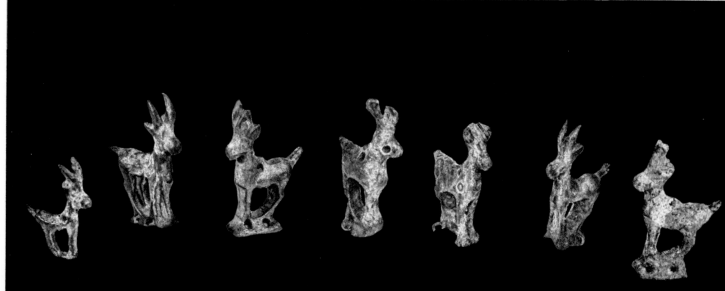

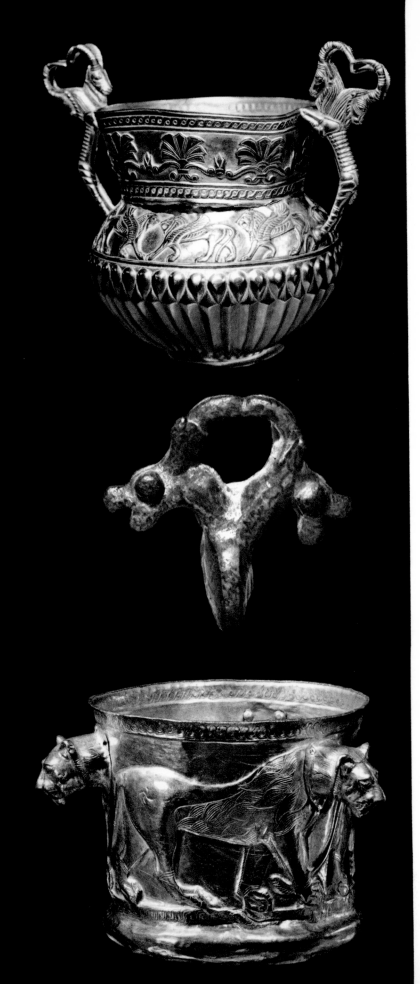

A fine gold bowl recently acquired by the Cincinnati Art Museum seems to have more in common with Medo-Cimmerian and Medo-Scythian work than with Achaemenian animal art. Its slightly carinated form recalls that of the pot-bellied, straight-necked bronze vases of Luristan. The flutings, instead of being smoothly rounded like those on Achaemenian cups, have sharp edges like those on a damaged gold goblet from Ziwiyeh. The lions on the shoulder, with their semi-shell-shaped wings, vertically incised manes and thick-set bodies, are quite unlike those of Achaemenian palace art. The geometrized palmettes on the neck had already appeared in the Ziwiyeh Treasure, and the border of two plaited bands is a motif often used both by the Ziwiyeh goldsmiths and by the Luristan bronze-workers. The animal-shaped handle is common in Achaemenian goldsmiths' work, but for the way the body of an ibex is treated, all in symmetrically marked ribs, there is no parallel in Achaemenian art, though there is at Ziwiyeh. Lastly, the structure of a two-headed animal (in bronze) brings to mind the fantastic creatures invented so frequently and with such gusto by the Luristan artists, who also fashioned double heads, with the horns soldered together, as in the case of the ibexes on the Cincinnati bowl.

To sum up, Achaemenian animal art aimed at being more realistic, though not excluding composite animals from its copious repertory of themes. For these reasons we feel justified in assigning this gold bowl to

125 - HAMADAN (?). BOWL (7th-6th CENTURIES B.C.)
126 - LURISTAN. ANIMAL (8th-7th CENTURIES B.C.)
127 - KALAR DASHT. CUP (8th-7th CENTURIES B.C.)
CINCINNATI MUSEUM, PRIV. COLL., TEHERAN MUSEUM

128 - KALAR DASHT. TERRACOTTA ANIMAL RHYTON (8th-7th CENTURIES B.C.) — TEHERAN MUSEUM

Median art of the sixth or seventh century B.C. Even assuming that it comes from Ecbatana (Hamadan), it may very well have been inherited by the Achaemenians along with the palaces of their predecessors, the Median kings.

A group of objects in gold and terracotta discovered by chance at Kalar Dasht, in a valley of the central Elburz (the range on the south shore of the Caspian), may be ascribed to Median art of the ninth to the seventh century B.C. The three lions spaced out in side-view, in relief, around the cylindrical body of a gold cup, with their heads presented frontally and in the round, has affinities (as regards this last feature in particular) with a series of bronzes from Luristan.

The same is true of a gold dagger very similar to the one carried by the god represented in the bronze statuette from Pusht-i-Kuh; noteworthy, too, is the double crescent in relief reinforcing the point of junction between the haft and the blade—a procedure also found in weapons of the Lurs.

As for the terracotta rhytons, they derive in nearly all respects from those of Sialk, Khurvin and Luristan. This is the period when the true, horn-shaped rhyton, its extremity adorned with an animal protome, first made its appearance. It is of interest to note that in Scythian investiture scenes the god is shown with a drinking cup of this type, replacing the usual diadem.

129 - KALAR DASHT. GOLD DAGGER (8th-7th CENTURIES B.C.) — TEHERAN MUSEUM

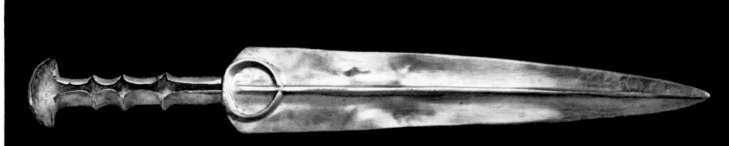

97

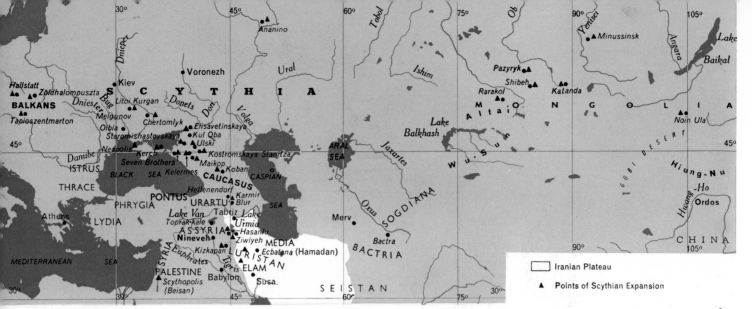

THE SCYTHIANS AND THE ROYAL TOMB OF ZIWIYEH

THE obscure Scythian phase of Iranian history was so to say 'materialized' by the chance discovery, made by peasants in 1947, of a buried treasure on the site of Ziwiyeh, near Sakkiz, south of Lake Urmia. In the seventh century B.C. this region formed part of the kingdom of Mannai, allied with the Medes against the Assyrians. After the defeat of the Mannaians (c. 660-659 B.C.) it was occupied by the Scythians, who soon annexed it to their own territory. It served as a base for their operations against the Medes and for their raids throughout Hither Asia. Whether or not the name of the chief town of the region, Sakkiz, was a derivative of 'Sakai' (the name by which the Scythians called themselves), the 'Ziwiyeh Treasure' proves that these warrior-horsemen were present in this part of Iran, where the political and artistic situation was particularly confused.

We have already alluded to this situation in indicating the contending forces at work in the region: on the one hand, the two great rival powers of Assyria and Urartu, each eager to extend its influence; on the other, the national aspirations of the Medes, the pressure exerted by the invading Cimmerians and Scythians, and finally the role of the indigenous peoples, who were well enough known for their skill in the arts and crafts for them to be courted by the Assyrians.

So much for the general state of affairs. But the important point for us to determine in this context is: What became of the Scythians after Madyes, son of Partatua, was defeated by Cyaxares, king of the Medes? Did they continue after this setback (c. 625 B.C.) to occupy the kingdom of Mannai? The problem has its importance since its solution will enable us to fix the date of burial of the Scythian prince interred at Ziwiyeh. It would seem that not all the Scythians withdrew to the Caucasus; since from 615 B.C. on we find them mentioned in Babylonian chronicles as allies of the Medes. True to their

98

policy of allying themselves with the strongest party, they may well have deserted the Assyrians and gone over to the side that was holding them at bay. Though unconfirmed by documentary evidence, the hypothesis that a Scythian kingdom in the region south of Lake Urmia continued to exist as the ally or vassal of the Medes seems well-founded. And if this Scythian kingdom was actually annexed by the Medes, this must have taken place in 590 B.C. at the latest, when —prompted by the Scythians—Media declared war on Lydia.

From Herodotus (iii. 92) we learn that in the late sixth or early fifth century B.C. the 'orthocorybant' Scythians, identified with the 'Tigraxauda' (i.e. 'the men with pointed caps'), dwelt in Media; and there seems little doubt that the Ziwiyeh Treasure came not from a cache, a crevice in the rocks where some robber lord had concealed the hoard, but from the tomb of a great Scythian king, buried in strict accordance with the Scythian tradition. The embalmed body of the dead king was first laid in state on a chariot, then conveyed from one tribe to another until the place of burial was reached. There it was placed on a bier in a tomb dug in the ground or given the form of a roofed chamber. 'Various members of the king's household are strangled and buried with him: one of his concubines, his butler, his cook, his groom, his steward and his chamberlain. With him are buried horses, and gold cups, and an assortment of his other treasures' (Herodotus, iv. 71).

132 - KOSTROMSKAYA STANITZA. SCYTHIAN BARROW: VERTICAL SECTION AND PLAN (6th CENT. B.C.)

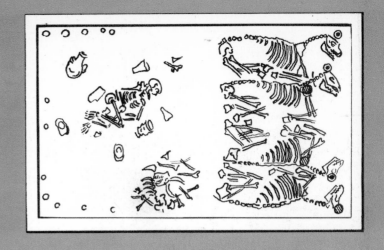

131 - HASANLU. GRAVE (8th CENTURY B.C.)

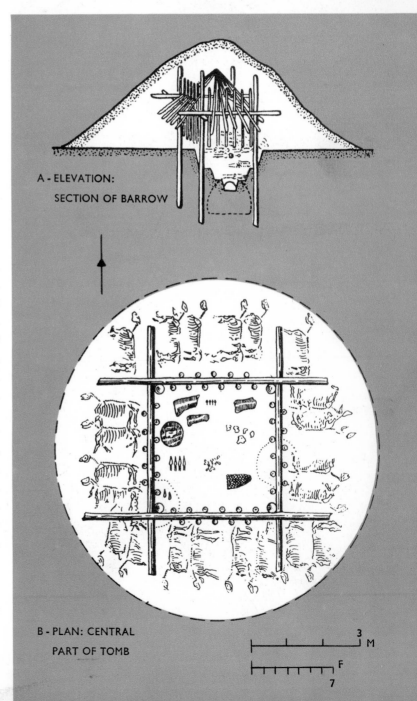

A - ELEVATION: SECTION OF BARROW

B - PLAN: CENTRAL PART OF TOMB

The remains of a bronze sarcophagus prove that the Ziwiyeh hoard came from a tomb. The objects in gold or silver—pectorals, a scabbard, a breast-plate, vases—and furniture adorned with ivory carvings were presumably the king's personal belongings. But some ornaments are specifically feminine. The variety of metals employed for the pins (4 in gold, 21 in silver, 15 in bronze) and fibulae (4 in gold, 38 in silver) seems to indicate differences of social status between the occupants of the tomb. Several hundred smaller pieces of gold served to adorn the robes of persons of high rank. The weapons in gold and silver must have belonged to the king, but the seven long iron spearheads suggest that the king's guards were immolated and buried with him. While the fragments of silver shields are indeed fit for a prince, what are we to make of the simulated shields in terracotta with a lion's head as *umbo?* The gold vases are part of a royal table service, but the pottery must have formed part of the grave goods of sacrificed servants. The possibility that a chariot and team of horses were buried with the king cannot be excluded, in view of the presence of eleven small bronze bells, miscellaneous horse-gear and bronze plaques which may have been affixed to a vehicle.

These objects reveal traces of the art of earlier Oriental civilizations (Assyria, Babylonia, Urartu, protohistoric Iran), combined with Median, Scythian, Cimmerian and perhaps Greek elements.

133 - ZIWIYEH. IVORY STATUETTE (7th CENTURY B.C.) — TEHERAN MUSEUM

134 - ZIWIYEH. IVORY PLAQUE WITH HUNTING SCENE (7th CENTURY B.C.) — PRIVATE COLLECTION

From earlier Oriental civilizations derive the techniques, iconography and decorative style of the works in the Ziwiyeh Treasure. There is no need to dwell on the striking resemblance between the designs on the Ziwiyeh sarcophagus and those on the ivory plaques adorning the throne of King Esarhaddon, which show the Medes, his vassals, bringing him tribute. So sweeping were the political changes then taking place in this part of Western Iran that a quarter of a century later it was a Scythian, instead of an Assyrian, king who received homage from the Medes.

Assyrian too are the horizontal and vertical plaques of gold and ivory used to decorate an article of furniture, perhaps a throne or a ceremonial bed. The horizontal hunting scenes with chariots start from a central circle containing ibexes on either side of a 'sacred tree' [524]—a motif that is thrice repeated. The vertical plaques are divided into three registers, representing a procession of dignitaries and warriors, a lion-hunt and a bull-hunt [525]. Since these vertical plaques [526] are identical with the only surviving revetment plaque in gold, it seems to follow that the decoration of the piece of furniture (whatever it was) must have been chryselephantine. On this fragment [527] we see the remains of two registers, with the procession of warriors marching to the right. And though the goldsmith made a slip, treating the left hand as if it were the right (or perhaps the engraver of the mould was responsible for the blunder), his technique by no means lacks a feeling for plastic values and realistic figuration. The warrior on the upper register is closely akin, in pose and details of costume, to the one on the upper left register of an ivory plaque from Ziwiyeh,

now in the Metropolitan Museum—a striking example of the influence of metal-work on ivory-carving. But to come back to the throne (or bed) itself —both the legs, joined by cross-bars, and the uprights were lavishly decorated. Two fragments, possibly terminals, seem to belong to this ensemble, which has much in common with late Assyrian works (e.g. bas-reliefs showing Assurbanipal hunting). While granting that the lion-hunt with chariots is a frequent theme in the art of the Mitannians, we do not think this work should be dated any earlier than the seventh century B.C.

There are good grounds for attributing the decorations of another article of furniture (?) in ivory to a local workshop. The motif is similar to the one which Esarhaddon caused to be represented in his palace at Nimrud, to celebrate the conclusion of a treaty with the Median chieftain Ramataia, and to the one that figures on the edge of the sarcophagus from the Ziwiyeh tomb. Likewise, a fragment of a plaque from a casket, which appears to commemorate a treaty concluded between two princes, may also be the work of a local artist. It throws new light on the art of Iran in the seventh century B.C., when it was developing a narrative style derived from that of the Assyrian empire, now almost *in extremis*. In this art, it seems to us, there are indications of the intermediary stages by which the Assyro-Babylonian heritage was transmitted to the Achaemenians.

The peculiar technique of massive inlays employed in small plaques[528] and an ivory statuette belonging to a casket (?) again raises the problem of origin. Phoenician ivory-carvers were of course familiar with this technique,

136 - ZIWIYEH. FIGURE CARVED IN IVORY (7th CENT. B.C.) — TEHERAN MUSEUM →

but as a rule confined it to smaller surfaces. It seems in this instance to correspond more closely to the taste of the Urartian artists, who produced many works in ivory, bronze and stone inlaid with glass paste or metal. The taste for polychromy so prevalent in Urartu could not fail to be appreciated at the court of a Scythian prince, where colours were applied even to gold objects.

Traces of Urartian influence can also be in a group of gold detected plaques which were cut into pieces by the peasants who discovered them. Among these were three pectorals, one crescent-shaped and the two others trapezoidal. All were divided into registers showing animals and hybrid beings converging on sacred trees placed in the centre of each composition. Our recent exhibition of Iranian Art in Paris, which brought together several fragments of these plaques now dispersed in various countries, gave us an opportunity of reconstituting them. As a result we had either two trapezoidal pectorals with seven registers, or two pieces of body armour, covering the chest and back of the wearer, which were presumably linked together by elements cut in the form of crescents, decorated with similar motifs and resting on the man's shoulders. The whole accoutrement was probably sewn on to bands of leather. It is possible that the thin strips of gold pierced with four holes and belonging to a coat of mail were attached to this cuirass, below and on the sides. Everything here conforms so closely to Assyrian iconography that one would be tempted to attribute these works to an Assyrian goldsmith but for the fact that, in Assyria and Babylonia, the pectoral was a peculiarly Urartian adornment. Even so, when we study in detail the decoration of these objects and note the striking deviations from Urartian practice (e.g. the trunkless tree of life and the way the winged hybrid beings are rendered), which drain them of their original meaning, we feel bound to reconsider any such attribution. There are in fact good grounds for believing that the Scythian prince buried at Ziwiyeh ordered these ornaments from some foreign workshop which merely copied the fantastic beings current in the iconography of Oriental art of the ninth-seventh centuries B.C. without understanding the religious and symbolic value attaching to such figurations.

It should be noted, moreover, that catering for the taste of his client, the artist introduced at each end of the two registers on the large crescent-shaped pectoral an animal theme (hare and recumbent feline) for which the Scythians showed a marked preference. In view of the peculiarities discernible in these objects (notably the tendency to give each human figure a different aspect), we should be inclined to assign them tentatively to a non-Urartian workshop, to artists who might well have been Medians; for in Median art many different strains—Urartian, Assyrian, local Mannaian, perhaps even Ionian— were undoubtedly intermingled during this period, the second half of the seventh century B.C.

Specifically Urartian work, however, is the annular gold mounting of a

137 - ZIWIYEH. GOLD PECTORAL (7th
CENT. B.C.) — TEHERAN MUSEUM →

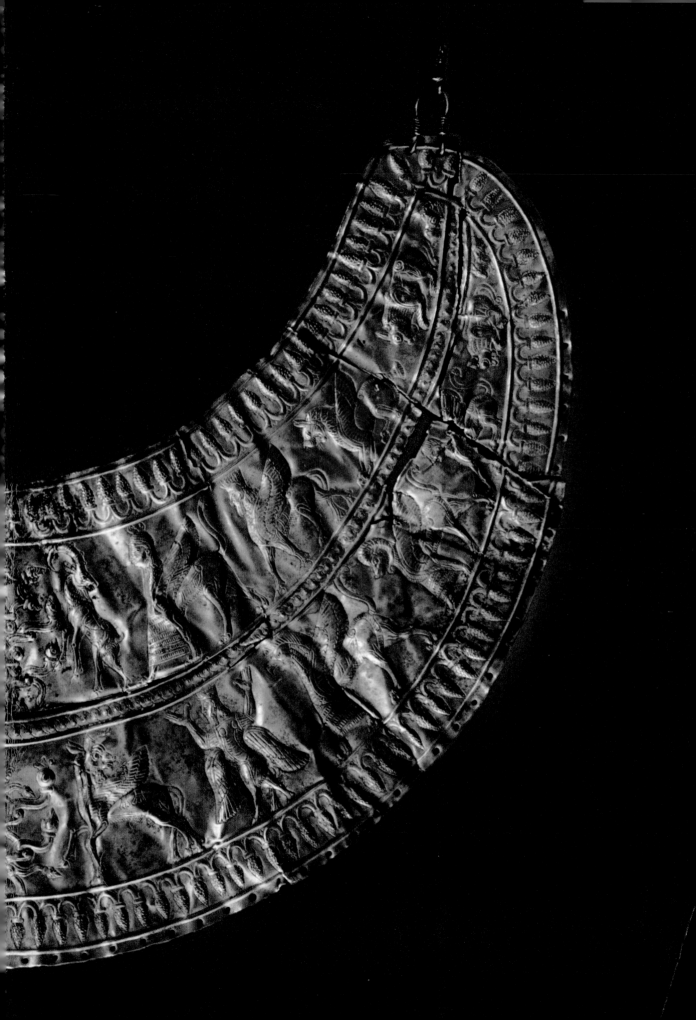

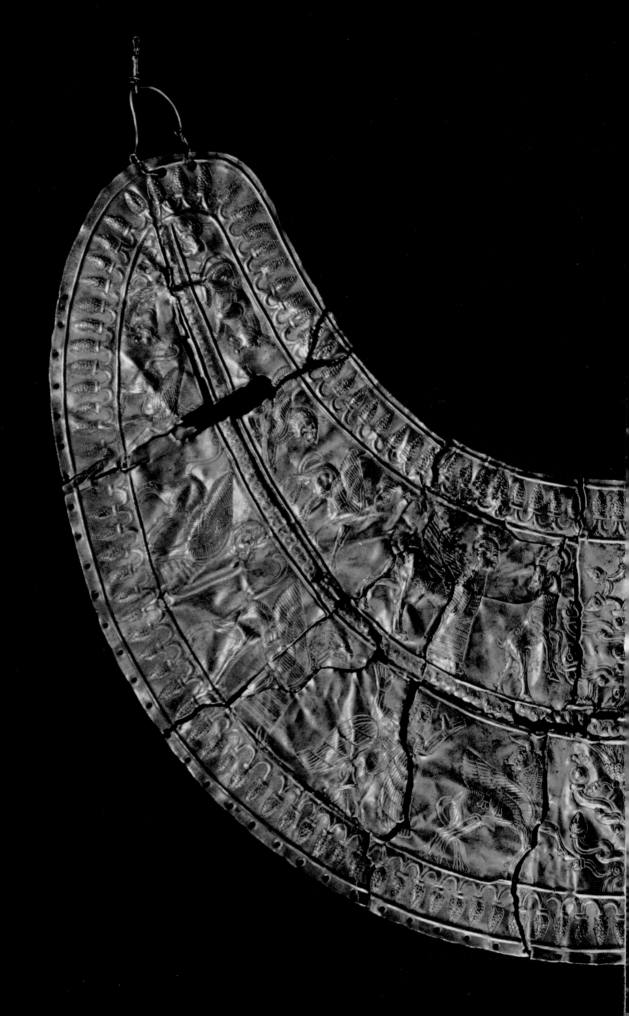

cylinder seal, consisting of two parts into which the cylinder was fitted (the stone itself has been torn out). Such objects, serving both as a stamp seal and a cylinder seal, were common in Urartu; a great many of them have been found at Karmir Blur.

The foreparts of griffins and lions from Ziwiyeh are also of Urartian workmanship. Regarded as possessing talismanic powers, they acted as guardians of the liquid in the funerary cauldron (missing), which they served to decorate, while also defending the tomb and its occupants. Certain stylistic idiosyncrasies of these protomes prove them to be neither Assyrian nor Scythian.

For it is in the art of Urartu that we find both the 'visor' covering the griffin's mouth and a double spiral of hair running downwards from the base of the ear. The round eye, moreover (which was probably inlaid), is treated exactly like that of the bull from Adelyevas, which is rightly believed to have been modelled on a metal figurine. The 'crest' in three tiers between the animal's eyes has nothing in common with the two protuberances figuring at the same place on the heads of Assyrian and Achaemenian lions. Behind the 'crest' rose that knob-like appendage which can be seen on Greek griffins. It should not be forgotten that the griffin does not appear in Greek art until about 700 B.C. and that its wings are always ostraceous, like those on Luristan bronzes. These bronzes, moreover, include griffins with a crest, composed of three elements, and a bird's head with a 'visor.' As for the lion, its type is no less Urartian in virtue of its chaps with long twisted folds, the squat, merlon-shaped nose, and the ears indicated by a small round boss inset in a fold of flesh; indeed it has obvious analogies with the bronze lion in the British Museum from the Toprak-kale throne.

Further objects from the Ziwiyeh tomb, Urartian in inspiration (though not in technique), might be cited, but as their general make-up is Scythian we shall discuss the most remarkable of them in dealing with the group of Scythian pieces.

142 - ZIWIYEH.   SILVER DISH WITH GOLD INLAYS (7th CENTURY B.C.) — TEHERAN MUSEUM

A silver dish inlaid with gold, with its edge turned slightly inward, carries an engraved design composed of ten concentric circles and various motifs, with a rosette of sixteen petals in the centre. The general effect of the design resembles that of the votive shield from the Regolini-Galassi tomb and the Toprak-kale shields. The subjects of the Ziwiyeh dish are Scythian (lynxes confronted or recumbent, running hares, heads of birds of prey), but certain elements derive from Asia Minor (heart-shaped ears of felines) and Urartu (hieroglyphic signs for the guidance of the craftsman who will have to assemble separately made pieces of the dish). The designs on this dish are of exceptional interest for the light they throw on Scythian art of the seventh century B.C. within the frame of reference of the Irano-Urartian *koine*.

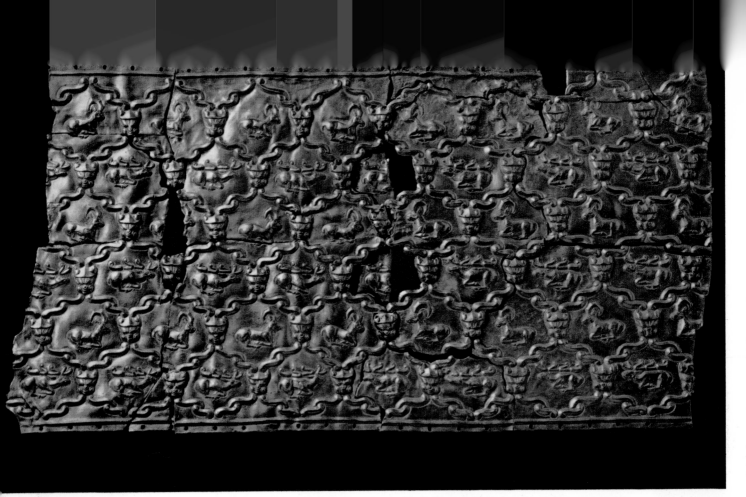

Belonging to the 'Asiatic' style of Scythian art (of which we shall have more to say) is a gold plaque with perforated edges probably intended to be fastened to a broad leather belt. While the double ('ogival') arches linked at their apexes by lions' heads reveal an Urartian technique, the recumbent stags in the spaces they enclose are in the purest tradition of Scythian art of the sixth century B.C., as exemplified in South Russia by objects found in the oldest tombs. The stags' heads are stretched forward, the muzzles slope sharply down from a median ridge, the ears, pressed down into the hollow of the neck, are pointed, as are the hoofs resting one upon the other. And while the shoulder is indicated by an oval bulge in which an Urartian touch is discernible, the neck, the antlers swept back over the animal's spine and the body are incised in surfaces sloping down in two directions from a central longitudinal ridge.

A plaque from a similar belt reveals a very different art. True, the ogee arches, the volutes and the palmettes of the tree of life are given the same prominent ridges, but the animals are not rendered in the Scythian technique. Indeed the design shows an entirely different approach: the artist seems to have a *horror vacui* and seeks to fill every inch of space available.

It seems clear that artists from different centres engraved the moulds that were used in the workshop serving the Scythian prince of Ziwiyeh. Local traditions, influenced by Urartian art (ears composed of a small round boss encircled by a volute), are evident in a lion's head which may have formed the butt-end of a belt. A point of interest is that here too the top of the animal's forehead is spanned by an ogee arch—a distinctively Urartian procedure of which we find another instance in the two lion cubs figuring on either side of the central part of the prince's bracelet. An inlay in the form of a rayed disk, perhaps of ivory, originally embellished the mane.

144 - ZIWIYEH. BUTT-END OF A BELT 145 - (A & B) BRACELET 146 - BELT PLAQUE (7th C. B.C.) — TEHERAN AND PHILADELPHIA

III

147 - ZIWIYEH. (A) BELT PLAQUE (B) DETAIL (7th CENTURY B.C.) — PRIVATE COLLECTION, NEW YORK

Two identical gold bands, one in the Teheran Museum, the other in the University Museum of Philadelphia, make it virtually certain that the artists from whom the Ziwiyeh prince commissioned the objects with a 'national style' decoration were trained in the ambience of the art of Asia Minor or were familiar with certain features characteristic of that milieu. The ornamentation running along the edge of these bands begins with two peculiar animals from the Scythian repertory. They are shown lying down, the back slightly arched, paws and tail ending in a circle, lips in the form of spirals and ears heart-shaped.

The point should here be emphasized: that this species of animal, frequent though it is on Scythian objects from South Russia, never appears there with heart-shaped ears; this is a feature peculiar to the art of Asia Minor. As for the birds with 'beakheads' which complete the ornamentation, their eyes, ears and circular feet were inlaid with enamel, and here we find another instance of that fondness for bright colour which the nomads acquired from their contacts with the ancient civilizations of Asia, mainly no doubt with Assyria, but also with Urartu.

On another, fairly thick gold band, the posture of the animals, whether back to back or facing each other, is contrary to the practice of Scythian art, which usually aligns them on a horizontal plane or superimposes them vertically. Thus the principles of the art of Western Asia were followed by the goldsmith working for his Scythian patron. It will be remembered that for a son of Heracles, whose name was Scythes, the belt was an attribute of power. Like armour, it served as a means of defence; it formed part both of the male and the female costume, and magic virtues were ascribed to it. No

112

148 - ZIWIYEH. BRACELET 149 - FRAGMENT OF A TORQUE 150 - BRACELET (7th CENT. B.C.) — TEHERAN AND PHILADELPHIA

belt as wide as those from Ziwiyeh appears to have been found in the Scythian tombs of South Russia, whereas some nearly as wide figure among the Luristan bronzes and Urartian artefacts. From Luristan again come the openwork pinheads on which animals are joined together by ogee arches. But the double arch, a motif common in Urartian art, was not invented in Luristan. So it would seem that Urartian artists must have been employed in the local workshop hitherto assumed to have produced uniquely Scythian works.

The taste of the Scythian prince of Ziwiyeh for massive, costly articles of personal adornment is further evidenced by some elaborately wrought gold bracelets. These, better than any object in the treasure, give an idea of the new art taking form in the north-west of the Iranian Plateau, drawing on the one hand on Assyro-Urartian sources, on the other on Scythian traditions. The two most splendid pieces carry lions' heads carved in the round at each extremity; one of them, being movable so as to allow the bracelet to slip over the hand, could be locked by means of a pin. Along the centre of the body of the bracelet runs a sharp edge, forming a triangular surface, on either side of which is a recumbent lion cub. These ornaments come from the same workshop and, like the belt-end discussed above, show technical features which derive from Scythian traditions influenced by Urartian art. The terminals of several other gold and silver bracelets of smaller size, which presumably were worn by women, are adorned with animal motifs of the Scythian type. A torque of solid gold is adorned with an unbroken series of moufflons' heads (a Scythian motif); together with its matching bracelet, it forms a very handsome decorative ensemble. Other torques and bracelets, though simpler in design, are hardly less fine.

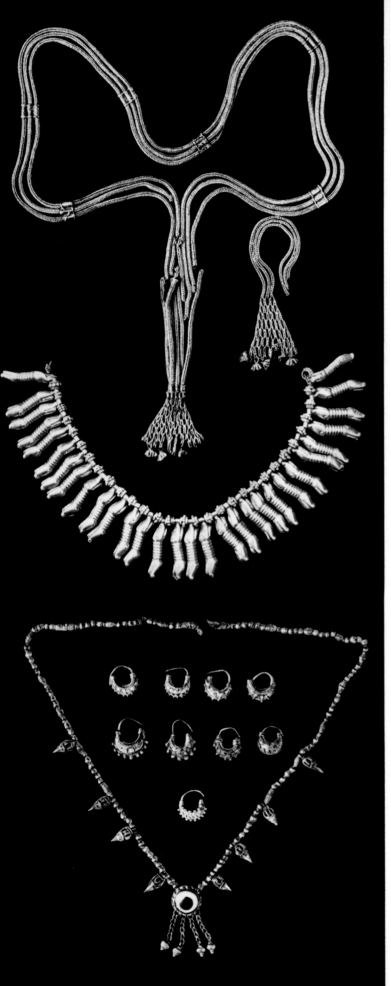

Apart from torques and bracelets, Scythian princes wore long gold chains, several of which have been found in Scythian tombs in South Russia, Hungary and Germany. The Ziwiyeh tomb contained at least two such chains. One, its three rows held together by sliding rings with granulated edges, ends in a tassel of interwoven strands supporting nine small bellshaped flowers. The necklaces are made of gold beads, spherical or pomegranate-shaped, the most elaborate ones being enriched with pendants.

Highly esteemed in Urartu, the technique of granulation enabled the decoration of the tiny surfaces of ear-rings and the settings of gold rings [529-530] with small grains of gold, disposed in floral or linear patterns soldered to the ground, while enamels of different colours enhanced the rosettes on women's headbands [531].

The Ziwiyeh tomb, for the first time in Iran, provided information regarding the use of various gold objects charged with 'protective' virtues, some in the form of an ibex, others stamped with rosettes, crosses, palmettes and merlons. Such objects were sewn on garments, a practice that remained in fashion under the Achaemenians [532-537]. The gold and silver fibulae are all of the same type; they have no spring, the pin being held in place by a loop at the tip of the arc opposite the hook. This type of fibula is very rare in Western Asia, but occurs, as we have seen, in Luristan and is common in the Caucasus.

151 - GOLD CHAINS — TEHERAN MUSEUM
152 - NECKLACE — PRIVATE COLLECTION, TEHERAN
153 - NECKLACE AND EAR-RINGS — TEHERAN
   MUSEUM. ZIWIYEH (7th CENTURY B.C.)

114

154 - ZIWIYEH. GOLD ORNAMENT IN THE FORM OF AN IBEX (7th CENTURY B.C.) — TEHERAN MUSEUM

As for the pins, which are as numerous as the fibulae, they are of the same type as those found by de Morgan in a tomb at Khalil Dehlil, in Kurdistan, more or less contemporary with the Ziwiyeh tomb. These pin-heads have some resemblance to the ornaments worn by the Ossete nomads, and similar ones figure among the Luristan bronzes.

Special interest attaches to a gauntlet[538] made of slender gold chains, with a clasp fastening it to the wrist; it was embellished with five rings adorned with pearls and small chains in relief. It was the fashion in Iran in the early first millennium B.C. to wear rings of this kind on all five fingers of one hand; we noticed this in the course of our excavation of Cemetery B at Sialk; and in a Scythian tomb in South Russia, at Chertomlyk, the body of a woman having rings on all ten fingers was found.

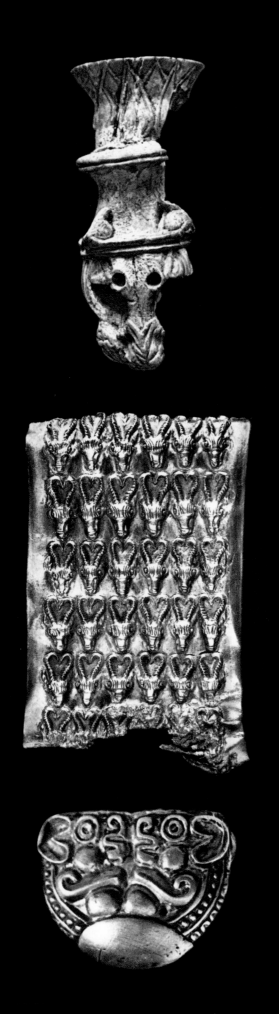

The intermingling of Oriental and Scythian art is also evident in such weapons as the ceremonial sword of gold and ivory, unfortunately broken, which is now divided between the Teheran Museum and the Metropolitan Museum of New York. Here the goldsmith has kept to the Scythian tradition, while the ivory-work shows traces of Irano-Urartian influence. We do not know for certain whether the scabbard had the form of an *akinakes*, that Scythian weapon *par excellence*. All the gold fragments belonging to it are decorated with the heads of saigas in front view, the number of heads diminishing as the scabbard tapers down to the place at which the chape was fastened. What this solid block of cast gold represents is a moot question; in our opinion, a human face, but others see two Scythian animals confronted. Contrasting with the age-old device of two confronted lions' heads in ivory, without lower jaws, 'spitting out' the iron sword-blade (now lost) is the ornamentation of the gold pommel with the curled-up form of a lion, with the upper part representing a row of lotus leaves in low relief.

We may well see in this pommel one of the finest productions of the workshop responsible for the objects of 'the Scythian group.' Disregarding appearances and giving rein to a creative imagination of no mean order, the craftsman indulged in inventions of a startling originality. The strongly marked corners heighten the impact of the frontally presented eye. It is clear that this artist is consciously

155 - ZIWIYEH. IVORY SWORD HILT — TEHERAN
156-157 - ZIWIYEH. GOLD SCABBARD AND CHAPE
(7th CENTURY B.C.) — TEHERAN

158 - ZIWIYEH.   GOLD SWORD POMMEL (7th CENTURY B.C.) — ERNEST ERICKSON FOUNDATION, NEW YORK

aiming at an effect of symmetrical convolutions binding the whole together, an effect that is implemented by the spirals defining the nose and shoulder-joint.   Similarly the relief-work shows a masterly comprehension of the art of simplifying forms and linking them together.   The hindquarters of the animal are modelled without being immobilized and its body tapers to a tail curled round in front of the jaws.

The paws, with their massive claws, are folded up under the head and body, rendered in a tensed pose less stylized than the rest and more nearly resembling the posture of a real animal.

159-160-161 - ZIWIYEH. DAGGER HANDLES   162-163 - UMBO AND FRAGMENT OF SHIELD (7th CENT. B.C.) — TEHERAN

To the blade of a tanged iron dagger is fastened a haft with a ribbed pommel, made of limestone covered with a thin sheet of silverfoil. Another iron dagger has a rib running down the middle of the blade and a square tang fitted with a haft of bone, lined inside with a thin sheet of bronze; the cone-shaped pommel is of solid silver.

All that remains of a third dagger is the ivory handle with the delicately carved head of a heifer; the shaft prolonging it is flanked by two rams' heads and ends in the jaws of two lions side by side; the tang of the blade entered the haft between the heads of two ibexes.

164 - ZIWIYEH. MACEHEAD   165 - ARROWHEADS   166 - SPEARHEAD (7th CENT. B.C.) — MUSEUM AND PRIVATE COLL., TEHERAN

Two bronze disks served, in our opinion, as the *umbones* of two shields, and a silver fragment with a palmette in relief and an incised design probably adorned a similar weapon. A pear-shaped ceremonial mace, made of veined marble, represents an attempt on the part of a local stone-cutter to create an object in the Scythian style by using beakheads, though in fact these were unsuited to the curved form of the weapon. The three-cusped arrowhead with socket and barb (the Scythians' most famed weapon) figures among a batch of arrows in bronze and bone, while seven iron spearheads represent the weapons carried by the guards.

Objects relating to the horse and its trappings seem to have bulked large in the contents of the Ziwiyeh tomb. Eleven small bronze bells, of various shapes, suggest that at least eleven horses were buried with the Scythian prince. Disk-shaped phalerae have also been found in large numbers. When the disk carries an engraved design showing galloping animals, this may perhaps be taken as a sign of Assyrian influence. A group of bronze phalerae, each composed of two disks, recall the shields of the Zinjirli warriors. As we know from Assyrian monuments, these phalerae adorned the breasts of the horses that drew the royal chariots. Undecorated, but fitted with three clapper-rings, these objects have a certain kinship with some of the Luristan bronzes.

Only one element of *psalia* (side-pieces of bits) has survived, but it is of some importance, for it confirms other evidence as to the identity of the person or persons buried in the Ziwiyeh tomb. It is of a type peculiar to the Scythian culture of 700-600 B.C. Distinctively Scythian, too, is part of a headstall shaped like a boar's tusk[539]. Carved in bone, it was held in place on the horse's head by two crossed straps. Such ornamental headstalls —already in use at the beginning of the second millennium B.C.—were employed by many peoples from eastern Siberia to Sweden. Judging by the bas-reliefs of the Xanthos tomb in Asia Minor, the Achaemenians adopted them, and they figure on the heads of the Scythians' horses on the Persepolis reliefs.

167 - ZIWIYEH. SILVER CHAMFRON (7th CENTURY B.C.) — TEHERAN MUSEUM

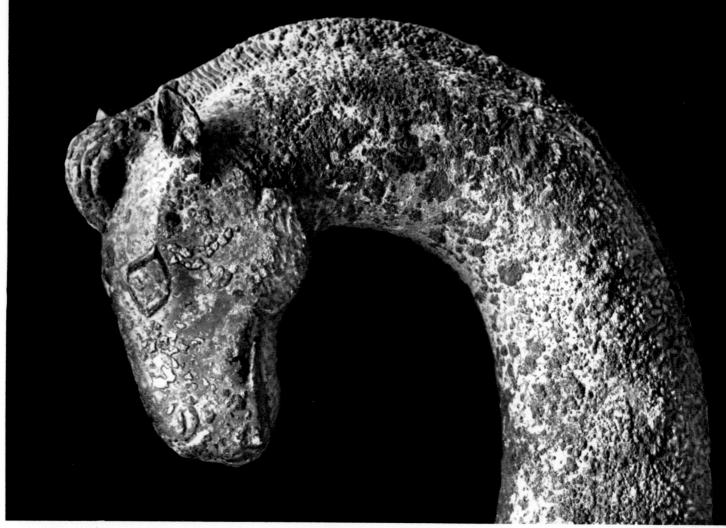

168 - ZIWIYEH. TERMINAL OF A CHARIOT SHAFT: HORSE'S HEAD (7th CENTURY B.C.) — TEHERAN MUSEUM

One of the most representative pieces of the Ziwiyeh group of works is a silver chamfron adorned with a leaping lion between two stylized trees. The animal's posture, with its forepaws thrust forward horizontally, is the same as that of the felines on the Gusci belt, whose Urartian origin is generally accepted. To balance his composition the artist has placed the palmette, inverted, at the foot of the column-trunk of a 'tree of life,' which, misunderstanding its significance, he has represented upside down! This palmette has similarities with the one in the centre of the *mitra* from Rethymnon (Crete).

There was at least one chariot, perhaps several, in the Ziwiyeh tomb. A horse's head forming the terminal of one of the shafts of a chariot might well be of Urartian workmanship. The way in which the eye is treated, enclosed in a lozenge and with the iris in relief, has unmistakable affinities with the technique of the bronze-founder responsible for the bull on the handle of an Urartian cauldron found in the Heraion of Argos. Finally we may draw attention to the pendants attached to straps level with the shoulders of draught-horses; they also figure on Assyrian monuments.

169 - ZIWIYEH. SILVER DRINKING-PIPE: HEIFER'S HEAD (7th CENTURY B.C.) — PRIVATE COLLECTION, TEHERAN

Of what seems to have been a large assortment of stone and metal vases deposited in the Ziwiyeh tomb, only a few pieces survive. First we have fragments of three vases of solid gold decorated in a technique that seems to link them up with the workshop that produced objects in the Scythian style. A straight-necked silver vase, on the other hand, seems to owe nothing to any of the workshops we have so far identified. Two small vases in bronze are shaped like water-skins[540]. It is difficult to say for what purpose they were intended; perhaps they were lamps hung in the tomb during the burial ceremony. Remarkable for the realism and precision of its workmanship is a heifer's head adorning a silver drinking-pipe. This must have been made in a well-equipped workshop, which may well have been Urartian.

Though very little grave furniture in hard stone has survived, enough remains to show that the Scytho-Median princes used the same kind of table-service as that which was in favour in Assyrian palaces. This, judging by fragments found in the excavations of the Treasury of Persepolis, was also much appreciated by the Achaemenian ruling class. Here again, the Medo-Scythian civilization appears to have acted as an intermediary between the great Oriental cultures of an earlier age and the future Achaemenian civilization which, as far as we can tell, only received that heritage by way of its immediate predecessors on Iranian soil.

The pottery placed beside the members of a lower class of society who accompanied their dead masters to the tomb at Ziwiyeh, is of particular interest. Both its forms and its ornamentation reveal the eclectic nature of this branch of Scythian art. The pitcher with a long beak-spout and the vase with a vertical cylinder-spout denote a continuation of the Iranian traditions of Sialk, Khurvin, Hasanlu and Luristan. Evidently a local product, this pottery includes pots and pitchers with lugs in the form of a recumbent feline, a characteristically Scythian motif, which also figures on the far more valuable gold objects. With its extremely fine, well-baked clay, its burnished red slip and its incised designs with nipples and grooves, it is the only pottery so far discovered which keeps to the technique of the Iranian potters whose products were inspired by those of metal-workers.

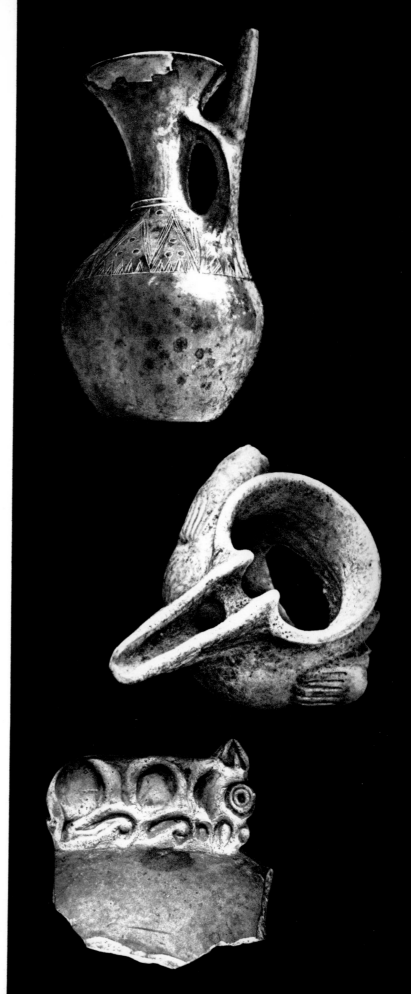

170 - ZIWIYEH. VASE WITH VERTICAL CYLINDER-SPOUT
171 - BEAK-SPOUT 172 - LUG OF A PITCHER (7th CENTURY B.C.) — MUSEUM AND PRIVATE COLL., TEHERAN

123

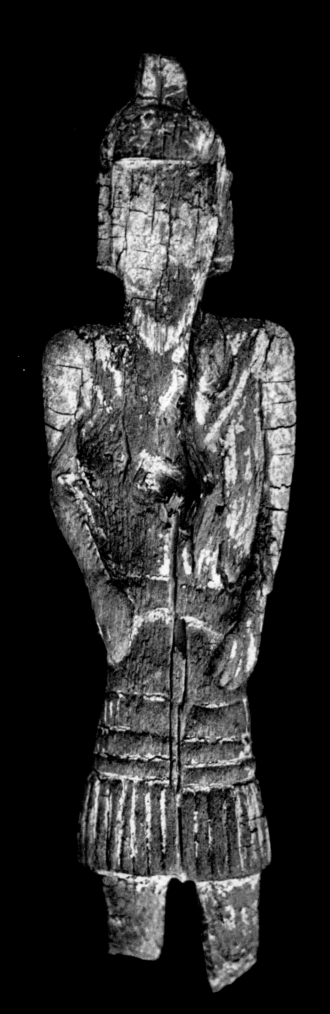

In the foregoing pages we have given a description of the various arts that figure in the Ziwiyeh Treasure. It would be incomplete, however, without some mention of an object that came as a complete surprise: a wooden statuette of a man, whose face, presumably made of ivory, is missing. The figure must have been overlaid with a thin sheet of metal, more probably of gold than of bronze, considering the magnificence of the tomb. We believe this to be one of the objects known as *sphyrelata* frequent in Greece and in use in Western Asia from very early times. It is the only known example of this technique. The costume is that of a nomad. The flat body, while keeping to the style of certain Luristan bronzes, also brings to mind the Greek works produced by the same process in the mid-seventh century B.C.

The variety of art currents discernible in the objects from the Ziwiyeh tomb reflects the many contacts—and conflicts—which the Scythians had with other peoples in Hither Asia in the course of the seventh century. It anticipates what were to be the characteristics of Iranian art under the Achaemenian Persians, and it also has much to tell us about Median art. So close were their material cultures that in the light of our present knowledge it seems impossible to differentiate the Medes from the Scythians and Cimmerians. Some later monuments, like the Persepolis bas-reliefs, prompted so acute a scholar as Herzfeld to maintain this view, and today there is ample evidence in favour of it.

173 - ZIWIYEH. WOODEN STATUETTE (7th CENTURY B.C.) — TEHERAN MUSEUM

As well as Assyrian artefacts, the Ziwiyeh Treasure also contained Urartian funerary (?) utensils and articles of local manufacture. But so numerous are those bearing the impress of Scythian art that there can be no doubt of the existence of a royal workshop producing ornaments in a style peculiar to itself and catering for the taste of the ruling princes.

Taken as a whole, this collection of works reveals no consistent artistic development, but rather a forward leap, the brusque, surprisingly successful adaptation of a great variety of styles, and behind this we sense a desire to build up a world of forms and symbols embodying the aspirations of a race still in the making. These elements were superimposed on the age-old traditions of this part of Asia, but were never truly integrated into them, and failed to achieve an organic unity. And though the technique has some admirable qualities, an unsureness of touch and a lack of imagination can be felt whenever the artist, presumably at his patron's bidding, diverges from the beaten path and strikes out in new directions.

The Ziwiyeh Treasure, unique of its kind, has added inestimably to our knowledge of the arts of Hither Asia and of South Russia, whose motifs lingered on for centuries to come. Just as at Begram the discoveries made by Hackin shortly before his tragic death threw a revealing light on the composite art deriving from the three great civilizations which divided the world between them in the early centuries of the Christian era—Rome, India and China—so at Ziwiyeh the tomb of a Scythian prince yielded a host of works reflecting the arts of a group of peoples and races having little in common.

The lessons to be drawn from the two discoveries, however, are very different. The three powers—Imperial Rome, the India of the Kushans, and Han China—whose arts met and mingled at Begram, were then at the height of their splendour. What we have at Ziwiyeh, on the other hand, is the 'swan song' of Assyria, heir of all the arts of Mesopotamia and Asia Minor, shortly before she was wiped off the political map of Asia. Urartu, also, was living on borrowed time; she survived a little longer, then, in turn, disappeared.

The void left by these two defeated antagonists was filled by other powers: the kingdom of the Medes, followed by the Persians and their world empire, whose art assimilated all that was to be learned from their predecessors and far outlasted the empire itself; and the Scythians who, like the Persians, imposed their art far and wide, both east and west: a composite art but one of great power and brilliant originality. Out of the fusion of Medo-Scythian art with that of the ancient Asiatic civilizations in the Irano-Urartian *koine*, sprang the unity of expression that characterizes the art of the Iranian Plateau. This unity remained intact in Achaemenian art, with which Scythian art, fertilized in the Pontus region by Greek art, never broke its ties.

| IRANIAN PLATEAU | | SITES |
MEDES	PERSIANS	SITES
10th century B.C.		
9th century B.C.		SIALK
825 - *Medes in the region of Lake Urmia*	834 - *Persians in the PARSA region*	
8th century B.C.		
		KHURVIN
DEIOCES (c. 728-675) *Founding of ECBATANA*	ACHAEMENES *Leader of the Achaemenians*	HASANLU AMLASH
7th century B.C.		
Cimmerian Invasion PHRAORTES (c. 675-653)	TEISPES (675-640)	LURISTAN
Scythian Invasion CYAXARES (c. 653-585)	CYRUS I King of PARSUMASH (c. 640-600) ARIARAMNES King of the Land of PARSA (c. 640-615)	ZIWIYEH treasure
6th century B.C.		
ASTYAGES (c. 585-550) MANDANE, daughter of ASTYAGES wife of CAMBYSES I	CAMBYSES I King of PARSUMASH and PARSA (c. 600-559)	OXUS treasure FARHAD-U-SHIRIN FAKHRIKA DUKKAN-I-DAU KIZKAPAN SAKAVEND
550 - *End of the Median Kingdom*		HAMADAN (Ecbatana) KALAR DASHT

PERSIA FROM THE ORIGINS TO THE ACHAEMENIANS

The arrival of the Iranians on the Plateau must have taken place about the beginning of the first millennium B.C. The art of Sialk—followed by the arts of Khurvin, Hasanlu and Amlash—formed an integral part of this new culture, which is reflected in the town-planning on these sites and in the decorative designs, first of potters, then of metal-workers. It achieved its most dynamic and original expression in the Luristan bronzes.

Towards the end of the eighth century B.C. the first Median kings, allied to the Scythians and Cimmerians, founded Ecbatana as a strong post on the invasion route followed by the Assyrian armies. Thus the composite art of the peoples of Elamo-Caspian origin was brought into contact with, and integrated into, that of the Medes, Scythians and Cimmerians. Out of this amalgamation emerged the arts of pre-Achaemenian Iran (Median rock tombs).

Then, on this vast artistic complex, there impinged in varying proportions Assyrian, Babylonian, Urartian and even Greek influences (Ziwiyeh Treasure).

ARCHITECTURE SCULPTURE	CLAY	METAL	IVORY BONE GLYPTICS	HITHER ASIA MESOPOTAMIA	URARTU
Terrace of the Ruler's Abode Upper and Lower Town **CEMETERY B**					
Tombs covered with stone or terracotta slabs forming a "gable-roof" Terrace Roof	Painted Pottery *Vases with Long Beak-Spout* Painted Pottery *Cups, Vases with Vertical Spout, Rhytons, Askoi*	Vases *Lead and Bronze* Jewellery *Silver and Bronze*	Cylinder Seals	SHALMANESER III (859-824)	*Formation of the Kingdom of URARTU* MENUAS King of URARTU (c. 810-781)
Cemetery *Shallow graves dug in the earth* Scythian Cemetery *Horse Sacrifices* Cemetery *Megalithic Tombs*	Monochrome Ware *Aryballoi, Kernoi, Askoi* Monochrome Ware *Vases in the form of a Human Figure* Statuette *Steatopygous Type* Figurines Rhytons	Warrior Statuette *Bronze* Jewellery - *Goldon Bitumen* Mirrors - *Bronze* Jewellery - *Gold and Stones* Cauldron Tripods and Horse Bits - *Bronze* Goblets *Gold and Silver* Figurines, Animals *Bronze*		SHALMANESER IV (783-773) *Annals* SARGON (722-705)	ARGISTIS I King of URARTU (c. 781-773) ARGISTIS II King of URARTU (c. 714-685)
Cemetery *Megalithic Tombs* Statuette *from Pusht-i-Kuh* *Temple of Surkh Dum*	 Painted and Glazed Pottery *Vases, Goblets, Rhytons*	Jewellery *Gold, Silver, Iron* Idols, Vases, Weapons Situlae, Bits, Pins *Bronze* Votive Pins with Large Round Heads *Bronze* Jewellery, Pectorals Weapons, Plate *Gold, Silver, Bronze*	Cylinder Seals Bone and Ivory Carvings	ESARHADDON (681-668) ASSURBANIPAL (668-626) *612 - Destruction of NINEVEH*	
Median Rock Tombs	 Red Terracotta *Rhytons*	Jewellery, Votive Plaques Figurines - *Gold* Spouted Jug with Handles - *Bronze* Cup - *Gold* Vases, Weapons - *Gold*		NEBUCHAD-NEZZAR II (604-562) *Beautifying of BABYLON* Ishtar Gate	*End of the Kingdom of URARTU*

175 - PASARGADAE. LION'S HEAD (6th CENTURY B.C.) — IN SITU

IV

ACHAEMENIAN PERSIA
ARCHITECTURE AND SCULPTURE

THE land of Parsua, to the south and south-west of Lake Urmia, is mentioned for the first time in the annals of the Assyrian king Shalmaneser III in 834 B.C. This seems to have been the region where the Persian tribes halted for a time before continuing their migration south-eastwards, following the valleys of the Zagros range. About 700 B.C. we find them established at Parsumash, in the foothills of the Bakhtiari mountains south-east of Susa, then part of the Elamite kingdom. In the tense atmosphere created by Elam's struggle for survival against Assyria, further aggravated by conflicts among the Elamites themselves, who were divided into pro- and anti-Assyrian factions, the small Persian kingdom founded by Achaemenes slowly gained ground.

Achaemenes' son and successor, Teispes (675-640 B.C.), already bore the title of 'King of the City of Anshan,' which we propose to identify with present-day Masjid-i-Sulaiman. With Elam now on the decline, he added to his kingdom the province of Parsa (present-day Fars). After his death the kingdom was divided between his two sons: Ariaramnes, king of Parsa, and Cyrus, who was to be the 'great king' of Parsumash. With the power of the Medes then in the ascendant under Cyaxares, the two small Persian kingdoms could not escape coming under the sway of the conqueror of Nineveh. Once they were reunited by Cambyses I (600-559), son of Cyrus I, a new era began for the Persian people who, following the victory of Cyrus the Great (559-529) over Astyages, king of Media, were united with the Medes.

← 174 - PASARGADAE. WINGED GENIUS
  (6th CENTURY B.C.) — IN SITU

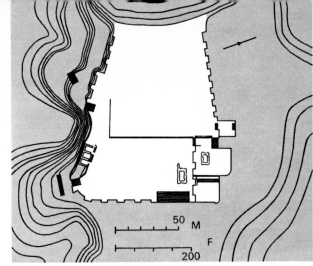

176 - MASJID-I-SULAIMAN. STAIRWAY (7th CENTURY B.C.)   177 - MASJID-I-SULAIMAN. PLAN OF THE TERRACE

It was, therefore, to the Achaemenians that Iran owed the conception and formation of a single Persian state. Cyrus the Great and Darius (521-485) incorporated in their far-flung dominions, the first great empire of recorded history, an aggregate of the civilizations of the ancient world: those of Mesopotamia, Syria, Egypt, Asia Minor, Greek cities and islands, and part of India. To force all these countries to fall in line with their own way of life would have had a retrograde effect, for as newcomers in the concert of peoples the Achaemenians could not fail to recognize the superiority of these ancient civilizations. Hence the large measure of autonomy granted by Cyrus; hence, too, the astute policy of Darius whereby the age-old cultures were left undisturbed and even favoured, perhaps at the expense of the stability of the central power. As long as the empire lasted, this unbalance was a latent, sometimes dangerous source of weakness and, given the expansionist tendency of the young, vigorous Persian people, proved to be one of the causes of its greatest setbacks and final downfall when, after the assassination of Artaxerxes III (338 B.C.), a new power, Macedon, appeared on the scene.

PALACES, TEMPLES AND TOMBS

Persian art under the Achaemenians was monarchical. In the capitals of the great King of Kings, it reflected the fortunes of the empire; hence its dazzling magnificence under Cyrus and Darius and, thereafter, its long stagnation, save for brief revivals under Xerxes and Artaxerxes.

Its outstanding monuments are the palaces. The history of their construction begins in the early seventh century B.C., when the Persian tribes were passing from a nomad state to a semi-settled way of life. As the imposing remains of Masjid-i-Sulaiman make clear, the man-made terrace abutting on a mountain-side, upon which stood the residence of the prince, was one of the elements used by these bold master-builders for producing a spectacular overall effect. Ten flights of stone steps, the main one some 80 feet wide, gave access to the terrace. The palace was surrounded by defensive walls, with projections and recesses, built of huge blocks of unbonded stone. Around the terrace lie the ruins of a fairly large village, with the foundations of its houses made of loose stones.

These building methods were something new on the Plateau. Though the local chieftains of protohistoric Iran had built their houses on terraces (as at Sialk), they knew nothing of Cyclopean masonry. The only country

178 - PASARGADAE. TAKHT-I-MADAR-I-SULAIMAN. TERRACE (6th C. B.C.)

thereabouts to make any considerable use of it was the kingdom of Urartu, on the edge of the Plateau, the immediate neighbour of the Persians during their sojourn in the vicinity of Lake Urmia. By the time they left this region the Persians were sufficiently well acquainted with Urartian culture to act as propagators of this type of construction, hitherto unknown on the Plateau but destined now to have a brilliant future.

It is to the Persians, then, that we attribute the terrace of Masjid-i-Sulaiman. Nor is this the only such terrace; there is another at Bard-i-Nishandah, fifteen miles to the north-east. But here the site covers a wider area and beside a cistern stand the ruins of an ancient settlement. It is quite possible that in these two places we have the first royal towns of the Persians, built perhaps by Achaemenes himself or by Teispes. The unification of the kingdom may have prompted Cambyses I to move his capital from Masjid-i-Sulaiman to Pasargadae, located in a more fertile region and more accessible to the Persian tribes now overrunning south-western Iran and advancing south of the great central desert in the direction of Kerman.

Although the art of Pasargadae is by and large a continuation of that of Masjid-i-Sulaiman, there is so great a difference in the architectural programmes of the two royal residences that only the rapidly rising prestige of Cyrus the Great can explain the transition from one to the other. Of the work attributable to Cambyses I there only remains the terrace, whose man-made part is wider than the surface of the natural rock overlooked by the mountain known as Takht-i-Madar-i-Sulaiman ('Throne of Solomon's Mother'). This terrace is similar to that of Masjid-i-Sulaiman. Its only novelty is the way the outer surrounding wall is built: its massive masonry consists of blocks of untrimmed stone fitted together by means of grooved joints. This technique is of Hittite origin. Adopted by the Phrygians, it spread to Urartu where the Persians familiarized themselves with it. The terrace has not yet been excavated; on it must have stood, in accordance with tradition, the buildings serving as the king's residence, no doubt made of unbaked bricks and wood; the town developed around it, within the defensive wall, on the west side of the mountain.

179 - PASARGADAE. RELIEF OF CYRUS (6th CENT. B.C.)   180 - DA-U-DUKHTAR. ROCK TOMB (7th-6th CENT. B.C.)

The built-up area covered a mile and a half from end to end. The great stone palaces enriched with decorative sculpture were built when Cyrus the Great became the ruler of the Medo-Persian kingdom (550 B.C.). He transformed Pasargadae, hitherto the fortress of a vassal prince, into the capital of an empire. This new palace area in the plain, with its enclosure wall, seems to have conformed to a carefully worked out plan. However, for an understanding of the developments in building methods that took place from the time of Cambyses I to that of Cyrus the Great it is essential, in our opinion, to study first of all the rock tomb of Da-u-Dukhtar, erected between Pasargadae and Masjid-i-Sulaiman for one of the first princes of the Achaemenid line. Standing as it does midway between the terrace presumably built by Cambyses and the 'imperial' buildings of Cyrus, it throws light on the Pasargadae complex. And as its attribution to Cambyses seems plausible, it lends support to the hypothesis that he was responsible for the lay-out of the Pasargadae terrace.

The monumental gate-house to the palaces of Cyrus stands at the south-east corner of the enclosure wall. It formed a large room, the roof of which rested on two rows of four columns. The main doors, opening on the narrow sides, were flanked by enormous winged bulls. Of the smaller doors on the long sides of the room, all that remains is a single jamb adorned with a bas-relief representing a four-winged genius, dressed in the Elamite manner and wearing an elaborate crown recalling the tiaras of Egyptian Horuses. Still visible in the early nineteenth century was an inscription above the genius, reading: 'I Cyrus, the King, the Achaemenid [built this].'

Two hundred yards to the north-west stood the Audience Hall with, on the east side, a raised hypostyle hall facing south and, on the west side, a triple portico with two corner rooms. The main portico, with two rows of twenty-four columns, faced north and extended over the whole width of the building. The elevation of the column is one of the characteristic features of this architecture: the smooth shaft, of white stone, stands on a square base of black stone enhanced with a fluted white torus; the capital, an impost block of black

132

stone, is adorned with protomes of bulls, lions and horses. The ornamental sculptures in the frames of the four doors of the main hall consist of human-headed, animal-bodied genii, guarding the entrances.

In the centre of an esplanade, amid what once were gardens watered by winding brooks, stands a second palace. We begin by crossing a portico *in antis*, facing south-east, that gives access to a door on the right leading to the hypostyle hall. Flanked on the north and south by rooms whose plan has yet to be elucidated, this hall communicated with a second portico having a room at each end. All the ceilings in the building were supported by rows of wooden columns with smooth shafts, originally frescoed. Their bases, of black and white stone, were square, with toruses. The same colour scheme, of alternating black and white, was repeated on the paved floor and the walls separating the porticoes. The two main doors of the central hall were framed with bas-reliefs representing the king followed by a servant with a sunshade. Here, for the first time, is an Iranian sculptor showing the folds of garments. True, in the royal robe inlaid with gold, relief is rather too sharply indicated and the effort to render the natural fall of the cloth fails to exclude traces of archaic rigidity. But the work marks, nevertheless, a notable advance; the difference between this bas-relief and the one at the monumental gate-house is striking. This inno-vation prepared the way for the decor-ations of the palaces at Persepolis.

Three types of trilingual inscrip-tions (in Old Persian, Elamite and Babylonian) have been found at Pasar-gadae. The most frequent is the type that figured above the winged genius and on the antae of the extant palaces. It perpetuated an ancient Elamite tradition exemplified, most notably, at Choga Zambil. The second type, engraved above the bas-relief of the king, shows a slight change; here Cyrus is styled 'the great king, son of Cambyses, the king, the Achaeme-nid. . .' The third runs along the folds of the royal robe: 'Cyrus, the great king, the Achaemenid.' The change in the royal title as borne by Cyrus and that of his father Cambyses is significant and suggests that the palaces were built after the Persian annexation of Media.

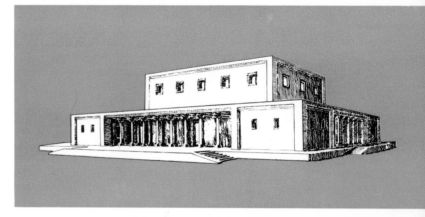

181 - PASARGADAE. AUDIENCE HALL (6th CENTURY B.C.)

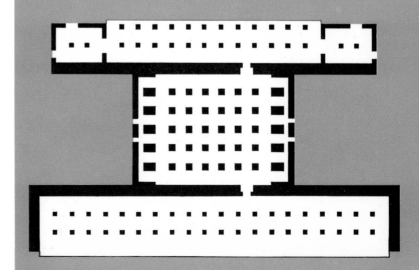

182 - PASARGADAE. RECEPTION HALL (6th CENTURY B.C.)

183 - PASARGADAE. FIRE ALTARS (6th CENTURY B.C.)

184 - PASARGADAE. RUINS OF THE
FIRE TEMPLE (6th CENT. B.C.)

Ernst Herzfeld assumed the second palace to be the king's private residence, but it seems to us more likely that it was employed exclusively for the receptions and banquets that followed the royal audiences. This would account for the lay-out in three parts of the buildings at Pasargadae, as also on the terrace at Persepolis: the monumental gate-house, the Apadana and the banqueting palace. It is to be noted, too, that the structure of the reception palace at Pasargadae is unique in Achaemenian architecture. One cannot help thinking of the vast tents in which the great nobles of Iran, less than a third of a century ago, still received their guests. Open at both ends, they enabled the assembled guests to sit outside under one or the other of two opposite awnings, according to the time of day and the position of the sun.

The architecture at Pasargadae is not exclusively secular; it also catered for the gods whom the Achaemenians worshipped. Within an enclosure wall of its own, a mile west of the terrace, stood a sanctuary of which all that remains is a pedestal with six steps, and two fire altars. Of the temple but a single wall survives, between the palaces and the terrace—last vestige of what once was a square tower of dressed stone, whose façade was adorned with blind windows. An identical tower, in an almost perfect state of preservation, can be seen at Naqsh-i-Rustam. The purpose of these edifices will be discussed when we come to deal with the religious architecture of Naqsh-i-Rustam.

with the old Iranian spirit, it grouped on a single terrace all that Cyrus had dispersed over a wide area. For an empire like that of Darius, stretching from Egypt to the Indus, from the Danube to the Jaxartes, a capital ensconced in a small valley of the Plateau was much too far from the vital centre of things. Pasargadae, nevertheless, was not abandoned. It remained the religious centre of Iran and, until the empire fell, the coronations of the Iranian kings were

The tomb of Cyrus, still revered today under the name of 'the Tomb of Solomon's Mother,' was built on the southern edge of the site, within a rectangular court surrounded by a wall of unbaked bricks. The funerary chamber stands on a stereobate of six stepped slabs of unequal height—which shows that it was not used as a stairway. On its north side is a low aperture four and a half feet high closed by an inner and an outer door. The masonry of the building consists entirely of carefully dressed blocks of fine white limestone, having the appearance of marble. Its gable-roof, made of five enormous slabs of stone, brings to mind a northern house and has similarities with the roofing slabs of the Sialk tombs (Cemetery B). With its seven storeys rising to a height of over 36 feet, this monument seems to have been inspired by a ziggurat of the Choga Zambil type, near Susa, which still remained intact in the time of Cyrus.

Pasargadae, whose ancient name is thought to have been Parsagada, meaning 'camp of the Persians,' has a disposition fully justifying this nomenclature. The town exemplifies on a vast scale an epoch of Persian art whose beginnings are still unknown, but to which Median art no doubt contributed. Composite as it is, with its Assyrian winged bulls, Hittite or-

185 - PASARGADAE. TOMB OF CYRUS II (6th CENTURY B.C.)

thostats, Babylonian polychromy and Egyptian symbols, this art reflects a national culture already of a high order. All the foreign elements have been recast, transposed and harmonized so as to form a new art predominantly architectonic in character, and owing something perhaps to the Greeks. What more likely than that the art of Persepolis originated in the Murghab valley? Concentrated in a smaller area, but drawing on the old traditions and infused

187 - SUSA. AERIAL VIEW OF THE PALACE AND THE APADANA

celebrated with due pomp and ceremony in its temple. For his political, diplomatic and administrative capital Darius chose Susa. The old Elamite city, which had been sacked and devastated about 640 B.C. by the army of Assurbanipal, lay only about sixty miles from the Persian Gulf, starting point of the sea routes to the Persian possessions in India and Egypt. Three overland routes connected Susa with Persepolis, by way of the 'Persian Gates' between Fahlian and Bishapur; with Ecbatana, through Luristan; and with Babylon, following the Tigris upstream.

On the Elamite acropolis stood the citadel; to the north of it, the royal palaces; south of these, the city proper. These three areas were surrounded by a great defensive wall; at the foot of the wall a moat was dug, through which flowed the river Shahur, diverted for this purpose from its course. Of the four essential parts of the Achaemenian palace (monumental gate-house, audience hall, reception hall, living quarters) only two have survived at Susa, and these in a very imperfect state: the audience hall and living quarters. The other buildings of the palace area have been too badly damaged, both in ancient and modern times, for any reliable conclusion to be drawn regarding their original lay-out.

The palace with the audience hall (Apadana) stood on a terrace, as at Masjid-i-Sulaiman and, in early times, at Pasargadae. A mound formed by previous settlements had been levelled and extended by walls of unbaked brick acting as caissons into which was poured an immense quantity of gravel. The Apadana, projecting from the north side of the palace, was acceded to by flights of steps starting from the forecourts which surrounded the Apadana on the north and west, and perhaps on the east side as well.

   ← 186 - SUSA. DETAIL OF A CAPITAL
(6th CENT. B.C.) — LOUVRE

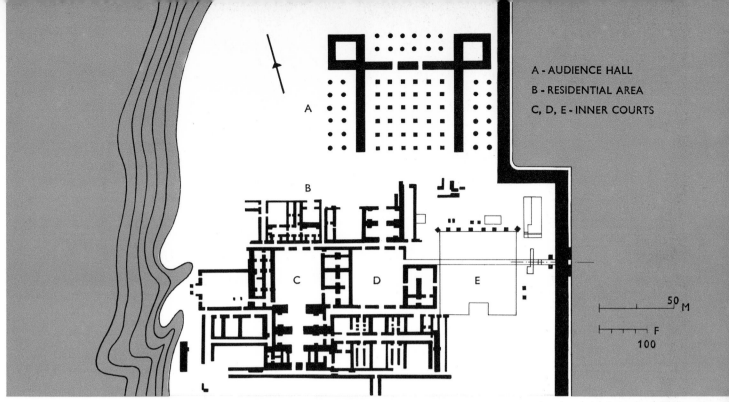

188 - SUSA.   PLAN OF THE PALACE AND THE APADANA

Excavations having enabled us to trace the position of the walls and to locate the north portico of the Apadana, there is no difficulty in establishing a ground plan.

The arrangement of the buildings at Susa is the same as at Pasargadae: a central hall with three porticoes, their north and east corners forming two square rooms.   The roof of the audience hall was supported by six rows of six stone columns each—wonderfully bold and light in structure.   With their fluted shafts, square bases and capitals of two bull protomes, they rise to a height of 65 feet, an architectural feat unparalleled in antiquity.   Though the Persian bull protomes imitate Assyrian and Babylonian models, their 'archaizing' style fails to conceal a new, distinctive tendency to naturalism appropriate in its context.   For fully plastic figuration of this kind contributed to the monumental effect intended.   Each portico comprised two rows of six columns whose bell-shaped bases were each adorned with a different design.   The whole structure was painted a pale yellow, giving it the appearance of marble and masking the imperfections of the stone beneath, a friable bituminous stone brought from the near-by Bakhtiari mountains.

We now know, thanks to excavations of the Elamite site of Choga Zambil, near Susa, that the palace of Darius at Susa followed the plan of the palaces of the Elamite kings, which may have stood on the same mound.   The main gate must have been located on the west side of the enclosure wall, opposite the west portico of the Apadana.   If, as seems likely, there was a reception and banquet room, it must have been at the north corner of the palace, to which the guests had access either by a stairway from the forecourt or on their way from the Apadana, without crossing the palace buildings.

189 - SUSA. FRAGMENT OF THE STATUE OF DARIUS (LATE 6th - EARLY 5th CENTURY B.C.) — LOUVRE

A long inscription discovered at Susa describes the building programme. After invoking the great god Ahuramazda, Darius enumerates the places from which the various materials came and the nationalities of the craftsmen who fashioned them. There was cedar from Lebanon, gold from Sardis and Bactria, lapis lazuli and carnelian from Sogdiana, turquoise from Chorasmia, silver and ebony from Egypt, mural decoration (?) from Ionia, ivory from Ethiopia and Arachosia, yaka wood from Kerman and Gandhara, stone for columns from Elam. The stone-cutters were Ionians and Sardians, the goldsmiths Medians and Egyptians, the wood-workers Sardians and Egyptians, the brick-makers Babylonians, the mural decorators (perhaps) Medians and Egyptians. The importance of this text is obvious, giving as it does a picture of the Persian Empire, a mosaic of many races, and of its all-powerful ruler summoning the best artificers in his dominions to pool their talents in a joint enterprise.

In another inscription Artaxerxes II informs us that the palace of Susa was burnt down under his grandfather Artaxerxes I, and that it was not rebuilt until he himself had this done. We believe that, in carrying out the reconstruction, he kept to the ground plan and decorations of the palace as it had been in the time of Darius.

All the ornamentation in the Apadana and the palace, without exception, consisted of glazed bricks. Stone was used only for columns and thresholds. Not a single fragment of carved stone has been found in the ruins of the great palace of Susa, except for the remains of a statue of Darius, apparently in the round. That the inner walls of the rooms were adorned with glazed brick appears unlikely, but the outside walls covered by it constituted a vast surface; the Apadana, for example, must have been over 65 feet in height. At Susa, as at Pasargadae, Darius placed the Apadana under the protection of benevolent genii, some of them in a setting of palmettes and rosettes. To these traditional subjects he added a representation of his guardsmen, the so-called Immortals, with whom he served in Egypt during its conquest by Cambyses, and who are believed to have helped him to regain his throne.

190 - SUSA. FRIEZE OF ARCHERS
(5th CENT. B.C.) — LOUVRE →

140

191 - SUSA. LION-GRIFFIN (5th CENTURY B.C.) — LOUVRE

Very different were the decorations on the stairways leading to the palace. Here, as at Persepolis, were files of servants carrying lambs for roasting and dishes ready to serve, kept warm in cups and bowls with lids.

What Darius fails to mention in the 'Foundation Charter' is that he—or one of his successors, perhaps—imported from Aswan (Egypt) the pink granite of which some of the column-bases were made. For others diorite was used; one of them seems to have been hewn out of an Elamite statue, or a statue imported from Babylonia by the Elamites.

For several decades, between the time it was burnt down and rebuilt, the palace of Darius was uninhabitable. But a capital as important as Susa could not long remain without a royal residence, and in the last quarter of the fifth century B.C. a 'miniature' palace was erected on the southern edge of the town, on the ruins of a sort of annexe which Dieulafoy called the 'Keep.' Available evidence (including inscriptions) proves that, above the 'Keep,' the two kings Artaxerxes I

192 - SUSA. WINGED BULL (5th CENTURY B.C.) — LOUVRE

193 - SUSA. LION. — LOUVRE →

194-195 · SUSA.   FRAGMENTS OF RELIEFS: CUP-BEARER AND WINGED LION (5th CENTURY B.C.) — TEHERAN

and Darius II erected a small hypostyle hall, replacing the Apadana, and a reception hall adjoining the living quarters.

All the fragments of stone bas-reliefs found at Susa come from this small palace. What is more, the carved ornamentation of this royal residence is, for the first time at Susa, entirely of stone. Keeping as it does, however, to the established iconographical tradition, it tends to be monotonous, though there are everywhere signs of a more delicate, more human touch, almost as if an Attic breeze were fanning the vast plain of Susiana. The gracious movement of the servant holding a cup adorned with a duck's head, the lifelike rendering of the folds and swelling surfaces of draperies, the vigorous naturalism of a roaring lion's jaws, and the technique of the relief work elegantly standing out against the ground plane—all these features might well have

196-197 - GREEK RELIEFS: WOMAN WITH DOVE AND BATTLE OF GIANTS, DETAIL (LATE 6th CENT. B.C.) — ROME AND DELPHI

stemmed from Greece. But the whole question of such influences must be treated with the utmost caution. Referring to the text of the 'Foundation Charter' of Darius, we find that the Ionians working on the king's palace were charged with the task of hewing columns, together with their bases and capitals, out of stone imported from 'the village named Abiradu, in Elam' (lines 45-49). Their share in the work was therefore limited to a single architectural element; the text expressly attributes the columns to them, nothing more. However, the Persians could not fail to be affected by Greek art, particularly that of Ionia, whose sculptors were renowned in even the most distant lands. It is frequently said that Achaemenian art remained unchanged during the two centuries of its existence, but this is not strictly true, as is shown even by the badly damaged fragments from the small palace of Susa.

199 - AERIAL VIEW OF PERSEPOLIS

Hardly was the palace of Susa finished when Darius, without abandoning Pasargadae, decided to build another capital at Persepolis, in his native province of Fars. Once again, keeping to tradition, the architects of the Great King of Kings built a terrace abutting—as at Pasargadae and Masjid-i-Sulaiman—on the mountain-side, here the Kuh-i-Rahmat ('Mountain of Mercy'), a projecting slope of which was levelled and artificially extended. On this terrace were erected the finest buildings ever seen in Asia up to that time.

Persepolis, however, was neither the diplomatic nor the administrative capital. Great statesman that he was, Darius saw the need to build an empire whose structure differed radically from that of all the great Asiatic powers —Babylonia, Elam, Assyria—that had preceded it in this part of the world. For the revolts that broke out on his accession had warned him of the separatist tendencies of the various peoples of the Persian empire.

← 198 - AERIAL VIEW OF PERSEPOLIS

200-201 - PERSEPOLIS. STAIRWAYS TO THE TERRACE. FIRST FLIGHT ON RIGHT AND LEFT SIDES

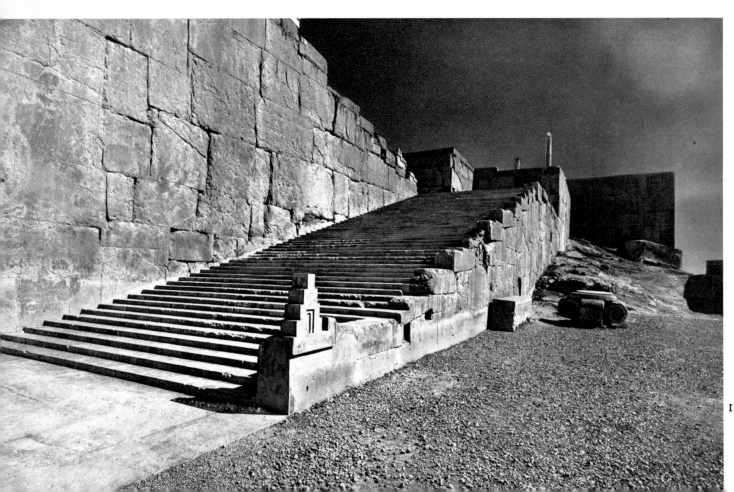

203 - PERSEPOLIS. GATE-HOUSE OF XERXES I (5th CENTURY B.C.) — IN SITU

202 - PERSEPOLIS. MONUMENTAL STAIRWAY TO THE TERRACE, OPPOSITE THE GATE-HOUSE OF XERXES I (LATE 6th CENTURY B.C.) — IN SITU

204 - PERSEPOLIS.   VIEW OF THE ROYAL TREASURY (5th CENTURY B.C.)

205-206 - PERSEPOLIS.   VIEWS OF THE HYPOSTYLE HALLS OF THE TREASURY (5th CENTURY B.C.)

Thus he decided for a centralized state, on the basis of equal rights and justice for all. Unwilling to stake his confidence on any but the dominant races, Darius chose from the leading Persian and Median families the satraps whom he charged with the administration of the provinces. Each nation preserved its own language, its own institutions, religion and art, but it had to recognize the sovereignty of the State of which it formed part. The empire had three official languages and functionaries corresponded with each other in a fourth, Aramaic, at that time widely used as a *lingua franca* from Egypt to India. As regards religion, the policy of Cyrus was maintained. There was no imperial cult common to all, but by the very fact that the king ruled by the will of Ahuramazda, the great god and creator of the universe, the Persian world came to acquire a kind of religious unity.

Everything at Persepolis was calculated to stimulate the sense of nationality and this was implemented by ceremonies taking place each year, at the beginning of spring, on the great feast-day of the Mazdaean religion: *Nov Ruz*, or New Year's Day. Under the auspices of the great god Ahuramazda and in the presence of the King of Kings, the dominant peoples, Persians and Medes, witnessed the processions of tribute-bearers from all the nations of this far-flung realm bringing their gifts to the foot of the throne in token of their fidelity and loyalty. No foreigners were admitted to the city—which accounts for the fact that no western writer so much as mentions the existence of Persepolis before the time of Alexander the Great. Even Ctesias, the Greek physician who lived at the court of Artaxerxes II (404-358), seems never to have heard of it. Long before the day of celebration, the grandees of the empire and the delegations of subject peoples arrived on the scene and pitched their tents by thousands in the vast plain, watered by the Pulvar, that stretches westwards from the terrace of Persepolis.

NEW YEAR'S DAY AT PERSEPOLIS

ON New Year's Day the highest dignitaries of the empire, Persian and Median noblemen, ascended the stairway leading to the terrace and, on the threshold of the monumental gate-house built by Xerxes, filed past the guardian animals, winged bulls, some of them human-headed.

These awe-inspiring genii, offspring of the Assyrian monsters, were chiefly intended to glorify the invincible might of the empire; they were not set up, as they had been in Assyria, to 'lay low rebels' or to 'overawe the King's subjects in order to gratify his heart.'

207 - PERSEPOLIS. ENTRANCE OF THE GATE- →
HOUSE OF XERXES I (5th CENTURY B.C.)

208 - PERSEPOLIS.   FOUNDATION PLAQUE OF THE APADANA (LATE 6th CENTURY B.C.)

After passing through the gate-house of Xerxes, the notables crossed the fore-court of the Apadana, a replica of the one at Susa.   At two different places in the substructure of the Apadana, Darius placed foundation deposits: two stone boxes each containing two foundation plaques, one in gold, the other in silver, accompanied by a few coins.   The text engraved on the plaques in three languages, Old Persian, Elamite and Babylonian, reads as follows:

'Darius, the Great King, King of Kings, King of the Countries, son of Hystaspes, the Achaemenid.   Saith Darius the King: This is the kingdom which I possess from the land of the Sakas on this side of Sogdiana as far as Kush, from India to Sardis.   Over this Ahuramazda has granted me dominion, he who is great above all the Gods. May Ahuramazda protect me and my Royal House.'

Two great stairways on the north and east sides gave access to the Apadana. Their ornamentation was threefold: first, the façade in the centre, showing eight guards presenting a royal inscription, while at each corner the triumph of good over evil is symbolized by a lion mauling a bull; next, the outer part of the ramp representing the setting in which the procession is to take place, while on the inner side Persian guards on the steps form a double row in front of which the King and grandees advance; lastly, on the back wall, forming the base of the Apadana, is a bas-relief representing the procession of the twenty-three subject nations of the empire, together with court notables, Persians and Medes, accompanied by their horses and the royal chariots, and escorted by Susian guards.

The pictured scenes gave the king's guests a preview of what they were soon to see. Not all the visitors, however, were privileged to come on to the terrace itself, and these scenes were intended to have a narrative value, appealing to the general public, apart from their decorative effect.

The king and his retinue watched the procession from a 'royal box,' projecting from the terrace, in front of

209 - PERSEPOLIS. S

the west portico of the hypostyle hall. The reliefs give us a vivid picture of what actually took place. The Susian tribute-bearers offered weapons and lions; the Armenians, vases of precious metals and horses; the Babylonians, cups, embroidered textiles and buffaloes; the Lydians, famed for their skill as goldsmiths, metal-work and horses; the Sogdians, sheep and textiles; the Cappadocians and Phrygians, horses and embroidered garments; the Tigraxauda ('pointed

157

211 - PERSEPOLIS. EAST STAIRWAY OF THE APADANA (6th-5th CENTURIES B.C.)

STAIRWAY RELIEFS OF THE TRIPYLON: MEDIAN NOBLES (6th-5th CENTURIES B.C.)

cap') Sakas, horses, jewellery and garments; the Indians, weapons and mules. The trees separating each delegation from the one behind are of the same species as those on the parapet of the ramp: the *Pinus Prutia*. They were copied from the trees planted by Darius on a vast esplanade at the foot of the terrace; their branches show them to be some ten to fifteen years old. All these reliefs were painted, in blue, red, almond green, yellow and purple.

212 - PERSEPOLIS.   GATE-HOUSE OF XERXES I.   'GATE OF ALL COUNTRIES' →

214 - PERSEPOLIS. STAIRWAY GIVING ACCESS TO THE TRIPYLON (6th-5th CENTURIES B.C.) — IN SITU

When the procession was over, king and grandees moved on to the Tripylon, a small building with three doors that must have served the same purpose as Xerxes' monumental gate-house. Mounting a vast stairway, attended by servants bearing his sunshade and fly-whisks (just as we see him represented on the north and south doors) and followed by his retinue of noblemen, the king walked across the small hall of four columns. Note how the artist, respecting the law of isocephaly, then already many centuries old in the Ancient East, places a dwarf and a giant on the same step and yet aligns both their heads with that of the figure in front of them or behind them. A Greek sculptor would have taken pains to represent them more realistically.

215 - PERSEPOLIS. STAIRWAY RELIEF OF THE TRIPYLON: PERSIAN DIGNITARY (6th-5th CENTURIES B.C.)

216 · PERSEPOLIS. EAST STAIRWAY OF THE APADANA: SUSIANS, ARMENIANS AND PERSIANS (6th-5th CENTURIES B.C.)

217 - PERSEPOLIS. EAST STAIRWAY OF THE APADANA: PERSIAN GUARDS (6th-5th CENTURIES B.C.)

218 - PERSEPOLIS. EAST STAIRWAY OF THE APADANA: SUSIAN GUARDS (6th-5th CENTURIES B.C.)

219 - PERSEPOLIS. EAST STAIRWAY OF THE APADANA:
PERSIAN GUARD (6th-5th CENTURIES B.C.) →

220 - PERSEPOLIS. EAST STAIRWAY OF THE APADANA: SYRIANS OR LYDIANS (6th-5th CENTURIES B.C.)

174

221 - PERSEPOLIS. EAST STAIRWAY OF THE APADANA: A BABYLONIAN (6th-5th CENTURIES B.C.)

222 - PERSEPOLIS. EAST STAIRWAY OF THE APADANA: AN ARMENIAN (?) (6th-5th CENTURIES B.C.)

223 - PERSEPOLIS. EAST STAIRWAY OF THE APADANA: BABYLONIANS (6th-5th CENTURIES B.C.)

224 - PERSEPOLIS. EAST STAIRWAY OF THE APADANA: SYRIAN OR LYDIAN (6th-5th CENTURIES B.C.)

225 - PERSEPOLIS. EAST STAIRWAY OF THE APADANA: SYRIAN OR LYDIAN (6th-5th CENTURIES B.C.)

226 - PERSEPOLIS. EAST STAIRWAY OF THE APADANA: PERSIAN DIGNITARY (6th-5th CENTURIES B.C.)

227 - PERSEPOLIS. EAST STAIRWAY OF THE APADANA: MEDIAN DIGNITARY (6th-5th CENTURIES B.C.)

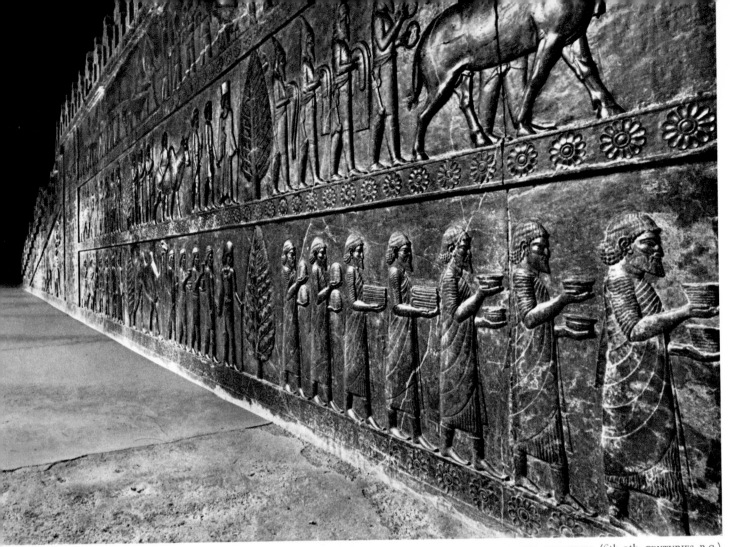

228 - PERSEPOLIS. EAST STAIRWAY OF THE APADANA: REPRESENTATIVES OF VARIOUS COUNTRIES (6th-5th CENTURIES B.C.)

18

230 - PERSEPOLIS.   EAST STAIRWAY OF THE APADANA: A BACTRIAN (6th-5th CENTURIES B.C.)

← 229 - PERSEPOLIS.   STAIRWAY OF THE APADANA, NORTH FAÇADE:
    REPRESENTATIVES OF VARIOUS COUNTRIES (6th-5th C. B.C.)

231 - PERSEPOLIS. EAST STAIRWAY OF THE APADANA: A CHORASMIAN (6th-5th CENTURIES B.C.)

232 – PERSEPOLIS. EAST STAIRWAY OF THE APADANA: AN USHER WITH A CHORASMIAN (6th-5th CENTURIES B.C.)

234 - PERSEPOLIS. SOUTH STAIRWAY OF THE TRIPYLON (6th-5th CENTURIES B.C.)

← 233 - PERSEPOLIS. TRIPYLON DOOR: DARIUS
BENEATH A SUNSHADE (6th-5th C. B.C.)

235 · PERSEPOLIS. STAIRWAY OF THE TRIPYLON: PERSIAN DIGNITARIES (6th-5th CENTURIES B.C.)

236 - PERSEPOLIS. STAIRWAY OF THE TRIPYLON: PERSIAN AND MEDIAN GUARDS (6th-5th CENTURIES B.C.)

237 - PERSEPOLIS. STAIRWAY OF THE TRIPYLON: A MEDIAN GUARD (6th-5th CENTURIES B.C.)

238 - PERSEPOLIS. STAIRWAY OF THE TRIPYLON: A PERSIAN GUARD (6th-5th CENTURIES B.C.)

239 - PERSEPOLIS. BAS-RELIEF IN FRONT OF THE PALACE OF DARIUS (5th CENTURY B.C.)

The banquet was served in the palace of Darius, whose approaches are decorated with servants shown coming up the steps and bringing the dishes and
animals to be eaten by the guests. Persian guards and servants standing on
the steps of the small south stairway of the Tripylon symbolically indicate the
goal towards which the guests en route to the palace are advancing.

240 - PERSEPOLIS. PALACE OF DARIUS: STAIRWAY RELIEFS (6th-5th CENTURIES B.C.)

It would seem that the palace of Darius, proving to be too small, was replaced under Xerxes by a larger building, whose function, however, as the decorations on the stairways show, remained the same. For these two palaces were not private residences; in them the king received his guests and gave official banquets.

241 - PERSEPOLIS. PALACE OF DARIUS: SERVANT   242 - TWO GUARDS (6th-5th CENTURIES B.C.)

243 - PERSEPOLIS. PALACE OF DARIUS: SERVANT (6th-5th CENTURIES B.C.)

245 - PERSEPOLIS. PALACE OF XERXES, WEST STAIRWAY: SERVANTS (5th CENTURY B.C.)

← 244 - PERSEPOLIS. PALACE OF XERXES, WEST
STAIRWAY: SERVANTS (5th CENTURY B.C.)

247 - PERSEPOLIS. EAST DOOR OF THE TRIPYLON, DETAIL: AHURAMAZDA (6th-5th CENTURIES B.C.)

When the meal was over, the king and his guests again repaired to the Tripylon, but this time by way of the east door, whose ornamentation again serves as a guide and informs us where they now were going. Here we see Darius seated on his throne, which is upheld by small figures personifying the twenty-eight nations; behind him stands the Crown Prince, Xerxes. Over the throne is a lavishly decorated baldachin, above which hovers the great god Ahuramazda. The 'imperial symbolism' of this scene relates to the audience the king is about to give to representatives of the subject nations.

← 246 - PERSEPOLIS. EAST DOOR OF THE TRIPYLON:
DARIUS AND XERXES (6th-5th CENTURIES B.C.)

249 - PERSEPOLIS. HALL OF A HUNDRED COLUMNS, SOUTH DOOR: BEARERS OF THE ROYAL THRONE (5th CENTURY B.C.)

These subject nations Darius proudly enumerates again and again in his inscriptions: on the south façade of the terrace of Persepolis, on the gold and silver plaques in the foundation deposit under the Apadana of Persepolis, on his tomb at Naqsh-i-Rustam—and each time he adds the names of the latest countries annexed to the empire.

Led by the king, the procession entered the Throne Hall, or Hall of a Hundred Columns, through the two doors on the south side. The inner sides of the doors were carved with reliefs; these repeat the theme on the east door of the Tripylon, showing the king enthroned, but Darius no longer figures in it. Now we see his grandson Artaxerxes I who, over a quarter of a century after Darius's death, finished building the edifice, most sumptuous of all those on the terrace, in which the King of Kings received the homage and gifts of his subject peoples.

Long before the king appeared and seated himself on his throne, the heads of delegations, with their attendants carrying the most precious objects, began moving towards the Throne Hall. Escorted by the Immortals, they climbed the main stairway to the terrace and passed through the gate-house of Xerxes, described in its inscription as the 'Gate of All Countries.' Coming out by the east door, they advanced down a long 'processional way' running along the north side of the wall around the Apadana. After passing through another monumental gate-house (never completed), they came out on a vast esplanade in front of the north portico of the Throne Hall. There the delegations awaited

← 248 - PERSEPOLIS. HALL OF A HUNDRED COLUMNS:
ARTAXERXES ENTHRONED (5th CENTURY B.C.)

250-251 - PERSEPOLIS. HALL OF A HUNDRED COLUMNS: 'ROYAL HERO' FIGHTING ANIMALS (5th CENTURY B.C.)

the king's summons, perhaps under the surveillance of the military commanders assembled in the hypostyle hall of the palace barracks.

One after another the heads of delegations were ushered into the hall and laid their gifts at the foot of the throne. There they could admire the gigantic reliefs on the east and west doors and ponder on the meaning of their symbolism.

252-253 - PERSEPOLIS. HALL OF A HUNDRED COLUMNS: 'ROYAL HERO' FIGHTING ANIMALS (5th CENTURY B.C.)

For the representations of the 'royal hero' subduing real or fabulous animals were clearly intended to remind them how surely and how ruthlessly any hostile forces would be crushed by the imperial power. Their mission accomplished, the delegations withdrew, again along the processional way, and were ushered out through the monumental gate-house of Xerxes.

We can only conclude, then, that the central part of what has hitherto been taken for the Treasury was actually a temporary throne room built by Darius. The fact is that in his time the greater part of the terrace of Persepolis was still a vast building yard; probably only his palace and the Tripylon were completed before his death. The Apadana was completed by Xerxes and the Throne Hall by Artaxerxes I.

But it was Darius who conceived the idea of building a new capital commensurate with the power and prestige of the Persian Empire, and already in his time the ceremonies described above must certainly have taken place there. A Treasury was obviously needed to house the tribute of the subject nations, and presumably it was built in the south-east corner of the terrace, on a site corresponding to the southern third of the buildings now known as the Treasury. But to receive delegations from the provinces Darius needed a throne hall, and this may be identified with the hall of ninety-nine columns (which gives on the courtyard with four porticoes where the two bas-reliefs mentioned above were found). This hall appears to have been erected hastily, for it was made of unbaked brick and wood, stone being used only for the column-bases. The columns themselves were made of wood plastered over and painted with a spiral pattern of blue, white and red—a decoration more lavish than anywhere else in the so-called Treasury.

Thus in the time of Darius the centre of gravity of this building complex presumably lay on the south side of the terrace. And the façade on this side would logically have been built first, for the ground level here is lower than that of the rest of the site. The procession of tribute-bearers must have taken place in the plain before this façade, whose central projection served as the 'royal box'—and this would account for the otherwise anomalous presence here of the trilingual inscriptions commemorating the foundation of Persepolis by Darius.

The Hall of a Hundred Columns, on the north side of the temporary throne room built by Darius, forms the third part of the Treasury. It too, in our opinion, was built by Xerxes. Did the inadequacy of the initial Treasury, which must soon have proved too small to contain the treasure hoard increased each year by the tribute of the king's subjects, lead to the decision to transform Darius's temporary throne room into a storehouse and accordingly to build a new temporary throne room? Or did Xerxes upon his accession consider it beneath his dignity to receive delegations in front of the bas-reliefs on the porticoes, which represented him as Crown Prince, standing respectfully behind his father's throne?

However this may be, one thing is certain: neither the hall of ninety-nine columns nor that of a hundred columns, both of which formed part of the 'Treasury' as it must have been when Alexander saw it, was originally intended to be a mere storehouse.

and certainly intended to decorate the place where they were found. They
represent the king in the attitude of a worshipper—the same scene that we
have already seen on the north door of the Throne Hall and on the east door
of the Tripylon. These reliefs must go back to the time of Darius, for he is
represented on them, followed by his son Xerxes and his attendants, one of
whom is armed with an *akinakes* (a short Scytho-Median sword) in a finely
wrought gold (?) scabbard. It seems strange that a work representing such
an important iconographic theme should have been relegated to a place where
only a few Treasury officials could see it. This must be the original which
Artaxerxes I caused to be copied on the north door of the Throne Hall.

255 - PERSEPOLIS. TREASURY: DARIUS GIVING AUDIENCE BEFORE TWO FIRE ALTARS (6th-5th CENT. B.C.) — TEHERAN MUSEUM

The reliefs on the north doors of the Throne Hall illustrate this culminating phase of the New Year's Day ceremonies at Persepolis. Here the king is represented enthroned. Seated in front of two fire altars, which separate him from the grand master of ceremonies and his assistant, he is ready to receive the tribute of his provinces, surrounded by fly-whisk bearers, heralds and his bodyguard, these last figuring on the five lowest registers. The precious objects presented to the king were at once removed to the Royal Treasury.

Now it so happens that excavations in the porticoed courtyard in the centre of the 'Treasury,' in front of a hall with ninety-nine columns, brought to light two bas-reliefs of the same size ($20^{1}/_{2}$ feet long), representing the same theme,

← 254 - PERSEPOLIS. HALL OF A HUNDRED COLUMNS (THRONE HALL),
NORTH DOOR: ARTAXERXES GIVING AUDIENCE (5th CENT. B.C.)

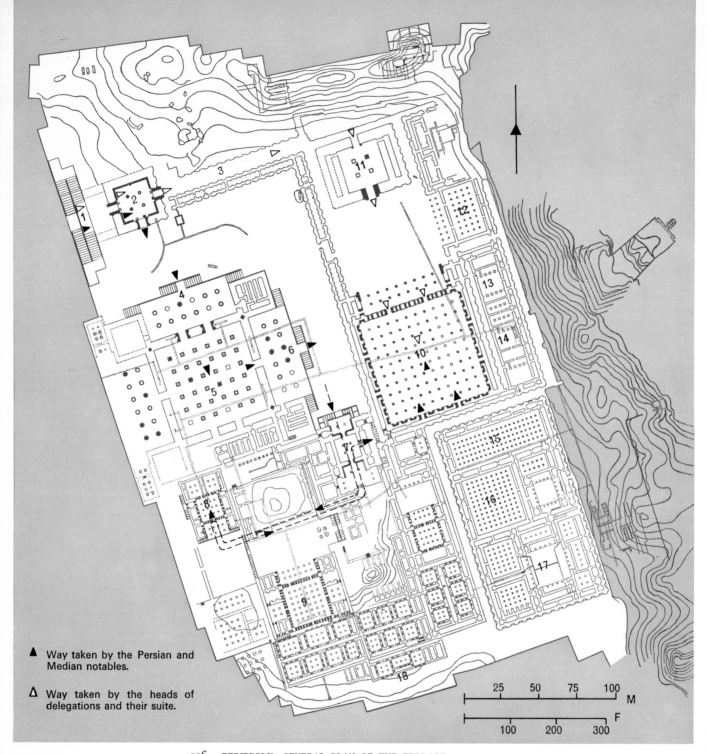

256 - PERSEPOLIS. GENERAL PLAN OF THE TERRACE

1 - Stairway to the Terrace. 2 - Gate-House of Xerxes, called " Gate of All Countries ". 3 - Processional Way. 4 - North Stairway of the Apadana. 5 - Apadana (Audience Hall). 6 - East Stairway of the Apadana. 7 - Tripylon. 8 - Palace of Darius (Banquet Hall). 9 - Palace of Xerxes (Banquet Hall). 10 - Hall of 100 Columns or Throne Hall. 11 - Unfinished Gate-House. 12-13-14 - Military Area. 15 - Hall of 100 Columns (3rd part of the Royal Treasury). 16 - Hall of 99 Columns (central part of the Treasury), temporary Throne Hall built by Darius. 17 - Storerooms of the Royal Treasury. 18 - South Façade of the Terrace overlooking the plain. In the centre, the Royal Box.

The general plan of Persepolis—due, we believe, to Darius and his architects —was a highly elaborate one, and it merits detailed study. The city was not intended to be a fortress—that much is certain. Darius wished Persepolis to be a rallying centre for the nations under his dominion.

We cannot agree with those who assume that the city was girdled with defensive walls and bastions, with the exception, of course, of the wall, flanked by towers, winding up the mountain-side behind the terrace. The terrace had only a low parapet, a few vestiges of which are still visible on the best preserved parts of the wall near the stairway leading up to it.

The pacific character of Persepolis is confirmed by the main stairway, which opens outwards and was obviously never meant to be defended. So it was not by reason of any ramparts, towers and bastions that Persepolis so powerfully impressed the subjects of the King of Kings; what they saw, rather, as they approached the city, was the dazzling spectacle of the most splendid palaces then to be found anywhere in the world, those magnificent edifices whose ruins can still be seen from many miles away.

Though laid out along a north-south axis, the architectural complex of Persepolis cannot be divided into an official northern sector and a private southern sector. To introduce any such division is to misunderstand the official role of the palace of Darius and Xerxes, to overlook the fact that the southern sector was the point of departure of the official activities on the terrace, and to take no account of the evidence offered by the inscriptions engraved there. To be sure, a private sector existed, confined at first to the very small area occupied by the harem ; it was subsequently much enlarged.

The building units were so disposed as to impress the beholder with the harmonious arrangement of their decorative elements. The colossal images of bulls flanking both the outer and the inner entrance of the gate-house of Xerxes must have been repeated on the 'unfinished' gate-house in front of the Throne Hall and they reappeared on the north portico of this hall. The gate-house of Xerxes seems, then, to have centred on the Throne Hall, not on the Apadana, and this assumption is borne out by Xerxes' inscription, by the decoration of the Throne Hall, and by the reconstitution of the ceremony held there, which indicates that all the monuments in question formed, as it were, the links of a chain.

The northern part of the terrace consisted of two independent units. The first, comprising the Throne Hall and two monumental gate-houses (that of Xerxes and the 'unfinished' gate), converges on the throne, hub of the empire, where all the subject nations met. The second, limited to the Apadana, which had a 'life' of its own, was the place where the king and his Persian and Median grandees conferred.

This explains why no such throne hall existed at Susa, where the ceremonies enacted at Persepolis did not take place.

257-258 - PERSEPOLIS.   UNIDENTIFIED RUINS.   STAIRWAY RELIEFS: SERVANTS (MID-4th CENTURY B.C.)

259 - PERSEPOLIS.   UNIDENTIFIED RUINS: TRIBUTE BEARERS (4th CENTURY B.C.)

260 - PERSEPOLIS. UNIDENTIFIED RUINS: LION ATTACKING A BULL (PERIOD OF ARTAXERXES III? - 4th CENTURY B.C.)

262 - PERSEPOLIS. NORTH COLUMN OF THE GATE-HOUSE OF XERXES I (5th CENTURY B.C.)

The column (the most original element of Achaemenian architecture), by the very nature of its animal-headed capitals, tended to emphasize the interdependence of the various sectors of the Persepolis terrace. Its elevation is identical with that of the Susa columns: square or bell-shaped base, fluted shaft, composite capital. The capital reflects, in its every part, an aspiration towards structural clarity and symmetrical precision. While its lower part, inspired by Egypt, imitates the cluster of leaves crowning the stem of the palm-tree, the cruciform upper part is devised to make a smooth transition from the circular to the rectangular plan; it consists of four double volutes, placed back to back on each side of the central rectangle and deriving perhaps from an architectural element already present in Median art. At the top of the column is an impost block composed of the foreparts of two animals, facing in opposite directions, between which was placed the master beam. This structural device was probably taken over from a northern timber building, in which the rafters were supported by a forked tree-trunk. Columns with the complete capital were reserved for the interior of buildings; columns with protomes resting directly on the shaft are found in the porticoes.

It is assumed that, once the work at Susa was completed, the artists employed there were transferred to Persepolis to help build the new capital. We know from Darius's 'Foundation Charter' that the columns were carved by Greeks and Lydians. Yet the Persian column as we know it is not Greek. Its bell-shaped base is foreign to Hellenic art, just as the verticality of its decoration contrasts with the horizontality of its Greek counterpart. No Greek column rises to the height of the Achaemenian column, nor is it ever crowned with a composite capital as ponderous and complex as the Persian impost block, which in fact is unique in ancient architecture. One can only conclude that if Greek artists took part in the building of Susa and Persepolis they did no more than execute work already planned out in detail by the Persians themselves.

The royal architects designed four different types of capitals at Persepolis. This variety, unexampled at Susa, may have been intended to act as a reminder

263 - PERSEPOLIS. COLUMNS (6th-5th CENTURIES B.C.)

of the interrelationship of the various buildings. The bulls guarding the entrance to the gate-house of Xerxes, which confronted the visitor as he reached the terrace, reappeared on the capitals supporting the roofs of the gate-house, the Apadana and the Throne Hall. Similar bulls guard the portico of the Throne Hall and crown certain columns of the north and west porticoes of the Apadana. The human-headed bulls of the gate-house of Xerxes looked towards the Throne Hall. Their presence on the columns in the portico of this room and on the columns of the Tripylon cannot have been due to chance. Since the Throne Hall was the meeting-point, the king who came from the Tripylon and the delegations coming from the gate-house advanced towards it. Capitals adorned with horned lions have been found both on the small columns of the south court of the Tripylon and on the tallest columns (62 feet high) of the portico of the Apadana. It was this latter portico through which the King of Kings entered and left the Apadana, while it was through the south court of the Tripylon that he entered and left his palace. Finally, beyond the north enclosure wall of the Apadana, two unfinished capitals composed of griffin protomes have just been discovered. (Protomes of lions and griffins were nothing new; they had figured, in gold, on a vessel of Urartian origin deposited in the Scythian tomb of Ziwiyeh.)

264-265 - PERSEPOLIS. BULL AND LION CAPITALS (5th CENTURY B.C.) — IN SITU AND TEHERAN MUSEUM

268 - PERSEPOLIS. CAPITAL WITH LION PROTOMES, DETAIL (5th CENTURY B.C.)

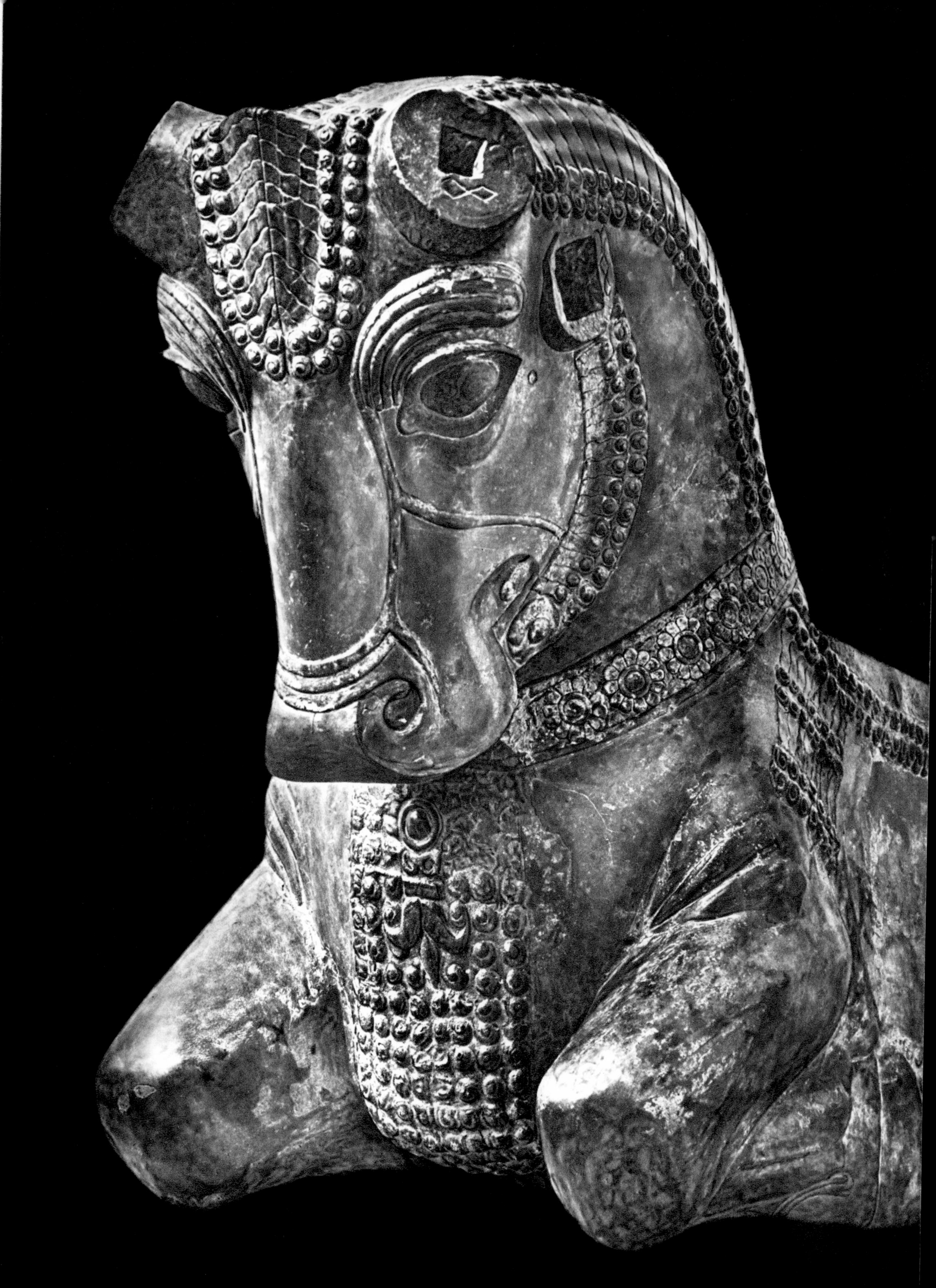

(5TH CENTURY B.C.) — NELSON GALLERY, KANSAS CITY

The extent of the borrowings by Persia from the old civilizations of the Ancient East must not be underrated. The Persians did not wait for their art to reach maturity by way of a slow internal evolution, but hastened to take over whatever served their turn from the Egyptians, Elamites, Babylonians, Hittites, Urartians and Assyrians.

The Iranian terrace derives from Urartu rather than from Mesopotamia. The plan of the Persepolitan palaces also seems to be of Urartian origin—unless we prefer to regard it as a further development of a type of house peculiar to northern Iran. Characterized by a porch supported by tree trunks, this type of dwelling may have inspired the Median architects, to judge by the rock tombs. Only the palace of Susa, necessarily adapted to the sultry climate of the plain, was built on the Elamite plan, with its various units disposed round an inner courtyard. The antecedents of Achaemenian architecture are to be found in Median art and in that of Western Asia; to these sources it owes much, though by no means all. For the assimilation of these elements never resulted in mere imitation but stimulated the growth of an architecture whose originality is unquestionable.

In dealing at length with the decorative sculpture of the palaces of Persepolis, our aim has been to challenge the commonly held view that it lacks the qualities of narrative art and has little or no intrinsic value. Indeed all Achaemenian art posterior to that of Persepolis has been regarded as a lifeless repetition of earlier work, incapable of breaking away from the conventions of the past.

But it must not be forgotten that the architectural lay-out of the Persepolis terrace was planned in detail by Darius and its execution took nearly a century (from about 520-518 B.C. in the time of Darius up to the reign of Artaxerxes I, who died in 424 B.C.). The fact that the original programme was strictly adhered to over so long a period does not necessarily mean that Achaemenian art was in any sense stereotyped and retrogressive.

True, the technique of Achaemenian monumental sculpture changed little, if at all. Leaving the possibilities of plastic expression unexplored and ignoring the third dimension, it neither freed itself from the shackling 'law' of isocephaly, nor represented figures otherwise than in profile. For

271 - PERSEPOLIS. ACHAEMENIAN
DRAPERY (6th-5th C. B.C.)

imparting a rhythm to figure groups represented in procession, it relied entirely on the intervals of empty space between them. Yet, for all its limitations, Persian art harmonizes admirably with the imposing aspect of the buildings it adorns. Calm and lofty, it reflects the national temperament, essentially dignified and pacific. We look in vain in its repertory for any of those scenes of battle and carnage that glorified the exploits of the Assyrian monarchs—as also for those intimate pictures of family life so often represented on the orthostats of the petty Aramaean kings of Northern Syria. The prime consideration here was the function of the several buildings; each served a specific purpose and was decorated accordingly.

In their palace art, as we see it everywhere prevailing on the terrace at Persepolis, the Achaemenians would seem indeed to have made a point of keeping to that archaism and 'frozen' severity of expression which they evidently regarded as the noblest heritage of an age-old tradition. Nevertheless, under Artaxerxes I, there was a discreet attempt both at Persepolis and at Susa to refine and vivify that tradition,

272 - PERSEPOLIS. STATUE OF PENELOPE (2nd HALF, 5th CENTURY B.C.)

for the Persian kings who built the palaces of Persepolis were not ignorant of the innovations of Greek art. That they appreciated both Greek statuary and ceramics is evidenced by the statue of Penelope, dating from the second half of the fifth century B.C., found in the Treasury of Persepolis, which must have been acquired by one of Xerxes' successors; and also by the Greek pottery of the second half of the fifth century found at Susa. But the fact remains that, as we have already pointed out, the Greek artists in the Persian service played only a very minor part in the creations of the Achaemenid kings employing them. This of course does not hold good for the westernmost territories of the Persian Empire; there, as we shall see in Part Two, Achaemenian art came into close contact with Ionian art and was subjected to its influence.

The Achaemenid kings were not content with a single residence. Before building Pasargadae, Cyrus had chosen Susa as his capital, then Ecbatana and Babylon. Darius, after a brief sojourn at Babylon, divided his time between Susa and Persepolis.

Besides a network of broad highways connecting the different centres of the empire and its capitals, a system of secondary roads was built to facilitate the royal journeys of a court continually on the move.

Among these narrower roads was the one connecting Susa with Persepolis. On this road, at Jin Jin, near Fahlian, are the remains of a royal pavilion with bell-shaped column-bases like those at Susa and Persepolis. It was here, no doubt, in the Zagros foothills, that the king and his court stopped for rest and refreshment. Situated near a broad river, in wooded country, the site was an ideal halting place to break a journey of several days, before beginning the long ascent by way of the 'Persian Gates' leading up to the Plateau, opposite Persepolis.

Another road, through Luristan, linked Susa with Ecbatana, where the court spent the summer months. All that now remains of this summer capital is a column-base in dark limestone composed of a double plinth surmounted by a torus. It bears an inscription in the name of Artaxerxes II.

The occupation of Babylon by the Iranians was not unattended with violence. Taken intact by Cyrus in 539 B.C. and respected by Darius, despite a revolt, the city was destroyed under Xerxes. But it must have been rebuilt almost at once, for it became once more the fourth capital of the empire under Artaxerxes I.

 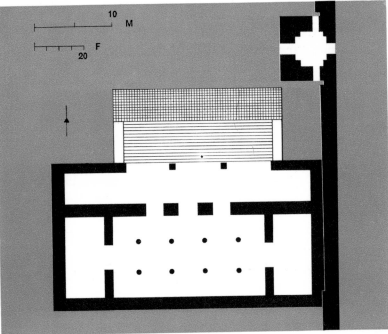

273 - JIN JIN. COLUMN-BASE   274 - BABYLON. PLAN OF AN ACHAEMENIAN BUILDING (5th-4th CENT. B.C.)

224

276 - NAQSH-I-RUSTAM. FIRE ALTARS (3rd-6th CENTURIES A.D.)

The temple of Naqsh-i-Rustam, in the form of a square tower, today called Ka'ba-i-Zardusht ('Ka'ba of Zoroaster'), stands in front of the tomb of Darius hewn in the rock. The Naqsh-i-Rustam tower (36 feet high and 23 feet wide), which exactly resembles the ruined tower at Pasargadae, is built of blocks of light-hued sandstone, carefully dressed and fitted, and decorated on the outer side with a rectangular honeycomb pattern. The roof, edged with a denticulated frieze, imitates the four sloping sides of a tent. Three rows of blind windows in black stone, on three sides of the tower, articulate the walls and give the tower the appearance of a three-storey building. On the fourth side is the entrance, led up to by a stone stairway. Inside is a single room (17 ft 5 in. by 12 ft 3 in.), its floor level with the blind windows of the first storey; it was closed by a double door whose hinge-sockets can still be seen.

primitive ceremonies presided over by the Magi. These ceremonies had their origin in the remote past of the Indo-European peoples.

To the Magi, a priestly caste of Median origin, were assigned important functions in the society of ancient Persia. They followed the armies so as to officiate at sacrifices; they interpreted dreams and were entrusted with the preparation of the *haoma*, an intoxicating beverage made from plants and drunk in the course of ritual observances; they were guardians of the royal tombs and tended the 'sacred fire' in the temples. Religious services were performed out of doors, beside the fire altars, which were generally grouped in pairs.

Monuments and texts throw light upon each other. The religious centre of Naqsh-i-Rustam, not far from Persepolis, was situated in a majestic, awesomely impressive landscape. The ancients, as is well known, did not readily abandon holy places consecrated by time and use. The famous sanctuary of the Hittites, for example, at Yazilikaya, near Boghazköy, occupied the site of a 'natural sanctuary' dating back to a very early age. At Naqsh-i-Rustam remains of Elamite bas-reliefs, carved in the rock-face, show that the Mazdaean Persians did no more than take over a holy place revered by the previous inhabitants of the region.

277 - NAQSH-I-RUSTAM.   FIRE TEMPLE (6th-5th CENTURIES B.C.)

As at Pasargadae, two altars were provided for religious services held out of doors; hewn in the rock, they were erected near the temple.   Their architecture, however, differs from that of the Achaemenian period, a fact that led Kurt Erdmann to assign them first to an earlier, then on second thoughts to a later age.   Actually they imitate the *chahar-tagh*, a pavilion open on all four sides, its four pillars supporting four arches crowned by a cupola.   It was

275 - NAQSH-I-RUSTAM. ROYAL ACHAEMENIAN TOMBS (6th-5th CENT. B.C.) AND SASSANIAN BAS-RELIEFS (3rd-4th CENT. A.D.)

This king, who had Babylonian concubines, seems to have resided in the city off and on. His successor, Darius II (Artaxerxes' son by one of his concubines), was satrap of Babylonia before mounting the throne.

We may safely presume that these kings and satraps built residences to their own taste. Only one such building, however, has so far been identified at Babylon: the so-called Apadana, which stood between the palace and the old enclosure wall, upon which it was built. A broad stairway led up to a vestibule whose roof was supported by two columns. In the room were two rows of four wooden columns each, with bell-shaped bases similar to those at Susa and Persepolis. The façade was decorated with glazed bricks representing men, women and horses; but the surviving fragments are so badly shattered that it has proved impossible to reassemble them.

Modern archaeology has shown Herodotus to be mistaken in supposing that the Persians had no temples, altars or images of their gods. Though in no way comparable to the religious edifices adjoining Assyrian palaces, the Mazdaean temples that have been brought to light give a reasonably clear idea of the religion and forms of worship of the Achaemenians. The Persians propitiated their gods with blood sacrifices which were enacted in the course of highly

225

around such pavilions as this that the
Sassanians held their religious ceremonies in the open.

The Persians made images of their
gods, pride of place being given to
Ahuramazda, shown in half-length
issuing from a winged disk. This,
reproduced an age-old motif of Egyptian iconography, used in figurations of
the sky-god Horus. Ahuramazda was
not the only god of the Persians, though
he often appears with Darius; represented above the king at Bisutun and
Persepolis, he gave an added lustre
to Darius's great achievements, which
the king acknowledged to be due to
divine grace and guidance. But from
the time of Artaxerxes II, the official
pantheon increased in number and
new names appear in the texts, notably
Mithras and Anahita. The former,
sun-god and god of contracts and
redemption, was a very old Iranian
deity; the latter, goddess of waters,
fecundity and procreation, may have
now reappeared under the influence
of non-Iranian cults.

Wikander believes the Naqsh-i-
Rustam tower to have been a temple
of Anahita containing a statue of the

278 - BISUTUN. BAS-RELIEF OF DARIUS: AHURAMAZDA (6th CENT. B.C.)

goddess whose cult served to unite all the peoples of the empire in the worship of a common deity. According to Berossus, images of the goddess were
adored at Sardis, Babylon, Damascus, Susa, Ecbatana, Persepolis and Bactra.
The Anahita of Bactra figures on the reverse of a coin of the Greco-Bactrian
king Demetrius (early second century B.C.). The triad Ahuramazda-Mithras-
Anahita was worshipped not only in Achaemenian Persia but also in Armenia,
where ancient historians report the existence of holy places with three altars
dedicated to these three gods. It is not unreasonable to assume that the two
Achaemenian altars at Pasargadae and Naqsh-i-Rustam, together with a third in
the near-by temple-tower, were dedicated to the same triad. This may have
marked a return to the triad Ahuramazda-Sraosha-Ashi (or perhaps Ahuramazda-
Mithras-Anahita), which figured on the Median tomb of Kizkapan.

Although we ourselves are convinced that the Naqsh-i-Rustam tower was one of those temples where the 'eternal fire' was guarded day and night, it is only fair to say that the exact purpose of the building is by no means clear and has given rise to different hypotheses. Some regard it as a tomb. As suggested above, it may well have been a temple of Anahita. Henning, basing his interpretation on the inscription engraved on the temple wall by Kartir, founder of the Sassanian national Church, sees in the tower a building erected for the purpose of housing the archives of that Church and, 'it may be conjectured, the master copy of the Avesta.'

It was in the Achaemenian period that the Mazdaean religion as reformed by Zoroaster began to spread throughout the empire. It found its most influential supporters among the aristocracy, who denounced the cruel practices and bloody rites of the old Aryan religions. Henceforth the dead could no longer be buried, burnt or immersed, lest the three sacred elements, earth, fire and water, should thereby be contaminated. Corpses were to be exposed on mountain-tops or on towers specially built for this purpose; after being picked clean by birds of prey, the bones were placed in ossuaries deposited in tombs either dug in the earth or situated in the open.

The Achaemenids were not Zoroastrians, for the monarchs were buried, from the time of Darius, in the cliffs of Naqsh-i-Rustam (tombs of Darius, Xerxes, Artaxerxes I and Darius II) and in the mountain-side behind the terrace of Persepolis (tombs of Artaxerxes II and III and Darius III).

The rock tomb of Da-u-Dukhtar ('The Nurse and the Princess') on the road from Pasargadae to Masjid-i-Sulaiman must have been that of an ancestor of Cyrus the Great. It maintained the traditions of the Median princes and was presumably the prototype of the rock tombs of the Achaemenid kings. Why Cyrus the Great departed from tradition we do not know. If, as suggested above, the steps of his tomb were intended to symbolize a mountain, the worship of the stars might explain its architectural design, which in that case would derive from that of the ziggurat.

Of the tomb of Cambyses II nothing remains but the ruins of a platform, Takht-i-Rustam, near Persepolis. Our knowledge of Achaemenian funerary architecture is based for the most part on the royal tombs in the cemetery of Naqsh-i-Rustam. The lay-out of this architecture was established at its inception by the tomb of Darius, and it was imitated by all subsequent kings. The tomb chamber comprises three rows of niches hewn in the rock; the ceiling, given the form of a gabled roof, recalls the roof of the tomb of Cyrus and that of the tombs in the cemetery of Sialk. The façade, nearly 73 feet high, has the form of a Greek cross. Divided into three zones, it contrasts the notion of a smooth wall acting as a structural element (lower part) with the notion of the wall as a formal element contributing to the general effect by its architectonic lay-out (central part) and decorative reliefs (upper part). It is precisely this latter

279 - NAQSH-I-RUSTAM. TOMB OF DARIUS
THE GREAT (6th-5th CENTURIES B.C.) →

230

280 - PERSEPOLIS. TOMB OF ARTAXERXES II OR III (4th CENTURY B.C.)

233

conception of a wall that we noted in the architecture of the Median rock tombs. What we have in both cases is an obvious imitation of the entrance of a palace, the wall surface being articulated by means of columns and figurations set in frames. In both cases we see a desire to associate Ahuramazda, god of gods, master of heaven and earth, with the king of kings, master and administrator of all the peoples of the earth.

Once again this religious and historical theme has been treated in a relief, fortunately supplemented by two long explanatory inscriptions. One, engraved on the upper part of the façade, enumerates the twenty-eight nations upholding the throne of the Great King. The other, engraved between the columns in the middle zone, reads like a 'profession of faith' on the part of the king—a fitting commentary on the reliefs glorifying his person and rule. Armed with a bow,

281 - PERSEPOLIS. VIEW OF THE PLAIN FROM WITHIN THE TOMB OF ARTAXERXES

Darius stands facing a fire altar, invoking Ahuramazda. The god floats in mid-air, followed by one of the familiar 'celestial abstractions,' represented here by a crescent within a disk—perhaps a symbol of the god Mithras. On either side of the scene stand members of the king's retinue; recognizable among them are Gobryas, bearer of his spear, and Aspachina, bearer of his battle-axe.

Everything here is static, hieratic. The sculptor responsible for this work made no innovations, but conformed to a tradition well established before his time. The bas-relief on the Bisutun rock, which represents Darius putting the upstart kings in irons, invokes the supreme god Ahuramazda and, while celebrating the triumph of the Great King of Kings, fixes once for all the principles of the decorative carvings henceforth to figure on royal tombs. The trilingual text running round the monument makes plain its lofty message.

The symbolism of this iconography, deriving from Assyria, was transmitted to the Persians by the Medes. The image of the god Assur inspired that of Ahuramazda, but the national sentiment of the Persian people imbued it with a more human ideology. The same idea had already found expression in the portrayal of the Median prince of Kizkapan, who had himself represented as an instrument of the divine will, armed with bow and arrow. Darius, a century later, claimed to be no more and no less.

Nothing is known of any other Achaemenian necropolis, apart from the

283 - BISUTUN.   ROCK RELIEF GLORIFYING
DARIUS THE GREAT (6th CENT. B.C.) →

284 - BISUTUN. ROCK RELIEF, DETAIL: DARIUS THE GREAT (6th CENTURY B.C.)

tombs, very poorly furnished, which have been found in the neighbourhood of
the terrace of Persepolis. The methods of burial recall those of the late Elamite
or Neo-Assyrian period, the dead being placed in terracotta sarcophagi consisting of two separate parts. A royal (?) tomb discovered at Susa by the Délégation
Archéologique Française had been dug into the Elamite stratum, where a
a hypogeum in unbaked brick seems originally to have stood. A bronze sarcophagus, shaped like a bath-tub with flared edges, contained a man's body accompanied by rich grave furniture.

What little we know of the architecture in the lower-class districts of Achaemenian towns derives not so much from vestiges of the houses themselves as from
business documents and artefacts found on the site of an ancient village about half
a mile from the Elamite acropolis of Susa. From them we gather that this was
a Persian community which in its early days (late eighth - early seventh century
B.C.) maintained for a while the tradition of the Sialk potters in a centre where

painted pottery had not been made for several centuries. The point is worth noting, for it shows that the Persian tribes from the Iranian Plateau were able to preserve their native traditions despite inevitable changes due to the growth and expansion of the Achaemenian Empire.

All the monuments we have studied come under the heading of 'palace art.' While by general consent this was of a hitherto unparalleled splendour, it has often been decried as being a rootless, composite art. This is a misconception, and our present-day knowledge of the history of Iranian art goes far to rehabilitate it. There is no denying that, like the arts of other countries, Achaemenian art made certain borrowings; it took over the Mediterranean column, the hypostyle hall of Egyptian inspiration, the Urartian façade, the lay-out and ornamentation of the Babylonian palace. But this is not the whole story, and to redress the balance we need to take a wider view of the art of the vast Persian Empire, as against the earlier approach, which made the study of Iranian art begin only with the Achaemenians.

The chronology of certain periods of Iranian art has always been a problem and it is no easy matter to form a connected idea of events. Moreover, one of its important factors, Median art, still remains almost an unknown quantity; we can only guess at its nature. Yet, though it cannot have lasted long, it was undoubtedly a formative element of Achaemenian art. The palaces of Cyrus did not spring out of nothing and the rock tombs of the Median princes, with their columns, capitals and reliefs, point us back to the palaces of Ecbatana, which have still to be excavated. Achaemenian cuneiform writing existed before Cyrus. The bas-reliefs of Pasargadae and their plastic renderings of bodies have more in common with those of the Kizkapan tomb than with Assyrian reliefs. All this adds up to a body of evidence quite adequate to prove that Achaemenian art was by no means exclusively shaped by foreign sources of influence. On the contrary, it was the outcome of a slow and steady development of Iranian art, taking the latter term in its widest possible acceptation. For to the Medes and Persians must be added the Cimmerians and Scythians, each of whom contributed appreciably to its evolution—and to its stabilization. It is not surprising then to find Achaemenian art so persistently addicted to specific ornamental and decorative formulas. Hence the repetition of themes on Achaemenian bas-reliefs, regardless of its monotonous effect. Hence, too, the Achaemenians' constant recourse to this same decorative repertory in the applied arts, which their predecessors of Sialk, Luristan and Ziwiyeh had practised before them.

286 - PERSEPOLIS. HALL OF A HUNDRED COLUMNS: DETAIL OF THE 'BALDACHIN'

285 - PERSEPOLIS. HALL OF A HUNDRED COLUMNS:
SCORPION MONSTER, DETAIL (5th CENT. B.C.)

287-288 - PERSEPOLIS. DETAILS OF THE TRIPYLON RELIEFS: TIPS OF SCABBARDS (5th CENTURY B.C.)

289 - PERSEPOLIS. TREASURY RELIEF: A DIGNITARY'S DAGGER, DETAIL (5th CENTURY B.C.)

291 - PERSEPOLIS. BRONZE SUPPORT: THREE LIONS (6th-5th CENTURIES B.C.) — TEHERAN MUSEUM

V

ACHAEMENIAN PERSIA
SUMPTUARY AND INDUSTRIAL ARTS

THE sumptuary and industrial arts were widely cultivated in Achaemenian Persia, and their development was influenced by contacts with crafts-men of many lands. Thanks to the introduction 'of coinage, trade was already flourishing on an international scale over a vast area, both by land and by sea. The Persepolis tablets, supplementing the information contained in the 'Foundation Charter' of Susa, make it plain that the arts were controlled by an imperial organization which had ramifications in all the countries of the Persian empire.

We have documentary evidence of this in a letter written from Susa, towards the end of the fifth century B.C., by Prince Arsames, satrap of Egypt, to Nehthor, steward of his Egyptian estates. The relevant passage reads as follows: 'Concerning the sculptor named Hanzani whom my servant Bagasaru has brought to Susa, give him and the women of his house the same supplies as were provided for the other assistants in order that he may make the statue of a rider...and let him carve a statue of the horse and rider corresponding to the one which he has already made for me, and other sculptures too. And urge the man to bring it to me promptly.' Thus not only were Egyptian sculptors brought to Persia, but Persian noblemen residing in Egypt employed them to embellish their homes.

The Persians' predilection for architectural revetment favoured the produc-tion of relief work at the expense of sculpture in the round. The latter seems to have been confined to small objects: heads and statuettes, for the most part mere votive offerings deposited in temples. According to the social standing of the subject, these statuettes were either likenesses or stock figures.

290 - HAMADAN (?). GOLD RHYTON: WINGED LION
  (5th CENTURY B.C.) — TEHERAN MUSEUM

The limestone head from Memphis, now in the Louvre, seems to belong to the same tradition. The head is of the same ethnic type as the one in the Stoclet Collection. But the execution of the Louvre head is bolder, volumes are more broadly rendered and it is clear that the sculptor's chief concern was to bring out his model's personality as an individual. The other head abides by the conventions of official art, details of hair and beard being carefully rendered, while stress is laid on the marks of hierarchical distinction (the taller cylindrical headdress). This is probably the portrait of a prince or a high dignitary of the royal palace, perhaps Arsames, presumed grandson of Darius the Great and author of the letter quoted above.

In much the same vein of inspiration is the face of a young man wearing a crown, in lapis lazuli paste, found at Persepolis and perhaps executed there. It embodies an ideal of nobility and physical beauty befitting a royal prince. And the eyes, originally inlaid with enamel, must have added overtones of vivaci y and vigilance to this pensive, strangely compelling face.

The only statuette in the round so far discovered is the bust of a Median (?) carrying a lion cub, executed in lapis lazuli. Here, as elsewhere in Achaemenian sculpture, hair and beard are indicated by parallel rows of small curls, while the moustache, twisted at each end, is striated. The aquiline nose and almond-shaped eyes suggest that this man was a Median of the

292 - HEAD OF AN ACHAEMENIAN PRINCE
293 - MEMPHIS. MAN'S HEAD (5th-4th C. B.C.) — PRIVATE COLL., LOUVRE

2

294 - PERSEPOLIS.   HEAD OF A PRINCE   295 - BUST OF A MEDIAN (5th-4th CENT. B.C.) — TEHERAN AND CLEVELAND MUSEUMS

traditional ethnic type—an identification borne out by the round 'pudding-basin' hat. The young lion in his arms, which he clasps with both hands to his breast, is roaring, its jaws agape and its paws, one of them standing out in high relief on the man's shoulder, disproportionately large (here we have a reminiscence of an earlier phase of Iranian art).

If this small bust really comes from Persepolis, its maker drew inspiration from the same theme as that of the figures lining the two stairways of the Apadana: offerings being brought by the peoples of the empire and laid at the foot of the throne. Full-grown animals that were offered were naturally confined in the royal parks, but a lion cub might well have been allowed into the palace as a pet for the young princes.

The 'votive portraits' dedicated to Egyptian gods by Achaemenian princes and nobles, always tolerant and broad-minded in their religious views, are outnumbered by the statuettes from the Oxus Treasure. We have already spoken of a certain number of objects which had been deposited in this hoard as early as the Median period. Under the Achaemenians, many offerings in precious metals were added to it.

296 - OXUS TREASURE. DONOR   297 - LURISTAN. WOMAN   298-299 - OXUS TREASURE. FIGURES — TEHERAN AND BRITISH MUSEUM

The 'canon' of palace art then in force throughout the empire finds expression in the silver statuette of an unidentifiable donor. Familiar elements reappear: the high cylindrical headdress held in place by a bandeau; the hair bunched up over the ears; a drooping moustache above a square-cut beard. Ethnic characteristics are well rendered: low forehead, arched eyebrows with no break in the middle, large almond-shaped eyes, long straight nose. Contrasting with the realism of the face, the body is treated along conventional lines in strict accordance with the law of frontality, and contains reminiscences of the art of Luristan. In the bronze statuette of an Iranian woman the figure has undergone a decorative stylization. Folds forming segments of a circle and placed one above the other cover the metal surface and create an optical illusion. These ripples (of which we saw a foretaste on the back of the Luristan figurine) extend over the entire length of the Oxus gold statuette, the engraver's skill thus compensating for the narrowness of the body. The broadly stated gesture, beginning at the shoulder and elbow of the man (he is holding a flower), overrides the limits of the geometric pattern imposed on the figure.

These well-defined and rigidly enforced plastic conventions made it impossible to give a full, convincing picture of man as he was in the setting and society of the Ancient East. What are we to make of this personage, carved in solid gold, wearing the short tunic of a horseman, over which he has

300 - OXUS TREASURE. MAN'S HEAD (6th-4th CENTURIES B.C.) — BRITISH MUSEUM

thrown a long mantle with richly patterned edges? Dalton thinks it to be a magus holding a *barsom;* and the artist has indeed invested the little figure with an air of rapt, otherworldly meditation. But the attribute, which might help to explain what manner of man this was, is not a *barsom* but a flower like the one held up in the same way by the Persian 'donor' described above. For our part we prefer to identify the figure as a high-ranking Bactrian dignitary. The goldsmiths responsible for some of these works were obviously attempting to render fully plastic volumes in three-dimensional space. All the same the technique of the bas-relief still held its ground. In striking contrast with these figurines is the portrait of a royal prince cut out in a plaque of gold. This art of flat surfaces, with hardly a hint of the third dimension, may have derived from the practice of overlaying one material with another, a legacy of an earlier tradition. It recalls the statue of Argistis I, king of Urartu, 'wearing the star-spangled tiara of the gods,' his hand making the gesture of benediction, which Sargon II found in the temple of the god Haldis at Musasir.

Next we have a 'portrait,' in gold repoussé work, the head of a beardless man, rendered with a somewhat naive forcefulness. In its original state, enriched with ear-rings, it must have conveyed a vivid impression of the culture from which it sprang. Even without these adornments, it clearly answers to the artistic norms of a semi-barbarian society.

247

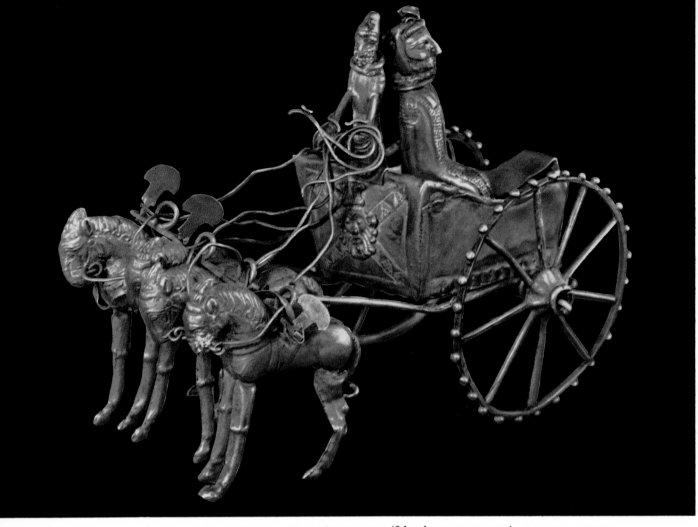

301 - OXUS TREASURE. FOUR-HORSE CHARIOT (6th-4th CENTURIES B.C.) — BRITISH MUSEUM

One of the most intriguing pieces in the Oxus Treasure is a gold chariot drawn by four horses. Beside the driver stands another figure; their costumes and personal adornments show them both to be Iranians. The team is similar to the one found in Barrow 5 at Pazyryk—a type quite different from any other so far discovered on this site. It is quite possible that Bactria (where the Oxus Treasure was found) was then already turning for inspiration to the vast open spaces of the Eurasian steppes. There can be no question of the votive character of the Oxus chariot—which suggests that the hoard as a whole was originally a temple treasure. The historical evidence, moreover, supports this hypothesis and brings us back to the kingdom of Urartu, whose civilization contributed so much to Iranian art.

The annals of Sargon II, to which we have already referred, tell us that, in addition to thirty-three silver chariots, the Assyrian king found in the temple of Musasir a 'statue of Ursa (Rusas I) with his two chargers and his driver, and their seat; all of this was in cast bronze, and (on the statue) his pride was expressed thus: With my two horses and my driver, my hands have conquered the kingdom of Urartu.' May not the Bactrian noble who had himself represented in the guise of a king of Urartu, have likewise dedicated his team of gold horses to his divine patron as a thanksgiving for some successful feat of arms? As a matter of fact, this chariot is not unique; there is another in the collection of the Earl of Lytton which may have the same origin.

The precious objects in the Oxus Treasure represent on the whole a composite art, sometimes marked by Urartian influence (lions rearing up on their hind feet), sometimes by Iranian traditions stemming from Sialk (eagles with pincer-shaped talons[543]) or from Luristan (sphinxes' wings ending in a bird's head[541]). A fine hunting scene on a silver-gilt *umbo*[542] repeats the lay-out of a similar scene on the bronze shield from Luristan in the Louvre. But the costumes, weapons, and trappings of the Oxus horsemen derive from those of classical Achaemenian art—as do the animals. The indication of muscles by dot-and-comma markings, for example, imitates the technique employed in the glazed brick animals at Susa. In sculpture in the round this technique sometimes achieves a mature style handled with remarkable proficiency.

The abundance of jewellery (bracelets and torques) makes it clear that these objects were mass-produced. However, in the finest of them we cannot but be struck by the vigour of the technique and the beauty of the materials employed, their splendour and radiance appealing equally to the sense of touch and to the eye.

Votive offerings also included seals, and here too the Persians maintained the age-old traditions of Oriental art. The themes—scenes of combat and divine apparitions—are the same as those of which so many examples have been found in Achaemenian palaces.

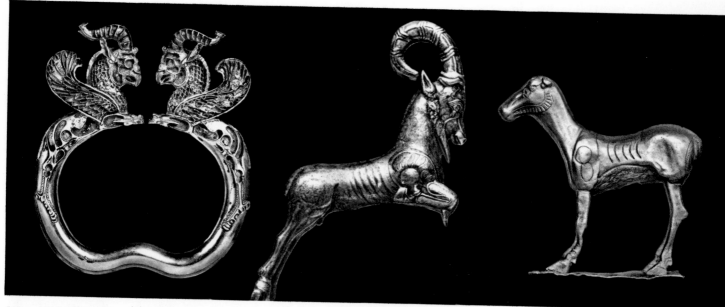

302 - OXUS TREASURE. (A) BRACELET (B) VASE HANDLE (C) DEER (6th-5th CENTURIES B.C.) — BRITISH MUSEUM

The quantity of precious objects in this hoard raises problems as to the location of the temple to which it must have belonged. It was said to have been found on the hill of Takht-i-Kobad. But we know that the largest sanctuary of the region, dedicated to the goddess Anahita, 'the Bactrian,' was the temple of Bactra, a town which lay across the river, a short distance from the left bank of the Oxus. Surely it is more plausible to assume that the treasure came from this temple, and that under the threat of invasion from the west, the priests hid it in a cache on the far side of the river. If the date of the objects composing the treasure could be shown to be no later than the fourth century B.C., the invader in question might well have been Alexander the Great. In any case, the fact remains that these offerings, made by women, shepherds, and warriors, answer to the characteristics of Anahita who, like the Babylonian Ishtar, was the tutelary goddess of all that ensured the continuity of life and, like Ishtar again, was at the same time a goddess of war.

The archives of the Achaemenian Empire were preserved at Ecbatana (present-day Hamadan). The Bible suggests as much (Ezra vi. 1 ff.) and the excavations of Susa and Persepolis have confirmed it. All the treasure seized by Alexander in the Persian capitals was deposited at Ecbatana under the guard of Parmenion.

The Hamadan Treasure, then, presumably included the precious objects which the Greek conqueror brought together in that capital. Some thirty years ago a sudden flood is said to have washed away a considerable part of the hoard and thrown it upon high ground. Several gold ingots, each bearing an inscription, are believed to have been melted down by the peasants who found them, together with a number of vases and some jewellery. All that has so far been recovered appears, as in the case of the Ziwiyeh Treasure, to be but a small fraction of what the peasants actually found.

In comparing the precious objects of the Hamadan Treasure with those discovered elsewhere, whether within the limits of the empire or beyond them, we find they are all very much alike. This uniformity was the result of Persian colonization, which gave currency to the procedures of imperial art over a wide area. It was also due to an inherited blend of older traditions, built up and transmitted by the North Iranians, Medes, Cimmerians and

303 - BASIN SUPPORTED BY EIGHT LION PROTOMES (6th-5th CENTURIES B.C.) — PRIVATE COLLECTION, NEW YORK

Scythians. All the same, the sumptuary arts of Achaemenian Persia were never paralysed by a slavish respect for the past. For, as we shall see, the evolution of all their art forms has a far more distinctive character than was long supposed. But if this vast production is to be fairly judged in its entirety, there is no dissociating the group of objects in the Hamadan Treasure from those which escaped the depredations of Alexander; all are products of the same creative inspiration.

Achaemenian realism excels in animal art. We have already drawn attention to this high proficiency in the monumental reliefs, in which the decorative motifs of the *objets d'art* attain their full development.

The stone ibex from Persepolis is one of the masterpieces of this art. Its sleek coat is rendered with a fine simplicity that brings out the beautiful play of surfaces around the neck and the base of the horns. The latter, forming one with the pointed, quivering ears, are swept back in a broad curve and join the body at the nape of the neck. The large hollow in the animal's back suggests that it had the same function as the three saiga ibexes which served as supports for a stone vase, in which the sculptor again came to grips with the problems of sculpture in the round. The conception of this very fine stone vase is not unrelated to that of the rhytons of the Hamadan Treasure, which likewise have bases consisting of animal protomes. But this vase stands on a triple base, reviving the ancient traditions of Elamite and Urartian art.

304 - LARGE SCULPTURED VASE IN STONE
305 - STONE IBEX (5th-4th CENTURIES B.C.)
PRIVATE COLL., GENEVA & NEW YORK

The demand for these vases sculptured in precious metal led to a slackening in the production of painted pottery. The rhyton, in its three different but related forms, was already in vogue in the Medo-Scythian period. This family of vases, represented by both plain and polychrome ware, opened up a fresh field of activity to the animal carvers, who became increasingly inventive and prone to naturalism—a field which includes the Iranian works of art of the entire Achaemenian period, and which was to be taken over also both by the Parthians and the peoples of Outer Iran.

The finest piece is unquestionably the gold rhyton in the Teheran Museum (from Hamadan?). It is composed of two parts: the protome of a winged lion and the recipient itself, the bottom of which, cut at a slant, joins the animal's body. The body is treated on traditional lines: puckered chaps and nose, round ears beaded along the edges, ruff composed of small strips of metal, a mane of 'hooked' triangles reaching to the flanks, jaws agape, and shell-shaped wings with three rows of feathers. The vase, adorned with horizontal fluting, has a classical design around the lip.

The gold rhyton in the Metropolitan Museum (also from Hamadan?) illustrates the same idea, though the technique is different: here the vase fits into the animal's body, whose hindquarters form the base of the goblet. Skilfully executed as it is, the animal gives an impression of greater rigidity and is distorted by superimposed designs stylized to such a point that the animal forms originally suggesting them have lost their natural characteristics.

These two rhytons are undoubtedly the products of separate workshops, but, in spite of differences between them, they derive from a common source of inspiration.

In the bas-reliefs of tribute-bearers at Persepolis, we have also noted identical objects with slight differences of design depending on their country of origin. The basic affinities between these variants are plain to see in two other rhytons, one of them, horn-shaped, from the Seven Brothers Barrow in the Kuban (Northern Caucasus), the other from Erzincan in Armenia. Here again the shape of the rhytons, in which the animal's head is prolonged by a vertical recipient, brings out the underlying unity of all Achaemenian vases, deriving as they do from Medo-Scythian forms. Thus a bronze prototype of the Median period is imitated in a horse-head rhyton in electrum, found in Mazandaran. The animal's harness is typically Median: boar's tusks and a row of ducks inset on a silver band around the neck. From Siberia comes another rhyton of the same group, in silver gilt, similar to the Hamadan rhyton, though technically superior.

Many were the countries of the empire that contributed metal vases to the ceremonies at Persepolis. Carrying on an ancient Iranian tradition, the handles have the form of animals. The arrangement of the figures is also familiar: facing in opposite directions, in a threatening attitude, they keep guard over

306 - HAMADAN (?). GOLD RHYTON: WINGED LION (5th CENTURY B.C.) — METROPOLITAN MUSEUM, NEW YORK

the vessel and its contents. These animal themes recur over a wide area, and are treated in the style peculiar to each region. A silver handle in the form of a bull, of local workmanship, has been found in Mesopotamia. A handsome winged ibex, in silver gilt, may be assigned to a Greek workshop on the strength of the Silenus mask on which the animal's paws rest. A silver-gilt vase of this group, which has recently entered a private collection in Paris, is said to come from Asia Minor and may perhaps have been made for a Persian noble-man. Its round base is bedecked with a rosette, flanked by two spouts through which the liquid was poured out. To the elegantly fluted body of the vase, whose shoulder is adorned with lotus flowers and palmettes, and to its flaring lip, are soldered two ibexes, both remarkable for their forceful expression and the graceful poise of their heads. This family of vases (including the amphora

308 - IRAN. OVOID FLUTED VASE (6th-5th CENTURIES B.C.) — TEHERAN MUSEUM

and the rhyton) long remained in favour with Iranian artists; its standard
types continued to be made throughout both Parthian and Sassanian times and
are, moreover, to be found far beyond the geographical limits of Iran proper.

Another silver vase, similar in form and again with a fluted body, has two
horse-shaped handles and the animals' heads are topped with a 'knob,' like
that of the Ziwiyeh griffin. Here the liquid is poured out in a different manner:
one of the two animals is hollow and under the slewed-round head there is
a short spout. Two of the subject peoples represented on the stairway reliefs

307 - FLUTED AMPHORA-RHYTON (LATE 6th-4th
CENTURY B.C.) — PRIVATE COLL., PARIS

of the Apadana at Persepolis carry vessels of this type, which obviously derives from traditions going back to the period of Cemetery B at Sialk. There, too, the liquid was poured off through a beak-spout, a longer one admittedly, but above it, too, figured the protome of a horse.

While in these animal motifs volumes are fully indicated, plant forms are reduced by skilful stylization to geometric designs that are essentially ornamental. In the group of precious-metal bowls with an *omphalos*, the decorative principle basic to the entire composition is a primary element (rosette or palmette) of Assyrian inspiration. Connecting motifs taken directly from nature ('hazel-nuts' fringed with tiny wings, almond-shaped 'drops,' lotus flowers or petals) implement the movements of translation and rotation which determine the spatial rhythm. Alternating variations on a single geometric schema serve to interlock or to separate its component parts, ringing the changes on a specific linear pattern.

In the Hamadan Treasure are some particularly fine bowls engraved with the names of the Great Kings of Kings. On a gold dish unique of its kind, decorated in the centre with a flying eagle, we find evidence of an ethnic survival: in keeping with an old tradition going back to the Luristan bronzes, the head, body and feet of the bird are represented in side-view, while wings and tail are shown frontally.

309 - HAMADAN (?). GOLD BOWL INSCRIBED WITH XERXES' NAME (5th CENT. B.C.) — TEHERAN MUSEUM

2

310 - HAMADAN. BOWL INSCRIBED WITH DARIUS'S NAME (5th CENTURY B.C.) — PRIVATE COLLECTION, GENEVA

311 - DISH: WINGED BULL (5th-4th C. B.C.) — PRIVATE COLL., NEW YORK

A large silver dish, which recently entered the Foroughi Collection in Teheran, is adorned with the *symplegma* which we also find represented in the stairway reliefs of the Apadana at Persepolis. But the goldsmith has outdone the sculptor in conveying the clash and strain of contending forms. On a silver cup from the Kasbek Treasure, in the Caucasus, the initial design has been enriched with swans' heads and necks addorsed on either side of a palmette [544]. The very high quality of the workmanship makes this object an outstanding example of its style.

The dating of Achaemenian bowls remains a matter of conjecture. The only one dating to the final period of the empire is the bowl found in the royal tomb at Susa [545]. By now the *omphalos* has disappeared, replaced by a design of spear-shaped leaves; this design also figures on some silver cups of the same period from Persepolis. The interior design has affinities with that of a small silver cup, with a broad smooth rim, discovered near Ardebil, in Persian Azerbaijan; within a ring of 'hazel-nuts' originally inlaid with gold, it has a central motif composed of five lotus flowers in relief. The bottom of a bronze bowl recently acquired by the Louvre conforms to the same ornamental principle, but the ostrich hunt incised all around it heralds the more spirited style of later Iranian works.

Over six hundred stone vases have been found in the two rooms of the Treasury of Persepolis excavated by the Oriental Institute of Chicago.

312 - DISH: TWO IBEXES (5th CENT. B.C.)
— PRIVATE COLLECTION, GENEVA

313 - DISH: LION ATTACKING A BULL (5th-4th CENTURIES B.C.) — PRIVATE COLLECTION, TEHERAN

Though all are in a fragmentary state, they complement the information given by the gold and silver tableware. Except for a few pieces deriving from looted palaces, such as a granite bowl[546] adorned with gold and precious stones and inscribed with the name of King Assurbanipal, the most noteworthy objects came from the workshops of the Royal Palace.

314 - PERSEPOLIS.   STONE CUP INSCRIBED WITH XERXES' NAME (5th CENTURY B.C.) — TEHERAN MUSEUM

The rim of one of these, a granite cup bearing the name of Xerxes, is adorned with the heads of twelve swans gazing down into the interior of the recipient —obviously a reminiscence of the figurative motifs which had played so great a part in the religious rites of the protohistoric Iranians.   There were, however, cases in which the primitive symbolism of the Sialk 'bird-vase' was treated by the Achaemenians from a purely plastic angle, that is to say without regard to its original significance.   Some tripods with lions' feet may have had a ritual or cultic function; one of them, in openwork, and given the aspect of a table, derives from much the same conception as that of a bronze support formed by three lions, undoubtedly the work of an Ionian craftsman.

There were also many *alabastra*, all made in Egypt.   The ones found in Susa are dated and prove that annual consignments of these small perfume bottles were sent from Egypt to Persia in the reigns of Darius and Xerxes.

A passage in Aristophanes' *Acharnians* mentions that an Athenian embassy travelling in Asia Minor was hospitably received by the Persians and given 'pure, very sweet wine' to drink in crystal and gold cups.   Judging by the small fragments found in the Treasury of Persepolis, glass tableware was as much in favour with the well-to-do as services in gold or silver.   A drinking bowl[547] found in the ruins of the Temple of Ephesus (burnt down in 356 B.C.) copies the designs on the bowls made by the silversmiths.   Fossing, who carefully examined this object, saw in it an Assyro-Babylonian work.

Apropos of a glass vase from Luristan we have spoken of the glass industry that flourished in Elam in the thirteenth century B.C. There are reasons for believing that glassware was manufactured on a commercial scale in this region and exported to distant lands. Presumably a bowl found in a tomb at Alguet in Georgia came from this source. Its decoration, like that of the silver drinking bowls which we assign to the fourth century B.C., answers to the descriptions of the drinking cups preserved in the treasuries of Greek temples of the same period. We are told that these had various types of decoration, 'feathers, darts, rays and spikes' and also calixes of flowers (here lotuses).

Works in precious metals incorporated in articles of furniture reproduced the themes and style of the architectural decorations. The bull, sometimes human-headed and having a symbolic significance, figured on the gold applied ornaments decorating doors and furniture. For the first, the metal-worker copied with meticulous precision models in stone or glazed brick. The model for the second was the human-headed bull executed in limestone; here we have the type figure of the genius, whose tall feathered headdress flanked by three pairs of horns ranked it among the lesser deities of the Mesopotamian pantheon. Both at Hamadan and Persepolis the applied arts show the persistent influence of Achaemenian monumental art. Another gold applied ornament represents a Bactrian camel in full gallop. Here the

315 - IRANIAN HORSEMAN (6th-4th CENT. B.C.) — BRITISH MUSEUM

316 - PERSEPOLIS. HORSES (5th-4th CENT. B.C.) — TEHERAN MUSEUM

317 - HAMADAN (?). BACTRIAN CAMEL (5th-4th C. B.C.) — PRIVATE COLL.

318 - SUSA. BRONZE LION (5th-4th CENTURIES B.C.) — LOUVRE

style is more realistic, limbs and muscles being accurately modelled.

Naturally enough bronze played an important part in the techniques of decorative metal-work. It was used not only for ornamenting furniture but also for the statuettes placed in temples as votive offerings and for interior decoration in private houses. Some of these statuettes were employed as stands for furniture.

Though these are more or less industrial products, some are works of art in their own right; for example an ornamental plaque with two yoked galloping horses. When we compare them with the horse ridden by a small, typically Iranian figure, they are seen to have none of the characteristics of the indigenous horse. Most probably the plaque was imported, perhaps on order, from Asia Minor; whereas the equestrian figurine is clearly an Achaemenian work, indeed one of the masterworks of Iranian art. The headdress of the rider and his *akinakes* hooked to his side are unmistakably Iranian, as is the horse with its tuft of hair, its stocky build, knotted tail and its trappings.

The small figure of a lion fitted with a ring, from Susa, seems to have been used as a weight. Here the bronze-smith's handling is specifically Persian.

The remarkable piece in which three grouped lions act as a support is very different in spirit and, like the tripod in the form of an openwork table, is certainly the work of an Ionian craftsman.

What strikes one most in Achaemenian jewellery is its strong family likeness to that of the Iranian civilizations preceding it. As in Luristan and at Ziwiyeh, the bracelets are of the open type and the ends are almost always decorated with the heads of real or imaginary animals. Set with round or oval stones, the rings keep to the traditions of the monumental art. One, which formed part of the Oxus Treasure, is engraved with the figure of a winged human-headed bull. Another, in solid gold, represents a similar genius with a tail ending in a scorpion's dart.

A large assortment of small *bracteae* [548-554] of engraved gold leaf (used for adorning garments), from the Treasure of Hamadan, is shared between the Oriental Institute, Chicago, and the Teheran Museum. The motifs are usually lions, represented either singly and in movement, or in pairs, addorsed and enclosed within a circle[555-556].

On the bas-relief in his palace at Persepolis Darius is shown wearing an ornament of this type on his robe. The Achaemenians were not the first to have small gold plaques sewn to their clothing; this practice had been in vogue in Mesopotamia as early as the second millennium B.C. But it had been limited to the garments of gods and of royalty on state occasions, and the decorative motifs were always geometric. Only in the Neo-Babylonian period did they become zoomorphic.

Two cylinder seals brought as trophies to the Treasury of Persepolis show *bracteae* of gold foil in the form of birds or quadrupeds sewn to the robe of a god (who may be Marduk). They were also employed in Urartu, where they adorn the garments of gods in the Temple of Musasir. Various objects from the Ziwiyeh Treasure show that these applied ornaments were currently used by the Scythians, who drew on the copious resources of their animal repertory. Though Luristan did not follow suit, it seems likely that some of

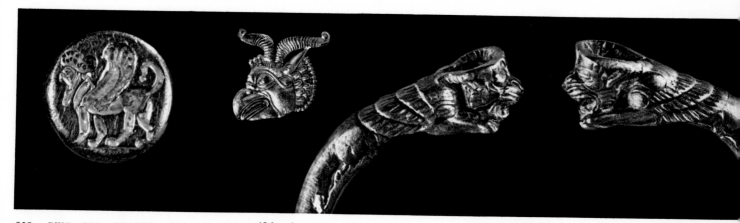

319 - RING   320 - BRACTEA   321 - BRACELET (6th-4th CENT. B.C.) — PRIVATE COLL., TEHERAN MUSEUM, LOUVRE

these motifs derived from the animal figurations of the Luristan bronze-smiths, and that both Scytho-Median art and Achaemenian art drew inspiration from this remarkably prolific source.

On a small gold *bractea* of another type we see a man wearing a 'fluted' headdress, with a flower in his left hand, and making with his right a gesture of salutation or benediction[557]. The image is enclosed in a circle thickening into a crescent below the figure.

This image recurs frequently in Achaemenian glyptic art. In our opinion it represents the supreme god Ahuramazda and, by implication, his representative on earth, the King of Kings, who infallibly, in everything he does, obeys the orders given him from on high.

The same idea is conveyed by a similar piece[558] from Sardis, dating to the sixth century B.C. Ahuramazda's head and shoulders are supported by five wings, as on the relief of the Kizkapan tomb. The fifth wing may be interpreted as a bird's tail in side-view.

At a later period, there was a return to the traditional lay-out, with the tail in front view and the bust of the god hovering above, upheld by four wings.

Among the jewellery, the circular ear-rings have pride of place. Those found at Susa come from the royal tomb described earlier. They date to the second half of the fourth century B.C. The outer bands of gold inset with lapis lazuli and turquoises, are often shaped like petals. They were fastened to the ears with hinged pins secured by keeper-pins.

Representative of the earliest phase of this type of jewellery, they derive from the classical Achaemenian ear-ring, the finest specimen of which, in gold, has been in the Louvre for nearly a century. Here the central part of the disk is adorned with an image in repoussé work, showing the god Bes gripping two ibexes, each preceded by a bird. The animals' fur is treated in the same style as on the Persepolis reliefs and appliqué plaques from Hamadan. The circumference is studded with gold pellets, as on the very simple ear-rings worn in Luristan.

322-323 - EAR-RINGS (4th AND 5th-4th CENT. B.C.) — LOUVRE   324 - EAR-RING (4th CENT. B.C.) — TEHERAN

Though there were certain changes in the ear-rings, their actual structure remained unchanged. The central aperture, however, tended to grow larger as time went on, and the decoration on the solid part of the disk, ceasing to be historiated, became purely decorative. Motifs which hitherto had merely edged or held together the basic concentric or modelled elements now become prominent. An openwork filigree of gold thread, sprinkled with gold beads or given granulated edges, imparted to these objects an aerial lightness. The Treasure of Akhalgori (in the Caucasus) has yielded very fine pieces of this type. In some, made in the form of crescents [559], the granulation of the ground helps to bring out the plastic values of the motifs in gold repoussé.

In the same treasure were forehead ornaments in gold, which could be fastened to braids in the hair. Each consists of a pair of horses (with a single saddle) and a vertical gold band crowned with a rosette rising from their backs. Though a fourth-century work, this 'barbarian' adornment illustrates the taste prevailing in the outlying regions of Iran and prefigures the bulky jewellery of the Parthian period (as represented, for example, on the Hatra statues).

An ancient Mesopotamian motif reappears in the crossed lions on two openwork pendants in gold repoussé attached to necklets. On a complete specimen of one of these pieces heads of horned lions, set in granulated gold mounts, hang from the gold tube forming the structural element [560].

325 - AKHALGORI (CAUCASUS). BRAID ORNAMENT (4th CENTURY B.C.) — TIFLIS MUSEUM

But it is not only the diversity of forms and beauty of the jewellery that demonstrate the high development of Achaemenian culture in this period. The ceremonial weapons carried on great occasions were no less impressive —for example the two gold swords of the Hamadan Treasure. One, in the Teheran Museum, has decorations inspired by the traditions of the Luristan metal-workers, certainly familiar to the Median craftsmen. The other, in the Metropolitan Museum of Art, though less lavishly decorated, shows similar influences.

The gold antelope-handles of whetstones also keep to the stylistic conventions of the Luristan craftsmen. But it is a gold belt-buckle that most clearly illustrates the affinities between Persian art and the arts of the Medo-Scythians. The decorative motif is an oddly shaped two-headed lion. The rendering of the muscular structure obviously derives from the abstract designs of 'dots and commas' or 'apples and pears' favoured by Achaemenian goldsmiths. The adjunction of a second head brings us back to the animal style of the Luristan bronzes, while the wispy coils incised on the flanks are also found on the animals of the Ziwiyeh hoard.

In a belt plaque on which the craftsman reverts to the back-to-back position on each side of a central axis, we find a different technique; the scalloped lions' manes, the tall, pricked-up ears, and the discoid terminals of the horns suggest that this plaque came from some region outside the Iranian Plateau.

326-327 - HAMADAN (?). BELT BUCKLE AND GOLD PLAQUE (6th-4th CENTURIES B.C.) — PRIVATE COLL. AND METROPOLITAN MUSEUM, NEW YORK

328 - HAMADAN (?). GOLD SWORD HILT (5th CENTURY B.C.) — TEHERAN MUSEUM

329 - CYLINDER SEAL OF DARIUS THE GREAT WITH TRILINGUAL INSCRIPTION (C. 500 B.C.) — BRITISH MUSEUM

The Achaemenians produced little work in ivory; their ivories were mostly imported from abroad. The fragments found at Susa[561-562] in a well of the small palace of Artaxerxes I and Darius II, on the 'keep,' may be assigned to Egypt, to Greece and to Asia Minor. They testify both to a wide appreciation of ivory-carving in the lands of Hither Asia and to the place this technique held in the repertory of applied arts favoured by the Achaemenid monarchs.

The invention of the Old Persian cuneiform script may probably be dated to the reign of Teispes (675-640 B.C.), since it figures on the gold tablet of Aria-ramnes, his son. At the time when the small kingdom of Fars was on its way to becoming an empire, the use of this script was confined to a small minority of the upper class. The rapid growth of the empire ruled out any possibility of translating Persian into all the numerous local languages. As it happened, the Aramaic language had spread out through Hither Asia as far as western Iran. By the Achaemenian period it had become, in fact, a *lingua franca* and was used, particularly for official transactions, from Egypt to India, where documents written in Aramaic have been found. The result was that although Elamite was written in Elam and Babylonian in Babylon, all the Persian chan-celleries employed the Aramaic script.

Tablets were inscribed in cuneiform characters and then, as a rule, signed by rolling a cylinder seal upon the clay. Papyrus and parchment were reserved for letters and documents written in ink in Aramaic, in Greek and in the languages of Asia Minor and Phoenicia. They were rolled up and the scroll was tied with a ribbon sealed with a clay bulla, which was then mar-ked with a stamp seal or a cylinder seal. It would seem that the Persians tended to restrict the use of the cuneiform script to inscriptions on rocks and monuments and otherwise employed Aramaic characters.

In the domain of glyptics Oriental symbolism was diverted from the religious to the secular plane. The king was represented standing on a lion[563] —like the gods in ancient Oriental imagery—holding a bow with one hand and three arrows in the other. From now on, the bow was to be the emblem of royal power; the king is shown carrying it, on cylinder seals as well as on the Bisutun and Naqsh-i-Rustam bas-reliefs and the Kizkapan tomb. Sometimes we see him represented twice, on two sides of a fire altar, and worshipping before two effigies of Ahuramazda who is facing in two directions so as to bless the king. Here the presentation of the scenes keeps to the methods of the ancient Oriental glyptic art, which took no account of the third dimension. The central theme—a god, an altar and a king—is governed by heraldic symmetry and the composition forms an harmoniously balanced whole. Even a scene of battle between Medes and Scythians is treated in this manner. Sometimes landscape is suggested by the presence of a single palm-tree, having no real connection with the subject.

On all the cylinders the king, glorious and invincible, symbolizes the might of the Achaemenian empire. Most famous is the seal of Darius the Great, inscribed with his name and title in three languages. Achaemenian monumental art had no influence on glyptics of the period. Only on a few intaglios do we find imitations of the contemporary applied arts, but recourse was had more frequently to ancient themes derived from the Sialk potters—another indication of the remarkable vitality of the procedures of early Iranian art.

330 - KING AT A FIRE ALTAR (6th-4th C. B.C.) — BIBL. NAT., PARIS

331 - MEDES AND SCYTHIANS FIGHTING (6th-4th C. B.C.) — BIBL. NAT.

332 - KING SHOOTING A LION (6th-4th CENT. B.C.) — VIENNA MUSEUM

Stamp seals kept to the ancient traditions of Asia Minor and were employed chiefly in the western territories of the empire; their technique and compositional structure resemble those of the cylinder seals. One of them, however, represents a high official, with his name engraved, a motif destined to bulk large in Sassanian glyptics.

From the fifth century B.C. on, under the auspices of Greek art, Persian gem engraving made rapid progress and production was intensified[564-566]. The freedom of movement in scenes of hunting and fighting, the use of subjects taken from everyday life and representations of animals at the flying gallop, differentiate this group of intaglios (from which figurations of the king seem to have been excluded) from the type which may be described as 'national.'

Some see in these elegantly finished objects the work of Greek craftsmen employed by the Persians. But this fails to take into account the traditionally Iranian methods of execution. These are no less evident in the remarkably low relief than in the characteristically Oriental practice of doubling the outlines of figures and animals. Despite the pains taken to render movement and suggest the third dimension, the basic elements of the composition lack coherence and the action of the participants, both men and animals, takes place in a strangely unconvincing space. Here everything, even the way details are stressed and meticulously rendered, points to the work of Persian craftsmen drawing inspiration from the Greeks. True, Persian art of this type is never a spontaneous creation and often utilizes foreign elements; yet it never copies them slavishly, but, after assimilating them, translates them into a language peculiarly its own. For the two worlds, Persian and Hellenic, intimate as were their contacts on the western confines of Hither Asia, never succeeded in amalgamating on the spiritual plane.

As for the coins issued by the Achaemenians, they remained unchanged throughout the whole period, and invariably represented the king armed with a bow, symbol of his power[567].

333 - SILVER AMPHORA (5th-4th CENTURIES B.C.) — PRIVATE COLLECTION, BASEL —

KINGS · DATES	SITES	ARCHITECTURE	SCULPTURE
6th century B.C.	MASJID-I-SULAIMAN PASARGADAE	Terrace Terrace	
CYRUS II (559-529) Founder of the Achaemenid Dynasty	PASARGADAE PASARGADAE PASARGADAE	Palace Tomb of Cyrus Fire Altars	Inscriptions, Reliefs, Capitals
CAMBYSES II (529-521)			
DARIUS I (521-485)	SUSA PERSEPOLIS BISUTUN NAQSH-I-RUSTAM	Palace with *Apadana* Palace: Terrace, *Tachara*, Tripylon, *Apadana*, Hall of 99 Columns Court with 4 Porticoes Tomb of Darius *Later Tombs of*	Inscribed Statue of Da Reliefs, Capitals Reliefs, Capitals Rock Relief Rock Reliefs
5th century B.C.		*Xerxes I, Artaxerxes I and Darius II*	
XERXES I (485-465)	HAMADAN PERSEPOLIS	 Palace: Gate-House Completion of *Apadana* Unfinished Portico Throne Hall, *Hadish*, Harem, Treasury	 Reliefs, Capitals Reliefs, Capitals Reliefs, Capitals Reliefs, Capitals Reliefs, Capitals
ARTAXERXES I (465-424)	PERSEPOLIS BABYLON	Palace: Completion of Throne Hall Palace: *Apadana*	 Bell-shaped Column Bases
XERXES II (424)			Reliefs
DARIUS II (424-404)	SUSA	Small Palace	Votive Portraits *Limestone, Lapis-Lazu*
4th century B.C.			
ARTAXERXES II (404-358)	SUSA	Reconstruction of *Apadana* Royal Tomb	
ARTAXERXES III (358-338) ARSES (338-335)	PERSEPOLIS	Unfinished Palace Tombs of Artaxerxes II and Artaxerxes III	Reliefs Reliefs Reliefs
DARIUS III CODOMANNUS (335-330)	PERSEPOLIS	Tomb of Darius III	Reliefs
334 - *Invasion of Persia by Alexander*			
330 - *Burning of Persepolis Murder of Darius III*			
End of the Achaemenians			

CLAY	METAL	IVORY GLASS	GLYPTICS EPIGRAPHY	MESOPOTAMIA	EGYPT	GREECE
Glazed Pottery	Foundation Plaques *Gold, Silver*		Trilingual Inscriptions Foundation Charter Trilingual Inscriptions	Capture of Babylon by Cyrus II (539) Cambyses II King of Babylon (529)	Psammetichus III (526-525) *Persian Domination* (525-404) Statue of PTAH-HOTEP	
	Treasure of HAMADAN Cup, Rhyton, Bowl Applied Arts *Gold, Bronze* Plate, Weapons Jewellery *Gold, Silver*	Imported Ivories Glass Rhyton	Cup, Bowl: Trilingual Inscriptions Greco-Persian Gems	Babylon 4th Capital of the Persian Empire	*Persian Domination* Alabastra sent to Persia Achaemenian Silverplate *Revolt in Egypt*	*First Persian War* (490) *End of the Persian Wars* The Parthenon (447-438)
...ieze of Archers and Lions *Glazed Brick*	Disk-shaped Ear-rings *Gold and Stones*		Stamp and Cylinder Seals *Alexander at Babylon* (331) *Death of Alexander at Babylon* (323)		NECTANEBES (378-350) *Second Persian Domination* (341-333) *Founding of Alexandria* (332)	PHILIP OF MACEDON (359-336) ALEXANDER THE GREAT (336-323)

United under a single crown, the Medes and Persians ruled over an empire composed of many different peoples, a cross-section of the civilizations of the Ancient Orient. The great Achaemenid kings, Cyrus the Great and Darius I, impressed by the achievements and prestige of these age-old civilizations, granted them a measure of autonomy, sometimes to the detriment of the central power. This instability was one of the causes of the downfall of the Persian empire, at the very time when a new political power, Macedon, was appearing on the scene.

The 'official' art of Achaemenian Persia celebrates the glory of the ruling monarch. Not only are the rock tombs of the Achaemenid kings (Naqsh-i-Rustam, Persepolis) adorned with relief-work, but long sequences of reliefs whose sole purpose is to glorify the monarch's person and prestige line the walls, stairways and gates of the palaces (Pasargadae, Persepolis).

In the development of the sumptuary arts craftsmen of many lands took part. Thanks to the introduction of coinage, trade was already flourishing on an international scale over a wide area (Persepolis reliefs showing the tribute-offerings of many nations).

Though the production of jewellery, vessels and plate of precious metal, and ceremonial weapons passed through several phases, the underlying conception remained unchanged. Their decorative motifs were taken over from monumental sculpture, and their technique and style, despite occasional signs of foreign inspiration, testify to the astonishing vitality of the art forms of ancient Iran.

PART TWO

335 - HASANLU. KERNOS WITH BIRD AND FIGURE, DETAIL (9th-8th CENTURIES B.C.) — TEHERAN MUSEUM

VI

CHRONOLOGY OF THE PROTOHISTORIC ART OF IRAN

SIALK DATINGS

OUR attribution of Cemetery B at Sialk to the Iranian tribes that had settled on the Plateau towards the beginning of the first millennium B.C. has not been contested. One of the most characteristic products of this new civilization is the bird-shaped vase with a long beak-spout, a type of vessel that is also found on other, slightly later sites of the Plateau, and remained in use to the very end of the seventh century B.C.

It is by examining the Sialk civilization in the context of other cultures on the Plateau that we have the best chance of determining the *terminus a quo* of its chronology.

At Giyan Level I the production of the so-called Hurrian painted pottery reached its zenith in the second half of the second millennium; after that, it steadily diminished and painted decoration gradually went out of use. Next came the tombs whose grave furniture and pottery are identical with those that have been brought to light at Babylon and date to the end of the period of

— 334 - SIALK. PAINTED VASE: WARRIOR-HUNTER (10th-9th CENTURIES B.C.) — PRIVATE COLLECTION, LUCERNE

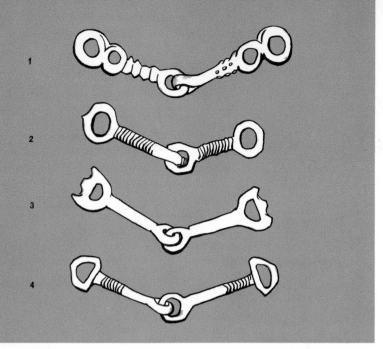

336 - CAUCASUS AND SOUTH RUSSIA: TYPES OF BITS (8th-7th c. b.c.)

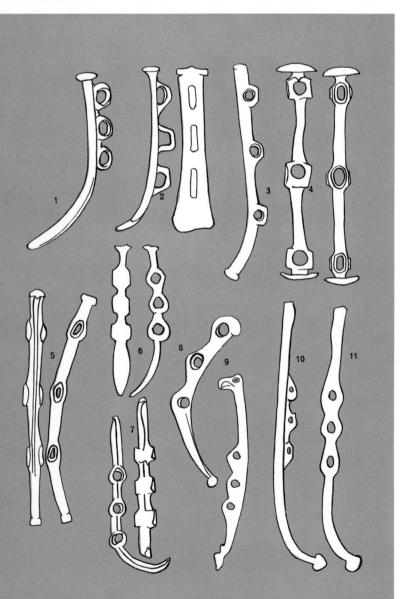

Kassite domination, that is, to the twelfth and eleventh centuries B.C. This period seems also to mark the end of the influence of the Western art currents which had prevailed for some centuries in the western portion of the Plateau, and it was now that currents from the east and north came into play. The first sign of the change is the appearance at Giyan of black or grey-black pottery characterized by knife-cut designs. This was almost the only type of pottery found in Cemetery A at Sialk (slightly earlier than Cemetery B). The insertion of a white substance in the incised geometric design was a new departure so far as the potters working on the Plateau were concerned. However a black pottery with similar designs is one of the type-elements of the domestic ware of Transcaucasia which Soviet archaeologists have succeeded in dating beyond all question to the extreme end of the second and the beginning of the first millennium B.C.

Though we are as yet unable to account for the appearance of this particular technique on the Plateau as being the result of any specific ethnic movement, we would stress the point that since it has become possible to align the date of Cemetery A to that of an identical culture, now authoritatively dated, existing in Transcaucasia, it seems to follow that the period of Cemetery A (the end of the second millennium B.C. at the earliest) may be assigned to a transitional phase of the cultures on the Plateau, during which the Bronze Age gave place to the Iron Age.

337 - CAUCASUS AND SOUTH RUSSIA: TYPES OF PSALIA (8th-7th CENTURIES B.C.)

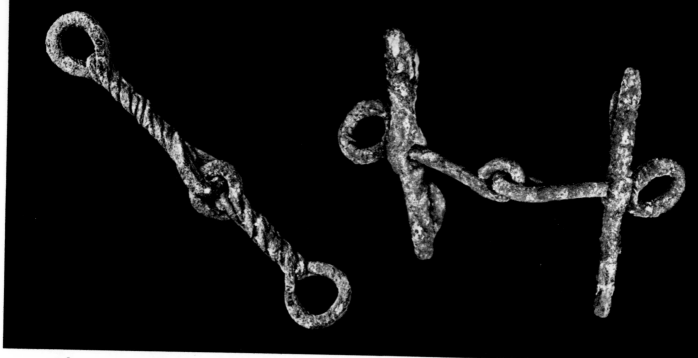

338 - HASANLU. BROKEN AND TWISTED BIT   339 - BROKEN BIT (9th-8th CENT. B.C.) — TEHERAN MUSEUM

Slightly preceding the civilization of Cemetery B and going back, at the earliest, to the end of the second millennium, Cemetery A invalidates the attribution of Cemetery B to the second millennium.

The *terminus ad quem* of the dating of this Cemetery can also be fixed with some assurance by an *argumentum a silentio*. For in over two hundred tombs that have been uncovered no trace has been found of fibulae or trilobal arrows, though among the grave goods are many hundreds of pins and laurel-shaped or rhomboidal arrowheads. These facts justify the view that the date we are seeking to establish cannot be placed later than the middle of the eighth century. For it was at approximately this time that fibulae and trilobal arrows made their first appearance on the Plateau, and they were invariably found near the Sialk tombs, but never inside them.

Light is also thrown on the problem of dating by a comparative examination, from the typological angle, of the pieces of horse-gear that have been discovered. Allowance must, however, be made for the remote position of the Plateau and the scantiness of our documentation for the first two centuries of the first millennium B.C. Of prime importance is a close examination of the Caucasian bits and *psalia*, which can hardly be dated earlier than 800 B.C. and of special interest is the fact that all the more elaborate *psalia*, having three holes and fastened with thongs to horse bits, date later than 1000 B.C. Sialk has yielded specimens of these as well as 'broken' bits with terminal rings also in iron, which suggests their dating to the first millennium B.C.

Iron bits and *psalia* independent of them like those of Sialk were in general use in the Kuban and Dnieper regions. They date to the sixth century and presumably were brought from Transcaucasia at the time when the cultures of the northern Caucasus and southern Russia were undergoing profound changes, probably due to the reflux of Scythian tribes. The Kelermes barrows (in the Kuban valley), dating to the first quarter of the sixth century at the earliest, have yielded bits whose rings are shaped like stirrups; they were a late development and they have also been found at Hasanlu, which was settled shortly after Sialk. In this context it should be noted that the transitional period when cavalry replaced chariotry in warfare (as attested by the Sialk monument) may be assigned to the first centuries of the first millennium B.C.

The only inscribed object found in Cemetery B at Sialk is a scarab bearing the name of Seti I. M. Boreux, who was the first to study it, pointed out the probability of its being a Syrian copy of an Egyptian original and therefore posterior to the end of the fourteenth century B.C. when Seti I was on the throne. Chronologically, evidence of this sort is far from being decisive; many cases can be cited of such small objects being continuously in use for many centuries despite far-reaching ethnic changes on the sites where they were discovered. Thus in Crete engraved pre-Hellenic precious stones have been found in tombs of the fourth century B.C. More importance, in our opinion, should be attached to the similarities between the cylinder seal from Cemetery B and an Assyrian seal of the ninth century B.C.

Finally, the fact that none of the megalithic tombs which constitute the most noteworthy feature of Cemetery B, made their appearance on the Plateau until the beginning of the first millennium B.C., conflicts with the tendency to date this cemetery to the second millennium. Thus we abide by our original dating of them to the tenth or ninth, even perhaps to the early eighth century— which is in accordance with the views of Przeworski, Akurgal and Diakonov.

340 - LURISTAN. BOWL INSCRIBED WITH THE NAME OF NARAM-SIN (24th CENT. B.C.) — PRIVATE COLL., TEHERAN

THE LURISTAN BRONZES: DATE AND ATTRIBUTION

THAT there was once a tendency to antedate the Luristan bronzes is generally admitted. Their points in common with ancient forms and themes had a misleading effect, since allowance was not made for the fact that at the time when the art of Luristan reached its zenith (in the second half of the eighth and in the seventh century) a sporadic revival of archaic types of art had been taking place in all parts of Hither Asia, even in Egypt. Albright has noted this in the Scriptures and Berta Segall in the Egyptian, Phoenician and Neo-Babylonian arts of the period.

As things turned out, this archaizing trend was followed (though on new lines, unprecedented on the Plateau) by the Luristan bronze-smiths, whose art bodied forth the religious myths of the Iranian tribes which had recently settled in the central regions of the Zagros range.

Here we come up against a much-debated ethnical problem, that of determining the people to which the Luristan bronzes should be assigned. König, in 1934, was the first scholar to suggest that they were Cimmerians. When Hancar, Cameron and Schefold discussed this theory they found nothing to say against it. But in view of the discoveries of Piotrovsky, Melikishvili and Diakonov (the last-named thinks the bronzes may be the work of Medians), it seems desirable to look more closely into the question.

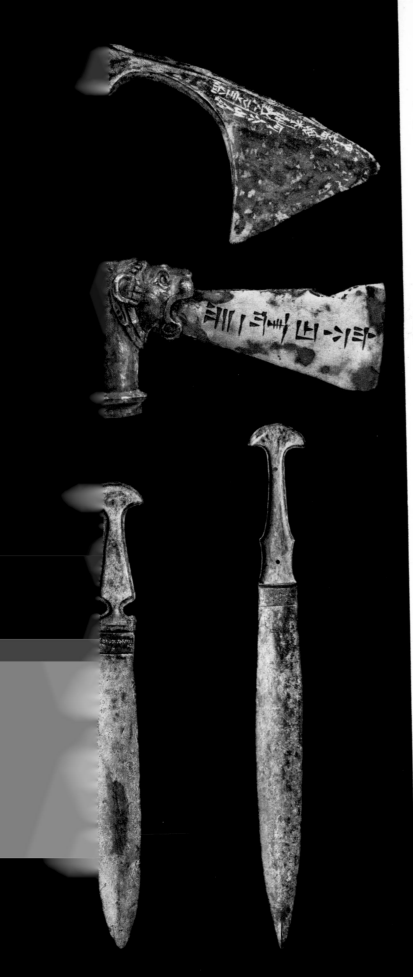

From the eighth century B.C. on, the Zagros range, forming the western frontier of Iran, was shared between three powers: the kingdom of Mannai, south of Lake Urmia; that of Ellipi covering the plain of Kermanshah; and Luristan (formerly inhabited by the Kassites) about whose political background little is known. In 702 King Sennacherib, son of Sargon, launched a campaign against Ellipi, but his first objective was the land of the nomad mountaineers south of that kingdom, that is to say Luristan. The Assyrians won a victory, carried off horses and mules as booty, 'settled' the local population in two fortresses, and foreign prisoners in a third, and continued their advance to Ellipi. The first phase of the campaign seems to have been intended to put the warriors of Luristan out of action, so as to prevent their joining forces with the Ellipians. In 689 the latter attacked Assyria, in alliance with the kings of Babylonia and Elam. But the Assyrians proved invincible; Babylon was taken and destroyed and part of Elam invaded.

Ten years later the Cimmerians attacked Assyria but were defeated by Esarhaddon in a battle whose site remains unidentified. Now a record of this same year (679 B.C.) tells of the sale of a garden at Nineveh and names one Ishdi-Kharran, captain of a Cimmerian regiment, among the witnesses to the transaction. Under these circumstances it seems unlikely that this regiment and its captain formed part of the Cimmerian army defeated by the Assyrians. Presumably these

341 - LURISTAN. AXE (11th CENTURY B.C.)
342 - CHOGA ZAMBIL. AXE (13th CENT. B.C.)
343 - LURISTAN. DAGGERS (2nd MILL. B.C.)
TEHERAN, LOUVRE, BRITISH MUSEUM

men were mercenaries serving in the Assyrian army during the campaign of 689, which resulted in the capture of Babylon and the invasion of Elam. Here perhaps we have an explanation of the presence of the weapons and inscribed bronze objects of Babylonian and Elamite provenance found in graves in Luristan. All may have been looted from Babylonian and Elamite temples by Cimmerian mercenaries serving in the Assyrian army. Engraved on most of them are the names of kings or officials of the end of the second millennium B.C., though there are some which must be a thousand years older.

The question now arises: Can these inscribed objects bearing dates whose authenticity there is no good reason to doubt help us to solve the problem of the dating of the tombs in which they were discovered? Not in all cases assuredly, as is proved by stone vases which have been found in the Persepolis Treasury, inscribed with the names of Kings Sargon (722-705), Esarhaddon (681-668), Assurbanipal (668-626) and Nebuchadnezzar (604-562). All had been looted in Assyrian and Babylonian palaces, then brought to one or other of the palaces of the Achaemenid kings.

Two bronze daggers found in Luristan graves, one bearing the name of Marduk-nadin-akhe of Babylon (c. 1110 B.C.), the other that of Shamash-kilani (?), 'officer of the king,' and also dating to the twelfth century B.C., have inscriptions beginning with the word *sa* which Langdon translates as 'property of...' But in the Foroughi Collection there is a bronze axe (found in a tomb in Luristan in 1957) which suggests a different interpretation of these inscriptions. On it is engraved *sa sarru* ᵐ*Sil-ha-ak* ᵈ*In-su-si-na-ak i-pu-su*, i.e. '[axe] that was made by King Shilhak-Inshushinak.' That is to say, the word *sa* qualifies an object commissioned by the king or a high official. The shape of the Foroughi axe shows that weapons of this class were not intended to be utilized. Our view that they were exclusively votive objects, made to be placed in temples, is borne out by the inscription on a bowl dedicated to the goddess Nin-egal.

Of much interest in this context is the bronze axe, its haft adorned with a boar in electrum, which was found in the temple of Kiririsha at Choga Zambil near Susa, where, along with some other objects, it had been overlooked by the Assyrian soldiery when the Elamite temples and palaces were plundered by Assurbanipal's army (c. 640 B.C.). It bears the inscription *I, Untash-Gal* and was evidently a votive offering made by the king of that name, builder of the Choga Zambil ziggurat.

All the inscribed objects found in the Luristan tombs came from temples plundered by the Assyrian troops. Hence the great variety of dates to which they are assignable, some of them going back to the third millennium B.C.— and this despite the fact that all alike come from megalithic tombs containing similar grave goods. None of the inscriptions on them, be it noted, refers to an Assyrian king or notable. Why, it may be asked, were these bowls, daggers and axes, most of them unutilizable, so greatly treasured by the looters that they had them buried in their graves? The reason is that any object bearing an inscription was thought to have a magical value and a power of averting evil from the man who owned or preserved it. It was a *maktub*, a thing with writing on it—which still today is venerated in the East.

True, among the Luristan bronzes, especially the weapons, some have forms corresponding to those current in Mesopotamia and Syria during the second millennium B.C. These resemblances have been rightly pointed out, but they apply to only a few of the several thousands of objects we are here concerned with. Moreover, we must not forget that certain types of weapons have an extremely long life.

An example of this is the dagger with an openwork, flanged hilt, found at the entrance of the temple of Ishniqarab at Choga Zambil, where it had been dropped in or about 640 B.C. by Assyrian or Elamite soldiers. Daggers exactly like it were found beside the dead in tombs of the Neo-Babylonian level recently cleared at Susa, and all resemble the type of weapon most commonly employed in Luristan.

Several authorities have attributed the Luristan bronzes to the Kassites. If this is so, how account for the fact that not a single bronze of the Luristan type has been found on any of the Kassite sites excavated in Mesopotamia, nor even any pottery akin to the Luristan objects? The use of the term 'Kassite' would be warranted here only in the connotation given it in Assyrian official records, where Luristan is referred to, as late as the seventh century B.C., as 'the land of the Kassites.' In pursuance of the same tradition of retaining archaic place names, Media was sometimes called 'the land of the Guti.' Yet at the time when these records were made the Indo-European element was already present in full force in Media and Luristan.

Whence came the Cimmerians who enlisted in the army of the King of Assyria, unlike those of Asia Minor who were allies of Rusas II, King of Urartu, from 676-675 B.C. on? The series of 'omen texts' recording answers given by the oracle between the years 675 and 650 tell us something of the part played by the Cimmerians in western Iran during this period. We also hear of Cimmerians as allies of the King of Mannai, with whom also Assyria was having trouble at the time.

A letter from a Babylonian priest in the service of the Assyrian king Esarhaddon alludes to negotiations with the Cimmerians then in progress, with a view to preventing them from intervening in the conflict between Assyria and Mannai. The writer warns the king against trusting the promises of the Cimmerians. There are many mentions of Cimmerians as allies of the Medes in the Median revolt of 673 B.C. The moving spirit of that revolt was Kashtariti (whom Herodotus calls Phraortes), son or grandson of Deioces, and his base of operations was Kar-Kashshi, i.e. the town (or colony) of the Kassites

—a name that brings us to the land of the Kassites and by the same token to Luristan, or some neighbouring region, such as the fertile plain of Nihawand. The rebellion was not unavailing, since the Median kingdom could now take form, on condition of paying tribute to Assyria.

An inquiry addressed by Assurbanipal to the oracle in which the Cimmerians are again mentioned helps to locate them more precisely. Before dispatching troops to attack the Ellipians, the King of Assyria asks if they will not 'fall into the hands of the Ellipians, the Medes or the Cimmerians,' and this enables us to determine approximately the geographical distribution of the three peoples. The route from the rich plain of Kermanshah to Hamadan (i.e. from Ellipi to Media) crosses a tract of hill country before abutting on another plain, that of Kengavar, where we are already in Median territory. These rugged uplands form part of a spur of the great mountain chain of Kuh-i-Jebet Nabalighan which skirts the northern frontier of Luristan and drives a wedge between the Kingdoms of Ellipi and that of Media, with which the Cimmerians, who dwelt just beyond it, then were allied. At the time of the Luristan revolt, some thirty years before, this section of the Kermanshah-Hamadan road was regarded as one of its 'danger points.'

The first recorded mention of Cimmerians in Hither Asia dates to about 722-715 B.C. when Assyrian spies in Urartu reported to their king that Rusas I, King of Urartu, had been

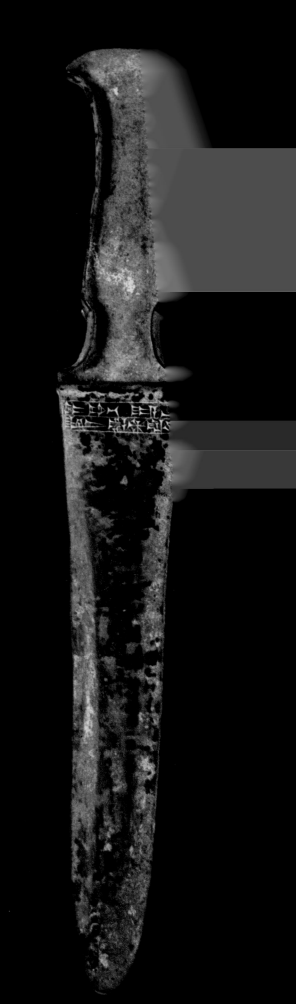

344 - LURISTAN. INSCRIBED DAGGER (13th CENT. B.C.) — PRIVATE COLLECTION, TEHERAN

severely defeated in his expedition into 'the land of the Cimmerians.' This was separated from Urartu by the land of Guriana, on the north-west of the Urartian sphere of influence. The fact that at this time there already existed in the eastern part of Asia Minor a 'land of the Cimmerians,' capable of defeating the powerful king of Urartu, suggests that the arrival of the Cimmerians south of the Caucasus must have preceded these events by a good number of years. In our opinion, their thrust into western Asia was not a mass invasion but a gradual infiltration beginning in the first half of the eighth century B.C. or perhaps even earlier.

Such are the geographical and historical data. In Part One of this work we attempted to show how much there was in common between the cultures of Sialk, Khurvin, Hasanlu and Amlash, while stressing the later date of the three last-named cultural centres. A marked progress in the art of metal-working, an improvement in the quality of weapons, a richer iconography, and an elegant stylization of abstract, fantastic motifs—all go to show that the Luristan culture is younger than that of Sialk and may be dated to the eighth-seventh centuries B.C., and that quite possibly it lasted well into the sixth century, or even later.

345 - MAKU. PAINTED HORSE RHYTON (8th CENTURY B.C.) — TEHERAN MUSEUM

DIFFUSION OF PROTOHISTORIC PAINTED POTTERY ON THE IRANIAN PLATEAU

L ITTLE is known as yet of the origins and development of the craft of painted pottery among the Iranians of the protohistoric period. Evidently its use was widespread, for traces of its survival until the end of the seventh century B.C.—that is to say at least two centuries after the end of the Sialk community —have been found in four distinct regions of the Plateau, two of which are some 1200 miles distant from each other. These four regions are Azerbaijan, Susiana, Luristan and Kurdistan. Here we shall deal only with the first two, since the continuing influence of the art of Sialk in the Luristan bronzes and the Ziwiyeh Treasure (from Kurdistan) has been discussed in our study of these groups of objects.

AZERBAIJAN

Near Maku in the north-west corner of Iran, not far from the Turkish frontier, a chance find brought to light a handsome rhyton in the shape of a horse. Made of fine-grained terracotta, polished to a light-brown lustre, this ritual vessel was filled through a funnel-shaped neck placed in the animal's back, while a small hole made in the breast served for pouring out the liquid. The horse is of a species bred in the highlands, famed for its strength and stamina. The decoration is in red, black being used chiefly for emphasizing outlines.

287

The maker of this rhyton took pains to render exactly the horse's trappings. Enclosed in a headstall, the forehead is protected by a rectangular frontlet, resting on a vertical stripe, and starting from each side of it are three slanting, wavy bands. There are fleur-de-lys designs on both sides of the neck; these are the *tamgas* (marks of ownership) branded by the nomads on their horses and cattle. Three broad straps spanning the horse's breast are attached to the saddle-cloth. The reins rest on the neck and the short mane is modelled in relief, as are the eyes and the tufted forelock, one of the traditional features of Iranian horses.

The saddle-cloth is of a type that became standardized under the Achaemenians; it seems to imitate a piece of felt or leather with incrustations, or perhaps one of the textiles woven in the nomads' tents. In recent years Soviet archaeologists have uncovered a whole series of very similar saddle-cloths in the frozen barrows at Pazyryk in the Altai range (South Siberia). Hence the special interest of the saddle-cloth so accurately reproduced by the maker of the Maku rhyton.

It is divided into two parts and the subject in both cases is a hunting scene. The ground line is indicated by the fringed border, and a sprinkling of rosettes suggests a landscape. The way the birds and animals are arranged shows a curious disregard of realism; one would expect to see the birds flying in the air, not placed below the feline, and the latter chasing the ibex, not being followed by it. None the less, the spirited renderings of the animals and the freedom of their movements give the scene, despite its curious improbabilities, a remarkable vivacity. This rhyton is clearly the work of a master-craftsman; the animals' bodies are composed of spaced-out reddish patches, between which, in the uncoloured zones, he has drawn black lines indicating muscles. Of no less interest is the attitude given the galloping animals, the same as that employed by the Urartian artists; it was adopted in Achaemenian art and had previously appeared in archaic Greek art.

Though the flowers are not drawn from nature, the attempt to render vegetation marks an advance on the art of Sialk. We have here a conventional art whose forms have already become more or less stylized, and the artist's chief concern is to achieve a rhythmically balanced composition.

In our opinion the Maku rhyton dates to the end of the eighth century B.C., in which case this art came after that of Sialk, but was anterior to a very similar rhyton to which we shall now turn.

346 - MAKU. DESIGN OF THE SADDLE-CLOTH ON THE HORSE RHYTON

347 - SUSA. PAINTED HORSE RHYTON (7th CENTURY B.C.) — TEHERAN MUSEUM

SUSIANA

In an early seventh-century Persian village, about half a mile from the Elamite acropolis at Susa, we found a horse-shaped rhyton resembling the one found at Maku. Another find (a few yards from the rhyton) was a large jar containing an Elamite tablet, datable to the last third of the seventh century B.C. This site has also yielded fragments of pottery.

The clay used for making this rhyton resembles that of the Maku piece and is practically the same as that employed by the Sialk potters. The decorations are in purplish-red on a buff ground. The animal's legs, part of its forelock and its tail are missing.

This Susian horse is not of the same breed as the one from Maku. Thinner and wirier, it is closer to the Arab type of horse. Whereas in China the ceramists of the Han dynasty made a point of emphasizing the differences between their native horses and those imported from the West (i.e. 'Outer' Iran), both the horses we are concerned with here were locally bred. It was presumably a cross of these two breeds that gave rise to the hardy, strongly built horse, with a slender neck and sturdy limbs, which, itself cased in scale armour, was capable of carrying a rider clad in a massive coat of mail, and to which the Parthian heavy cavalry owed its renown throughout the East.

The obvious affinities between the two rhytons seem all the more remarkable when we remember the distance, over 1200 miles, between the sites where they were found. At Susa as at Maku, the horse's ears, eyes, forelock and mane are moulded in relief, and the headstall contains a triangular frontlet. The arrangement of the reins is identical, the decoration of the saddle-cloth is similarly divided into two parts, and the *tamga* appears on the horse's shoulders, though, while still shaped like a fleur-de-lys, it here is of a simpler order. Note, however, the decorative value given the breast-strap attached to the saddle-cloth which covers almost the entire back of the animal. A rectangle in the centre, starting from the withers, contains the orifice of the recipient; painted red, it seems to represent a cushion serving as the rider's saddle.

Though the arrangement of the decorations on the saddle-cloth is the same as that of the Maku rhyton, the subjects differ. Here, in each compartment, two boars in antithetical postures are depicted; they are separated on one side by reeds and on the other by the chequered surface of a pool of water. Above each scene a bird is hovering. The artist, working probably a century later than the Maku artist, pays more attention to details, for example the animals' heads and flattened snouts. The upstanding bristles of the wild boars preparing to charge an assailant are particularly effective. Here for the first time we see a representation of the 'flying gallop,' which was to characterize Iranian animal figurations for many centuries. The natural setting, too, is more graphically indicated than the Maku painter's abstract landscape. This motif of confronted animals with birds flying overhead was also current in the art of Sialk. But at Susa there has been a notable advance; not only in the landscape setting but also in the more realistic treatment of the animals. Yet, somehow the painter, try as he may, fails to make these animals 'come alive'; they seem oddly static, all movement arrested. And this immobility, so characteristic of the early phase of Iranian art, was destined to persist despite improvements in techniques.

The idea of making recipients in the form of quadrupeds may well have originated with a potter in one of the outlying regions of the North, such as Cappadocia, where rhytons were in favour over a long period. Also to the same source may perhaps be assigned the polychrome designs, though these sometimes occur on the Plateau, particularly in Luristan (cf. some vases in the Teheran Museum). But the figuration of the quadruped as a horse is an essentially Iranian conception, appropriate to a race of mounted warriors who owed the gradual conquest of the country they had invaded to their cavalry.

By a fortunate coincidence these two rhytons, from Maku and Susiana, give solid historical proof of the presence of this race in both the northern and the southern parts of the region. Furthermore they prove that this uniform expansion did not entail a similar uniformity in their art forms—a fact that has also been observed in the course of researches into the prehistory of the Plateau and the arts of archaic Iran.

In the ancient world the horse was constantly associated with the sun god. Thus Xenophon, in a description of Cyrus going forth to make a sacrifice, speaks of 'horses which have to be slain as offerings to the sun.' In the arts of Europe and Hither Asia, in regions which from the late second or early first millennium B.C. were overrun by the Indo-Europeans, horses are associated with solar symbols. And on pottery decorated in the geometric style the image of a horse is often combined with a circle surrounded by dots—a motif that also figures on the breast and neck of the Susiana horse.

Given, then, the religious and symbolic values of the horse, these rhytons may be presumed to have been funerary ware. 'A mystical relationship between the horse and Death, or the dead, seems to have existed in the prehistoric age of the Indo-European peoples, and it still exists in the folklore of some modern nations.' With some races this notion found expression in the practice of burying the horse with the deceased or burning it over his tomb. This explains why terracotta horses were placed in graves in Greece and in Han China, and horses carved in wood in Siberian graves. They were intended to act as substitutes for the animal best fitted to transport the dead man's soul to the Other World. The sacrifice of horses, still practised at funerals in Siberia by the Buriats and Yakuts, has the same significance. And even now the hearse of a great military commander is followed by his horse (which in earlier times would have been immolated on its master's grave). It was in connection with this last journey that the notion of a 'Pegasus' developed, earlier it would seem in Iran than in Greece. For the image of a winged horse carrying the dead man to his new abode occurs both at Sialk and at Hasanlu.

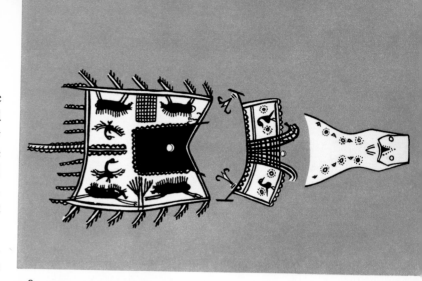

348 - SUSA.   DESIGN OF THE SADDLE-CLOTH ON THE HORSE RHYTON

349 - SIALK.   PAINTED VASE (10th-9th CENT. B.C.) — TEHERAN

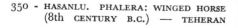

350 - HASANLU. PHALERA: WINGED HORSE (8th CENTURY B.C.) — TEHERAN

351 - SUSA. FRAGMENT OF A PAINTED VASE: ANIMAL AND PLANT DESIGN (7th CENTURY B.C.) — TEHERAN MUSEUM

A fragment of a ewer dating to the seventh century B.C. and assignable to the Susian school of painted pottery—it was discovered in the same village as the rhyton—displays unusual features, which seem to be innovations. The ewer in question belongs to the family of Sialk vases with flattened spouts, slanting up from the beginning of the neck. At Susa the spout acquired the trilobal form that it was to keep throughout the 'imperial' period of Achaemenian art, though pottery still carried painted decorations. Around the starting-point of the spout and neck was a ring of festoons and a herring-bone design. (Festoons, it may be noted, are a distinctive feature of the Susian rhyton.) A plant, towards which points the head of a bird with a very long neck (a wader?), is painted on a large area to the right of the spout. The rendering of this plant-and-animal motif is obviously the work of a highly skilled craftsman; with two well-placed brushstrokes he deftly suggests the graceful poise of the head of a water-bird. Here we have an early example of that predilection for the heads of ducks and swans which was characteristic of Achaemenian plastic art, whether in stone carving or in repoussé work on precious metal.

This humble fragment forecasts the Persian palace art of a century later. But it also illustrates the vast progress made by Iranian painting in the many centuries that had elapsed since it made its début at Sialk. Its culminating point was to coincide with its eclipse. For, to the best of our present knowledge, the Susian fragment had no sequel, and only monochrome pottery was produced on the Plateau from the sixth century on.

353 - LURISTAN (?). BRONZE CAULDRON HANDLE (8th-7th CENTURIES B.C.) — TEHERAN MUSEUM

VII

THE IRANO-URARTIAN 'KOINE'

IN the mid-ninth century B.C. the many small principalities of the country of Nairi, in the Lake Van region, were amalgamated into one vast kingdom bearing the name Urartu. By the end of the century this young, dynamic state, taking advantage of the decline in Assyrian power, had greatly extended its frontiers and brought many neighbouring lands under its control. Between 810 and 743, in the reigns of Menuas, Argistis I and Sarduris II, the Urartians secured outlets on the Mediterranean and the Black Sea, and by occupying Aleppo in the West and the land of Kulkhai (Colchis) in the north, were brought into active contact with the outposts of the Greek world.

During this period, according to the Assyrian annalists, the Persians occupied the region west and south-west of Lake Urmia, while the Medes held the south-east, in the vicinity of Hamadan. It is now that Iranian names begin to figure in the army of the kings of Urartu. The Persians do not seem to have prolonged their stay in north-western Iran. In the eighth century they were on the move and gradually advanced south-east by way of the Zagros foothills. How long they remained under Urartian domination is unknown. It is clear, however, that when they left the region of Urartu and before their final conquest of Fars, they had acquired a working knowledge of Urartian culture in general and in particular of certain architectural methods that we find employed at Pasargadae and Persepolis.

352 - VETULONIA. URARTIAN CAULDRON HANDLE
(8th-7th CENTURIES B.C.) — FLORENCE

Meanwhile Media had become the principal theatre of operations in the Assyrian conflict with Urartu and, under alternating Urartian and Assyrian rule, was included in the region, famed for its metal industry, which extended from the northern frontier of Elam to (perhaps) the shore of the Black Sea, and which contained a great variety of ethnical elements. Among these the Urartian element seems to have provided a favourable milieu for the development of the arts of the Iranians, who also studied to advantage those of the Assyro-Babylonians and Elamites. For, far from conflicting, the Urartian and Iranian arts complemented each other. Both alike drew inspiration from the ancient sources in Hither Asia, which the Hurrians, kinsmen of the Urartians, had so skilfully exploited, and together they created a *koine* in the field of metalworking, to which each made contributions of its own.

Even in their earliest settlements, the Iranians had imitated Urartian architecture. Thus we find an early instance of the terrace at Sialk; of cyclopean architecture in the terrace of Masjid-i-Sulaiman, and of rustic work in the walls at Pasargadae. Both cyclopean and rusticated masonry, employed in the temple of Haldis at Toprak-kale in Urartu, were unknown on the Plateau and in Mesopotamia, as was also the use of alternating black and white blocks of stone, common to the palaces at Pasargadae and the Toprak-kale temple.

The houses at Tushpa, the capital of Urartu, had (according to Moses of Chorene) several storeys, and a bronze plaque from Toprak-kale represents

presumably an edifice of this kind. Exceptional in the Ancient East, this type of building inspired the makers of the Ka'ba-i-Zardusht at Naqsh-i-Rustam. May not the two types of Urartian houses—those in the hot plains with a central courtyard and those in the inclement highlands with a central room (replacing the courtyard) round which the other rooms were grouped—lie at the origin of Achaemenian architecture, the lay-out of the second type pointing the way to that of the palaces at Persepolis? The gabled roof of Cyrus's tomb is seen to be of Urartian origin when we compare it with the temple of Musasir, an important political and religious centre which remained under Urartian domination down to the Sargonid period.

354 - TOPRAK-KALE. BRONZE PLAQUE REPRESENTING A URARTIAN BUILDING (8th-7th CENT. B.C.) — BRITISH MUSEUM, LONDON

2

355 - TOPRAK-KALE. LUG OF A CAULDRON (8th-7th CENTURIES B.C.) — BRITISH MUSEUM

We have spoken of the function of the animals in relief which figure on the Sialk, Khurvin, Hasanlu, Amlash and Luristan vases. They seem to have served the same purpose on the cauldrons and vases of Urartu, some of which have only an animal's head flanked by wings, while on others, as in Iran, the animal is gazing down into the recipient. Still more striking is the common usage by both peoples of handles or lugs having the form of 'sirens'[568]. The effigies (exactly similar) on the Luristan vessel and the one from Hamadan convey the same idea—of protection or surveillance—as does the winged male torso on Urartian cauldrons. Another point of interest is that these bearded heads wearing a typically Scythian pointed cap are bifacial, like the bronze votive 'idols' of Luristan which, in our opinion, represent the god Sraosha. The function of these tutelary beings was clearly indicated by the potters of Hasanlu and Luristan in a vase with a long beak-spout which is held by a figure of this kind. The bearded 'mermen' of Urartu have feminine

356 - VETULONIA. CAULDRON HANDLE: WINGED TWO-FACED FIGURE (8th-7th C. B.C.) — FLORENCE

357 - URARTU (?). LAMP STAND (8th-7th CENT. B.C.) — ERLANGEN

counterparts, and these, too, were taken over by the Iranians.

In both lands figures of men and animals served as stands for vases (usually in the form of tripods). From Urartu comes a female statuette standing on a tripod adorned with birds' heads; this type of tripod was also found in Luristan and resembles the one from Toprak-kale. Elsewhere, figures form the uprights of supports. When human limbs or bulls' feet are used for this purpose in Irano-Urartian tripods, the idea is the same—and it, too, came to Iran from Urartu.

The well-known bronze statuette representing a goddess, front face, seated on two horse protomes reminds us of the large part played by the horse in the political and economic life of Urartu. In the inscriptions of Urartian kings mention is made of 'ranches' in the highlands where horse-breeding was practised on a large scale, and it is highly probable that there were deities associated with the horse. In that case this bronze statuette may represent a *potnia hippon* (mistress of horses), a function also assigned to Athena in Greece, judging by a bronze discovered on the Acropolis of Athens. A similar statuette found in Luristan and showing two figures seated on horse protomes[569], has recently been acquired by the Maleki Collection.

In Iran, as in Greece, the deities concerned with horses were very varied. Poseidon was Athena's equestrian associate in Attica and they shared an altar in Athens. But at Olympia it was Ares who partnered Athena. Whether alone or in the company of a male deity, the 'horse goddess' is represented in Urartian art in exactly the same manner as in the art of Luristan; indeed it is sometimes hard to tell whether a given work comes from Urartu or Luristan.

358 - TRANSCAUCASIA. GODDESS SEATED ON TWO HORSE PROTOMES (8th-7th CENTURY B.C.) — BRITISH MUSEUM

2

We believe the worshipper statuettes found in the Toprak-kale temple to be imported Iranian bronzes, and would draw attention to the similarities between a Urartian bronze in the Louvre and the warrior statuette from Khurvin in the Maleki Collection. The latter's equipment —notably the crested helmet like those worn by the Urartian warriors represented on the Balawat gates— may have been of Urartian origin and adopted by the Iranians. A bronze helmet, very similar in its ornamentation, comes from a Luristan tomb.

As for the votive offerings, dedicated shields and quivers were placed in temples in Urartu, just as they were in Luristan (Temple of Surkh Dum). Chariots were also donated; Sargon II found thirty-three in the Urartian temple of Musasir, and one in gold, the work of a Bactrian master-craftsman, was included in the Oxus Treasure. In both arts the metal-workers employed the same techniques: the *cire*

359 - URARTU. BRONZE WARRIOR (8th-7th CENT. B.C.) — LOUVRE

perdue process for the cast bronzes and the thin plaques in repoussé work; the treatment of the eye in relief, surrounded by a raised rim; the filling of the wings of animals with hatchings; and the rendering of animals' fur with dots or thin short parallel lines. Of much interest is the special type of decoration on the helmet of Argistis, King of Urartu, with volutes set with monsters' heads, closely resembling the decoration of the Median gold scabbard in the Oxus Treasure. The use of the pectoral, too, we believe, originated in Urartu; one in bronze has recently been found in Luristan.

It was not only the arts and techniques of Urartu that were transmitted to the Iranians. Like King Rusas of Urartu who won his throne thanks to his horses and his chariot-driver, Darius too (if Herodotus can be trusted) won his crown and kingship thanks to his horses and a trick of his groom. Moreover, some of the traditions of Urartian administration were followed by the Persians. For it is not in Babylonian or Elamite texts but solely in those of Urartu that we find royal inscriptions divided into clauses, each beginning with 'Saith (name inserted) the King..,' the formula employed by the Achaemenids.

361 - VAN (ARMENIA). BRONZE CAULDRON HANDLE (8th-7th CENT. B.C.) — PRIVATE COLLECTION, PARIS

SCYTHIAN ART AND THE IRANO-URARTIAN 'KOINE'

Soviet archaeologists accept the view that the Timber-Frame Tomb (*Srubnaya*) culture which grew up west of the Volga about 1000-900 B.C., represents a proto-Scythian phase and replaced in South Russia the so-called Catacomb culture of the Cimmerians. The advance of the Scythians, however, did not cease with the occupation of these regions but continued in the direction of the Caucasus, for we find traces of Scythian occupation in Transcaucasia in the eighth and, perhaps even earlier, in the ninth century B.C. Here, to defend themselves against the kingdom of Urartu, the Scythians organized, it seems, a confederation of the nomad tribes and, reinforced by a new wave of invaders from South Russia, overran the regions south of Transcaucasia in the seventh century B.C. For the succeeding period historical records, in particular Assyrian texts, throw light on their activities.

We have already seen how, after allying themselves with the Medes during the revolt of Kashtariti (Khshathrita) in 673 B.C., the Scythians changed sides and joined forces with the Assyrians. Esarhaddon's letters to the oracle of the god Shamash mention the presence of their armies 'in the country of the Mannaians.' From this time (c. 674 B.C.) their fortunes seem to have been bound up with those of the kingdom of Mannai, south of Lake Urmia (present-day Kurdistan). This fact, vouched for by written records, supports the theory of a previous infiltration of the Scythian element before this nomad race finally established itself in the region. This would also account for the Scythian characteristics of the Hasanlu tomb.

— 360 - URARTU (?). STATUETTE OF A PRINCE
(8th-7th CENTURIES B.C.) — BOSTON

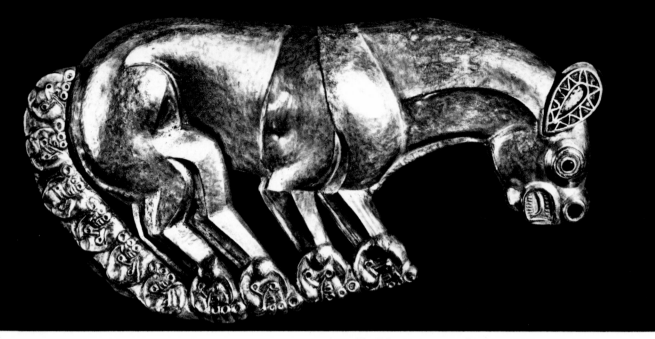

Around 660-659 B.C. the Mannaians, who had taken part in the Median revolt, were defeated by Assyria; their fortified towns, among them Ziwiyeh, were captured and the whole country was pillaged. This disaster was followed by an uprising of the populace, the king was assassinated and his son appealed to Assurbanipal for help against his own people, with what result we do not know. In any case the Assyrian king seems to have lost interest in the conquered territory, for he now abandoned it to the Scythians.

It seems probable that a Scythian kingdom had existed in Transcaucasia prior to the invasion in the seventh century. The possibility that the kingdom of Mannai was annexed by the Scythians after the events of 659 cannot be ruled out if we bear in mind, not only the political, geographical and ethnical relations of the peoples involved, but also the fact that the Scythians were allies of Assyria and as such defended the eastern flank of the Assyrian kingdom against the Medes. Moreover, Assyrian records refer to Partatua, the Scythian, as 'king' and not as 'leader,' the title assigned to his predecessor Ishpakai.

Well suited to the needs of nomad hordes of warrior horsemen, this region was used by the Scythians as a base of operations for their numerous campaigns. They not only harried Urartu but pressed forward into Cappadocia where they defeated the Cimmerians, allies of Urartu. In a series of devastating raids they attacked and pillaged Syria and Palestine and even reached the frontier of Egypt (Herodotus, i. 105). In 653-652 they launched an attack on the Medes, their eastern neighbours, and held them in vassalage for twenty-eight years. They were finally driven out of Media in or about 625. There are conflicting views regarding the outcome of this defeat. We incline to the view that the Scythian kingdom continued to exist in the region south of Lake Urmia until it was annexed by the Medes some time before 590 B.C., after the Medes had brought their war with Lydia to a successful end.

Thus from the historical viewpoint the Scythian civilization had four phases. The scene of the first was the region north of the Caucasus; of the second, Transcaucasia; of the third, Kurdistan (the land of Mannai); of the fourth, the Kuban valley, north of the Caucasus, and the lower reaches of the Dnieper.

That the best known Scythian art is that of the fourth phase is due to the discovery, many years ago, of the Scythian royal tombs in the Kuban valley (Kelermes, Kostromskaya Stanitza) and on the Dnieper (Litoi Kurgan and the Melgunov Treasure).

The oldest of them (Kelermes) can hardly be dated earlier than 580-570 B.C. These barrows consist of large chambers roofed with wooden beams in which the dead king was buried together with members of his court and his horses, as well as an abundance of grave goods composed of weapons and objects in precious metals.

Scythian animal art of this period already has a fully developed iconography of its own. The characteristic Scythian motif is a stag in a special posture, with its antlers lying flat upon its back, its neck stretched forward, legs folded beneath the body and pointed hoofs set one above the other. This is undoubtedly a cultic animal or symbol, a survival from the remote time when stags were used as mounts. Other animals are represented: the feline figuring on the edge of a plaque along with stags whose feet, eyes and ears are stylized into circles; a 'beakhead' bird; and another feline curled up cat-wise.

363 - KOSTROMSKAYA STANITZA. GORYTUS ORNAMENT IN GOLD (6th CENTURY B.C.) — HERMITAGE

303

Here a tendency to naturalism is counteracted by the magical or symbolic function of these animals. Indeed it would seem that the origins of this animal style were of a religious order, linking up with totems and an animist ideology. The motifs are always set out vertically or horizontally. Though the animals are not in overt action, somehow they convey a sense of tension. Whether in an elongated or a curled-up pose, they give an impression of suddenly arrested motion. For the iconography of this phase is predominantly static. The way in which the natural outlines of bodies are split up into several double surfaces joined by a ridge makes for abstraction. It may well have derived from a technique of carving wood, bone or horn that was practised when this art originated.

Along with specifically Scythian images, and often on the same objects, we find others taken from the iconography of the arts of western Asia: animals in heraldic poses, and hybrid creatures. Some peculiarities in their execution show that Greek artists had a hand in them; this applies, for instance, to the Kelermes mirror, in which Scythian, Asiatic and Greek elements are intermingled.

It has been suggested that in the bone carvings found near Kerch, at Temir Gora, we have examples of the Scythian art of the first phase. While their date, 650 B.C., may seem relatively late, it is generally agreed that these types of Scythian imagery must have been end-products of a long development.

364-365 - KELERMES. IRON SWORD AND
GOLD AXE (6th CENTURY B.C.)
HERMITAGE, LENINGRAD

366 - (A) KELERMES. SILVER MIRROR (6th CENT. B.C.) (B & C) TEMIR GORA. HARNESS PIECES (7th CENT. B.C.) — HERMITAGE

Their burial practices throw light on the customs of the Scythians during their sojourn in Transcaucasia (our 'second phase'). In a tomb near Lake Sevan the bodies of thirteen sacrificed 'slaves' were found alongside that of a local chieftain. Other tombs with similar sacrifices of men and horses have been discovered at Hellenendorf in Azerbaijan. It should be noted that the bronze swords and ribbed black pottery figuring among the grave goods have much in common with the objects brought to light at Khurvin.

BLACK SEA
COLCHIS
CASPIAN
40°
45°
40°
40°

Khiehuni
Khaldi
Lake
Sevan
Argistikhinili
Teishebaini
(Karmir Blur)
Erivan
Dzovinar
Menuahiniti
Irepuni (Arine-Berd)
Erzerum
Mt Ararat
Araxes
U R A R T U
BIAINA
Arasani
Lake Van
Toprak-kale
N
A
I
R
I
Tushpa (Van)
Melitene
Mt Nal
Lake
Urmia
Tigris
Great Zab
Mt Nibur
MUSASIR
LAND OF MANNAI
ASSYRIA
Mt Simirrua
Nineveh
Hamadan
Kalakh
(Nimrud)
Mt Kallar
M E D I A
Aleppo
Euphrates
Khabur
Little Zab
Assur
PARSUA
Diyala
35°
35°
SYRIAN
DESERT
Tadmor
(Palmyra)
40°
45°
LURISTAN

367 - THE KINGDOM OF URARTU

Once the Scythian tribes had secured a solid foothold in Transcaucasia, east and north-east of the frontiers of Urartu, they came into direct contact with that kingdom, and Urartian inscriptions mention the presence of these dangerous neighbours. To defend themselves against Scythian aggression, especially in the second half of the eighth century B.C. when Urartu was having difficulty in maintaining its ascendancy in northern Syria and eastern Asia Minor, the Urartians built a string of fortresses along their eastern frontier. One of these, Teishebaini (Karmir Blur), has been excavated by a Soviet expedition and many vestiges of Scythian objects of the period before the capture of this fortress by the Scythians (in the early sixth century B.C.) have been found. However, the relations between Scythians and Urartians were not of an exclusively military order; the nomads came under the civilizing influence of their more cultured neighbours, widely renowned for their arts and metal industry. Piotrovsky, who led the Karmir Blur expedition, did not fail to note the part played by Urartu in shaping Scythian art and culture, and the Ziwiyeh tomb confirmed the findings of the Russian archaeologists.

We shall now turn to the third or 'Asiatic' phase of Scythian art. In our survey of Median art we drew attention to the mixed character of the rock-hewn tomb at Kizkapan, which is obviously a replica in a different medium of

306

one of the Scythian timber-frame barrows found on so many sites from South Russia to Transcaucasia. This suggests that the Ziwiyeh tomb is not the only one assignable to the Scythians. We have no direct knowledge of the structure of the Ziwiyeh tomb, but some fragments of the sarcophagus have survived, enough to give an idea of its form and of most of its decorations. It was shaped like a flat-bottomed bath-tub. Incised on the broad raised rim riveted to the sides was a continuous motif representing two processions. The vertical joints were secured by riveted bands decorated with ibexes standing on marguerites. Sarcophagi of this type, now in the British Museum and at Birmingham, were found at Ur. Others, in terracotta, also composed of two parts (which, however, were not joined), have been found at Babylon—they date to the Neo-Babylonian period—and also at Assur, where they are described as 'post-Assyrian.' The crucial question is whether the Ziwiyeh sarcophagus was commissioned by the Scythian king and made in an Assyrian or Babylonian workshop, or whether it came from a royal Assyrian tomb which had been looted at some undetermined date. If the first alternative were proved, it could be dated to the period of Scythian domination, earlier, that is to say, than 625 B.C. If, however, the second alternative is correct, the tomb must be assigned to a date later than 612, the year that witnessed the downfall of the Assyrian empire and the plundering of its great cities.

368 - UR. BRONZE SARCOPHAGUS (7th CENT. B.C.) — BRITISH MUSEUM

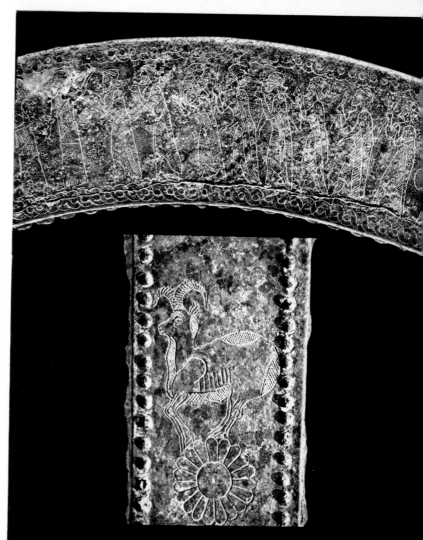

369 - ZIWIYEH. EDGE AND PLAQUE OF A SARCOPHAGUS (7th CENTURY B.C.) — METROPOLITAN MUSEUM

7

When discussing the Ziwiyeh pectorals we suggested that they were the products of a workshop influenced by Urartian art. There is no trace of the use of pectorals in Assyria and Babylonia, whereas they figure frequently in the arts of Urartu. A pectoral adorns the breast of the bronze statuette in the Berlin Museum; and one is hung below the neck of the bronze sphinx from Toprak-kale; another is worn by the Urartian 'siren' found in Etruria[568]. It was doubtless during their sojourn in Transcaucasia that the Scythians adopted the Urartian practice of wearing pectorals; this is borne out by the half-moon shaped bronze pectoral found in a Scythian tomb at Beshtau. A similar bronze pectoral from Luristan has recently been found.

Not all the pectorals worn in Urartu were given the form of crescents. On the bronze handle of a cauldron in the Marquis de Vogüé Collection are two winged 'sirens' whose chests have rectangular slots perforated with mortise-holes which evidently served to fix to the figures inlaid plaques of bone or precious metal. Presumably these plaques simulated rectangular pectorals (much as in the carving of another siren we find the representation of a crescent-shaped pectoral). An example of the rectangular type of pectoral was found at Hasanlu in a tomb which we believe to be a Scythian's, in view of the sacrificed horses it contained and the stag's head depicted on the pectoral, the stag being a characteristic motif of Scythian iconography.

370 - TOPRAK-KALE. STATUETTE WITH PECTORAL (8th-6th CENTURIES B.C.) — BERLIN

The Assyrian kings are never shown wearing pectorals. Exceptionally, an amber statuette of a prince in the Boston Museum has on its chest a gold pectoral on which eight-petalled rosettes alternate, on seven registers, with chevrons pointing in different directions. Like the pectoral of the bronze statuette from Toprak-kale in the Berlin Museum, on which are five cupules which once contained incrustations, the Boston statuette was perhaps embellished with precious stones.

The treatment of the Boston figure, whose skilful modelling shows that the sculptor wished to create the illusion of a living being, is quite different from that of Assyrian sculpture in the round. It may well be that this was the work of a Urartian craftsman who, in giving the figure a cylindrical aspect, was conforming to Assyrian precedents. In any case the 'column-statue' type of figure is also found in Urartian statuettes.

Ziwiyeh is the only Scythian royal tomb to show that pectorals were in use among the Scythians. None was found in the richly furnished Scythian graves of South Russia dating to the period when the Scythians had retreated north of the Caucasus. The only explanation of the presence of the Ziwiyeh pectoral is that the buried chieftain had been in close touch with Urartu and had adopted its customs. There is no knowing whether he commissioned it and had it decorated with themes familiar to him, or (as seems less probable in view of the distinctively Scythian elements) if it was a

371 - TOPRAK-KALE. SPHINX (8th-7th CENT. B.C.) — BRITISH MUSEUM

372 - HASANLU. BRONZE PLAQUE: STAG'S HEAD (8th CENTURY B.C.) — TEHERAN MUSEUM

373 - CAERE. PECTORAL (8th-7th C. B.C.) — MUSEO GREGORIANO, ROME

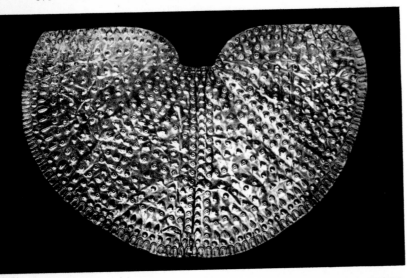

374 - DALBOKI. PECTORAL (5th C. B.C.) — ASHMOLEAN MUSEUM, OXFORD

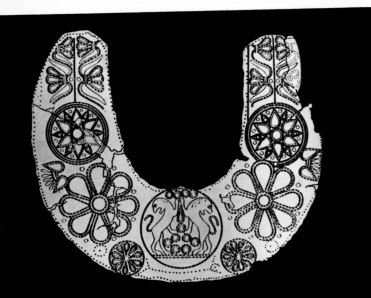

gift. This much is certain: that the Scythians of South Russia never took to wearing such ornaments.

Things were different in the western world. Pectorals in precious metals have been found in Etruscan tombs in Italy, and it would seem that only Etruscans wore them. The gold pectoral from Caere (Regolini-Galassi Tomb) carries decorations on eighteen registers, consisting of rows of human beings and animals, mostly winged and treated in much the same spirit as at Ziwiyeh. From the Etruscans the pectoral made its way into the Roman army and that it was also adopted by the western Scythians is proved by the pectoral of Dalboki (in Bulgaria), datable to the fifth century B.C. A rigorously geometric arrangement of circles, olives and languets is combined with animals' heads, viewed from above, in quite the Scythian manner. The gold pectoral from Trebenishchei appears to be an earlier work.

The great diversity, not to say incongruity, of the decorative elements on the Ziwiyeh pectorals, to which we now revert, sets some difficult problems. This crescent-shaped pectoral, hung on a chain when worn, has two concentric registers, edged with a frieze of pine-cones, and separated by a braid. The sacred tree in the centre of each register differs markedly from the tree that figured in Assyrian art, especially from the ninth century onward, and is distinctively Urartian. Also the attitude of the ibex and the bull flanking it is not Assyrian. The bull-man in the

375 - TREBENISHCHEI. PECTORAL (6th CENTURY B.C.) — SOFIA MUSEUM

3

posture of an Atlas figures in Assyrian art, but is always upholding a weight. The wings of all these hybrid creatures have the same straightness and rigidity that we find in those of Urartian winged beings. Sphinxes with 'aprons' sometimes figured in Assyrian art, which took them over from the Phoenicians, but here their 'aprons' are made of feathers with vertical striations and differ from those on the pectoral.

When we turn to the human faces of some of these fantastic beings, our difficulties increase. The face of the sphinx on the highest register is round and plump; the bulging nostrils, the nose-ridge and forehead form a single straight line; far from showing any trace of Oriental naturalism, the ear is given the form of a volute. This device is also employed—but here the volute is double—for the *lamassu* (human-headed bull) following the sphinx and, departing from the Assyrian tradition (retained in Achaemenian art), the *lamassu* has human ears, not the pointed ones of animals. Its body, like that of the Atlas bullman, is not of the Oriental type, but long and slender, resembling that of the small seated sphinx in the lowest register.

The same peculiarities have been stressed by Kunze in his study of the orientalizing Cretan bronzes, and he sees in them an early indication of Greek workmanship. The headdress of the sphinx in the top register—a round cap with two volutes above it—is a characteristic element of the decoration of the bronze bands of shields from Olympia.

376 - ZIWIYEH. (A) PECTORAL (7th CENT. B.C.)
(B, C) DETAILS — TEHERAN MUSEUM

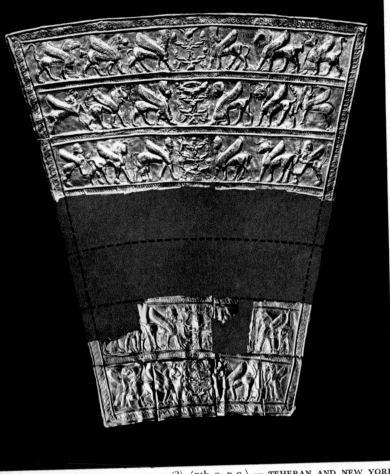

Turning to the pectoral in the Metropolitan Museum we find still more anomalies. Three of the registers are in a good state of preservation. Seemingly by the same hand as the pectoral described above, it has, however, a trapezoidal form. On each register figure two identical processions on either side of a sacred tree, but differing from one register to another. The same type of composition is found in Achaemenian art, in the decorations of the Apadana at Persepolis. There is nothing Oriental in the heads of the sphinxes, particularly those on the second register; they resemble, rather, the head on a cauldron handle from Delphi which Kunze classifies as a Greek work. The *lamassu* are bearded but without moustaches.

The artist's flagrant incomprehension of the subject is evident above all in the postures and placing of the winged ibexes on the second register and the rearing sphinxes on the third; given their attitudes, they should have flanked the central tree, instead of coming at the tail-end of the processions. True, the shape of the lower part of the pectorals, progressively narrowing down towards the bottom, allowed less and less space for the processions but this did not necessitate any change in the order of the animals.

On a fragmentary pectoral in the Teheran Museum (only the two lower registers remain, much damaged and smaller than the one described above) the artist makes a mistake in placing the winged genius with the head of a bird of prey (who, as on Assyrian bas-reliefs, holds a pine-cone) at the rear of the procession. The function of this genius, as his gesture shows, is to fertilize the palm-tree, not to sprinkle the scorpion-tail of the winged lion in front of him.

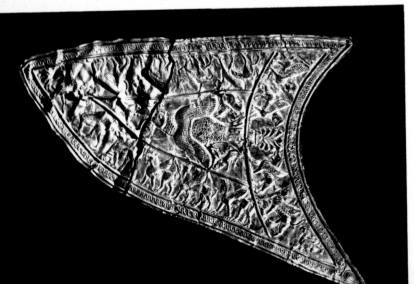

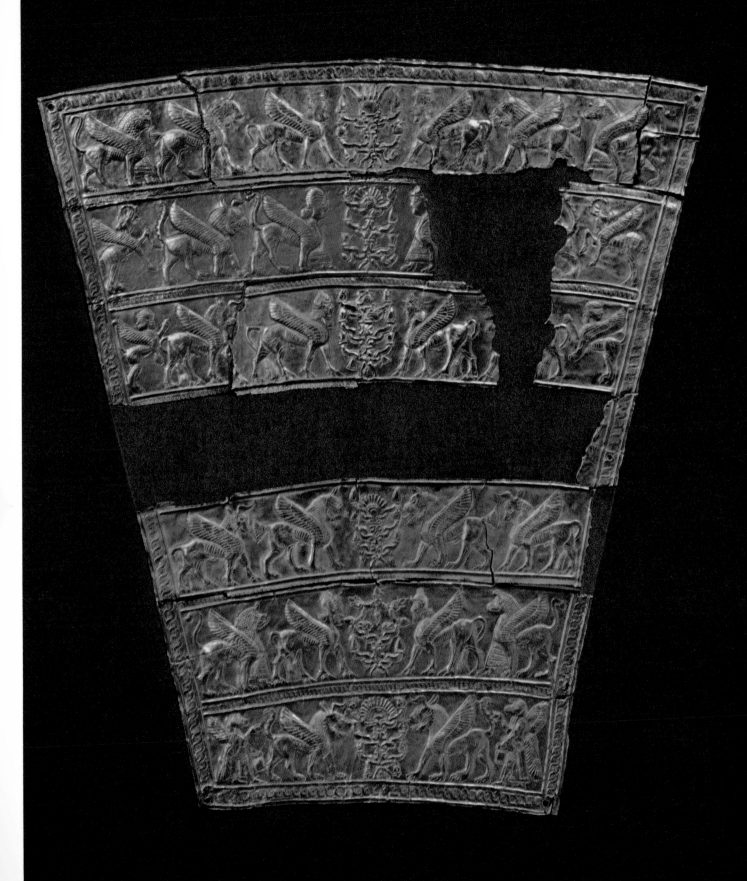

380 - (A) CAUCASUS (B) LURISTAN. PECTORALS (8th-7th CENT. B.C.) — PIATIGORSK MUSEUM AND PRIVATE COLL., TEHERAN

The peculiarities and mistakes apparent in the three Ziwiyeh pectorals suggest that they were made by artists who were subjected to Assyrian and Urartian influences. These artists, however, do not appear to have belonged, by birth and background, to either of these two great art traditions, though their debt to that of Urartu is unmistakable.

We have Urartian work in the much-damaged fragments in thick gold of a cauldron decorated with griffins and lions similar to those on the bronze cauldron from the Barberini Tomb, which the goldsmith obviously copied. In this context our readers' attention may be drawn to the objects discussed at an earlier page and assigned by us to 'the Urartian group.' The gold plaque of a belt in the Asiatic Scythian style, shared between the Teheran Museum and the University Museum of Philadelphia, has some distinctively Urartian features. The ogival arch, in particular, deriving from a 'continuous design' employed in Western Asia as early as the second millennium B.C., enjoyed a great vogue in Urartu. We find this motif incised on a stone slab from Toprak-kale[570] and, in a lay-out like that of the Ziwiyeh belt, it figures on a Urartian bronze belt[571] found at Zakim in the Kars region. There is also a winged archer, who reappears on a Urartian belt from Gusci[572] and also on the sheath of a Scythian *akinakes* from the Melgunov Treasure, where he is metamorphosed into various hybrid beings. He also figures on a sword sheath from Kelermes, which seems to be the work of an artist who, while trying to keep in step with the art of Western Asia, has garbled the traditional iconography by introducing uncalled-for complications.

The posture of the lion on the Zakim belt, with forelegs stretched forth horizontally, recurs on the Gusci belt, and we have already drawn attention to it on the silver chamfron from Ziwiyeh. It is also found on the saddle-cloth of the rhyton from Maku. This was, we believe, a Urartian speciality. Noteworthy, too, is the similar stylization of the age-old motif of the Tree of Life[573-579] in the art of Urartu and that of the Scythians. This is illustrated by the inlaid bone plaque in which the ogee-shaped branches of the Tree of Life are tipped with pomegranates and pine-cones.

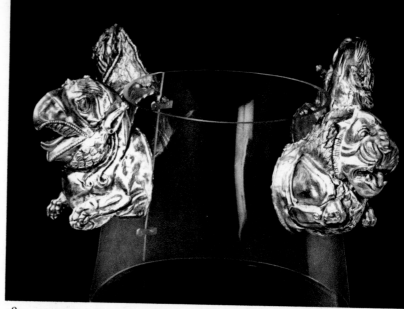

381 - ZIWIYEH. LUGS OF CAULDRONS (7th CENT. B.C.) — TEHERAN

382 - PALESTRINA (BARBERINI TOMB). CAULDRON (8th-7th C. B.C.) — VILLA GIULIA, ROME

383 - ZIWIYEH. PLAQUE (7TH CENT. B.C.) — METROPOLITAN MUSEUM 384 - LURISTAN. PINHEAD (8th-7th C. B.C.) — PRIVATE COLL., PARIS

The connection between Scythian art and the art of Luristan has been called in question. A study of the Ziwiyeh Treasure justifies a reconsideration of the problem.

A handsome gold plaque from Ziwiyeh (in the Metropolitan Museum), trapezoidal in form, has decorations inspired by Assyrian themes but is clearly not by an Assyrian hand. The column with a huge palmette sprouting from it has an Aeolian (?) capital much resembling the one on a mirror from Kelermes dating to the first quarter of the sixth century B.C. (It also figures on the frescoes dating to the second half of that century which have been brought to light at Gordion.) Though deriving from models current in Assyria in the seventh century, the two rampant lions with a single head differ from Assyrian animal art in the emphasis on details (e.g. the fur on the animals' backs and bellies, the stylization of the ribs) and by such 'exotic' features as slotted eyes ending in volutes and wings treated in the Urartian technique. The marked analogies between this plaque and the Luristan bronzes prove that the craftsman was familiar with the latter and may even have been an inhabitant of that region. The animals' plaited fur resembles the braided hair we see on Luristan pinheads with a human face in the centre.

316

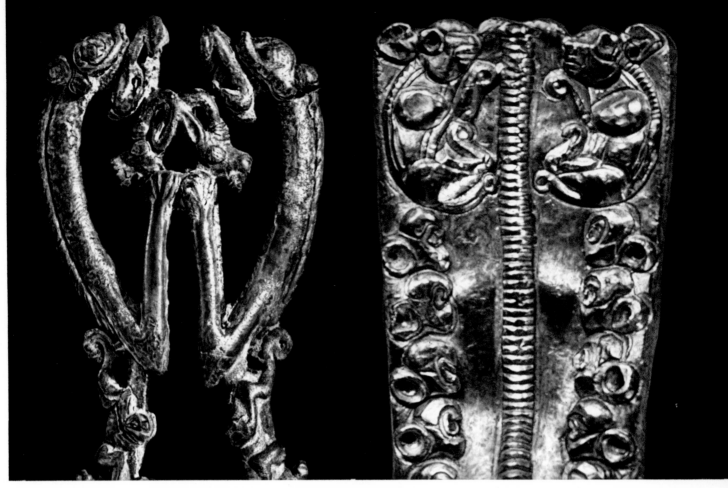

385 - LURISTAN. IDOL (8th-7th CENT. B.C.) — LOUVRE   386 - ZIWIYEH. BELT (7th CENT. B.C.) — PHILADELPHIA

The resemblance is even more striking when we compare this gold plaque from Ziwiyeh with a pinhead on which is engraved the same motif (relatively rare in Assyrian iconography) of two lions with a single head. Here we find the same treatment of the mane in hatched lozenges and of the fur in tresses as in one of the Ziwiyeh lions. The affinities are too pronounced to be regarded as accidental. Nor are these exceptional cases.

It is also interesting to compare the handling of a horse's head on a Luristan bit with that of a Scythian horse, or the handling of a Luristan stag with that of the Kostromskaya stag. On the Luristan bits we have an early example of the 'zoomorphic juncture' typical of so much Scythian art, parts of another animal being added to the body of the animal represented. The birds' heads bordering a plaque from Ziwiyeh reappear on a diadem from Luristan. And may not the small animals which, in Luristan, went to form the bodies of the large ones, have been the original idea from which the later figurations of Scythian art developed? The iron dagger from Ziwiyeh is merely a replica of the iron sword from Luristan. Pins with 'pomegranate' heads and two cross-bars, and fibulae without springs, are common to Ziwiyeh and Luristan. Moreover the Ziwiyeh pottery shows how closely allied were the two cultures.

We agree with Schefold that 'the Luristan finds help us to understand more clearly the essential elements of the Scythian style, unaffected by Greek influence.'

The compound bow represented on a Luristan belt supports the view that the Lurs, Medes and Persians were closely allied. It is of the type found at Baghuz (Yrzi) on the left bank of the Euphrates, and dates to the Parthian period. It is also found at Susa and Persepolis on several Achaemenian monuments depicting the king's archers. The introduction of this improved type of bow has accordingly been attributed to the Medes and Persians. But the hunting scene on the belt from Luristan proves that the compound bow, with the ends of the arms curving forward, was already in use among the Lurs.

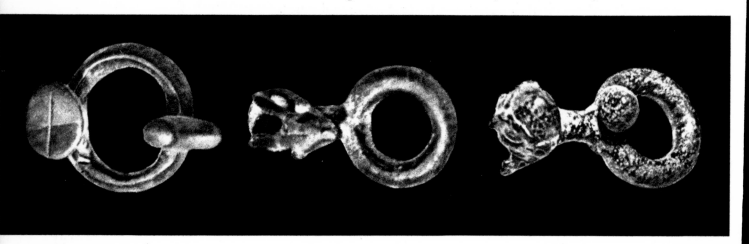

389 - LURISTAN. ARCHERS' RINGS FOR BENDING THEIR BOWS (8th-7th C. B.C.) — MUSEUM AND PRIVATE COLL., TEHERAN

The bas-relief on the Kizkapan tomb shows a slightly different type of bow, which also figures on a gold sheath from the Oxus Treasure where it is carried by a Median prince. This was the 'Scythian' or 'Cupid's' bow, known to the ancients as the type of bow used on the shores of the Black Sea (Strabo, ii. 5. 22; Ammianus Marcellinus, xxii. 8. 37; Pliny, *Hist. Nat.* iv. 24). Its extremities are turned back to form a hook, while the central part curves sharply inward. By reason of its smallness this weapon was chiefly used by riders, and it was adopted by the Median cavalry. The larger (earlier) type of bow was usually carried by foot-soldiers or by warriors in chariots.

The use of this new bow, far harder to draw and bend, led to the invention of a special ring, in bronze, silver, sometimes gold. Rings of this kind have been discovered over a wide area, extending from Western Asia to the frontiers of Chinese Turkestan. None precedes the coming of the Iranians to the Plateau which now bears their name. The fact, moreover, that most of them come from Luristan goes to show that this new accessory was, like the new type of bow, an Iranian invention. These bows were stiffer and harder to manipulate, but gave the arrow much greater driving force than that provided by the ordinary, more flexible bow. This is why great kingdoms like Assyria and Urartu sought to include in their armies, whether as allies or as mercenaries, the famous Iranian bowmen — who usually ended up by

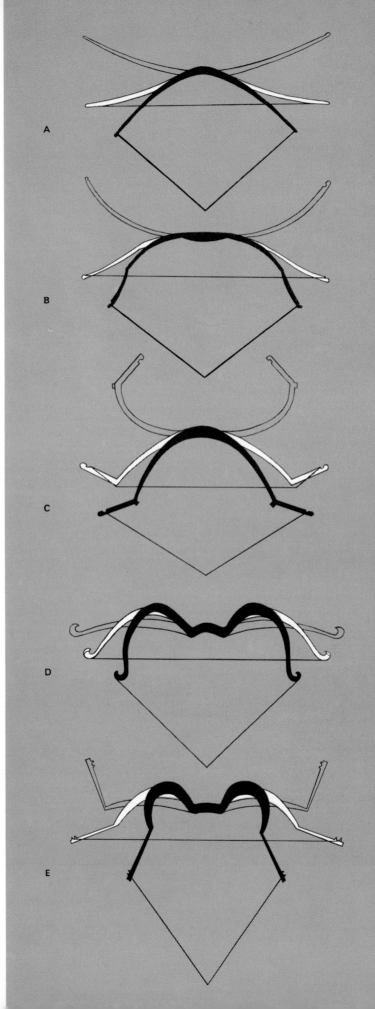

390 - TYPES OF BOWS. (A) ASSYRIAN (B) FROM YRZI (C) FROM TURKESTAN (D) SCYTHIAN (E) SASSANIAN

391 - LURISTAN. VASE (8th-7th C. B.C.) — PRIVATE COLL.

vanquishing their former employers or overlords. Indeed it was thanks to this weapon that they became the masters of the ancient world.

In the Ziwiyeh pottery we have yet further evidence of the basic homogeneity of the Medo-Scythian-Cimmerian civilization whose evolution we have traced and whose beginnings we assign to the tenth century B.C. The shape and imagery of the vases retained their funerary significance and varied but little on the Plateau during these four centuries.

Meanwhile the influence of metalwork on the forms of pottery steadily intensified. In a red terracotta vase from Ziwiyeh the beak-spout frankly imitates the foreparts of a bird, which had been merely hinted at in the Sialk vases. Beak-spouts with an open channel were still attached to vases of a traditional shape, but we now find two hands clasping the vase on each side of the belly—a curious motif to which we drew attention apropos of a piece from Luristan. More elaborate modelling is found on a shoe-shaped pot—this was a Khurvin creation—with the seams on its upper part indicated by incised lines. A sauce-boat fitted with a strainer has a handle on the side with a thumb-rest shaped as an animal's head; the body is grooved, with alternating stripes of red and light buff. There are also some elegant bottles with fluted bellies, a ring of beads on the shoulders and two loops by which to hang them. We have already stressed the importance of the lug on a dish whose animal style establishes the

392 - ZIWIYEH. LION (7th C. B.C.) — PRIVATE COLL., PARIS 393 - PRINIAS. LATE GEOMETRIC LION — PRIVATE COLL., BERLIN

existence of a Scythian type of pottery: round eyes, curling muzzle, heart-shaped ears, paws ending in volutes and a body made of two bulging surfaces. The inner edge of the dish is painted purplish red. Here the meticulous execution keeps very close to that of the metal-workers, but besides plastic ornamentation in the round, in relief or incised, the decoration includes painting, though always on a very small scale.

To the same family of pottery belong two modelled, hollow lions' heads, cut short at the neck, which may have served as *umbones* on simulated shields (as in Greece) or as handles on cauldrons. And to it also belongs an assortment of almost a hundred and fifty terracotta beads in the Teheran Museum, relics perhaps of necklets worn by immolated soldiers or menials.

Some monochrome and polychrome rhytons in glazed terracotta link up with the group of objects from Ziwiyeh. Bahrami assigns them to the hoard itself, whereas Godard describes them merely as 'coming from Ziwiyeh or near by.' For obvious reasons attributions of objects found in unscientifically conducted excavations can never be wholly relied on. Nevertheless Bahrami's positive and Godard's vaguer statements carry weight, especially if we preclude the notion of a cache (in which it seems unlikely that pottery would be included). These objects point to the existence of a flourishing ceramic industry; in view of their abundance, their dimensions and the craftsmen's skilful handling of colour, they occupy a place in the grave goods of the Ziwiyeh tomb midway between the royal table-service in precious metal and the finely worked articles in earthenware which presumably belonged to members of the court or servants buried with their master.

394 - ZIWIYEH. DUCK RHYTON (7th CENT. B.C.) — TEHERAN MUSEUM

We may assign the rhytons to four separate groups determined by their forms.

Form A. — Made in the shape of a duck, the rhyton has a hole in its back for filling and an outlet pierced in its beak for pouring out the contents. The ground colour of the glazing is dark violet; the breast and scale-like breast-feathers are violet and yellow; the feathers of the wings, alternately brown and yellow, are separated by dark maroon lines; the tail has streaks of brown and green.

Form B. — Here we have only the animal's head, its neck being prolonged by a vertical container—clearly a prototype of the Achaemenian gold rhytons in the Hamadan Treasure. This animal, the saiga, is a 'speciality' of the Scythian artefacts found at Ziwiyeh.

Made of very fine highly polished red clay, it was given an all-over coat of blue-green glaze. The eyes are black, the horns red and dark green. The modelling is simple, but expert; the circular eyes have not the parallel folds demarcating the tops of the eyes of the other animals in the group. Two hollow lines join the eyes to the nostrils and two small holes figure just below the places where the horns begin. The ear, in low relief, is pressed against the head.

To the same group may be assigned, in virtue of its form, a damaged rhyton with a bull's head in which the slanting movement is particularly marked. What little has survived of the glazing shows it was originally green or blue.

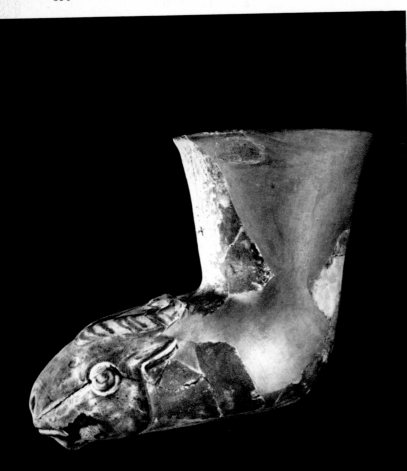

395 - ZIWIYEH. RHYTON: SAIGA'S HEAD (7th CENTURY B.C.) — TEHERAN MUSEUM

3

396 - ZIWIYEH. RHYTON: SAIGA'S HEAD 397 - ZIWIYEH. RHYTON: MOUFFLON'S HEAD (7th CENTURY B.C.) — TEHERAN MUSEUM

Form C. — To this group belongs what is the most remarkable rhyton from the artistic viewpoint.   It has the shape of a goblet widening out at the mouth, the lower part consisting of a moufflon's head. Despite the damage it has undergone, the globular, protruding eyes, framed in a nest of creases, have lost nothing of their expressive power.   The eyebrows stretch to the root of the ears, laid flat beneath the curves described by the majestic sweep of the horns. Fleece is suggested by evenly distributed rows of beads.   Finally the potter has ingeniously simulated ring and clasp fastenings, with two rivets, as used on metal rhytons.   Technically akin to this rhyton is one with a saiga's head, in yellow, brightly polished clay.

398 - ZIWIYEH. GLAZED JAR (7th CENT. B.C.) — TEHERAN MUSEUM

Beside these rhytons were found two small glazed terracotta jars. On the shoulder is a rosette with pointed petals, alternately pale buff and light green. The body is adorned with a band three inches wide on which the same motif figures twice: ibexes kneeling on each side of a rosette with thirteen petals of the same hue as those on the shoulder. The rest of the vessel is dark green. A jar of the same size, with the same decoration in almost the same colours, was found in a tomb at Assur dating to the end of the Assyrian, possibly to the post-Assyrian period. Its contents, partly burnt human bones, showed it to be a funeral urn. The close resemblance between these vessels suggests that, if the Ziwiyeh jars were not actually made by Assyrians, they can at any rate be assigned to craftsmen of the same school.

In this case all the rhytons we are discussing, whose exceptionally high quality suggests the work of those great experts in animal art, the Assyrians, may be given the same attribution.

The animal-head rhyton used as a drinking vessel seems to have been in high favour in Media in the eighth and seventh centuries B.C.

A bronze rhyton found south of Lake Urmia has recently been acquired by the Foroughi Collection, Teheran. The gazelle's head has a plain bronze lining on the inner side, and a thick coat of bitumen separates the lining from the outer casing. The eyes and eyebrows had been inlaid with precious stones or ivory. Framed

399 - NORTH-WEST IRAN. RHYTON: GAZELLE'S HEAD (8th-7th CENTURIES B.C.) PRIVATE COLLECTION, TEHERAN

between the lyre-shaped horns in high relief, worked over with a burin, is an engraved motif representing a stylized sacred tree flanked by ibexes. Three birds are perched on the top branches. The lip of the rhyton is bordered with two braided lines with, between them, two rows of ibexes which meet above the tree. A collaret of curls forming a double spiral, beginning at the root of the ear, runs round the lower jaw as on one of the rhytons described above. Here

400 - LURISTAN. GOLD EAR-RING (8th-7th CENT. B.C.) — TEHERAN

we have one of the handsomest specimens of this relatively rare type of ceremonial drinking vessel. Whether the work is Assyrian or Urartian we cannot say. Two of its features argue in favour of the second alternative: the two rows of ibexes, resembling the rows of animals on some Urartian shields, and the way the birds' crests are rendered—by a rectangle of wavy lines across the forehead and enclosing the eyes—much as the bulls' heads are treated on a Urartian cauldron.

That the gazelle's head motif, so frequent in the bronzes and in their imitations by the potters, was also employed by goldsmiths is proved by a gold ear-ring from Luristan now in the Foroughi Collection. It is yet another instance of the fondness of the Medians in the seventh century B.C. for this eminently graceful creature. The lion also figured among the animal forms employed in rhytons of this group. One of them, made of thin bronze leaf, was found in 1957 south of Lake Urmia, in other words in the heart of the Mannaian region. Judging by the execution, which is much inferior to that of the two above-mentioned rhytons, it must have been of local manufacture.

In the Mannaian rhyton with a lion's head we have but a pale reflection of the art obtaining west of this small kingdom.

401 - NORTH-WEST IRAN. RHYTON: BRONZE LION'S HEAD (7th CENTURY B.C.) — TEHERAN

5

Form D. — To this fourth group belongs the rhyton shaped like an animal's horn, found at Kalar Dasht, and ending with the head of a gazelle (or ibex).

During the period we are concerned with here, rhytons were in common use throughout Media. The fact that they were given four forms and executed in gold, bronze and terracotta (plain or glazed) proves the popularity of this type of drinking vessel with all classes of the Iranian population. Did the Ziwiyeh duck, the Maku horse and the Susa horse perpetuate a tradition already existing as early as the fourth millennium among the potters on the Plateau? There is no knowing, since no elements exist to bridge the gap of nearly three millennia between the known examples.

The three other types of rhyton are of more recent origin; their appearance on the Plateau cannot have been previous to the coming of the Iranians. In groups A and C we have 'true' rhytons, since they have a second aperture located in the animal's mouth or breast. The other two, B and D, form, typologically, a class apart.

We may surmise that Form C, having the shape of a goblet with an animal's head at the base, was the prototype. It came into use in Assyria at the end of the eighth century B.C. at the time when the Sargonids were steadily forcing their way towards the Plateau. Form B appears to have developed out of Form C, and the Achaemenians subsequently adopted it.

402 - KALAR DASHT. RHYTON: GAZELLE'S HEAD (?) (7th-6th CENTURIES B.C.) — TEHERAN MUSEUM

Some years ago Svoboda published a study of the origins of the rhyton. Let us hope it will be followed up, so as to include the many newly discovered pieces stemming from Iran, where this form of drinking vessel seems to have been particularly appreciated.

The significance of some of the elements of the grave furniture of the Scythian tomb at Ziwiyeh still awaits solution. For despite the recent discovery of texts throwing light on certain historical events of the period, the information they provide relates almost exclusively to the part played by the two great powers, Assyria and Babylonia, less to the activities of Urartu, and tells us next to nothing about those of the Medo-Scythians. Yet it was precisely this last group, it seems, that did most to bring about the downfall of Assyria and Urartu— just as less than a century later the Persians played a leading part in the fall of Babylon.

403 - ASSYRIAN BAS-RELIEF REPRESENTING A BANQUET

First of our problems is the date of the Ziwiyeh Treasure and the stylistic factors discussed above provide considerable latitude in this respect. It seems most unlikely that any of the objects assignable to Assyrian workshops can be dated earlier than the eighth century B.C., and this gives us a *terminus post quem*. The *terminus ante quem* is furnished by the Scythian tombs of Kelermes, in the Kuban, considered the earliest ones in South Russia; in an exhaustive study of the subject Maximova dates them to about 580-570. We had suggested 625 as the terminal date, but Barnett is inclined to fix this as late as 600 and Piotrovsky even later. If the year 600 is accepted, we must assume that Cyaxares' liberation of Media from the Scythians (c. 625) did not involve the collapse of the Scythians as a military power, and that if the Scythians joined in the coalition which brought about the downfall of Assyria, they did so not in the capacity of mere auxiliaries of the Medes but as their allies. On this assumption the Scythians must have retained their kingdom, which included the ancient land of Mannai and in which the tomb of a rich and powerful ruler, one of the successors of Madyes, was brought to light. Thus something in the nature of an enclave must have remained, for several decades, embedded in the western

part of Media, and survived until 600 B.C. at the earliest. In short, the Medo-Scythian symbiosis must have lasted a good deal longer than used to be supposed.

However this may be, there can be no doubt that when the Scythians established themselves in Western Asia—in Transcaucasia to begin with, then south of Lake Urmia—they enriched their art with all that the Irano-Urartian *koine* had to offer. For the art of Urartu and that of Luristan furnished the staple elements of Scythian art and affected it more profoundly than did Assyrian art, many specimens of which figure among the grave goods found at Ziwiyeh.

Fertilized on Asiatic soil by the ancient civilizations of Mesopotamia, Syria and Asia Minor, archaic Scythian art, which in its early days had made do with the humblest of materials—bone, horn and wood—took to the use of precious metal, as a result of the rapid enrichment of the peoples for whom it catered, and who brought back an immense war booty from campaigns as far afield as the frontiers of Egypt. It was in the palaces of the Kings of the East that the Scythians acquired their taste for luxury and lavish colour, and they never lost it, even after their return to the steppes of South Russia. But their art always remained what it had been at its inception: an applied art, appropriate to 'the nomad's gear.' Conditions in Iran favoured its integration into Medo-Cimmerian art, which likewise tended to 'a theriomorphic conception of the world.'

404 - NORTH-WEST IRAN. RHYTON: GAZELLE'S HEAD (8th-7th
CENTURIES B.C.) — PRIVATE COLLECTION, TEHERAN

406 - GREECE. LURISTAN VASE AND PENDANT (8th-7th CENT. B.C.) — SAMOS AND HERAKLEION MUSEUMS

THE IRANO-URARTIAN 'KOINE' AND THE WEST

AT the time when the Urartian kingdom was taking form the Greeks were gradually colonizing the coast of Asia Minor. Their presence at Al Mina, a Syrian port at the mouth of the Orontes, may go back to 800 B.C., if not earlier. There are indications of three main centres of Greek activity, each serving a different trade route coming from the East: (1) Eastern Greece, along with Samos and Ephesus, (2) Crete, and (3) Corinth.

In 757 B.C. the Milesians founded a colony at Trebizond and Greek settlements began to proliferate on the southern shore of the Black Sea. It does not, however, follow that this was the first appearance of Greek merchant-adventurers in these waters; the Urartian artefacts procurable on the Black Sea coast may well have attracted their attention. Moreover the foundation of a colony and the selection of its site must have involved preliminary contacts with the local population, whether deliberate or accidental. Typical of the latter was the case of Colapios of Samos who, on a voyage to Egypt, was driven by adverse winds beyond the Pillars of Hercules (Gibraltar) and discovered Tartessus, where he did some profitable trading (Herodotus, iv. 152).

On the Pontic coast Greek traders procured iron, wax, flax, wool, precious metals, cinnabar, wood, bronzes, bronze furniture from Urartu, Elamite and Median textiles and embroidery. At about this time the Iranian cock made its first appearance in Greece. But it was not the only exotic merchandise imported. A bronze vessel from Luristan with a long beak-spout, found in the Heraion of Samos, and a bronze pendant, also from Luristan, found in a tomb at Knossos (both from buildings of the seventh-eighth centuries B.C.) show that Iran took part in the commerce between Greece and the East.

405 - CHIUSI. JUG WITH WOMAN'S HEAD (6th CENTURY B.C.) — ANTIQUARIUM, BERLIN

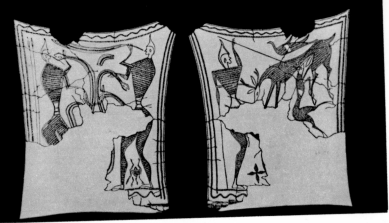

407 - GREECE. BOEOTIAN FIBULA (8th CENT. B.C.) — PHILADELPHIA

408 - GREECE. FIBULA (8th CENT. B.C.) — ANTIQUARIUM, MUNICH

409 - GREECE. ATTIC BOWL (8th CENT. B.C.) — COPENHAGEN

May not these two objects—not to mention the Perachora bronze, apparently of the same provenance—have made their way to Greece by the two great northern and western trade routes, by which, it would seem, Iranian wares followed those of Urartu? Be this as it may, from the third quarter of the eighth century B.C. on, when Greek art became susceptible to Oriental influences, Iranian art must have been included in the art currents now setting towards Greece.

We are far from asserting that the painted pottery of protohistoric Iran (meaning that of Sialk) played a key part in shaping the evolution of Greek vase painting. All we wish to do is point out the similarities between the characteristic subjects and techniques of the two arts. If these resemblances were limited to a few isolated cases, any such rapprochement might seem far-fetched. But they are so numerous and suggestive that we feel justified in drawing attention to a fact that has been overlooked in even the most comprehensive studies of this period of Greek art.

From the mid-eighth century B.C. on, the strict disciplines of the Greek Geometric style are gradually relaxed, the design is loosened up and gains in poise and balance, though ancient traditions are still respected. The 'tyranny of ruler and compass,' basic to the Geometric style, is challenged and 'its structure broken up.'

New rules and rhythms are introduced and we also find attempts to render plastic values. This applies to Greece as well as to Iran; the two

410 - THEBES (GREECE). PAINTED AMPHORA (C. 700 B.C.) — NAT. MUSEUM, ATHENS

arts, at slightly different periods, are following the same path. The human form, losing its angular contours, becomes suppler, more alive. Represented, to start with, as a uniform patch, it is gradually separated into articulated parts by the introduction of clearly marked divisions, forming 'belts' encircling the narrowest parts of the body. We find this highly distinctive mode of rendering the human form employed both on Sialk vases and on Boeotian fibulae of the end of the eighth century B.C. The same technique is applied to the bodies of animals which, larger than those on the Geometric vases and drawn at first in silhouette, are similarly intersected by 'belts' or 'collars' both at Sialk and on the fibulae. The boars on the saddle-cloth of the horse rhyton from Susa are treated in this manner, which also prevailed in Greek art of the period, in depictions of men with flowing locks and animals with shaggy manes.

Human figures are often shown in movement. Greek vase painters employed the Pegasus-and-rider motif that had already figured in Iranian pottery. The horse, moreover, often had a special significance in Greek art, as it is related to a chthonian deity and had symbolic associations with Death. In the Pyrrhic dance scenes, already represented by a Sialk painter, much care is taken to impart to the human body realistic movements, suggesting the rhythm of a war dance.

The hunting scene on a Sialk vase depicts what was presumably an inci-

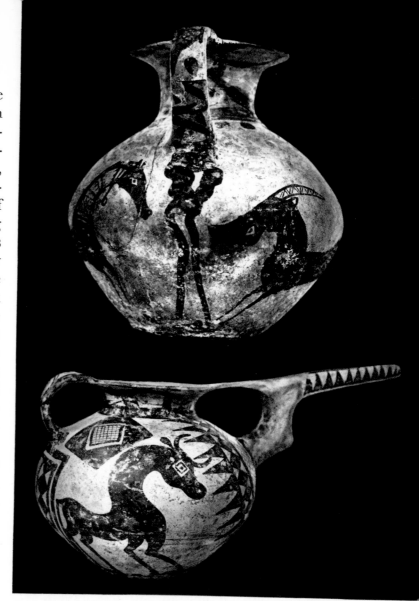

411 - SIALK. PAINTED VASES (10th-9th CENT. B.C.) — TEHERAN

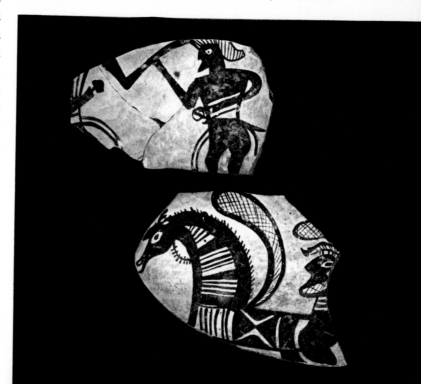

412 - SIALK. POTSHERDS: DANCER AND RIDER (10th-9th C. B.C.) — LOUVRE, TEHERAN

413 - AEGINA. STAGS FIGHTING (8th CENT. B.C.) 414 - LURISTAN. STAG GRAZING (8th-7th CENT. B.C.) — TEHERAN

dent in an epic cycle, a series of episodes based on primitive heroic legends; we find these scenes engraved on Boeotian fibulae—the first time they appear in archaic Greek art. In this hunting scene distinctively funerary allusions (the lion, emissary of death, is associated with the man leaning on his spear) are combined with a symbolism linked up with the conception of an heroic age. The rectangular shield has a painted checker-board design like that of the shield carried by the Molionides on a Sub-Geometric pitcher.

The lion with a raised paw was to become a standard motif of archaic Greek imagery; we see it on a kantharos in the National Museum, Athens; with its head and jaws edged with a thin, pale line, it may almost pass for a copy of the lion on the Sialk vase. Above the beasts of prey often figure the *disjecta membra* of the animals they have torn to pieces; this motif is also found on one of the round-headed pins from Luristan. Similar lions in exactly the same posture, but forming an antithetic group, occur in the art of Sialk. They also adorn a hydria, regarded as one of the earliest Greek vases showing orientalizing trends; the underside of the belly is decorated with a row of grazing stags, a motif used by the bronze-smiths of Luristan. Again we see a lion, in a mena- cing attitude, with one paw thrust forward, on an Attic painted vase whose ground, like that of the Sialk vase, is patterned with a series of triangles making a crown of petals from which the body of the vessel emerges like the bud of a flower out of its calyx. On a Sialk jug two seated lions, face to face, sink their claws into each other, suggesting the beginning of a combat, and this heraldic figuration points the way to the imagery found on the bands of Greek shields.

Like the lion, the stag was an animal motif that originated in the East. When at the beginning of the proto-Corinthian period a painter depicts two stags fighting, this scene, done from life, has obvious affinities with the art of Sialk in which the theme of fighting or confronted animals was often used.

334

That the Iranian weavers had a feeling for the beauty of landscape, pure and simple, is proved by the saddle-cloth represented on the Maku rhyton. These textiles (from which the potters, too, drew inspiration) were among the Iranian objects most likely to catch the eye of a Greek artist; what seem to be reminiscences of them are found in the scenes on Boeotian fibulae.

When representing animals in movement Iranian potters show them either with all four legs (the Sialk vases) or with only two (as on the Maku saddle-cloth). Both types are found together on a silver plaque from Luristan. They were, later, to become one of the most frequent decorative motifs of Greek vase painting, from the end of the proto-Corinthian style onward [580].

It would seem that the makers of the Luristan bronzes were the first to have the idea of the animal with two bodies and a single head [581], imitated by the goldsmiths working for the Scythian chieftain buried at Ziwiyeh. The vase painters of Rhodes as well as those of Greece seem to have had a predilection for this composite animal form towards the close of the seventh century B.C. Creatures with double bodies [582] (whose Oriental origin used to be denied) figure on several vases and also in Etruscan art of the same period. The threefold division of the decoration on the round Sialk vase became the rule on aryballoi [583] produced in Rhodes and Crete; moreover, from the eighth century B.C. on, these

415 - ANALATOS (GREECE). PAINTED HYDRIA (BEFORE 720 B.C.) — ATHENS

416 - SIALK. VESSEL WITH LONG BEAK-SPOUT (10th-9th CENTURIES B.C.) — PRIVATE COLLECTION, LUCERNE

417 - CRETE. PYXIS WITH VOLUTE DESIGN (7th CENT. B.C.)

418 - LURISTAN. HELMET WITH VOLUTES (8th-7th C. B.C.)

aryballoi combined a very large number of orientalizing decorative motifs and their component parts were treated as independent units. Broad volutes ending in monsters' heads, of Urartian origin, figure prominently in the decoration of King Sarduris's helmet, in that of a pyxis from Aphrati and in that of the sword sheath in the Oxus Treasure. On another pyxis, found in the Heraion of Argos[584], there figures a 'sacred tree' much resembling the one that occurs in Urartian art. Finally, many motifs of a minor order (chequer patterns, squares, lozenges, crosses, rosettes with stems ending in tiny disks, beribboned handles painted with wavy lines or braids) are common to the ceramics of both regions.

Modelled vessels in the form of wine-skins, shoes and birds, are as frequent in Greece as in Iran, where they were being made on all the known sites from the early first millennium on. Painted vases embellished with a modelled griffin's, lion's or (later) human head began to appear in Crete only about 700 B.C., whereas heads of animals in relief, and even human faces, were in current use as ornamental adjuncts among potters on proto-Iranian sites, the metal-workers of Luristan and Median goldsmiths. In short Iranian or Irano-Urartian priority in this field seems unquestionable. On the other hand, the decoration of the small Cretan cauldrons with quarter-palmettes in the angles of the design is certainly of Elamite origin. It must have been transmitted from Elam to Luristan.

419 - CRETE. CAULDRON ADORNED WITH GRIFFINS (660-640 B.C.)

420 - OLYMPIA. WOMAN'S HEAD (7th C. B.C.) — BERLIN   421 - LURISTAN. GODDESS'S HEAD (8th-7th C. B.C.) — PRIVATE COLL.

The large round pinheads from Luristan, with a woman's face in the centre cut short at the chin, may lie at the origin of the round bronze plaque with a woman's head, without the neck, discovered at Olympia. For this way of treating the human face is not Greek, but one of the idiosyncrasies of Iranian iconography, first evidenced at Sialk. Though unquestionably the work of Greek craftsmen, the Olympia disk, with its V-shaped face, archaic smile and inlaid eyes, reminds us of certain Luristan bronzes of typically Iranian conception and execution.

Although no direct affiliation between them can be demonstrated, there is a striking similarity between the figurations on the bronze plaques of Luristan quivers and on those which, on certain Greek shields, held in place the loops through which the arm was passed. Thus in Luristan in the eighth and seventh centuries B.C., as in Greece in the seventh and sixth, art is put to the service of mythology.

Black bucchero pottery was in general use in Iran in the first centuries

422 - OLYMPIA. BAND OF A SHIELD (7th CENTURY B.C.) — OLYMPIA MUSEUM
423 - LURISTAN. PLAQUE OF A QUIVER (8th-7th C. B.C.) — PRIVATE COLL., PARIS

7

424 - GREECE. WINGED DEMON CARRYING OFF THE DEAD — BERLIN

425 - XANTHOS. HARPY TOMB (C. 500 B.C.) — BRITISH MUSEUM

of the first millennium B.C.; it is also common in Etruscan tombs. The hybrid theme of the bird-woman, given plastic form in vases or vase handles, is of Irano-Urartian origin. Subsequently Greece and Etruria adopted the funerary symbolism implicit in the conception of a composite being who carries off the dead. It was this belief, evidenced in so much Sialk pottery, that gave rise to the legend of Phineus and the Harpies, which a Greek artist in the service of a Persian nobleman represented on his master's tomb, while another artist envisaged the 'ravisher of the dead' as a winged demon, exactly like the one represented by an Etruscan goldsmith.

To this bird-woman corresponded the bearded bird-man on the handles of bronze vessels from Luristan and Hamadan (also on the handles of Urartian cauldrons). This was the Greek Thanatos, whom we see depicted on a lekythos in the act of dragging away a corpse.

The lion and the horse are emissaries of Death, as is the griffin placed above the bronze cauldrons used as funerary monuments in Greece and also found in Etruscan tombs. Here we see affinities with the cauldron placed beside the Scythian chieftain in his tomb at Ziwiyeh. Though regarded as a 'demon,' the griffin is not always malignant. Sometimes it acts as a tutelary being, even when the receptacle which it watches over is intended for a tomb. Nor was the griffin regarded as in any sense malevolent when, in Greece, it formed part of an offering to a much-revered deity.

426 - RHODES. LEKYTHOS WITH THANATOS CARRYING OFF A DEAD MAN — BRITISH MUSEUM

427 - RHODES. GRIFFIN (7th-6th CENT. B.C.) — BRITISH MUSEUM 428 - SUSA. GRIFFIN (8th-7th CENT. B.C.) — LOUVRE

Though the Urartian origin of these cauldrons is unquestioned, there is a tendency to doubt whether the bronze griffins ornamenting them were the work of Urartian craftsmen. The Ziwiyeh griffin is not the only one from Iran; excavations at Susa have brought to light the head of a similar griffin cast in bronze. Unfortunately its ears are broken and there is no knowing whether they had above them a conical knob like those of the Ziwiyeh griffin.

Though, in Greek copies, griffin's ears are not shaped in the same way, the Ziwiyeh type of figure may have been used as a model, if we assume that the 'knob' pointed the way to the tall, elongated 'pavilion' of the ear (a Greek invention). And it would seem that the shell-like concavity of the Oriental ear, converted into a bulge, served as a base for all this elaborate superstructure.

339

429 - TARQUINIA. HEAD OF ACHELOUS — ANTIQUARIUM, BERLIN   430 - LURISTAN. UMBO (8th-7th CENT. B.C.) — TEHERAN

In our account of the votive shields of Luristan, we commented on the absence of shields with zoomorphic *umbones*. However, judging by the hunting scenes on bas-reliefs, these were in use among the Assyrians. In Urartu they were hung as votive offerings on the walls of the temple of Musasir. For the same purpose, shields were placed in the Idaean Cave (Crete) and also in Etruscan tombs. The device of three lions forming a triangle on the *umbo* of an Etruscan shield[585] gives the impression of being an interpretation by a Greek or Etruscan artist of an Iranian theme.

We have already noted the Irano-Urartian origin of the *umbones* representing human faces. In the West, Etruria was the only land to adopt this use of a face as an apotropaic device. The Gorgon's head was an emblem of this kind, and a curious amalgamation of the male with the female face (both of which were common in Iranian art) gave rise to that of a bearded woman. The first representations of the Gorgon do not go back earlier than the mid-seventh century B.C. The head alone, which appears first, is much more frequent in the art of this period than the full-size Gorgon. It is generally agreed that the conception of the Gorgon's head as a means of averting danger lay at the origin of the myth that grew up around this monstrous being. This seems to suggest a more remote source of the Gorgon image, formerly thought to be of Assyrian or Phoenician, possibly Egyptian origin. According to Nicolaus Damascenus, the hero Achaemenes, legendary forbear of the Persian dynasty of the Achaemenids, was the son of Perseus, nor must we forget that Aeschylus (*Prometheus Bound*, 792 ff.) speaks of the Gorgons as living in 'the fields of Kisthenes,' on the south-east coast of

340

431 - GREECE. VASE PAINTING, DETAIL: GORGON'S HEAD (C. 600 B.C.) — BRITISH MUSEUM

the Black Sea, supposedly the habitat of the Phorcides, those 'ancient maidens with swans' bodies' (sirens). The geographical reference is vague, but it may be that the earliest effigies of Harpies, Sirens and the Gorgon came from this region and that memories of this origin were embodied in the Greek legends.

In his study of the votive shields from the Idaean Cave (Crete) Kunze failed to see any trace of Urartian influence in their designs. But also found there was a lion's head in painted earthenware like the one from Prinias, dating to the late eighth or early seventh century B.C. The Ziwiyeh tomb has yielded similar pieces, which may originally have been fastened to votive shields executed in ceramics. Here, once again, we have indications of the links that must have existed between the Cretan and Iranian art traditions. One of the bronze shields from the Idaean Cave shows riders seated with their backs to the horses' heads, shooting arrows at lions, and this obvious recall of the 'Parthian arrow' motif can only have come from Iran. It reappears, long after, in the fourth century A.D., on a Sassanian silver plate in the Teheran Museum—which presumably fixes the *terminus ad quem* of this figurative motif.

432 - CRETE. DESIGN ON A SHIELD (7th-6th CENTURIES B.C.) — HERAKLION MUSEUM

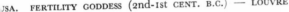

On an Etruscan ivory statue found at Marsiliana, we have another instance of the vitality of a relatively unusual theme, only two examples of which, with nearly a thousand years' interval between them, are known. The statue represents a naked woman (perhaps a goddess) pressing one hand to a breast and with the other holding a cup to catch the milk. This is a theme unknown to Greek art and attempts have been made to find Oriental or Aegean equivalents. It was employed in Iran during the Parthian period and may very well have originated there.

Some characteristic features of Etruscan jewellery and toilet articles have affinities with those of Iran: for example, human heads having the form of 'masks' adorning bracelets, and the masks, Iranian in origin, combined with lions' heads on an Etruscan bronze belt-buckle. May not a trade route have existed along the shore of the Black Sea leading westward to Etruria, and may there not be reminiscences of this in the tale of the Argonauts? Jason and his companions, it will be remembered, after leaving Colchis and many months of seafaring, had reached a point west of Italy, in other words off the Etrurian coast, when they were caught in a violent storm that swept them still further westward.

The role played by Greek pins has been elucidated in a recent study by Jacobsthal. Considering their great number, the range of forms is surprisingly limited. The sobriety and simplicity of the pins of archaic Greece

434 - ETRURIA (MARSILIANA D'ALBEGNA). NAKED GODDESS (7th-6th CENT. B.C.) — FLORENCE

strike a contrast with the ostentation and exuberance of the types favoured by the Iranians. In both lands, however, the pin came to be used not only as an article of personal adornment but also as a token of religious piety. Hundreds of votive pins have been found in the temple of Surkh Dum and a similar practice obtained in Greece—to a greater extent than in any other country of the West. Vast quantities of votive pins have been found in Greek temples; the Heraion of Argos alone yielded no less than 2800 of them. At Argos and at Paphos the pins bore the names of the goddesses to whom they were dedicated. Those of Luristan have no inscriptions, but the scenes represented on them often give us a clue to the deity for whom they were intended. Those found in temples of Zeus and Apollo may have been votive offerings to goddesses ranking beside the titular gods, and the same perhaps applies to those in the Surkh Dum temple. The fact that some Greek pins bore dedications to a specific deity shows that they had never been worn. It is equally clear that the Luristan pins with round heads must have served a ritual or votive purpose. Finally, in Greece as in Luristan, a great number of pins were offerings to the dead.

So close a kinship between the religious traditions of Greeks and

435 - LURISTAN. GOLD BRACELET (8th-7th CENT. B.C.) — LOUVRE

436 - ETRURIA. BRONZE BELT BUCKLE (7th-6th C. B.C.) — FLORENCE

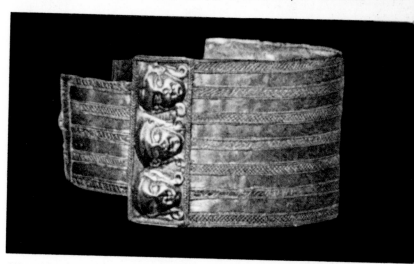

437 - ETRURIA. GOLD BRACELET (7th-6th CENT. B.C.) — FLORENCE

Iranians cannot have been due solely to commercial and artistic contacts and it seems practically certain that these beliefs and practices stemmed from a common source. And, while admitting that fundamentally the human mind tends to work on much the same lines in all countries, despite their manifold diversities, we suggest that in this case the 'common source' was the Irano-Urartian *koine*.

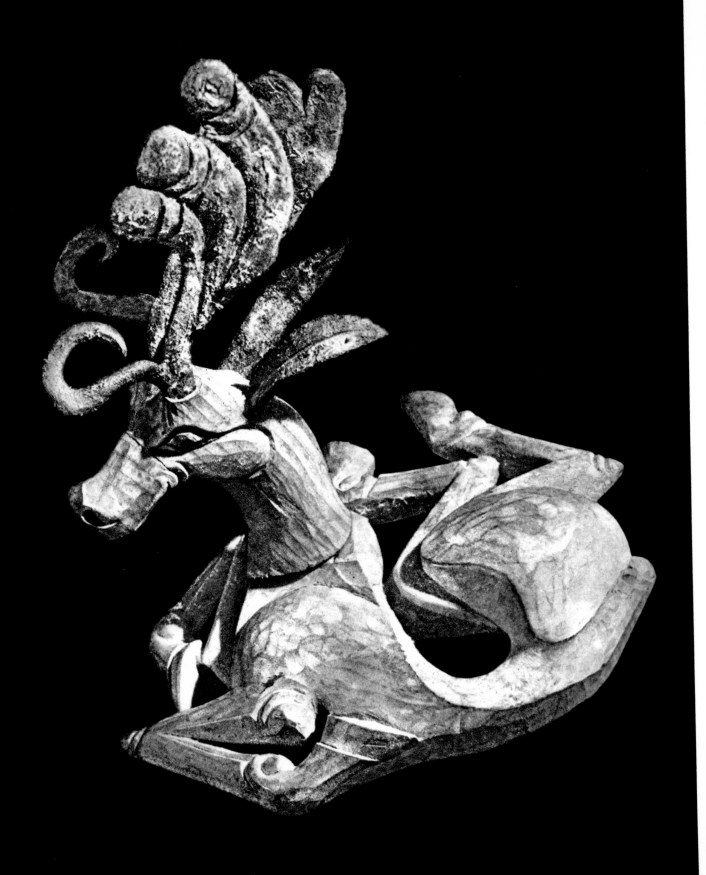

439 - PAZYRYK. LEATHER SADDLE ORNAMENT (4th-3rd CENTURIES B.C.) — HERMITAGE, LENINGRAD

VIII

THE LEGACY OF ACHAEMENIAN ART

THE works dealt with in the preceding chapters furnish, if not actual proof, rewarding indications of the general trends of the many-sided art that flourished in Achaemenian Iran. We have seen how the spirited inventions and unbridled fantasy characteristic of the art of Luristan were followed by an art more suited to the dominant part the Iranians were now to play in shaping the destinies of Western Asia. After the turmoil of the second half of the seventh century B.C. and the integration of the Median elements, it became incumbent on the young State to move beyond the narrow confines of the applied arts and to create a monumental art worthy of a great power.

Nothing, however, is known about this transitional phase. It coincided with the period when Greek art, breaking with Orientalism and freeing itself from the servitude of archaic conventions, struck out on its chosen path. Thanks to the stimulus of colonization, the development of city-states and the rapid flowering of the Hellenic genius, Greek art now achieved immortal fame with the creations of her Attic artists. Now, too, a cleavage took place and an ever-widening gulf developed between the Greek aesthetic and that of Iran.

438 - PAZYRYK. WOOD AND LEATHER BRIDLE ORNAMENT (4th-3rd CENT. B.C.) — HERMITAGE, LENINGRAD

In Iranian art of the sixth century B.C. there is no sign as yet of the eclecticism that was to mark the great achievements of such enlightened rulers as Cyrus and Darius. This would no doubt be confirmed by Ecbatana, were it not that the remains of the acropolis have so far kept their secret intact. Already the Median kings had found it needful to enlist the aid of the men who built the Assyrian towns (recently reduced to ruins) and of the artists who had contributed to the splendours of the last Babylonian dynasty. Darius's task proved easier since his kingdom became an empire and foreign artists from many countries, ranging from Egypt and Greece to India, were called in to exercise their skills under Persian superintendence. Iranian genius absorbed their contributions and shaped them to its needs, without ever breaking with its past, and as a result Achaemenian civilization attained a fine stability. Its art is, so to speak, Janus-faced; on one side it finds expression in urban architecture and monumental decoration, both owing something to the West, while its other face is turned towards the nomad world, from which the Persians stemmed and whose animal art was integrated into the architectural themes without losing anything of its atavistic vitality.

In its major creations Achaemenian art could not, or would not, relinquish its addiction for the grandiose, for dignity and immobility; moreover, it was always guided by the concept of the strict subservience of the people to the monarch and of the monarch to the Supreme God. For the Greeks, with their love of freedom, both political and religious, and their classical art (contemporary with the Achaemenids) whose aesthetic, as Hanfmann rightly points out, was charged 'with emotional elements,' Persian art could have no appeal; it was something alien, not to say inhuman. Even though the Parthenon frieze may give an impression of being akin to the 'continuous decoration' that the Great King imposed on the stairways of the Apadana, the two arts differed *toto caelo*, in technique and style no less than in spirit. While in Athens the processions of free citizens passing before the statue of their patron goddess may well have felt a thrill of affectionate devotion, and the city took pride in seeing her immortalized in the cella frieze of the Parthenon, the subject peoples who with their tribute offerings filed past the King of Kings must have felt very differently towards the stairway reliefs of the Apadana which proclaimed their servitude and glorified the 'master race.' Only the King and his Persian and Median grandees could take pleasure in this picture of a muster of the peoples of the empire, whose purpose was to magnify the monarch's power in the eyes of his subjects.

Achaemenian palace art was unaffected by the dazzling successes of the contemporary art of Greece. Only in the reign of Artaxerxes I do we find slight traces of Hellenic art currents. Surprisingly enough, considering that it was the heir of the art of Luristan, in which movement was a *sine qua non*, official Achaemenian art is essentially static, and in this sharply opposed to the spirit of its precursors. It would seem that Elamite rock-cut monuments, such as those at Kurangun and Malamir, lay at the origin of these spectacular arrays of unmoving stereotyped figures in 'frozen' attitudes. None the less Persian reliefs reveal a concern for plastic values and we even see attempts to break with conventional techniques, particularly in the treatment of drapery folds. However, though sometimes regarded as an innovation, this was no novelty in Oriental art.

As far back as the third millennium B.C. Akkadian artists had sought to render the natural fall of drapery and the makers of the Gudea statues made similar attempts, though with an extreme timidity. The folds of Achaemenian garments were already indicated on the Pasargadae reliefs.

440 - EREGLI. SCENE OF SACRIFICE (5th CENTURY B.C.) — ISTANBUL

Applied exclusively to the loose-fitting robes of the Medes—a significant fact— these folds remained unchanged until the fall of the empire. In the imagery of Persepolis some garments are devoid of draped effects; in others, however, we see on the backs of figures parallel lines imitating those of the folds which Babylonian artists had already used in their figurations.

All this was poles apart from Greek art, which at this very time was seeking to suggest the beauty of the human body under the rippling flow of garments, and was breathing life into them. The assumption that the double vertical band and stacked folds on the lower parts of the garments of Persian notables represented on the Persepolis reliefs were of Greek origin is by no means universally accepted. It is impossible to come to any definite conclusion, in view of the absence of any Persian monuments previous to those of Pasargadae. As we have already seen, the back of a Luristan statuette of a woman dating to the sixth century B.C. shows semicircular folds, like those on the silver statuette from the Oxus Treasure. This latter may well date to the Median period, in which case the front part of the garment would mark a step towards the treatment of drapery folds found on the Pasargadae reliefs.

Achaemenian monumental art seems to have been quite uninfluenced by what was being produced in the West. Yet the Great Kings appreciated things of beauty, Greek statuary in particular. Pliny (*Hist. Nat.* xxxiv. 68) tells us

347

441 - EREGLI.   PROCESSION (5th CENTURY B.C.) — ISTANBUL

that the sculptor Telephanes of Phocaea worked for Darius and Xerxes. And the latter, after the sack of Athens, carried back some Greek statues. The statue of Penelope dating to the second half of the fifth century B.C. which was found in the Treasury of Persepolis proves that Greek works were appreciated by the Achaemenids. This is confirmed by the discovery at Susa of Greek pottery of the first half of the fifth century B.C.

In the western provinces of the empire, however, at the courts of the satraps and in the residences of the nobility, Achaemenian art took a different course.   There it came in closer contact with Ionian art, and was influenced by it from the second half of the fifth century B.C. on.

We have already mentioned the conclusions to be drawn regarding the numerous so-called Greco-Persian intaglios in which the two arts are juxtaposed without intermingling.   The same conclusions are reached when we study the relief from Dascylion (Eregli), capital of the satrapy of Phrygia (Asia Minor). It can be dated to the second half of the fifth century B.C.   The theme of the relief was a procession accompanied by a scene of sacrifice.   The processional figures, men on horseback and women riding mules, moving in single file, are exactly like those at Susa and Persepolis.   But the scene of sacrifice is evidently by a different hand, though its setting remains Achaemenian.   For example, the door in front of which the priests are posted closely resembles the door on the Tomb of Cyrus at Pasargadae and that of the 'Ka'ba-i-Zardusht' at Naqsh-i-Rustam.   Head-dresses, garments, ritual objects and the attitudes of the priests prove that the theme has been carefully studied down to its smallest details.

None the less, there are differences in treatment: eyes are shown in side-view, the garments, held in place by a belt, fall in folds and other folds

442 - ÇAVUCH KOI.   FUNERARY STELE
(4th CENT. B.C.) — ISTANBUL

are indicated at the elbows. We also find a feeling for three-dimensional form in the handling of the *barsoms* and attempts to render perspective in the representation of the bundle of twigs. In short, while subject and composition are Persian, the execution is inspired by Greek techniques.

Three other fragments of this relief are extant, but broken into so many pieces that it is impossible to determine its function. Some have thought it formed part of an altar or served to decorate a religious edifice. The existing fragments enable us to gauge more or less its size: over $7\frac{1}{2}$ feet long and about 3 feet 9 inches high. The lowness of the door invites comparison with the west side of the 'Harpy Tomb,' which is actually a trifle lower, just over 3 feet in height; in which case this edifice may have been a *heroon*.

Greco-Persian symbolism is even more marked in a funerary stele, with two registers. In the hunting scene the garments worn by the figures are Persian, as are the horse's trappings, the tuft of hair on its head and the knotted tail; moreover, it is moving at the Assyro-Persian gallop. But the freedom of movement and arrangement of the scene are Greek. The funerary stele was unknown in Persia and the banquet represented in the lower register is taking place in a Greek setting.

F.J. Tritsch has pointed out the analogies between the bas-reliefs of Darius and Artaxerxes I, and one side of the Harpy Tomb. This tomb was situated at Xanthos, in Lycia, a region conquered in the reign of Cyrus by Harpagos, a Median general, whose descendants thereafter ruled the country. Here the Greek sculptor has treated the ruler in the heroic style, giving him the posture of the King of Kings. This two servitors behind the throne have a Greek aspect and the high official confronting Harpagos has been transformed into a menial presenting the king with a cock. True, the offering of this animal conformed to an age-old Lycian tradition, but we also know that, for the Persians, the cock was an attribute of Sraosha, god of Judgment. Behind the servitor is another menial holding a dog on a leash, a motif very frequent on Hellenic stelae.

Here again the ideas behind the imagery are basically Persian, though they are presented in a Greek garb. Of interest, also, in this context is the fact that the practice (attested by Firdausi) of burying a monarch seated on a throne obtained in Persia.

443 - PERSEPOLIS. ROYAL AUDIENCE
(6th-5th c. b.c.) — TEHERAN
444 - XANTHOS. HARPY TOMB (c.
500 b.c.) — BRITISH MUSEUM

445 - XANTHOS. FUNERARY BAS-RELIEF (C. 470 B.C.) — BRITISH MUSEUM

On another tomb, at Xanthos, we see a Persian dignitary travelling in a chariot to his last abode. The dead man's horse, led by a groom, heads the procession, and a rider follows it. This funerary symbolism, figuring forth a horse acting as envoy of the powers of the netherworld and as a 'herald' sent to escort the dead man, was common both to Greeks and Persians. But for two details indicating the dead man's country of origin there would be nothing to connect this scene with Persia. First there is the nature of the horses' trappings; the boars' tusks painted on the cross-straps on the horses' brows are specifically Iranian (they often figure on the Persepolis reliefs). The second clue has been pointed out by B.O. Vitt, an authority on the breeds of horses in the ancient world, to whom we owe an exhaustive study of the horses in the Pazyryk barrows. He has shown that the build of the dead man's saddle-horse and the way it holds its head prove it to be a stallion bred in Media or Central Asia. Smaller than those of Persia, Greek horses are harnessed to the chariot. There is a striking similarity between this work and the so-called Sarcophagus of the Satrap (dated a century later) from the cemetery of Sidon; the dead man, striking an 'heroic' attitude, figures on the left of the composition, shifting the centre of gravity to the left, while a scene of the chase commemorates his exploits as a hunter.

The Achaemenian Empire had passed away when the most magnificent and most representative of these funerary monuments of Iranian inspiration was executed: the so-called Sarcophagus of Alexander the Great, also from the royal cemetery of Sidon. Here we see Persians and Greeks figuring in a battle scene and a hunting scene.

446 - SIDON. SARCOPHAGUS OF THE SATRAP (MID-4th CENTURY B.C.) — ISTANBUL

447 - SIDON. SARCOPHAGUS OF ALEXANDER (4th CENTURY B.C.) — ISTANBUL MUSEUM

Hitherto only Alexander had been recognized among these figures. Recently, however, Jean Charbonneaux has also identified Antigonus Cyclops ('one-eyed') and his son Demetrius Poliorcetes who were first among Alexander's successors to assume the title of King and wear the royal diadem (in 306 B.C.); traces of it can be seen on Demetrius's head in the relief.

This sarcophagus probably contained the body of Abdalonymos, last king of Sidon of Persian blood, who had been raised to the throne by Alexander in 333. Battle and hunting scenes were a stock theme with the engravers of 'Greco-Persian' intaglios since they answered to the taste of their Iranian clientele. And the carvings on the Alexander Sarcophagus, coloured by sycophancy or subservience, are merely a transposition into a purely Greek plastic language of a type of imagery long current in the Ancient East and frequently resorted to in Roman historical reliefs of the imperial age.

The back-to-back protomes of bulls from Bostan-esh-Sheikh, near Sidon, while handled in much the same spirit as the Sarcophagus of Alexander, conform to Persian architectural traditions. Similar bull capitals figured in the residence of a satrap (?) at Sidon dating to the Achaemenian period. But the provincial sculptors failed to suggest the massive power required of animals called upon to bear a tremendous load. This motif of weight-bearing animals underwent further changes as it made its way from Bostan-esh-Sheikh, via Delos, to Thasos. In the end its functional purpose was forgotten and it became a purely decorative element.

It has been pointed out that the bull protomes at Bostan-esh-Sheikh, not

448 - SIDON. CAPITAL WITH BULL PROTOMES
(5th-4th CENT. B.C.) — BEIRUT MUSEUM

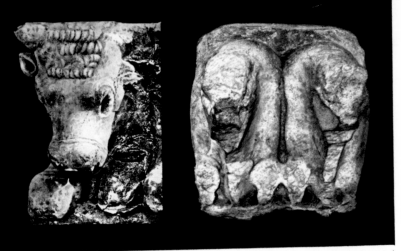

449-450 - DELOS. BULL CAPITALS (2nd CENTURY B.C.)

451 - DELOS. HOUSE B. HELLENISTIC CAPITAL

subjected to the analytic technique characteristic of Achaemenian protomes, are less conventional, the movement of the heads being more realistic. Affinities with the protomes of the famous Altar of Horns at Delos have been noted. There was a pronounced taste in Delos for this architectural formula; it is used in several edifices, for example in the Sanctuary of the Bulls and the House of the Trident in which the animals are paired, whereas in House B they are separated.

There is no question of the origin of these structural elements, but what, one may wonder, led to their wide diffusion? Assuming that a kinship exists between the Alexander Sarcophagus and the protomes of Bostanesh-Sheikh, Demetrius Poliorcetes may well have had a share in this, so far as the monument near Sidon is concerned. He is known to have visited Delos in 301 B.C., and Delos was included in his dominions. The capital at Delos is reduced to a head alone, the animal's forelegs being omitted, as on the Portico of Antigonus, which dates to the second half of the third century B.C.

At Thasos a winged horse replaces the bull and, no longer serving as an architectural support, illustrates the obsolescence of the functional values of such elements.

In a handsome capital found at Salamis (Cyprus) in the palace of Evagoras I (411-374 B.C.) we have a striking instance of an organic deviation from the Achaemenian capital, whose prototype was the trunk of a forked

452 - DELOS. CAPITAL ON THE PORTICO OF
ANTIGONUS (2nd HALF, 3rd C. B.C.)

sapling. Here the space between the protomes is occupied by caryatids upholding an abacus on which rested a cross-beam. That supernatural, semi-divine creature, the Achaemenian bull, has given place to a sturdy animal replete with energy. The conventional curls are absent, the animal's hair is represented by wisps covering its forehead only, while the eyes, sunk deep beneath the superciliary ridges, and the folds of skin under the head (bent lower than in the Achaemenian capitals) convey an idea of brute force.

This capital might be said to reflect the personality of that truculent, enterprising vassal king Evagoras, in whom Hellenistic and Oriental strains were intermingled. For no less than ten years (390-380 B.C.) Artaxerxes II waged war on his revolting vassal, then ended up by forgiving him and restoring him to the throne. He has sometimes been described as the precursor of the Hellenistic period. Judging by his deeds, it would seem that this Oriental monarch, a fervent proselyte of Hellenism, was less impressed by the power of the King of Kings than by the splendour of his palaces at Susa and Persepolis.

453 - THASOS. HELLENISTIC CAPITAL WITH WINGED HORSE

454 - SALAMIS. CAPITAL OF EVAGORAS I (4th C. B.C.) — BRITISH MUSEUM

Syrian architects expanded the impost-block made of the foreparts of two bulls into a true capital with four protomes emerging from a bed of acanthus leaves. The French archaeologist Henri Seyrig, who published the capital recently found at Arados, in Syria, has shown how Persian prototypes led to the creation of the 'foliated scroll with protomes' used in Roman architectural decoration and subsequently reproduced in metal-work.

That jewellers, too, employed the theme of animals' foreparts is evidenced by a pin discovered at Paphos (Cyprus) datable to the third century B.C.

455 - PAPHOS. SANCTUARY OF APHRODITE. PINHEAD IN THE FORM OF A CAPITAL (3rd CENT. B.C.) — BRITISH MUSEUM

In the third and second centuries B.C. this motif of weight-bearing animals, of Persian origin, enjoyed widespread favour. It came into general use all along the eastern coast of the Mediterranean. Josephus has given a description of the *baris* built by Hyrkanus, a member of the family of the Tobiads (175-174 B.C.): an edifice near the Jordan whose façade bore a frieze of lions (reminiscent of the Persepolis reliefs), and the beams of which rested on bull protomes.

For the Jews of Palestine during the Seleucid period, when they were engaged in constant struggles with their overlords, this revival of Achaemenian traditions may have had a symbolic value. It may also be interpreted as a token of their esteem for the monarchs who had granted them religious freedom, and of their antipathy to their present rulers.

457 - HEAD OF A PRINCE (5th CENT. B.C.) — PRIVATE COLL., BRUSSEL

The Labranda Sphinx, from Asia Minor, seems to have had the same function as the bulls in the portico of the Throne Hall at Persepolis. It figured in the antae of a building on the upper terrace in the sacred precinct of the town, which was famous for the cult of Zeus Labrandeus, whose symbol was the Double Axe (a survival of an ancient local cult). We have its prototype in the male sphinx of the Palace of Darius at Persepolis. It wears the *kalathos* of the Labranda Zeus (cf. the coins issued by the satraps), a headdress also figuring on the small Achaemenian heads carved in the round. The sphinx's hair falls over its shoulders in two long wavy locks ending in volutes like those of the bulls on the Susa capital. The deep-set eyes, however, lack the relief normally given them in Achaemenian sculpture and, no longer ending in curved tips, the moustache merges into a long, uncurled beard. Finally, our western artist has thought it more logical to give a human head human ears. More logical, too, is the way in which the wing starts off not from the sphinx's chest but behind its shoulders. These slight differences reflect variations due to local conditions and cultural particularities within a more or less identical frame of reference. Such was the case with Labranda (in Caria), which was detached in 395 B.C. from the satrapy of Sardis and brought under the rule of a local dynasty of satraps, first of whom was Hecatomnos (395-367 B.C.).

— 456 - LABRANDA (ASIA MINOR). SPHINX DECORATING THE ANTAE OF A BUILDING (4th CENTURY B.C.)

Achaemenian architectural traditions ultimately affected India, but it was not until three-quarters of a century after the collapse of the Persian empire that Iranian elements made their appearance there. One of the consequences of the Achaemenian occupation of Western India was the creation of the first Indian alphabet, *kharoshti*, derived from the Aramaic script, which, as we have seen, was employed by the central administration and thus came into general use throughout the Persian empire.

Under King Asoka (c. 274-237/6 B.C.) the hypostyle royal palace at Pataliputra, his capital, owed much to Achaemenian inspiration. Typical of the art favoured by the king were the inscribed columns consisting of a sandstone shaft (sometimes extremely high) topped with a bell-shaped capital of the Susian or Persepolitan type. It serves to support a group of animals carved in the round, for the most part seated lions treated in the Iranian style. At Lauriya-Nandangarh, in particular, they clearly play the part of the guardian animals of Persepolis. Handsomest of these is the Sarnath column at the gates of Benares; the three foreparts of standing lions, back to back, at the top of the capital, clearly derive from Persian arrangements of three weight-bearing animals. Capitals of addorsed animals were widely adopted in Indian architecture, but the sculptors did not divide up the impost-block between the animals; as a result, one is shown entire while only the protome of the others is visible (Mathura, first century A.D.).

458 - SARNATH. LION CAPITAL (3rd CENTURY B.C.) — NATIONAL MUSEUM, NEW DELHI
459 - AMARAVATI. PILASTER WITH WINGED LIONS (3rd CENTURY A.D.) — MUSÉE GUIMET, PARIS

460 - BEGRAM. IVORY CARVING (1st-2nd CENT. A.D.) — KABUL   461 - MATHURA. CAPITAL (1st CENT. A.D.) — MATHURA

Similar decorative motifs, with lions or bulls, figure on first- and second-century ivories from Begram, and we find them again in the third century on a pilaster from Amaravati; here, above a bell-shaped base of floral ornament, two winged lions uphold an architrave carved with an animal frieze, as on the baldachin of the king's throne at Persepolis.

Indian craftsmen long drew on the traditions of the Persian master-builders, who in the popular imagination were envisaged as a species of supermen. It is thought that Asoka's columns were made in a workshop near the capital where native sculptors were employed under the supervision of Iranian experts. But, though in their works we find traces of Persian and even western art, such was the basic originality of these Indian craftsmen that they never slavishly copied foreign models, but boldly adapted them to the tastes and ideology of their fellow-countrymen.

The belated emergence of this art (belated with respect to its prototypes) suggests that its origin goes far back, to contacts that had been established between India and the Seleucid empire. In that case its seminal centres may have been those two great cities, Seleucia-on-the-Tigris and Susa, which, as a result of their proximity to the Persian Gulf, played an important part in the sea traffic and trade relations with India.

The view that Persian-Hellenistic influences were instrumental in shaping Maurya art has found a vigorous exponent in Mario Bussagli, who sees in India the last land where reminiscences of Achaemenian art at its best can be discerned, and this despite the essentially autonomous character of Indian art.

357

462 - KUBAN. RHYTON (5th CENT. B.C.) — HERMITAGE   463 - CHERTOMLYK. SWORD HILT (4th CENT. B.C.) — HERMITAGE

According to Rostovtzeff the art of South Russia always had two aspects, one European, the other Oriental (in large part Iranian). Darius's attempt to conquer Scythia had failed. The founding of a string of Greek colonies along the north coast of the Black Sea created a new cultural milieu in which Scythian animal art developed along new lines. Greek craftsmen working for Scythian patrons naturally catered for their taste, but modified the 'warlike' art of the nomads by introducing Greek procedures. Achaemenian art and Scythian art, both of them born in a period of Medo-Scythian symbiosis, followed separate paths as a result of differing historical conditions. But both alike retained that predilection for animal forms which was their common birthright.

That the Scythians of South Russia appreciated the Achaemenian gold- and silver-work is demonstrated by objects discovered in their royal tombs. A notable example is the silver rhyton in the form of a winged ibex (datable to the fifth century B.C.) from the Seven Brothers Barrow in the Koban, near Taman.

Similarly, the gold hilt of an iron sword dating to the first half of the fourth century B.C., which was found in a tomb at Chertomlyk, on the Dnieper, is almost certainly the work of an Achaemenian craftsman. It is topped by two

358

464 - OXUS. SWORD SHEATH (7th C. B.C.) — BRITISH MUSEUM 465 - KARAGODENASHK. RHYTON (4th-3rd C. B.C.) — HERMITAGE

heifers' heads with a palmette between them, while the rest of the haft is divided into two parallel fields showing six men on horseback hunting gazelles. This motif reproduces, with only slight variants, the hunting scenes represented on the gold sword sheath from the Oxus Treasure, which in our opinion is undoubtedly a Median work.

Some of the figurations on Scythian objects of the fourth century B.C. (and even later) seem to derive from Achaemenian Persia, though no exact contemporary equivalents have so far been found there.

The themes are of a religious order, such as the investiture of a king by a god or goddess or the consecration of the king's power by a sacred potion proffered by a divine being in a ceremonial rhyton. (Rhytons were as generally used in Scythia as in Iran.)

The investiture scene on the Karagodenashk rhyton (dating to the third or fourth century B.C.) represents Ahuramazda presenting to the king the emblems of his power; both king and god are on horseback, each of them trampling underfoot a vanquished foe—symbolizing the victory of Good over Evil. This theme often figures on Sassanian rock reliefs, which suggests that it had existed under the Achaemenians.

466 - PAZYRYK. WOOL CARPET OF PERSIAN ORIGIN (4th-3rd CENT. B.C.) — HERMITAGE, LENINGRAD

Influences of Achaemenian art can also be seen in objects of the fourth and third centuries B.C. found in the frozen tombs of the nomad chieftains of Pazyryk that have been uncovered in the Altai range in southern Siberia. Most striking of these objects are the carpets and textiles.

The central zone of a small carpet of Persian origin is decorated with rows of four-rayed stars, a motif also found on Luristan bronzes. The borders, in the purest Achaemenian style, represent two processions: one of horsemen, one of elks. Here, moreover, we find certain distinctive features of the fringes composed of merlons of the saddle-cloths represented on Greco-Persian intaglios.

467 - PAZYRYK. DETAIL OF THE CARPET: HORSEMAN AND GRIFFINS —

468 - PAZYRYK. HANGING, DETAIL (4th-3rd C. B.C.) — HERMITAGE

469 - PAZYRYK. SADDLE-CLOTH, DETAIL (4th-3rd C. B.C.) — HERMITAGE

A wall hanging in wool from the Pazyryk barrows depicting queens sacrificing at a fire altar again shows Achaemenian influence. Here the censer resembles one which figures beside Darius's throne on one of the Persepolis bas-reliefs.

The typically Persian frieze of lions passant occurs on a saddle-cloth. The indications of the animals' muscular structure on the shoulders and thighs by specific decorative motifs— circles, commas, figures of eight with polychrome inlays—are obvious imitations of the style of the Achaemenian gold and silver smiths.

The silhouettes of lions' heads with oddly tousled manes, cut out of leather and appliqued to a felt carpet, clearly derive from a frieze in glazed bricks at Susa or from the gold plaques of Hamadan.

All these felt carpets from Siberia decorated with painted leather cutouts, in which the figuration of animals' muscles keeps to the convention of commas and circles, are in the direct lineage of the saddle-cloths that potters of Susa and Maku painted on their horse rhytons in the earliest phase of Iranian art.

But the artist's vision of the animal world has changed; that world has now become a scene of savage, murderous conflict, and his renderings of the quivering flesh of mortally wounded beasts have an emotive, almost compassionate quality that hitherto was lacking. A changed spirit is breathing over the vast Eurasian steppes, heralding a new phase of Iranian art.

470 - PAZYRYK. APPLIED ORNAMENTS ON FELT CARPETS (4th-3rd CENT. B.C.) — HERMITAGE, LENINGRAD

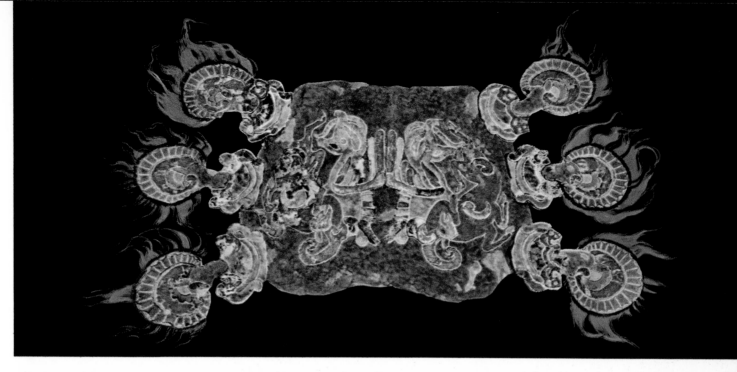

471-472 - PAZYRYK. FELT SADDLE-CLOTH WITH PAINTED LEATHER ORNAMENTS: WHOLE AND DETAIL (4th-3rd C. B.C.) — HERMITAGE

473 - PAZYRYK. (A, B) HUMAN HEADS (C) HORSE'S HEAD (D) ARROW SHAFT (4th-3rd CENT. B.C.) — HERMITAGE

The same technique, involving the use of painted leather cut into specific shapes, was applied to elements of horse-gear. Here, as in the wooden masks serving as pendants, we find the familiar Iranian motif of faces cut short at the chin.

The decorations on shafts of arrows derive from those that the painters employed at Persepolis had used for the wooden columns of the Treasury (which had done duty, provisionally, for the Hall of a Hundred Columns, not yet built).

Several horses accompanied the dead man to his tomb at Pazyryk, some of them wearing leather masks given the form of stags' and reindeers' heads. One such ornament contains a motif in painted leather enhanced with very thin gold plaques, representing a combat between a griffin-lion and a tiger. The mane is tucked into a felt sheath bedecked with applied ornaments having the form of cocks (animals that often figure in the art of Luristan).

The purpose of this mask was to disguise the horse as a reindeer, an artifice of exceptional interest for the researcher into the ethnic background of the culture we are concerned with. For it recalled the bygone age when the reindeer was used as a mount, playing the same part as the stag in the life of the Scythian nomads of the Altai region. The Pazyryk reindeer and griffin, like the stag and griffin of the Scythians, symbolized a victory of darkness over light. Closely linked to the cult of the dead, these animals made their appearance at the moment when the dead man, leaving the familiar realm of light, descended into the world of darkness. After being superseded by the horse as a means of transport, the reindeer, elk and stag still figured in the primitive mythology and in funerary art, as did the horse among the Greeks and the Iranians.

474 - PAZYRYK. STAG'S HEAD IN THE JAWS OF A GRIFFIN. WOOD AND LEATHER (4th-3rd C. B.C.) — HERMITAGE

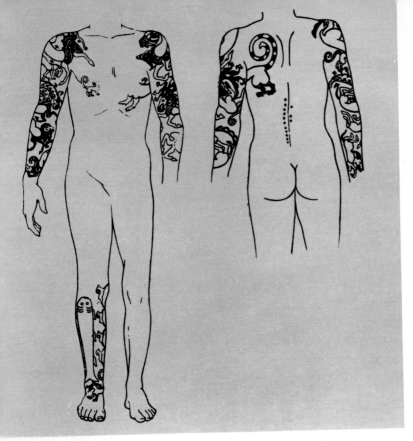

475 - PAZYRYK. TATTOOINGS (4th-3rd CENT. B.C.) — HERMITAGE

The embalmed body of a man found in Barrow 2 at Pazyryk had elaborate tattooings (perfectly preserved) on the back, arms and one leg. Besides an unbroken sequence of highly fantastic animals in the most unlikely postures, there were images of the animals which he had hunted or tended in his lifetime. These figurations may indicate the high rank of the deceased, but they may equally well have served a magical, evil-averting purpose.

That the practice of tattooing had already existed in Luristan is proved by a bronze statuette that recently appeared on the Teheran art market. It represents a middle-aged man with a long beard, composed of tiers of chevrons, and, except for a loin-cloth, naked. Incised on his chest are two snakes, zigzagging up his body and resting their heads on his shoulders. On the back, under a rather crudely delineated mountain ibex, is what looks like a sign. A cord, fastened to one of its hind legs, is looped round the man's waist.

The tattooings on this statuette go to show that the Lurs continued to keep in touch with the nomad peoples who had established themselves in their original homeland.

As in India, influences of Achaemenian art were felt in Siberia, at the very time when the dynasty of the King of Kings was extinct or on the brink of extinction.

But whereas in India the local traditions were strong enough to assimilate and transform Iranian data, the nomads of the Altai region adopted Achaemenian formulae in their applied arts without making any attempt to modify them. Thus Persian art, itself deriving from and conditioned by the nomad way of life, found in the Altai communities a soil that lent itself to the propagation of Iranian influence.

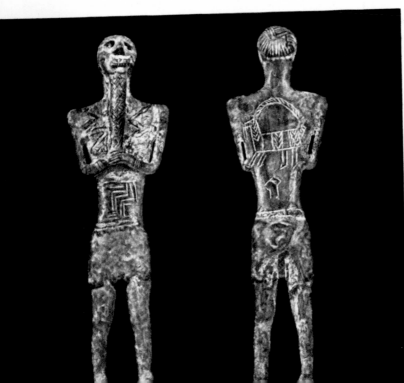

476 - LURISTAN. STATUETTES WITH TATTOOINGS (8th-7th C. B.C.) — TEHERAN ART MARKET

477 - PAZYRYK. TATTOOING, DETAIL — HERMITAGE

IRANIAN PLATEAU	HITHER ASIA ASIA MINOR	URARTU	GREECE
10th century B.C. **PROTOHISTORIC ART** *Medes and Persians in Iran*	969-936 - Temple of Jerusalem		**PROTO-GEOMETRIC ART**
9th century B.C. _____ SIALK ____ (Cemetery B)	883-859 - ASSURNA-SIRPAL II *Nimrud* 835 - SHALMANESER III *in Media*	*Formation of the Kingdom of* URARTU	**GEOMETRIC ART**
8th century B.C. _____ **PROTOHISTORIC ART** *Founding of Ecbatana* KHURVIN *by the Medes* HASANLU *Achaemenes, Leader* AMLASH *of the Achaemenians*	737 - TIGLATH-PILESER II *in the Teheran Region* 722-705 - SARGON II *Khorsabad*	*Expansion of the Kingdom of* URARTU TOPRAK-KALE AND ____	**PROTO-CORINTHIAN ART**
7th century B.C. _____ **PROTOHISTORIC ART** LURISTAN **MEDIAN ART** *Rock Tombs* ZIWIYEH	668-626 - ASSURBANIPAL *Nineveh Reliefs* End of Elamite Kingdom 612 - *Fall of Nineveh* Neo-Babylonian Empire *Cimmerian Invasion*	KARMIR BLUR *Architecture Metal-work*	**PROTO-CORINTHIAN ART** *Luristan Bronzes in Crete and Samos*
6th century B.C. _____ 550 - End of Median Kingdom **ACHAEMENIAN ART** 559-529 - CYRUS II PASARGADAE 521-485 - DARIUS I SUSA PERSEPOLIS	596 - *Taking of Jerusalem by Nebuchadnezzar* 539 - *Taking of Babylon by Cyrus* Harpy Tomb at Xanthos (Lycia)	*End of the Kingdom of* URARTU	*First Kouroi* **CORINTHIAN ART** c. 559 - Artemisio of Croesus at Ephe *Black-Figure Vases* 525 - Siphnian Treasury
5th century B.C. _____ 485-465 - XERXES I PERSEPOLIS 465-424 - ARTAXERXES I PERSEPOLIS SUSA BABYLON 404-358 - ARTAXERXES II SUSA	Dascylion Reliefs (Eregli) *Greco-Persian Gems* Labranda Sphinx (Caria)		*Red-Figure Vases* The Parthenon (447-438)
4th century B.C. _____ 358-338 - ARTAXERXES III PERSEPOLIS 330 - *Burning of Persepolis* End of Achaemenian Dynasty	Palace of Evagoras - *Capitals* (Salamis, Cyprus) Funerary Stele of Canc-Koy (Istanbul) 306 - Sarcophagus of Alexander		387 - *Founding of the Academy by Pla* PHILIP of Maced (359-336) ALEXANDER the Great (336-32 *Hellenistic Period*

THE DIFFUSION OF PERSIAN ART

Drawing on the ancient art traditions of Hither Asia, which the Hurrians before them had exploited, the Urartians and Iranians established a *koine* in the field of metallurgy, whose influence took effect in the Scythian world and radiated westwards.

Though enriched by the old civilizations of Western Asia, Scythian art always remained what it had been in its inception: an applied art, adapted to 'the nomad's gear.' Conditions in Iran favoured its integration into Medo-Cimmerian art. Later, in South Russia, while acquiring a taste for the gold- and silver-work of the Achaemenians, the Scythians adopted certain formulas of Greek art.

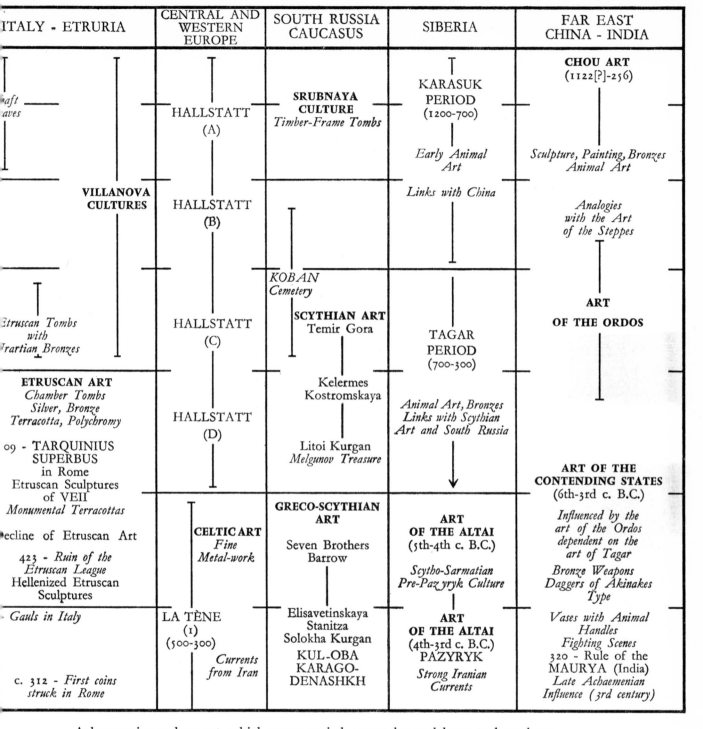

ITALY - ETRURIA	CENTRAL AND WESTERN EUROPE	SOUTH RUSSIA CAUCASUS	SIBERIA	FAR EAST CHINA - INDIA
…aft …aves	HALLSTATT (A)	**SRUBNAYA CULTURE** *Timber-Frame Tombs*	KARASUK PERIOD (1200-700)	**CHOU ART** (1122[?]-256)
			Early Animal Art	*Sculpture, Painting, Bronzes Animal Art*
VILLANOVA CULTURES	HALLSTATT (B)		*Links with China*	*Analogies with the Art of the Steppes*
Etruscan Tombs with Urartian Bronzes	HALLSTATT (C)	*KOBAN Cemetery* **SCYTHIAN ART** Temir Gora	TAGAR PERIOD (700-300)	**ART OF THE ORDOS**
ETRUSCAN ART *Chamber Tombs Silver, Bronze Terracotta, Polychromy*	HALLSTATT (D)	Kelermes Kostromskaya	*Animal Art, Bronzes Links with Scythian Art and South Russia*	
o9 - **TARQUINIUS SUPERBUS** in Rome Etruscan Sculptures of VEII *Monumental Terracottas*		Litoi Kurgan *Melgunov Treasure*		**ART OF THE CONTENDING STATES** (6th-3rd c. B.C.)
●ecline of Etruscan Art	**CELTIC ART** *Fine Metal-work*	**GRECO-SCYTHIAN ART** Seven Brothers Barrow	**ART OF THE ALTAI** (5th-4th c. B.C.) *Scytho-Sarmatian Pre-Pazyryk Culture*	*Influenced by the art of the Ordos dependent on the art of Tagar Bronze Weapons Daggers of Akinakes Type*
423 - *Ruin of the Etruscan League* Hellenized Etruscan Sculptures				
● *Gauls in Italy*	LA TÈNE (1) (500-300)	Elisavetinskaya Stanitza Solokha Kurgan KUL-OBA KARAGO-	**ART OF THE ALTAI** (4th-3rd c. B.C.) PAZYRYK	*Vases with Animal Handles Fighting Scenes* 320 - Rule of the MAURYA (India)
c. 312 - *First coins struck in Rome*	*Currents from Iran*	DENASHKH	*Strong Iranian Currents*	*Late Achaemenian Influence (3rd century)*

Achaemenian palace art, which never varied, seems by and large to have been un-affected by the new trends of Greek art. In the western provinces of the Persian empire, however, there were contacts with Ionian art, traces of whose influence can be discerned from the second half of the fifth century B.C. on (e. g. 'Greco-Persian' intaglios).

The diffusion of Achaemenian art extended not only to India but also to Siberia, where it gained ground at the very time when the Achaemenid dynasty was tottering to its fall. There, among the peoples of the Altai region (Pazyryk), Persian art found a soil well suited to the propagation of its influence.

CONCLUSION

$\mathbf{L}$IKE a 'middle empire,' Iran was surrounded by two vast cultural areas, each as large as a continent. One contained the settled population of the valleys of the Tigris, Euphrates, Oxus, Jaxartes and Indus. The other, forming an outer belt, was the world of the nomads, the mobile population of the Eurasian steppes to the north and north-east, and of the Arabs to the south-west.

From the Eurasian hinterland came the successive waves of Iranian peoples who occupied the Plateau: Medes and Persians to begin with, soon followed by Cimmerians and Scythians. Seven centuries later a further migration took place, bringing the Parthians to Iran.

The coming of the Iranians led to sweeping changes in the life of the Plateau: changes in religious beliefs, in burial customs, in social and political life. Proto-Iranian art evokes 'the world of the dead,' with which it associates 'the world of the gods.' It is in this early phase that the Iranian peoples have artistic aspirations much resembling those of the Greeks in the eighth and seventh centuries B.C. To the Greek fibula corresponds the bronze pin of Luristan.

But the art of Luristan has none of the brightness and insouciance of Greek imagery. The Luristan bronzes stem from a world of mystery, magic symbols, savagely conflicting powers. Have we here the ultimate source of Etruscan art, whose iconography was destined in the course of time to enrich Celtic art, then the art of the *Völkerwanderung*, and finally Romanesque sculpture, which has been described as 'steeped in the glamour of Eurasia.' Just as Celtic art dominated the minor arts of the Roman provinces, so the art of Luristan fecundated that of Iran, transmitting to it its inorganic structure, its creative fantasy, its remarkable originality.

478 - HAMADAN (?). GOLD DISH ADORNED WITH AN EAGLE
(5th-4th CENT. B.C.) — PRIVATE COLL., NEW YORK

In this phase of Iranian art a whole world of fantastic forms charged with magic intimations, scene of a never-ending conflict between hostile and benevolent powers, came into being, and with them a phantasmagoric vision of the world beyond the grave. Many modern artists are producing similar works, freed from the restraints imposed by the conscious mind, and their roots are often found to lie in an immemorial past. Breaking with the classical forms of Greco-Roman civilization, our contemporary art is harking back to traditions that were thousands of years old when Greek art was born. Like so much modern art, the art of Luristan 'rings the changes on instinct, reason and pure fantasy.'

During the first four centuries of the first millennium B.C., when the Plateau was in process of being Iranicized, it looked westwards and its art drew inspiration from the west. This tendency, however, was counterbalanced by a diffusion of its own art forms among the new, emergent civilizations. The tidal wave of the Scythian incursions, followed by their withdrawal towards South Russia, created a link between the arts of the nomads and those of the Plateau, and, further afield, with the age-old cultures of the Ancient East. These ties between the arts of the barbarian tribes and those of the eastern world henceforth remained unbroken.

The early, formative period of Iranian art is still inadequately documented. Two wide gaps in our knowledge have yet to be filled. On the one hand we have the unsolved problem of Median art as it existed at the time of the Median kingdom; on the other, the mystery enveloping the prehistory of the Persians.

Historians have been prone to belittle Achaemenian art as being overmuch indebted to the arts of other peoples. It is true that, in the natural course of events, it fell heir to the great civilizations that had preceded it in the Ancient East; that it took over the art forms and techniques of Urartu and Elam in particular, and to a lesser extent those of Assyria and Babylonia. But to this heritage which enabled it to rise almost at once to heights commensurate with the destinies of a great empire, Achaemenian art added something new—a spirit of grandeur and magnificence, of power and domination peculiar to itself.

For Achaemenian art, an art worthy of a King of Kings, faithfully reflects the political synthesis which this young, vigorous nation, so recently converted from the nomad way of life, achieved in creating the first world empire and, more noteworthy still, a form of government which, for the first time in human history, on so large a scale, was animated by a genuine spirit of justice and tolerance for all, regardless of race, colour and creed. From the artistic and spiritual heritage embodied in Achaemenian art, marked with the seal of its own originality and transmitted to the future, what emerges is neither 'the world of the dead' nor 'the world of the gods.' It is 'the world of the living' alone which triumphs in a vision diffused through many lands and which justifies Iran's great historical mission in antiquity as an intermediary between the settled peoples of the West and the still mobile East.

PART THREE

APPENDIX OF ILLUSTRATIONS
GLOSSARIAL INDEX
BIBLIOGRAPHY
LIST OF ILLUSTRATIONS

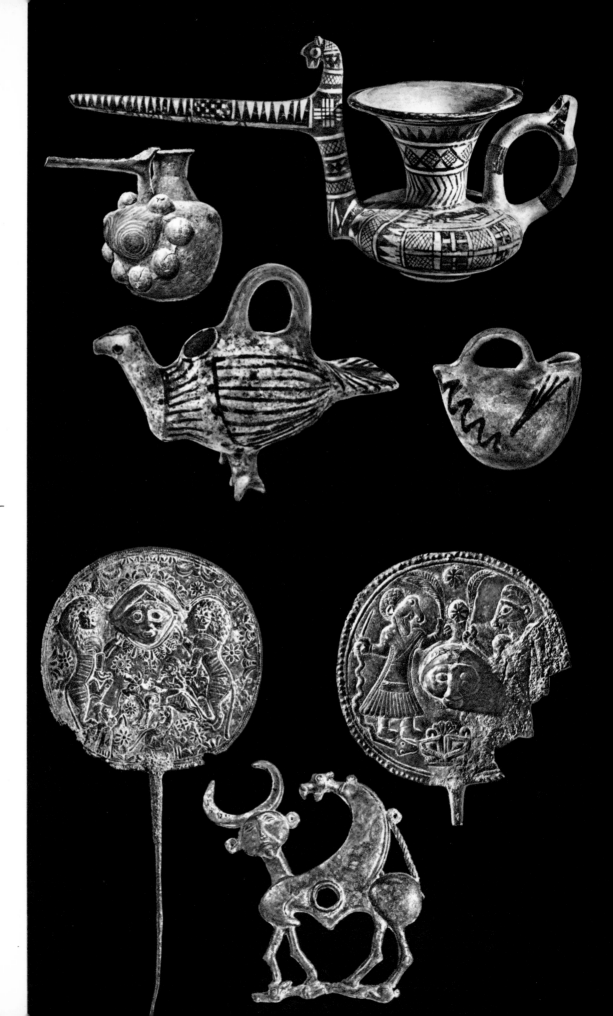

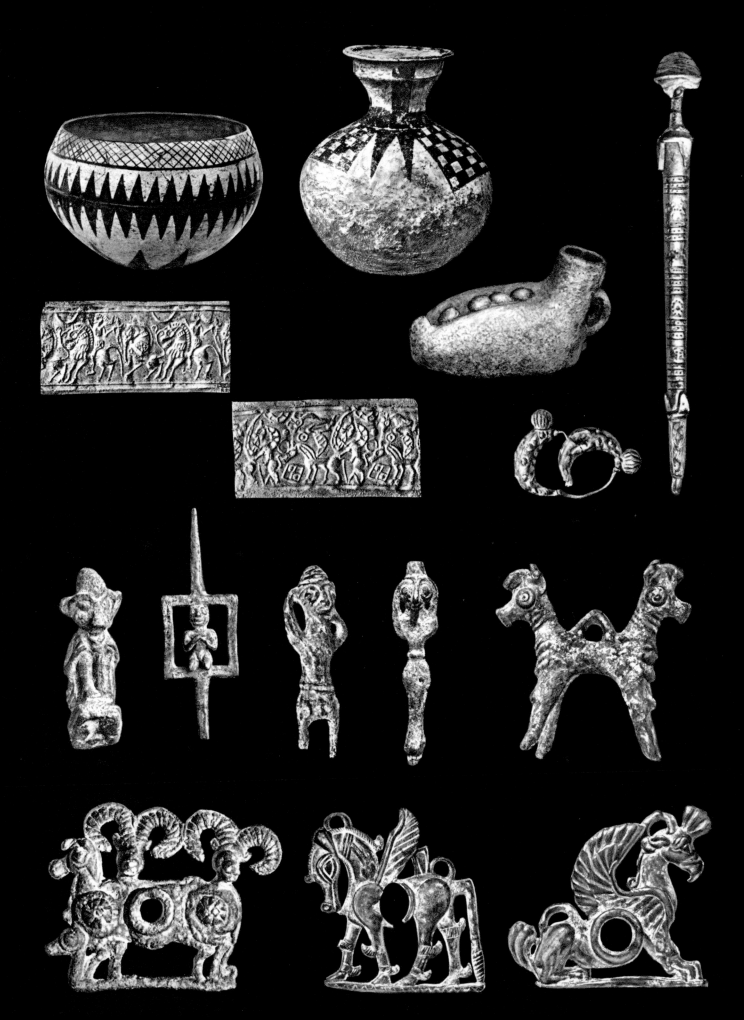

501 to 505

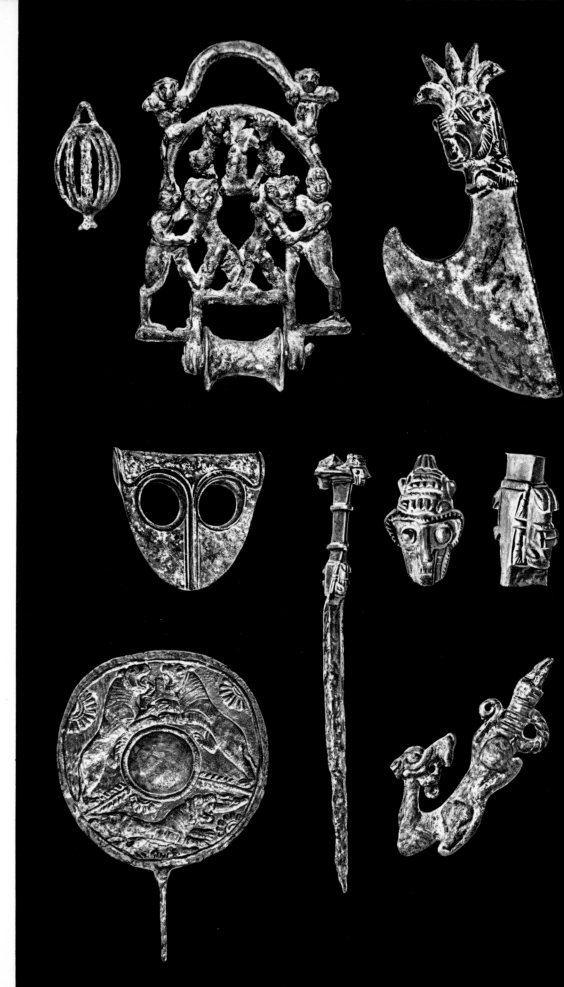

506 to 511

512 to 517

CHAPTER III

518 to 523

524 to 527

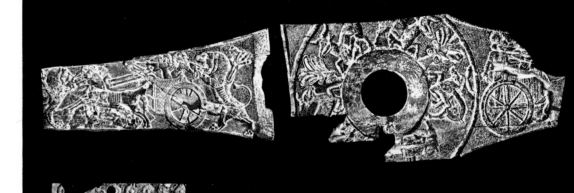

528 to 537

538 to 540

378
379

CHAPTER V

541 to 545

546 to 554

555 to 559

560 to 563

564 to 567

380
381

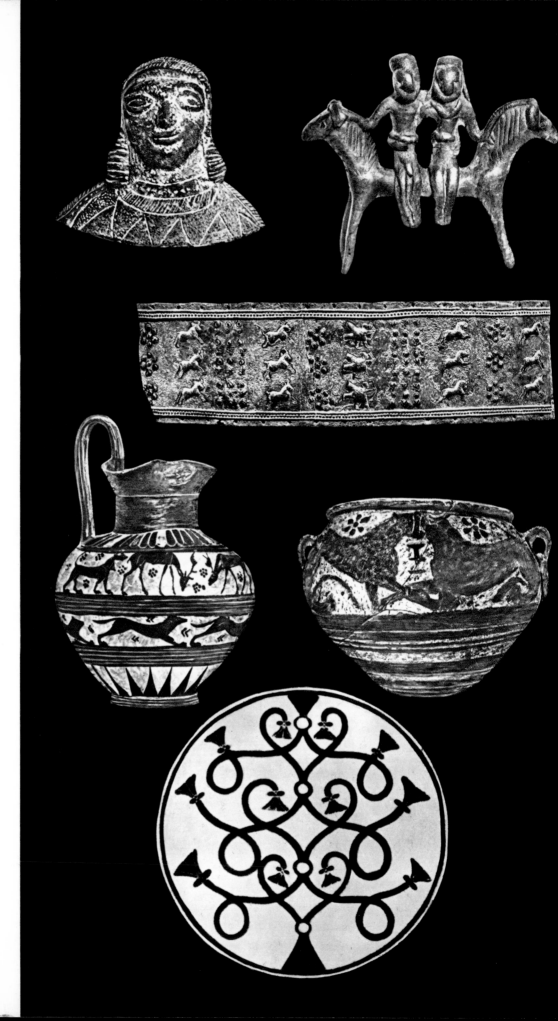

568 to 571

572 to 579

580 to 583

584 and 585

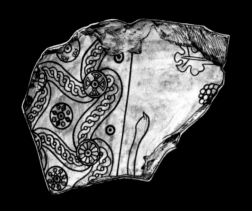

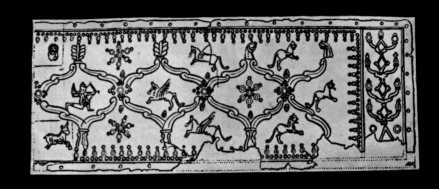

GLOSSARIAL INDEX

Each work reproduced is listed under the place where it was discovered.

ABACUS — Slab forming the uppermost member of the capital of a column. . . . . *p.* 353

ABDALONYMOS — Last king of Sidon, Persian by birth. Alexander the Great restored him to the throne in 333 B.C. . . . . *p.* 351

ACHAEMENES — Founder of the Achaemenid dynasty (c. 700-675? B.C.). . . . *p.* 129, 131, 340

ACHAEMENIANS or ACHAEMENIDS — Persian royal dynasty whose name derives from Achaemenes, first of the line, who reigned c. 700 B.C. With Darius III, vanquished by Alexander the Great, the dynasty came to an end (330 B.C.) *p.* 22, 59, 61, 62, 68, 70, 74, 78, 85, 89, 90, 94, 97, 108, 114, 120, 123, 124, 125, 128-270, 283, 288, 293, 296, 299, 311, 312, 318, 322, 326, 340, 345-372

ACHELOUS — River god of Greek mythology, taking his name from the longest river in Greece (the present-day Aspropotamos) . . . . *fig.* 429

ADELYEVAS — Site on the north-western shore of Lake Van, where remains of an Urartian inscription and bas-relief have been found. . . . . . *p.* 108

AEGEAN CIVILIZATION — Links with Iran. . . *p.* 59, 342

AEGINA — Island in the Gulf of Aegina, near Athens. *fig.* 413

AESCHYLUS (525-456 B.C.) — One of the greatest of the Greek tragic poets, founder of the Greek drama. . . . . *p.* 340, 341

AHRIMAN — The power of evil and of darkness, brother and enemy of Ahuramazda. According to an ancient myth, both were the progeny of a bisexual being, Zurvan. Ahriman, as the first-born, had in the beginning ruled the world and Ahuramazda had to contend with him in order to establish his dominion. . . . . *p.* 51, 52, 71 *fig.* 64

AHURAMAZDA — Supreme god in the ancient Persian pantheon and also in the reformed religion introduced by Zoroaster. Creator of the world, he was named 'the Wise, the Lord.' Son of the androgynous deity, Zurvan, he was in perpetual opposition to his twin brother Ahriman, lord of evil, whom in the end he was to vanquish . *p.* 44, 51, 52, 71, 88, 89, 140, 154, 156, 157, 199, 229, 233, 234, 264, 269, 359 *fig.* 64, 247, 278

AKHALGORI — Site in the Caucasus (Georgia). . *p.* 265 *fig.* 325, 559

AKINAKES — Short Scythian sword. *p.* 13, 90, 116, 206, 262, 315

AKKAD — Ancient city and state of Mesopotamia, whose founder, Sargon of Akkad, conquered the Sumerians. His dynasty ruled all Mesopotamia for nearly two centuries (2470-2285 B.C.) . . *p.* 2, 347

AKURGAL (Ekrem) — Turkish archaeologist and art historian. Professor at Ankara University. Director of Turkish archaeological research. . . *p.* 280

ALABASTRUM — Small narrow-necked perfume bottle or ointment jar, without handles or with lugs. . . . . *p.* 260

AL-BIRUNI, see BIRUNI.

ALBRIGHT (W.F.) — American Orientalist (born 1891). Former director of the American School of Oriental Research in Jerusalem and Professor of Semitic Languages in the Johns Hopkins University, Baltimore. . . . . *p.* 281

ALEPPO — City in northern Syria, already mentioned in tablets found at Mari (18th century B.C.) *p.* 295

ALEXANDER THE GREAT (356-323 B.C.) — King of Macedon, son of Philip II. Freed the Greek states of Asia Minor, occupied the Phoenician cities, founded Alexandria, invaded Egypt and advanced into Mesopotamia. After his victory over Darius III (331 B.C.) all the capitals of the Persian Empire (Babylon, Susa, Persepolis, Ecbatana) opened their gates to him. Parthyene, Hyrcania, Aria, Arachosia, Bactria and Sogdiana were subdued and reorganized (329-328) and new Alexandrias founded at strategic points. Entering the Indus valley, Alexander advanced to the Hydaspes, but here his exhausted troops refused to go any further. He built a fleet and instructed Admiral Nearchus to reach the Persian Gulf. Then he returned to Susa where the end of the campaign was celebrated with five days' festivities (February, 325); he went on to Babylon, where he died (323) when everything seemed set for a new conquest, that of Carthage *p.* XII, XIII, 154, 207, 250, 251, 351, 352 *fig.* 447

ALGUET TOMB — Site in the Caucasus (Georgia) . *p.* 261

AL MINA — Port on the coast of Syria, at the mouth of the Orontes . . . . *p.* 331

ALTAI — Mountainous region in South Siberia *p.* 77, 288, 360, 364, 366

AMARAVATI — Ruined city in the eastern Deccan between the deltas of the Godavari and Kistna rivers. Capital of the mighty kingdom of the Andhra dynasty (early 2nd century B.C. to early 3rd century A.D.), which made a stand against the Greco-Scythian tribes established in North India. Amaravati stood for an 'Indian India', last refuge of the truly national genius. The art of this region helps to bridge the gap between the ancient schools of Bharhut and Sanchi and medieval Hindu art *p.* 357 *fig.* 459

AMLASH — Locality in the mountainous region south-west of the Caspian Sea. Objects from megalithic tombs of the 8th and 9th centuries B.C. *p.* XVI, 6, 30-39, 41, 77, 286, 297

AMMIANUS MARCELLINUS — Roman historian born at Antioch about A.D. 330. Served under Constantius II and accompanied the Emperor Julian in his campaign against the Persians (363). His history (*Rerum Gestarum Libri XXXI*), though incomplete, contains much useful information about Iran and the Iranians . . . . *p.* 319

AMPHICTYONY — A league of neighbouring communities grouped round a sanctuary and observing the same cults . . . . *p.* 42

AMPHORA — Large vessel for wine or oil, having a handle on each side of the neck and usually ending in a point so that it can be fixed in the ground. *p.* 253 *fig.* 307, 333, 410

AMU DARYA — Modern name of the river Oxus, which forms the boundary between Afghanistan and the U.S.S.R. It flows into the Aral Sea *p.* 90

ANAHITA — Goddess of the waters, fertility and procreation. Her full name *Ardvi Sura Anahita* seems to signify 'Lofty, mighty, immaculate.' She was also associated with warfare *p.* 88, 229, 230, 250

ANATOLIA — The Asiatic territory of modern Turkey, roughly corresponding to Asia Minor. . . . *p.* 29

ANNUBANINI — King of the Lullubi (3rd millennium B.C.), represented on a bas-relief near the village of Sar-i-Pul-i-Zohab in western Iran . . . . *p.* 2

ANSHAN — Town founded by Teispes, son of Achaemenes. Site unknown, but probably identifiable with Masjid-i-Sulaiman. . . . . *p.* 129

ANTIGONUS CYCLOPS (382-301 B.C.) — One of the generals of Alexander the Great and father of Demetrius Poliorcetes. After Alexander's death he was governor of Greater Phrygia, Lycia and Pamphylia. Killed in the battle of Ipsus in Phrygia (301) . . . . *p.* 351, 352 *fig.* 452

APADANA — Large audience hall in Achaemenian palaces *p.* 94, 138-140, 144, 156, 157, 201, 207, 209, 215, 225, 245, 256, 258, 312, 346

Architecture :

Sculpture :

APHRATI — Site in Crete. . . . *p.* 336 *fig.* 419

APOLLO — Greek god of light, music, poetry and prophecy. . . . . *p.* 343

ARACHOSIA — Province of the Persian Empire between Drangiana on the west and India on the east. Now forms part of Baluchistan. . . *p.* 140

ARADOS — Phoenician city and island linked by a bridge to the continent and facing Antarados which served as its port. Present-day Ruad, north of Tripoli off the Syrian coast. . . . . *p.* 353

ARAL SEA — Inland sea in Central Asia, east of the Caspian. . . . . *p.* XI, 4

ARAMAIC — Lingua franca of the Achaemenian Empire. . . . . *p.* 154, 268, 356

ARAXES — River in the Caucasus, flowing into the Caspian Sea. Now the boundary between U.S.S.R. and Iran. . . . . *p.* 302

ARDEBIL — Town in northern Iran, near the Caspian Sea . . . . *p.* 258

ARES — Greek god of war, assimilated to the Roman Mars . . . . *p.* 298

ARGISTIS I — King of Urartu (781-760 B.C.) *p.* 38, 247, 295, 299

ARGONAUTS — Greek heroes who sailed in the Argo, under Jason, to Colchis in quest of the Golden Fleece. . . . . *p.* 342

ARGOS — City in the eastern Peloponnese, ancient capital of Argolis . . . . *p.* 121, 336, 343

ARIARAMNES (640-615? B.C.) — Son of Teispes and grandson of Achaemenes. On a gold tablet found at Hamadan he is described as 'Great King, King of Kings, King of the land of Parsa' (or Persis, present-day Fars). . . . . *p.* 129, 268

ARISTOPHANES (c. 450-386 B.C.) — Greatest comic poet of ancient Greece . . . . *p.* 260

ARMENIA — Region of high plateaux in Hither Asia, overlooking on all sides the neighbouring lands: Transcaucasia, Azerbaijan, Persia, Kurdistan and Cappadocia. The proto-Armenian kingdom regained its independence after the destruction of Nineveh (612 B.C.), then was conquered by the Medes and Persians. After Alexander's victories it was made over to the Seleucids of Syria. In 149 B.C. the Parthian king Arsaces established in Armenia, on behalf of his brother Valarsaces, the dynasty of the Arsacids of Armenia, one of whose most famous members was Abgar, who made Edessa his capital and in whose reign the Christian religion was preached in Armenia. The Sassanians, however, tried to stamp out Christianity and replace it with Mazdaeism. In the 7th century A.D. the Sassanians were superseded by the Caliphs. Today Armenia is divided between the U.S.S.R., Turkey and Persia. *p.* 157, 229, 252

ARSAMES — Achaemenid king (590-550? B.C.). On a gold tablet found at Hamadan he is described as 'Great King, King of Kings, King of Parsa, son of Ariaramnes the king, the Achaemenid.' Arsames was the father of Hystaspes and grandfather of Darius the Great . . . . . *p.* 243, 244

ARTAXERXES I — Achaemenid king (465-424 B.C.), son of Xerxes. 'His reign witnessed an extension of cultural relations between Persia and Greece, which explains some changes in the art of his time. This was the age in which Herodotus wrote his *History* and probably Democritus would not have developed his atomic theory had he not been in contact with Babylonian scholars.' *p.* 140, 142, 201, 206, 207, 222, 223, 225, 230, 268, 346 *fig.* 248

ARTAXERXES II — Achaemenid king (404-358 B.C.), son of Darius II. 'What Darius and Xerxes failed to achieve with their mighty war-machine, Artaxerxes achieved with his gold, which he employed unscrupulously for diplomatic ends. But at the very moment when his power seemed at its height and he had the Greeks of Europe at his mercy, the revolt of the satraps in the western provinces brought the Empire to the verge of disintegration. Though his sole aim throughout his reign was to safeguard his frontiers, the task proved to be beyond his powers.' *p.* 140, 154, 224, 229, 230, 353 *fig.* 280

ARTAXERXES III — Achaemenid king (358-338 B.C.), son of Artaxerxes II. A strong ruler, though brutal and ruthless, he reconquered Egypt and re-established the unity of the Persian Empire. Killed by an assassin and succeeded by his son Arses (338-335). *p.* 130, 230 *fig.* 280

ARYBALLOS — Vase shaped like a pouch drawn tight at the neck. . . . . *p.* 15, 19, 335 *fig.* 583

ASHI ('the good') — Iranian deity, sister of Sraosha. Fertility goddess, protectress of newly wed couples and animals in the rutting season. She dowered women with beauty, happiness and wealth. . *p.* 46, 48, 50, 94, 229

ASIA, CENTRAL — Links with Iran. *p.* 3, 17, 76, 350

ASIANIC — Relating to the indigenous, non-Indo-European population of Western Asia, before the coming of the Indo-Europeans in the 2nd millennium B.C. . . . . *p.* 3, 4, 48, 86

ASKOS — Vessel for water or wine shaped like a leather bottle. . . . . *p.* 15, 20

ASOKA — Emperor of India (c. 274-237/6 B.C.), belonging to the Maurya dynasty. . . *p.* 356, 357

ASSUR — Oldest of the capital cities of Assyria, on the west bank of the Tigris, below the confluence of the Great Zab. Present-day Qalaat Shergat. *p.* 3, 307, 324

ASSUR — Patron god of the city of Assur and supreme god of the Assyrian pantheon . . . . . *p.* 234

ASSURBANIPAL — King of Assyria (668-626 B.C.), son of Esarhaddon *p.* 102, 138, 259, 283, 285, 302

ASSYRIA — Northern part of Mesopotamia, overlapping the region between the Tigris and Euphrates, including the whole Mosul basin on the north,

and touching the western outskirts of Iran on the east. The Iranians always kept in close touch with the arts, religion and politics of Assyria . *p.* 4, 42, 59, 66, 85, 90, 98, 100, 104, 112, 125, 129, 147, 154, 234, 282-285, 301, 302, 308, 309, 316, 319, 326, 327, 372

ASTYAGES — Last king of Media (585-550 B.C.). Defeated by Cyrus the Great, his vassal, who was the son of Cambyses I and Mandane, Astyages' daughter. . . . . *p.* 129

ASWAN — Town of Upper Egypt, on the Nile, south of the First Cataract . . . . *p.* 142

ATHENA — Greek goddess, daughter of Zeus and Metis. In her were combined the qualities of both: power and 'good counsel.' She was protectress of States and all that caused prosperity. Patroness of agriculture, she invented the plough and other agricultural implements. She gave the Greeks the olive-tree. One of her functions was to see to the observance of the laws and the maintenance of order in courts of justice. She was also regarded as a goddess of war; hence the practice of representing her helmeted and carrying a lance . . . . . . *p.* 298

ATHENS — The leading city of ancient Greece, in the plain of Attica, dominated by the 'altar-rock' of the Acropolis on which the Parthenon stands. *p.* XII, 298, 346, 348

ATLAS — Male figure employed instead of a column to support a superstructure (cf. CARYATID) *p.* 311

ATREK — River flowing into the south-eastern corner of the Caspian and forming the boundary between Iran and the U.S.S.R. . . . . *p.* 3

ATTICA — Region of ancient Greece, around Athens. The Attic art of classical Greece is noted for its characteristic purity and refinement *p.* 298, 334, 345 *fig.* 409

AVESTA — Collection of sacred books pertaining to the Mazdaean religion, attributed to Zoroaster. *p.* 44, 45, 94, 230

AZERBAIJAN — Province of north-west Iran, occupying a high mountain plateau. Ancient Atropatene. *p.* 258, 287, 305

BABYLON — Capital of Babylonia. The ancient city stood on both banks of the Euphrates. At the height of its glory in the Neo-Babylonian period, especially in the reign of Nebuchadnezzar II (604-562 B.C.) *p.* XII, XIII, 3, 138, 224, 225, 229, 268, 282, 283, 307, 327 *fig.* 274

BABYLONIA — Ancient Mesopotamian empire, capital Babylon *p.* XII, 2, 4, 59, 100, 104, 142, 147, 282, 308, 327, 372

BACTRA — Present-day Balkh in Afghanistan. Capital of the Greco-Bactrian kingdom founded about 250 B.C. and overthrown by an invasion of Iranian nomads about 130 B.C. Situated north of the Hindu Kush and south of the confluence of the Balkh river and the Oxus (Amu Darya) . . . . . *p.* 229, 250

BACTRIA — Ancient country in the great plain of northern Afghanistan, between the Hindu Kush on the south and the Oxus on the north. . *p.* XI, 75, 90, 94, 140, 248

BADAKHSHAN — Province of north-eastern Afghanistan. Mines of balas rubies and lapis lazuli *p.* 76

BAGHUZ (YRZI) — Site on the left bank of the Euphrates, opposite Dura Europos . . . *p.* 318 *fig.* 390 b

BAHRAMI (M.) — Iranian Orientalist, died 1951 . *p.* 321

BAKHTIARI — Mountains in the western part of the Iranian plateau, forming part of the Zagros range. Named after the tribes inhabiting the district. *p.* 129, 139

BALAWAT — Site in northern Mesopotamia (Iraq), with the ruins of a palace built by Shalmaneser III. *p.* 299

BARBERINI TOMB — Tomb of an Etruscan prince at Praeneste (modern Palestrina), some 20 miles east of Rome. Excavated in 1855-56 *p.* 314 *fig.* 382

BARD-I-NISHANDAH — Site 15 miles north-east of Masjid-i-Sulaiman in the province of Khuzistan. *p.* 131

BARESMAN, see BARSOM.

BARIS (or VAR) — Stronghold said to have been built by the hero Yima (Jamshid) mentioned in the *Avesta* . . . . *p.* 355

BARNETT (R.D.) — British Orientalist, Keeper of the Department of Western Asiatic Antiquities at the British Museum. . . . . *p.* 327

BARROW — Ancient grave mound. *p.* 252, 280, 303, 307, 358

BARSOM — Bundle of branches tied together, symbolizing vegetal life in cult ceremonies . *p.* 48, 50-52, 87, 90, 91, 94, 247, 348 *fig.* 109

BASHLYK — Woollen cap peculiar to the nomad races. Shaped like a pointed hood, it had two long ribbons to fasten it round the neck. Still worn in Russia. . . . . *p.* 94

BEAKHEAD — Stylized head of a bird of prey, a characteristically Scythian motif. *p.* 112, 119, 303

BEGRAM (KAPICI) — Ancient town some 40 miles north of Kabul, probably founded by a Greco-Bactrian king. Summer capital of the Kushan dynasty . . . . *p.* 125, 357 *fig.* 460

BENARES — Ancient Indian city on the Ganges, a great religious centre since the 6th century B.C. *p.* 356

BEROSSUS — Babylonian priest (4th-3rd century B.C.), author of a once famous history of Chaldaea and Assyria, now known only by extracts preserved by later writers . . . . *p.* 129

BES — Egyptian god, of non-Egyptian origin, whose cult became widely diffused in the first millennium B.C. Much revered by the Achaemenians as protector of women and children, also of men in battle. Several heads of Bes in frit were found in excavations at Susa. . . . . *p.* 264

BESHTAU — Caucasian site on the mountain of that name . . . . *p.* 308

BIRUNI — Arab scholar and historian (A.D. 973-1048), of Iranian origin . . . . *p.* 4

BISHAPUR — Royal city in the province of Fars, founded by the Sassanid king Shapur I in the third century A.D. Near the modern town of Kazerum. Excavated by a French expedition from 1935 to 1941 . . . . *p.* 138

BISUTUN (BEHISTUN) — In the province of Kurdistan, east of Kermanshah. Site of the bas-relief of Darius the Great and three Parthian bas-reliefs. *p.* 89, 234, 236, 269

— View of the site (wash drawing) . . . . *fig.* 282
Sculpture:
— Bas-relief of Darius : Ahuramazda . . . *fig.* 278
— Rock reliefs: Darius the Great . . . *fig.* 283, 284

BLACK SEA — The Pontus Euxinus of the ancients, inland sea connected with the Mediterranean by the Bosporus and the Hellespont (Dardanelles) *p.* XI, 295, 296, 319, 331, 341, 342, 358

BOEOTIA — Region of ancient Greece, north of the Gulf of Corinth, capital Thebes . . . . *p.* 333-335 *fig.* 407, 410

BOGHAZKÖY — Capital of the Hittite kingdom, east of Ankara . . . . *p.* 226

BOREUX (Charles) — French Egyptologist, former Curator of the Louvre. . . . . *p.* 280

BOSTAN-ESH-SHEIKH — Site near Sidon, in Phoenicia . . . . *p.* 351, 352

BRACTEAE — Stamped gold plaquettes perforated with holes or fitted with rings so as to fasten them to garments. *p.* 263, 264 *fig.* 154, 320, 264, 548-555, 557, 558

BRONZE AGE — Prehistoric period preceding the Iron Age, characterized by the use of bronze for tools, weapons and artefacts. Begins in Iran about 2000 B.C. . . . . *p.* 278

BUCCHERO NERO — Pottery made of a black paste covered with a black glossy slip. . . . *p.* 25, 337

BUKHARA — Ancient city in Russian Turkestan *p.* 3

BURIATS — Siberian tribe living east, south and west of Lake Baikal. . . . . *p.* 291

BUSSAGLI (Mario) — Italian Orientalist, specializing in the arts and civilizations of India and Central Asia. . . . . *p.* 357

CAERE — Etruscan city (modern Cerveteri), some 20 miles north-west of Rome. . . *p.* 310 *fig.* 373

CAMBYSES I — Achaemenid king (600-559 B.C.), father of Cyrus the Great . . . . *p.* 129, 131-133

CAMBYSES II — Achaemenid king (529-521 B.C.), son of Cyrus. Conquered Egypt . . *p.* 140, 230

CAMERON (G.G.) — American Assyriologist and historian, head of the Oriental Institute of the University of Michigan. . . . . *p.* 281

CAPPADOCIA — Inland district in the centre of Asia Minor, between Pontus and Armenia *p.* 290, 302

CARIA — District of Asia Minor bounded by the Aegean Sea and the eastern Mediterranean. Subdued by Cyrus, the native rulers being appointed satraps. After being conquered by Alexander the Great, Caria was incorporated into the kingdom of Syria, then into the Roman Empire . . . . *p.* 22, 355

CARYATID — Female figure employed instead of a column to support a superstructure . *p.* 23, 77, 353 *fig.* 23, 101

CASPIAN SEA — Inland sea between the U.S.S.R. and Iran . . . . *p.* XI, 3, 4, 31, 86, 97

CATACOMB CULTURE — A Bronze Age culture of South Russia, in the steppe country of the lower Volga, Don and Dnieper, characterized by burials in catacombs. . . . . *p.* 301

CAUCASUS — Mountain range between the Black Sea and the Caspian. *p.* 4, 37, 59, 76, 98, 114, 252, 258, 265, 279, 286, 301, 303, 309 *fig.* 336, 337, 380

ÇAVUCH KÖI — Site near Panderma (Asia Minor) on the south shore of the Sea of Marmara. *fig.* 442

CELTIC ART — Art of the Celtic peoples in western and central Europe in the first millennium B.C. *p.* 371

CHAHAR-TAGH ('four arches') — Pavilion with four pillars supporting four arches surmounted by a cupola. Served in religious ceremonies of the Sassanian period, the sacred fire being lit in this kiosk-like building open on all four sides . *p.* 229

CHARBONNEAUX (Jean) — French archaeologist and art historian. Curator of the Department of Greek and Roman Antiquities at the Louvre and member of the Institut de France . . . . *p.* 351

CHERTOMLYK — Site with a Scythian royal tomb of the 4th century B.C. Situated north-east of Olbia in South Russia, in the great bend of the Dnieper. *p.* 115, 358
— Gold sword hilt . . . . *fig.* 463

CHINA — Links with ancient Iran. Cf. CONTENDING STATES and HAN . . *p.* 51, 57, 79, 125, 289

CHIUSI — Etruscan city (ancient Clusium) in Tuscany, 50 miles south-east of Siena . . . . *fig.* 405

CHOGA ZAMBIL — Site in the province of Khuzistan, 30 miles from Susa, with remains of an Elamite city founded in the 13th century B.C. and destroyed by Assurbanipal about 640 B.C. . . *p.* 81, 133, 135, 139, 283, 284
— Axe . . . . *fig.* 342

CHORASMIA — Region extending over both banks of the lower Oxus (Amu Darya) and around the Aral Sea. It formed part of the 16th Satrapy under the Achaemenians. From the 3rd century A.D. an independent kingdom. Inhabitants of Iranian origin . . . . *p.* 4, 140

CHTHONIAN — Relating to the gods or spirits of the underworld . . . . *p.* 51, 333

CIMMERIANS — A people of Iranian origin, from South Russia, who crossed the Caucasus and settled in western Iran and Asia Minor in the 8th (?) century B.C. *p.* 4, 41, 42, 57, 72, 77, 85, 86, 124, 237, 250, 281, 282, 284-286, 301, 302, 361

CINVAT — The bridge which man crosses after death and which, if he has led a good life, will guide him to Paradise. If he has led an evil life the bridge becomes narrower and narrower till it is like a knife-blade, with the result that he loses his footing and falls into Hell, where he will undergo torments proportionate to his sins. . . . . *p.* 45, 52

CIRE-PERDUE — Technique of metal-casting. *p.* 299

COIFFARD (Jacques) — Former French Ambassador to Iran, who when on duty at Teheran assembled one of the finest private collections of Luristan bronzes (now in the Louvre) . . . . *p.* 26

COLAPIOS — Early Greek navigator, from Samos, who discovered Tartessus in south-western Spain (Herodotus, iv. 152). . . . . *p.* 331

COLCHIS, see KULKHAI.

CONTENAU (Georges) — Famous French archaeologist, historian and Assyriologist. . . . . *p.* 56

CONTENDING STATES — A period of political struggle in China, lasting from the 6th to the 3rd century B.C. . . . . *p.* 51, 79

CORINTH — In the Peloponnese, one of the most prosperous cities of ancient Greece and a rival of Athens and Sparta. Destroyed by the Romans, 146 B.C. Now a port on the Gulf of Corinth, at the entrance of the Isthmus . . . . . . *p.* 331

CRETE — Greek island in the eastern Mediterranean, birthplace of Zeus and home of the famous Minoan civilization *p.* 121, 331, 336, 340, 341 *fig.* 417, 419, 432

CTESIAS — Greek physician and historian (fl. late 5th century B.C.) who spent nearly twenty years at the Achaemenian court under Artaxerxes II. *p.* 154

CYAVANA — According to a Brahmanic legend, the wealthy Cyavana persuaded Indra to admit to the company of the gods the Nasatya twins who had given him eternal youth. . . . . *p.* 70

CYAXARES — Median king (633-584 B.C.), son of Kashtariti (Phraortes). . . . *p.* 85, 86, 98, 129, 327

CYPRUS — Greek island in the eastern Mediterranean. . . . . *p.* 90, 352, 353

CYRUS I — Achaemenid king (c. 640-600 B.C.), son of Teispes, received as his share of the Persian kingdom the province of Parsumash, while his brother Ariaramnes became king of the land of Parsa. Cambyses I, son of Cyrus I, reunited the Achaemenian kingdom. . . . . *p.* 129

CYRUS II, THE GREAT (559-529 B.C.) — Founder of the Persian Empire, son of Cambyses and Mandane, daughter of Astyages, King of Media. Few kings have achieved such high and honourable renown as Cyrus. A great military commander and leader of men, generous and broad-minded, he refrained from forcing new forms of government on the kingdoms he brought under his control. The Persians called him 'father,' the Hellenes whom he had conquered saw in him a worthy ruler and law-giver, and the Jews regarded him as 'the Lord's anointed.' In an historical text written in Babylon, Cyrus speaks as follows. 'After visiting all lands in search of an upright ruler, a king after his own heart, whom he could take by his hand, Marduk has made known the name, "Cyrus of Anshan," and designated him to rule the world.' *p.* 10, 129-133, 135, 136, 154, 224, 230, 237, 290, 296, 346, 348, 349 *fig.* 179, 185

DALBOKI — Site in Bulgaria with Scythian tombs of the 5th century B.C. . . . . . *p.* 310 *fig.* 374

DALTON (O.M.) — British Orientalist and Byzantine scholar. . . . . *p.* 247

DAMGHAN — Town some 200 miles east of Teheran, with the ruins of a Sassanian palace . . . . *p.* 2

DANUBE — River of Central Europe, flowing through the Balkans and emptying into the Black Sea. Its importance as an age-old traffic artery and cultural link between Western Europe and the Near East is attested by archaeological evidence, by traditions and myths, and by historical events . . . *p.* 136

DARIUS I — Achaemenid king (521-485 B.C.), son of Hystaspes. 'He created a powerful, centralized, national State. The feudal society that had prevailed under Cyrus the Great was replaced by an administrative and fiscal system in which the different nationalities were respected. His great inscription at Bisutun is a kind of credo glorifying the enlightened imperialism of a just and merciful monarch. Achaemenian civilization in his reign reached the height of its power and glory.' *p.* XII, XIII, 78, 89, 90, 130, 136, 138-140, 142, 145, 147, 154, 156-158, 192, 193, 199, 201, 206, 207, 209, 222, 224, 227, 229, 230, 233, 234, 244, 260, 263, 269, 299, 346, 347, 355, 357, 362, *fig.* 189, 233, 246, 255, 279, 283, 284, 310, 329

DARIUS II — Achaemenid king (424-404 B.C.), son of Artaxerxes I. His whole reign was marked by intrigues and corruption; Persian gold was largely responsible for the catastrophe that befell Athens in the Peloponnesian War against Sparta. The state of affairs in the palace and the Court, where the royal family was constantly embroiled in feuds, reflected Darius's tortuous foreign policy *p.* 142, 225, 230, 268

DARIUS III CODOMANNUS — Last Achaemenid king (335-330 B.C.), he was a courageous man but, too confident in the might of his army, he under-estimated the danger of Alexander's 'crusade' against the Persian Empire. After his defeat he fled to Ecbatana, then to the northern provinces. He was betrayed, imprisoned and stabbed to death near Damghan by Bessus, his satrap, viceroy of Bactria. . . . . *p.* XIII, 230

DASCYLION (DASCYLIUM), see EREGLI.

DA-U-DUKHTAR — Site in the province of Fars, between Pasargadae and Masjid-i-Sulaiman, with a rock tomb attributed to Cambyses I *p.* 132, 230 *fig.* 180

DEIOCES — Median chieftain (c. 715 B.C.), said by Herodotus to have been the founder of the Median royal dynasty. . . . . *p.* 4, 86, 284

DELOS — Aegean island, smallest of the Cyclades. Seat of the worship of Apollo and active trade centre. *p.* 351, 352 *fig.* 449-452

DEMETRIUS — Greco-Bactrian king who between 180 and 170 B.C. reconquered north-western India after the collapse of the Maurya dynasty . *p.* 229

DEMETRIUS I POLIORCETES ('Besieger') — King of Macedon (294-286 B.C.), son of Antigonus Cyclops . . . . *p.* 351, 352

DIAKONOV (I.M.) — Soviet Assyriologist and historian. . . . . *p.* 86, 250, 281

DIAKONOV (M.M.) — Soviet Assyriologist and historian . . . . *p.* 42, 280

DIEULAFOY (Marcel) — French archaeologist (1844-1920) who, with his wife, excavated the Apadana of Susa (1884-86). . . . . *p.* 142

DNIEPER — River in South Russia flowing into the Black Sea . . . . *p.* 279, 303, 358

DUKKAN-I-DAUD — Median rock tomb near the modern town of Sar-i-Pul-i-Zohab (western Iran), on the road from Baghdad to Kermanshah *p.* 87 *fig.* 111, 112

DUMEZIL (Georges) — French Orientalist, philologist and historian of comparative religion. Professor at the Collège de France . . . . *p.* 70

DUSSAUD (René) — French Orientalist, historian of art and comparative religion (1868-1958) *p.* 48, 51, 70

ECBATANA (HAGMATANA) — The modern city of Hamadan (western Iran). Capital of the Median then of the Achaemenian kingdom, and summer capital of the Parthians. Said to have been founded by Deioces in the late 8th century B.C. *p.* 42, 80, 85-87, 94-97, 126, 138, 224, 229, 237, 250-252, 256, 261, 263, 264, 266, 285, 295, 297, 322, 338, 346, 362
Bronzes:
— Ibexes . . . . *fig.* 124
— Jug. . . . . *fig.* 122
Goldwork:
— Belt buckle and plaque. . . . . . *fig.* 326, 327
— Cup . . . . *fig.* 125
— Cup with Darius's name . . . . *fig.* 310
— Cup with Xerxes' name . . . . *fig.* 309
— Dish with an eagle. . . . . *fig.* 478
— Sword . . . . *fig.* 328
— Winged-lion rhyton . . . . . . *fig.* 290, 306
Appendix . . . . *fig.* 548-557, 560

EGYPT — Links with Iran *p.* XII, XV, 80, 130, 135, 136, 140, 154, 214, 222, 245, 260, 268, 281, 302, 331, 340, 346

ELAM — Ancient kingdom (now western Iran) including the plain of Susiana and the Zagros mountains bordering it. Its conquests extended as far as Isfahan on the east and Babylon on the west. Fell to Assurbanipal (c. 640 B.C.) and thereafter declined *p.* XV, 2, 4, 59, 75, 81, 129, 140, 145, 147, 261, 268, 282, 283, 296, 299, 336, 372

GRYLLI — Intaglios and gems regarded as possessing a prophylactic or talismanic value. They usually represent various types of human and animal heads combined into a single grotesque or fantastic figure. A number of seal impressions taken from such gems, and dating to the Achaemenian period, have been found at Ur . . . . *p.* 63

GUDEA — Sumerian ruler (*patesi*) of Lagash in southern Mesopotamia (21st century B.C.). Several statues of Gudea, found by the French expedition to Telloh (Lagash), are in the Louvre. . . . *p.* 347

GUENNOL COLLECTION — Private collection in New York containing many superb works of the Achaemenian and Sassanian periods . . . *p.* 251

GURIANA — District near the north-western frontier of the kingdom of Urartu. . . . . *p.* 286

GUSCI (GUSHCHI) — Site near Lake Urmia where a fragment of a bronze belt was found (now in the Metropolitan Museum, New York) . . *p.* 121, 315

GUTI — A mountain tribe of Asianic or 'Zagro-Elamite' origin, living in the central zone of the Zagros range. Their invasion of Mesopotamia at the close of the 3rd millennium B.C. put an end to the Akkadian dynasty. . . . . *p.* 2, 284

HACKIN (Joseph) — French Orientalist, former Chief Curator of the Musée Guimet, Paris, and head of the Délégation Archéologique Française in Afghanistan. Joined the Free French forces during the war and went down with a torpedoed ship in 1941. . . . . *p.* 125

HALDIS — Supreme god of the Urartian pantheon. One of a triad, along with the god Tesheba and the goddess Ardini. His chief temple was at Musasir, west of Lake Urmia. . . . . *p.* 66, 68, 247, 296

HAMADAN, see ECBATANA.

HAN — Imperial dynasty of China (206 B.C.-A.D. 220). *p.* 125, 289, 291

HANCAR (F.) — Austrian Orientalist, ethnographer and historian. Professor at Vienna University *p.* 281

HANFMANN (G.M.A.) — American archaeologist and classical historian. Professor at Harvard and in charge of excavations at Sardis (Asia Minor). *p.* 346

HAOMA — The Indian Soma. At once a god and a beverage partaken of in the religious ceremonies of the early Iranians. It was made of a plant having mystical virtues. To the earthly *haoma* corresponded the celestial *haoma* which, in the resurrection, was to give men immortality. . . . . *p.* 50, 226

HARPAGOS — A Median general of the 6th century B.C. who joined forces with Cyrus and was made governor of Lydia. . . . . *p.* 349

HARPIES — Flying goddesses who carried off those whose disappearance was desired by the gods. They were originally depicted with beautiful flowing locks and wings on their backs. Later, the Greeks represented them as ugly monsters: birds with women's heads, long claws and ghastly, emaciated faces. . . . . *p.* 14, 338, 341, 349 *fig.* 425, 444

HASANLU — Site near the market town of Solduz, south-west of Lake Urmia (Azerbaijan) *p.* XVI, 6, 24-29, 41, 60, 77, 79, 123, 280, 286, 293, 297, 301, 308
— Tomb . . . . *fig.* 131
Bronzes:
— Bits. . . . . *fig.* 338, 339
— Lion . . . . *fig.* 28, 29
— Phalera: winged horse . . . . *fig.* 350
— Stag's head . . . . *fig.* 372
Goldwork:
— Bowl. . . . . *fig.* 30, 31
— Ear-ring . . . . *fig.* 27a
— Necklaces. . . . . *fig.* 27b-c
Pottery:
— Kernos . . . . *fig.* 24, 335
— Libation vase . . . . *fig.* 25

HATHOR — Egyptian goddess, often represented with a cow's head or ears . . . . *p.* 47

HATRA — Capital of a small kingdom in northern Mesopotamia, near Mosul. Extensive ruins of the 2nd century A.D. . . . . *p.* 265

HECATOMNOS — Satrap of Caria (395-367 B.C.). *p.* 355

HELLENENDORF — Protohistoric site with cemeteries, in Transcaucasia. . . . . *p.* 305

HELLENISTIC ART — Greek art after the classical period, from the time of Alexander the Great to the first century B.C. . . . . . *p.* 353, 357 *fig.* 451, 453

HENNING (W.B.) — English Orientalist, epigraphist, philologist, specialist in ancient Iranian languages. Professor at the School of Oriental Languages, London, and the University of California, Berkeley. *p.* 230

HERACLES — One of the great gods and heroes of Greek mythology, son of Zeus and Alcmene, famous for his Twelve Labours . . . . *p.* 13, 112

HERAION — Temple dedicated to the Greek goddess Hera, sister and wife of Zeus. Most famous were the temples of Argos and Samos *p.* 121, 331, 336, 343 *fig.* 406, 584

HERODOTUS — Greek historian (c. 484-425 B.C.), called the Father of History, who travelled widely in Asia, Africa and Europe, gathering material for the *History* that occupied him all his life *p.* 85, 86, 88, 94, 99, 225, 299, 302, 331

HEROON — Shrine dedicated to a hero. . *p.* 349

HERZFELD (Ernst) — German Orientalist, epigraphist, archaeologist and historian (1879-1948). Formerly professor at Berlin University and in charge of American excavations at Persepolis. Formerly at Princeton University. . . . . *p.* 124, 134

HISSAR — The existence of a prehistoric settlement in the neighbourhood of Damghan was suggested as early as 1880 by accidental discoveries of painted pottery. The exact site, Hissar, was identified by Herzfeld in 1925. E.F. Schmidt brought to light a palace and a fire temple containing stucco ornaments and dating to the period of the Sassanid king Kavad I (A.D. 488-531) . . . . *p.* 2-4

HITTITES — An ancient people who settled in Anatolia in the early 2nd millennium B.C. and formed a powerful kingdom. Capital, Boghazköy *p.* 131, 135, 222, 226

HOMER — The great epic poet of Greece (late 9th century B.C.?), author of the *Iliad* and the *Odyssey*. *p.* 21

HORUS — Egyptian sun god . . . . . *p.* 132, 229

HUART (Clément) — French Orientalist (1854-1926). *p.* XIV

HUNGARY — Scythian tombs . . . . . . *p.* 114

HURIN-SHEIKH-KHAN — Rock relief some 12 miles north of Sar-i-Pul-i-Zohab (Kurdistan) *p.* 2

HURRIANS — A people dwelling in the 3rd millennium B.C. in northern Mesopotamia and the Lake Van region. In the 2nd millennium they spread out into Syria and Palestine. Subsequently, under Semite pressure, they were forced to retreat and by the end of the 2nd millennium were confined to the region west and south of Lake Van. They had a language of their own, neither Semitic nor Indo-European, usually regarded as belonging to the Caucasian group. . . . . *p.* 3, 4

HURVIN, see KHURVIN.

HYDRIA — Large water jug . . . *p.* 334 *fig.* 415

HYRKANUS — Member of the family of the Tobiads (175-174 B.C.). Achaemenian influence can be seen in the façade of his residence near the Jordan *p.* 355

IBEX — Mountain goat with long, ridged horns *p.* 47, 96, 251, 264 *fig.* 44, 49, 305

IDAEAN CAVES — On Mount Ida in central Crete where, according to tradition, the 'Birth Cave' of Zeus was located. This was one of the places where his cult was celebrated. . . . . *p.* 340, 341

INDIA — Links with ancient Iran . *p.* XII, 4, 125, 268, 346, 356, 357, 366

INDRA — Supreme god in the Vedic pantheon, wielder of the thunderbolt, dispenser of rain and lord of the elements. . . . . *p.* 70

INDUS — River rising in the Himalayas, flowing through Kashmir and Pakistan to the Arabian Sea. *p.* XI, XII, XIV, 136, 371

INSHUSHINAK — Supreme god in the Elamite pantheon. To him was dedicated the Choga Zambil ziggurat . . . . *p.* 81

IONIA — Ancient Greek region on the west coast of Asia Minor, including Ephesus, Miletus, Phocaea and the adjacent islands (Samos, Chios). Brought under Persian domination by Cyrus the Great (559-529 B.C.) *p.* XI, 104, 140, 145, 223, 260, 348

IRON AGE — Period when iron came into general use for tools and weapons. Begins in Iran about 1000 B.C. . . . . *p.* 37, 73, 278

ISHNIQARAB — Elamite god . . . . . . *p.* 284

ISHPAKAI — Scythian chieftain who about 670 B.C. allied himself with the Mannaians and was killed in the campaign against the Assyrians. His name is said to derive from *aspaka* (horseman) or *spakaya* (from *spaka*, i.e. dog) . . . . *p.* 302

ISHTAR — Assyro-Babylonian goddess of love, fertility and warfare . . . . *p.* 250

JACOBSTHAL (Paul) — English art historian, formerly professor at Oxford . . . . *p.* 342

JANUS — Roman god with two opposite faces. A combination of two gods, of the sun and the moon. *p.* 47, 346

JASON — Greek hero who led the Argonauts in quest of the Golden Fleece . . . . *p.* 342

JAXARTES — River of Central Asia (the modern Syr Darya), flowing into the Aral Sea . *p.* 136, 371

JIN JIN — Town in the province of Fars, 4 miles west of Fahlian. Relay station on the road from Susa to Persepolis. Remains of a royal pavilion *p.* 224 *fig.* 273

JORDAN — River in Palestine, flowing into the Dead Sea . . . . *p.* XII, 355

JOSEPHUS, FLAVIUS (c. A.D. 37-93) — Jewish historian, author of a contemporary chronicle of the events which led to the end of the national existence of the Jews. . . . . *p.* 355

KA'BA-I-ZARDUSHT — Square tower at Naqsh-i-Rustam, actually a fire temple of the Achaemenian period . . . . *p.* 227, 296, 348

KALAR DASHT — Group of tombs in a valley of the Elburz chain, south of the Caspian Sea (Mazandaran). . . . . *p.* 97, 326
— Animal rhyton. . . . . *fig.* 128
— Cup . . . . *fig.* 127
— Gazelle's head rhyton . . . . *fig.* 402
— Gold dagger. . . . . *fig.* 129

KALATHOS — Tall cylindrical headdress worn by the Persians in the Achaemenian period. . *p.* 355

KANTHAROS — Two-handled vase or drinking cup. *p.* 334

KARAGODENASHK — Barrow in the Kuban valley (Caucasus). . . . . *p.* 359
— Rhyton. . . . . *fig.* 465

KARMIR BLUR — Urartian stronghold on the Upper Araxes (Transcaucasia), recently uncovered by Soviet archaeologists. . . . . *p.* 108, 306
— Helmet of King Sarduris . . . . . . *fig.* 119

KARS — City in north-eastern Turkey (Armenia) *p.* 315

KARTIR — Zoroastrian priest of the 3rd century A.D., founder of the official Sassanian Church. . *p.* 230

KASHTARITI — Son of the Median chieftain Deioces, called Phraortes by Herodotus (died 653 B.C.) *p.* 42, 85, 284, 301

KASSITES — A people of Asianic or 'Zagro-Elamite' stock, inhabiting the central Zagros area (present-day Luristan). Conquered Babylonia where a Kassite dynasty reigned from the 16th to the 12th century B.C.. . . . . *p.* 3, 4, 42, 70, 71, 282-285

KAZBEK — Ancient site in the Caucasus, where a treasure of the Achaemenian period was discovered *p.* 258

KELERMES — In the Kuban region (northern Caucasus), where burial mounds with royal Scythian tombs of the 6th century B.C. have been explored. *p.* 28, 77, 279, 303, 304, 315, 316, 327
— Applied ornament: lioness (?) . . . . *fig.* 362
— Axe . . . . *fig.* 365
— Mirror. . . . . *fig.* 366a
— Sword . . . . *fig.* 364

KENGAVAR — Village in Kurdistan, between Kermanshah and Hamadan, with remains of a Seleucid temple dedicated to Anahita. . . . . *p.* 285

KERCH — Seaport in the Crimea (Strait of Yenikale) on the site of the ancient Panticapaeum founded by Greek colonists . . . . *p.* 304

KERMAN — Town in the province of the same name, in south-eastern Iran . . . . *p.* 131, 140

KERMANSHAH — Town in the province of Kurdistan. . . . . *p.* 41, 80, 87, 282, 285

KERNOS — Ritual vessel holding one or more vases or cups intended to receive small quantities of offerings from worshippers. *p.* 19 *fig.* 17, 18, 24,335

KHALIL DEHLIL — Site in Kurdistan where Jacques de Morgan discovered three tombs, one of them containing pins contemporary with those of Ziwiyeh. *p.* 115

KHAROSHTI — First alphabet of Western India, derived from the Aramaic script . . . . . . *p.* 356

KHURVIN — Village in the southern foothills of the Elburz chain, about 50 miles west of Teheran, where a proto-Iranian cemetery was discovered by local peasants. *p.* XVI, 6, 17-23, 25, 26, 41, 58, 73, 76, 77, 79, 97, 123, 286, 297, 299, 305, 320
— Belt . . . . *fig.* 22
— Ear-rings. . . . . *fig.* 488
— Figurines. . . . . *fig.* 19, 20
— Kernoi. . . . . *fig.* 17, 18
— Mirror. . . . . *fig.* 23
— Pendants. . . . . *fig.* 21
— Pin . . . . *fig.* 489
— Vases . . . . *fig.* 15, 16, 487

KIRIRISHA — Elamite goddess who had a temple at Choga Zambil. . . . . *p.* 283

KISHESIM — Median town in north-western Iran represented on an Assyrian bas-relief . . . *fig.* 110

KISTHENES — Legendary land south-east of the Black Sea where, according to Aeschylus, the Gorgons lived . . . . *p.* 340

KIZKAPAN — Rock tomb cut in the mountain side near the bend of the Little Zab and the Shahrizor valley, in Iraqi Kurdistan, near Surdash. *p.* 88, 89, 229, 234, 237, 264, 269, 306, 319
— Rock tomb . . . . *fig.* 115, 116

KNOSSOS — Inland Cretan town in the plain of the river Kairatos. The discovery here of a Luristan bronze of the 8th or 7th century B.C. shows that Iran played a part in the give-and-take between the East and the Greek world . . . . *p.* 331

KOBAN — Site in the Caucasus, about 130 miles north of Tiflis, with an Iron Age cemetery. . . *p.* 72

KOFLER-TRUNIGER COLLECTION — Private Collection, Lucerne. . . . . *p.* 12

KOINE — A hybrid style, or artistic 'lingua franca,' used over a large area. *p.* 10, 27, 68, 78, 82, 109. 125, 295-343

KÖNIG (F.W.) — Austrian philologist and historian, professor at Vienna University . . . . . . *p.* 281

KOSTROMSKAYA STANITZA — Site in the Kuban (northern Caucasus) with barrows containing Scythian royal tombs of the 6th century B.C. *p.* 303, 317
— Gorytus ornament. . . . . *fig.* 363
— Scythian tomb . . . . *fig.* 132

KUBAN — A province of Ciscaucasia and the name of a river flowing through it into the Black Sea. *p.* 28, 252, 279, 303, 327, 358
— Rhyton. . . . . *fig.* 462

KUH-I-JEBET NABALIGHAN — Mountain chain on the northern outskirts of Luristan. . . . *p.* 285

KUH-I-RAHMAT ('Mountain of Mercy') — Mountain on which the terrace at Persepolis abuts. *p.* 147

KULKHAI (COLCHIS) — Ancient kingdom, east of the Pontus Euxinus (Black Sea) and south of the Caucasus . . . . *p.* 295, 342

KUNZE (E.) — German archaeologist and classical historian, head of the German Archaeological Institute in Athens . . . . *p.* 311, 341

KURANGUN — Site in the Fars province, northwest of Fahlian, with an Elamite rock relief. *p.* 346

KURDISTAN — Region north of Luristan, including the mountains and valleys of the northern Zagros. Through southern Kurdistan winds the ancient caravan route, along which are to be found most of the monuments of ancient Iran, erected by the Elamites, Medians (?), Achaemenians, Seleucids, Parthians and Sassanians. Aptly called 'the Gateway of Asia' by Ernst Herzfeld. *p.* 88, 115, 287, 301, 303

KUSHANS — A people of Iranian origin who in the first century A.D. ruled over a vast empire, including present-day Afghanistan, most of India, and parts of Russian and Chinese Turkestan . . . . . *p.* 125

LABRANDA — Town in Caria (Asia Minor), east of Miletus, north of Mylasa, famous for the cult of Zeus Labrandeus, which probably grew out of some ancient local cult. The god's symbol was the *labrys* or double axe. . . . . *p.* 355
— Sphinx. . . . . *fig.* 456

LABRYS — The double axe. . . . . *p.* 22

LAMASSU — Protective genius in the form of a winged human-headed bull, guarding the entrance of Assyrian palaces . . . . *p.* 311, 312

LANGDON (S.H.) — English Assyriologist (1876-1937). . . . . *p.* 283

LAURIYA (NANDANGARH) — Ancient site in India, on the confines of Nepal and the ancient kingdom of Magadha, with a pillar inscribed with an edict of Asoka. . . . . *p.* 356

LE BRETON (Louis) — French archaeologist, former member of the Susa expedition. . . . . . . *p.* 94

LEKYTHOS — Cylindrical vase made to contain oil or perfumes, often ornamented with paintings. *p.* 338 *fig.* 426

LITOI KURGAN — Locality in the government of Kherson, on the lower Dnieper, where in 1763 General Melgunov discovered a Scythian royal tomb of the 6th century B.C.. . . . . *p.* 303

LULLUBI — Mountaineers of Asianic or 'Zagro-Elamite' stock, occupying a region in the northern Zagros range extending to Lake Urmia and perhaps even farther north. In the time of the kingdom of Urartu (8th-7th centuries B.C.) their country was called Zamua, from the name of one of their tribes. The Georgians are thought to be descended from the northern branch of the Lullubi. At the end of the 2nd millennium B.C. a powerful Lullubi kingdom seems to have come into existence, against which the Assyrians waged war. After the 9th century B.C. the generic term 'Lullubi' disappears, replaced by 'Zamua' . . . . *p.* 2

LURISTAN — Mountainous province in the Zagros range, in western Iran, famous for the bronzes found there. *p.* XVI, 6, 21-23, 35, 26, 37, 40-83, 88-91, 94-97, 108, 113-115, 120, 123, 124, 138, 224, 237, 246, 249, 256, 261, 263, 264, 266, 281-287, 290, 297-299, 308, 316-320, 329, 331, 334-338, 340, 343-347, 360, 364, 366, 371, 372

Bronzes :
— Animal. . . . . *fig.* 126
— Axes. . . . . *fig.* 79-82, 341, 503-506
— Bell . . . . *fig.* 501
— Belts. . . . . *fig.* 92, 388, 510
— Bits . . . . *fig.* 72-75, 497-500
— Bowl of Naram-Sin . . . . *fig.* 340
— Bracelet . . . . *fig.* 94
— Cauldron handle . . . . *fig.* 353
— Clapper hanger . . . . *fig.* 76
— Daggers . . . . *fig.* 83, 343, 344
— Diadem . . . . *fig.* 511
— Fibula. . . . . *fig.* 514, 515
— Gazelle. . . . . *fig.* 71
— God Sraosha . . . . *fig.* 50, 51
— Harness piece. . . . . *fig.* 502
— Head of a Goddess. . . . . *fig.* 421
— Helmet. . . . . *fig.* 418
— Ibex. . . . . *fig.* 70
— Idols. . . . . *fig.* 52, 53, 55, 385
— Loop handle of shield . . . . . . *fig.* 88
— Mirrors . . . . *fig.* 100, 101
— Nude goddess. . . . . *fig.* 49, 56
— Pectoral . . . . *fig.* 380*b*
— Pendant . . . . *fig.* 496
— Pinheads. *fig.* 54, 57-63, 96-99, 384, 490, 491, 512, 513
— Quiver plaques . . . . *fig.* 91, 423
— Rein rings . . . . *fig.* 77, 78
— Rings for bending bows. . . . . . *fig.* 389
— Rhyton. . . . . *fig.* 105
— Situla . . . . *fig.* 107
— Stag. . . . . *fig.* 414
— Stamp seal . . . . *fig.* 492
— Statuettes. . . *fig.* 68, 69, 297, 476, 494, 495, 569
— Tool. . . . . *fig.* 493
— Umbones. . . . . *fig.* 87, 89, 90, 430

— Vase handle . . . . *fig.* 103
— Vases . . . . . . *fig.* 106, 406, 522, 523
— Whetstone handles. . . . . . . *fig.* 84-86
— Worshippers . . . . . . *fig.* 65-67, 519-521

Glass :
— Bottle . . . . *fig.* 517

Gold :
— Belt . . . . *fig.* 93
— Bracelet . . . . *fig.* 435
— Ear-ring . . . . *fig.* 400

Iron :
— Sword . . . . *fig.* 507-509

Pottery :
— Vases . . . . . . *fig.* 26, 102, 108, 391, 516

Silver :
— Plaques . . . . *fig.* 64, 95

LURS — Inhabitants of Luristan. . . *p.* 97, 318, 366

LYCIA — Ancient district of Asia Minor, on the Mediterranean coast. Incorporated in the Persian Empire by Cyrus the Great (559-529 B.C.). After the conquest of Persia by Alexander, it formed part of the Seleucid Empire, until the defeat of Antiochus by the Romans. . . . . *p.* 349

LYDIA — Ancient district of Asia Minor, bounded on the west by the Aegean Sea, on the south by the Meander, capital Sardis. Incorporated in the Persian Empire by Cyrus the Great. After Alexander's conquest, it passed to the Seleucids, then to the kings of Pergamum, and finally to the Romans. *p.* 22, 99, 302

MACEDON — Ancient country in the Balkan peninsula, north of Greece. Hellenized from about the 7th century B.C. on. Under Philip II (359-336 B.C.) it asserted its predominance over the Greek city-states, and his son Alexander the Great conquered a large part of the Oriental world (334-323). *p.* 130

MADYES — Scythian king of the 7th century B.C., son of Partatua (Protothyes) and a contemporary of Assurbanipal, King of Assyria . . . . *p.* 98, 327

MAGNA GRAECIA — The name given to the Greek colonies in South Italy (Tarentum, Sybaris, Crotona, etc.), most of them founded in the 8th century B.C. . . . . *p.* XI

MAH — Moon goddess in the pre-Zoroastrian religion of Iran . . . . *p.* 88

MAKU — Site in Azerbaijan, in north-western Iran, where a horse rhyton was found in 1924. *p.* 287-290, 315, 326, 335, 362
— Horse rhyton . . . . *fig.* 345, 346

MALAMIR — Plain in the province of Khuzistan (present-day Izeh), with Elamite rock reliefs. *p.* 346

MALEKI (Dr A.) — Professor at the Faculty of Medicine, Teheran University, and an eminent collector . . . . *p.* 299

MALLOWAN (M.E.L.) — English archaeologist and historian (born 1904), professor of Western Asiatic Archaeology at the Institute of Archaeology, London University, and in charge of British excavations in Iraq. . . . . *p.* 85

MANNAI — Kingdom of the Mannaians, south of Lake Urmia, capital Isirta, 30 miles east of the modern town of Sakkiz. *p.* XVI, 24, 29, 42, 80, 98, 282, 284, 301-303, 327

MANNAIANS — A people of the 'Zagro-Elamite' family, related to the Lullubi and the Hurrians. From the 9th or 8th century B.C., Iranian names begin to appear among the Mannaians. Their kingdom is mentioned for the first time in the second half of the 9th century B.C.; in the 8th, it was perhaps the most powerful in the region, after the kingdom of Urartu, and by the end of the century had over-shadowed the latter. In the 7th century the Scythians appear in the land of Mannai as allies of the Mannaians in their struggle against Assyria. Assurbanipal (668-626) devastated the kingdom, which became the vassal of Assyria and was finally annexed by the Medes after their victory over Assyria. *p.* 85, 98, 301, 302

MARDUK — Supreme god of the Babylonian pantheon. *p.* 56, 263

MARDUK-NADIN-AKHE — King of Babylonia (c. 1110 B.C.). A bronze sword in the Louvre is inscribed with his name . . . . *p.* 283

MARLIK — Ancient site with cemeteries in the mountains south-west of the Caspian Sea. Here were found the objects of the so-called Amlash culture (9th-7th centuries B.C.) . . . . *p.* 38

MARSILIANA D'ALBEGNA — Etruscan site a few miles inland from Orbetello on the Tuscan coast. *p.* 342
— Nude goddess . . . . *fig.* 434

MARUTAS — Aryan divinity in the Vedic mythology of India. . . . . *p.* 70

MASJID-I-SULAIMAN — Locality in the province of Khuzistan, 30 miles south-east of Shushtar, with an ancient terrace on which the fortified residence of a prince once stood. Probably the first capital of the Achaemenid kings. . *p.* 129-132, 138, 147, 230, 296
— Plan of the terrace. . . . . *fig.* 117
— Stairway . . . . *fig.* 176

MASSON-OURSEL (Paul) — French Sanskrit scholar (1882-1956) . . . . *p.* XVII

MATHURA — Modern Muttra, south of New Delhi, on the Jumna river. . . . . *p.* 356
— Capital. . . . . *fig.* 461

MAURYA — Great Hindu dynasty founded about 322 B.C. by Chandragupta. It ruled the whole of northern India and part of the Deccan until about 185 B.C. Maurya art was influenced by that of Hellenistic Iran, which still reflected all the grandeur of Achaemenian art. . . . . *p.* 357

MAXIMOVA (M.) — Soviet archaeologist and art historian. . . . . *p.* 77, 327

MAZANDARAN — Province of Iran south of the Caspian Sea. . . . . *p.* 252

MAZDAEISM — The religion of the ancient Iranians, revealed by Ahuramazda (or Ormuzd) to the prophet Zoroaster and formulated in the *Avesta*. *p.* 154, 225, 226, 230

MEDIA — Ancient country of western Iran, extending north to the Elburz range, east to the central desert of the Plateau, and to the Zagros mountains in the west and south. Capital, Ecbatana (present-day Hamadan). *p.* XV, 1, 17, 81, 85, 86, 90, 129, 133, 284, 285, 296, 324-327, 329, 350

MEDIA PARAETACENE — Region of central Iran, with modern Isfahan as its principal city. . . *p.* 17

MELGUNOV TREASURE — Discovered in a Scythian barrow in South Russia by General Melgunov in 1763. . . . . *p.* 303, 315

MELIKISHVILI (G.A.) — Soviet philologist and historian, specialist in Urartian inscriptions *p.* 42, 281

MEMPHIS — Ancient city of Lower Egypt . *p.* 244
Sculpture :
— Head of an Achaemenian prince. . . . *fig.* 292
— Head of a Man . . . . *fig.* 293

MENUAS — King of Urartu (810-781 B.C.) *p.* 28, 38, 295

MESOPOTAMIA — Region between the Tigris and Euphrates (modern Iraq), seat of the ancient civilizations of Sumer, Akkad, Babylonia and Assyria. *p.* XI, XII, XIV-XVI, 2, 16, 17, 33, 37, 44, 46, 62, 74, 81, 125, 130, 222, 253, 263, 265, 284, 329

METOPE — The space between the dentils of a cornice or between the triglyphs of a frieze . *p.* 15, 79

MILESIANS — Inhabitants of Miletus (Asia Minor), seaport on the Aegean. . . . . *p.* 331

MITANNIANS — A people of Indo-European origin who formed a kingdom (Mitanni) on the Upper Euphrates in the 2nd millennium B.C. . *p.* 3, 4, 102

MITHRAS — Persian god of light, of contracts, and of justice, mediator between Ahuramazda and Ahriman. Assisted by Sraosha and Rashnu, he judged the souls of the dead. His cult spread throughout the Roman world, along the Rhine and Danube, and even to Brittany. Mithraism gradually gave way to Christianity but only after long resistance. Mithraic symbolism is illustrated on many surviving monuments. *p.* 21, 44-46, 51, 70, 88, 121, 229, 234

MITRA — Military belt worn round the waist, at the bottom of the cuirass, as a protection to the belly (cf. *Iliad*, iv. 137) . . . . *p.* 21, 121

MIYANDUAB — Modern town south-east of Lake Urmia . . . . *p.* 28

MOHENJO-DARO — Ancient site on the Indus (West Pakistan), nearly 200 miles north of Karachi. *p.* 59

MOLIONIDES — Twin giants of Greek mythology. *p.* 334

MORGAN (Jacques de) — French mining engineer, archaeologist, historian, epigraphist, numismatist and writer (1857-1924). Former Director General of Egyptian Antiquities and head of the French archaeological expedition to Susa. Discovered oil in Iran. . . . . *p.* 115

MOSES OF CHORENE — Armenian writer of the 5th century A.D. The *History of Armenia* which bears his name appears to date to the 9th century. *p.* 396

MURGHAB — River watering the plain of Pasargadae. *p.* 135

MUSASIR — Region and city west of Lake Urmia. In the city stood the greatest temple of Urartu, dedicated to Haldis, the supreme god of the Urartian pantheon. The temple was looted by Sargon II of Assyria during his campaign against Urartu in 714 B.C. The city was located on the upper course of the Great Zab, a tributary of the Tigris. *p.* 10, 66, 247, 248, 263, 296, 299, 340

NABU — Babylonian god of scribes and writing, son of Marduk, the supreme god. . . . . *p.* 85

NAIRI — Region lying east of the sources of the Euphrates, including Lake Van and extending as far as the valley of the Araxes. United by one of its princes in the 11th century B.C., it became the kingdom of Urartu (Ararat) . . . . *p.* 295

NANDANGARH, see LAURIYA.

NAQSH-I-RUSTAM — An ancient site some four miles north of Persepolis, with four rock tombs of Achaemenid kings and some Sassanian bas-reliefs cut into the cliff. Opposite these stand a fire temple and two fire altars. *p.* 134, 201, 226-231, 269, 296, 348
— Achaemenian tombs and Sassanian bas-reliefs. *fig.* 275
— Fire altars . . . . *fig.* 276
— Fire temple. . . . . *fig.* 277
— Tomb of Darius the Great . . . . . *fig.* 279

NARAM-SIN — King of the Akkadian dynasty (c. 2300 B.C.), son of Sargon of Akkad. The Stele of Naram-Sin (Louvre) was found by Morgan at Susa. *p.* 2 *fig.* 340

NASATYA — Pair of benevolent divinities in the Vedic pantheon, gravitating round Indra. . . *p.* 70

NEBUCHADNEZZAR II — King of Babylon (604-562 B.C.). . . . . *p.* 283

NEO-BABYLONIAN PERIOD — Begins with Nabopolassar (625-605 B.C.), founder of the Neo-Babylonian dynasty, and ends with Nabonidus (539 B.C.), defeated by Cyrus the Great. . . . . *p.* 263, 281, 284, 307

NICOLAUS DAMASCENUS — The last of the Neo-Platonists, born at Damascus about A.D. 480. *p.* 340

NIHAWAND (NIHAVEND) — Town in Iran, some 60 miles south of Hamadan, with remains of a Hellenistic temple. About 10 miles away is the prehistoric site of Tepe Giyan. The decisive battle between the armies of Yazdgard III, last Sassanid king, and the Arab conquerors took place in the plain of Nihawand in A.D. 642. . . . . *p.* 285

NIMRUD — Ancient Kalakh, one of the capitals of the kingdom of Assyria, on the Tigris north of Assur. *p.* 85, 102

NIN-EGAL — Babylonian goddess, 'lady of the palace.' *p.* 283

NINEVEH — One of the three capitals of the kingdom of Assyria, on the Upper Tigris. *p.* XII, XIII, 66, 129, 282

NINNI — Mesopotamian goddess . . . . . . *p.* 2

NOV RUZ — New Year's Day, the most important feast day in the Mazdaean religion . . . . *p.* 154

NUZI — Site in northern Mesopotamia, near Kirkuk. *p.* 82

OIKOS — House, place of residence. . . . . . *p.* 4

OLYMPIA — Small plain in Elis (Greece) where the Altis, the sacred grove of Zeus, was located. This was an ancient centre of worship, with many temples, statues and public monuments. Here the Olympic games were held, beginning (according to tradition) in 776 B.C.. . . . . *p.* 69, 298, 311, 337
— Band of a shield . . . . *fig.* 422
— Disk with woman's face. . . . . . . *fig.* 420

OMPHALOS — The round central boss of a dish, shield or chariot wheel . . . . . *p.* 74, 256, 258

ORONTES — River in central Syria (now called Nasr el-Asi) flowing into the Mediterranean. *p.* XI, 331

ORTHOSTATS — Stone reliefs set along the base of a wall, which they reinforced and decorated at the same time. . . . . *p.* 135, 223

OSSETES — A people of Iranian origin settled in the central Caucasus . . . . *p.* 115

OX (HUMPED) — Animal often represented by the potters and metal-workers of Amlash. Presumably the species of buffalo still found in that region. *p.* 35 *fig.* 34, 40

OXUS — River of Central Asia (modern name Amu Darya), rising in the Pamirs and flowing into the Aral Sea. Now forms the frontier between Afghanistan and the U.S.S.R. . . . . . *p.* 90, 250, 371

OXUS TREASURE — Treasure hoard found on the right bank of the Oxus, near Bactra (Afghanistan), now in the British Museum. *p.* 90-94, 245-250, 263, 299, 319, 347, 359
Gold :
— Bracelet . . . . *fig.* 302a
— Bractea. . . . . *fig.* 541
— Chariot . . . . *fig.* 301
— Disk with eagle . . . . *fig.* 543
— Figures. . . . . *fig.* 298, 299
— Figure with barsom . . . . *fig.* 109
— Man's head. . . . . *fig.* 300
— Scabbard. . . . . . . *fig.* 118, 387, 464
— Stag . . . . *fig.* 302c
— Votive plaques . . . . *fig.* 120, 121
Silver :
— Donor . . . . *fig.* 296
— Umbo . . . . *fig.* 542
— Vase handle . . . . *fig.* 302b

PAMIRS — A mountainous region of Central Asia (Russia and Afghanistan), forming a plateau with an average height of over 15,000 feet and known as 'the Roof of the World' . . . . *p.* 76

PAPHOS — Ancient city on the west coast of Cyprus. *p.* 343, 353
— Pinhead . . . . *fig.* 455

PERSEUS — Hero of Greek mythology, son of Zeus and Danaë. He slew the Gorgon Medusa as she slept, cutting off her head while with averted eyes (to avoid being turned to stone) he looked at her reflection in a mirror. He gave the head to Athena, who placed it in the centre of her shield . . *p.* 340

PHALERAE — Roman term for metal ornaments fastened to horses' harness, hung on their breasts, heads and cruppers. . . . . *fig.* 350

PHINEUS — In Greek legend, the blind king of Salmydessus on the coast of Thrace, endowed with the gift of prophecy. Tormented by the Harpies for having mistreated his sons. . . . . . . *p.* 338

PHOENICIA — Ancient maritime power on the eastern Mediterranean seaboard (present-day Lebanon), with Tyre and Sidon as its principal ports. *p.* 82, 102, 268, 281, 311, 340

PHORCIDES — Sirens who in Greek mythology inhabited the fields of Kisthenes . . . . . *p.* 340

PHRYGIA — Ancient kingdom of Asia Minor (8th-7th centuries B.C.), whose most famous ruler was King Midas. Its capital was Gordium, on the river Sangarius. . . . . *p.* 22, 348

PHRYGIANS — A Thracian people of Indo-European stock, who migrated from the Balkans to Asia Minor. After settling first in the north-western corner of Asia Minor, they were driven further inland, occupying the western part of the great central plateau of Anatolia . . . . *p.* 131

PIOTROVSKY (B.B.) — Soviet Orientalist, professor at Leningrad University and a specialist in Urartian civilization, in charge of excavations at Karmir Blur . . . . *p.* 42, 281, 306, 327

PISÉ — Stiff clay or kneaded earth used for building purposes. . . . . *p.* 2

PLINY THE ELDER (A.D. 23-79) — Roman naturalist, born at Comum (Como), author of the *Naturalis historia*, an encyclopaedic work in 37 books covering all the arts and sciences of Antiquity. *p.* 319, 347

POLOS — A high headdress tapering off at the top and fastened at the bottom with a broad ribbon. *p.* 74

PONTUS — An ancient country of north-east Asia Minor bordering on the Euxine (Black Sea). Made a satrapy of the Persian Empire under Darius I (521-485 B.C.), it became in time an independent kingdom. Later incorporated in Alexander's empire. *p.* XI, 125

POSEIDON — Greek god of the sea and of navigation, identified with the Roman god Neptune.. . *p.* 298

POTNIA HIPPON — 'Mistress of horses'. . *p.* 298

POTNIA THERON — 'Mistress of animals', ancient goddess with whom were associated the animals she tamed and rode . . . . *p.* 46

PREHISTORY — Period of unrecorded history, knowledge of which is based almost entirely on a study of the artefacts and human remains found by archaeologists. In Iran, prehistoric times come to an end about 1000 B.C. . . . . *p.* 2, 4, 9, 10, 42, 290, 291, 372

PRINIAS — Ancient site in Crete . . . . . *p.* 341
— Lion. . . . . *fig.* 393

PROTOHISTORY — Phase of civilization beginning at the end of prehistoric times (c. 1000 B.C. in Iran) and ending when epigraphically recorded history begins (6th century B.C. in Iran). *p.* 9, 14, 16, 38, 60, 73, 81, 100, 131, 260, 277, 287, 332

PROTOME — Foreparts of an animal as represented in art. *p.* 14, 59, 61, 73, 97, 108, 133, 139, 214, 215, 251, 252, 256, 298, 351, 352, 353, 355   *fig.* 72, 138, 139, 267, 268, 303, 358

PRZEWORSKI (Stefan) — Polish Orientalist. *p.* 280

PSALIA — Side-pieces of a horse's bit. *p.* 28, 60, 120, 279 *fig.* 337

PULVAR — River watering the plain of Persepolis. *p.* 154

PUSHT-I-KUH — Mountains in south-west Luristan where a bronze statuette of an armed divinity was discovered. . . . . *p.* 55, 97

PYRRHIC DANCE — War dance of the ancient Greeks, executed in battle array, at a quick step, to the piping of flutes . . . . *p.* 14, 333

PYXIS — A small box or jewel case *p.* 336 *fig.* 417

RAMATAIA — Median prince (7th century B.C.). *p.* 85, 102

RASHNU — Iranian god who presided over judgment by ordeal. With Mithras and Sraosha, he judged the dead on the bridge of Cinvat. . . . *p.* 45, 46

REGOLINI-GALASSI TOMB — Etruscan tomb at Caere (Cerveteri), north-west of Rome, taking its name from its discoverers. . . . . . . *p.* 109, 310

RETHYMNON — Site on the north coast of Crete. *p.* 121

RHODES — Aegean island off the south-west coast of Asia Minor . . . . *p.* 335 *fig.* 426, 427

RHYTON — Drinking vessel in the form of a horn or an animal's head *p.* 15, 32, 79, 97, 251, 255, 287-288, 289-291, 315, 321-327, 333, 335, 358, 359, 362 *fig.* 34, 35, 47, 105, 128, 290, 306, 307, 345-348, 394-397, 399, 401-402, 404, 462, 465

ROMANESQUE — Style of art and architecture in medieval Europe (c. 950-1150), much influenced by the earlier arts of Byzantium and Hither Asia. *p.* 371

ROSTOVTZEFF (Michael) — Russian-American Orientalist and historian (1870-1952), former professor at Yale and promoter of American excavations at Dura Europos . . . . *p.* 358

RUDBAR — Small modern town near the river Sefid Rud (Kizil Uzun), in the mountainous region south-west of the Caspian Sea, not far from the ancient site of Marlik . . . . *p.* 38

RUDRA — Storm god in the Vedic mythology. He lives on the mountains and rules the sky and the atmosphere . . . . *p.* 70

RUSAS I — King of Urartu (c. 732-714 B.C.) *p.* 248, 285, 299

RUS

SIA

RUSAS II — King of Urartu (678-654? B.C.). *p.* 284

SAIGA — A species of antelope found in Eastern Europe and Western Asia . . *p.* 116, 251, 322-324 *fig.* 395, 396

SAKAS (SACAE) — A Scythian tribe of Chinese Turkestan who joined with the Yueh-chi to conquer the Greco-Bactrian kingdom (130 B.C.). *p.* 156, 158

SAKAVAND (or DEH-I-NAU) — Village in Kurdistan, south of Bisutun, where two rock tombs are located, one of them surmounted by a relief. . *p.* 88, 89
— Rock tomb. . . . . *fig.* 117

SAKKIZ — Iranian town south of Lake Urmia, near the site of Ziwiyeh where in 1947 peasants discovered a royal treasure hoard that has thrown new light on the Scythian episode of Iranian history . . . *p.* 98

SALAMIS — The chief city of ancient Cyprus, located on the east coast of the island . . . . . . *p.* 342
— Capital of Evagoras I . . . . *fig.* 454

SAMOS — One of the principal islands of the Aegean Sea, a centre of the arts and sciences of ancient Ionia. . . . . *p.* 331

SARDIS — City of Asia Minor, capital of the kingdom of Lydia. Residence of Croesus, then of the Persian satraps of Lydia after the conquest of the region by Cyrus the Great in 546 B.C. *p.* 140, 156, 229, 264, 355

SARDURIS II — King of Urartu (c. 760-743 B.C.). *p.* 295, 336 *fig.* 119

SARGON II — King of Assyria (722-705 B.C.) *p.* 66, 247, 248, 282, 283, 299

SARGONID PERIOD — Period of Assyrian domination under Sargon II (722-705 B.C.) . . . . *p.* 296, 326

SAR-I-PUL-I-ZOHAB — Locality in Kurdistan, in the Holwan district, with bas-reliefs carved in the rock-face. . . . . *p.* 2

SARNATH — Ancient site near Benares (India). The deer park where the Buddha first preached is marked by a monolithic pillar with a capital of Iranian inspiration . . . . *p.* 356 *fig.* 458

SASSANIANS or SASSANIDS — Ruling dynasty of Persia (A.D. 224-650) . . . . . . *p.* XIII, 229

SCHEFOLD (Karl) — Swiss Orientalist and classical scholar, professor at Basle University. . . *p.* 281, 317

SCHMIDT (Erich F.) — American archaeologist and Orientalist (born 1897), in charge of excavations at Persepolis from 1934 to 1939. . . . . . . *p.* 48

SCYTHIANS — Nomads of Iranian origin who migrated to western Asia from South Russia, probably by way of the Caucasus. They are mentioned by Herodotus, and in Assyrian and Urartian annals, also in the Bible under the name of Ashkenaz. The joint invasion of western Asia by the Scythians and Cimmerians took place in or about the 8th century B.C. Among the Scythians were warlike tribes which, led by their chieftains, served as mercenaries (probably paid in war booty) in the Median and Assyrian armies. Their invasions, in the course of the 7th century B.C., impinged on many countries from the Caucasus to Palestine and from Urartu to Iran. Their name survived in the vocabulary of several regions. The Scythians seem to have been driven back north of

the Caucasus in the early 6th century B.C. *p.* 4, 27, 28, 29, 37, 45, 60, 61, 71, 73, 76, 85, 86, 88, 90, 96. 97, 98-125, 215, 237, 251, 263, 269, 297, 301-329, 358-359, 371, 372
Map :
— Area of Scythian expansion . . . . . . *fig.* 130

SEGALL (Berta) — American Orientalist . . *p.* 281

SEHNA — Village on the road between Kermanshah and Hamadan, in western Iran. Near by is a Median rock tomb of the 7th or 6th century B.C.. . . *p.* 87

SELEUCIA — Town in Babylonia, on the right bank of the Tigris, founded by Seleucus Nicator in 307 B.C. First capital of the kingdom of Syria under the Seleucids. . . . . *p.* 357

SELEUCIDS — A Greek dynasty founded in Syria by Seleucus (356-280 B.C.), later styled Seleucus Nicator, one of Alexander's generals. Successors of the kings of Persia, they were hard put to it to impose Greek culture on the Iranians, though more successful in Asia Minor. They founded new cities, Seleucia and Antioch, and promoted commerce between their empire and India. . . *p.* XIII, 355

SENNACHERIB — King of Assyria (705-681 B.C.), son and successor of Sargon II . . . . . . *p.* 282

SETI I — Egyptian king of the XIXth Dynasty (1312-1298 B.C.). His son and successor was the great Ramses II. . . . . *p.* 280

SEVAN — Mountain lake in Transcaucasia (present-day Armenian Soviet Socialist Republic), in a region that formed part of the kingdom of Urartu . *p.* 305

SEVEN BROTHERS BARROW — Scythian royal tomb in the Kuban (northern Caucasus). *p.* 252, 358

SEYRIG (Henri) — French Hellenist, Orientalist, historian and numismatist (born 1895). Member of the Institut de France, director of the Institut Archéologique Français at Beirut, and former director of the Musées Nationaux de France . . *p.* 353

SHAMANISM — One of the most primitive religions of the East, prevailing chiefly among the peoples of Siberia and the Altai region. . . . . . *p.* 45

SHAMASH — Babylonian sun god and upholder of justice. . . . . *p.* 301

SHAMASH-KILANI — An officer of the king, whose name is inscribed on a bronze dagger found in a Luristan tomb (12th century B.C.). . . . . *p.* 283

SHAPUR, see BISHAPUR.

SHILHAK-INSHUSHINAK — Elamite king (12th century B.C.), son of Shutruk-Nakhunte. His name is inscribed on a bronze axe in the Foroughi Collection, found in 1957 in a Luristan tomb. . . *p.* 283

SIALK — Prehistoric and protohistoric site explored by the French expedition in 1933-34 and 1937. Located near Kashan, some 150 miles south of Teheran, on the western fringe of the great central desert of Iran *p.* 1, 2, 3, 4, 6, 9-16, 17, 18, 19, 21, 22, 26, 41, 42, 51, 60, 62, 73, 77, 79, 82, 97, 115, 123, 131, 135, 230, 236, 237, 249, 256, 260, 269, 277-80, 286, 287, 288, 289, 290, 291, 293, 296, 297, 320,332, 333, 334, 335, 337, 338
Architecture :
— Cemetery. . . . . *fig.* 4
— Terrace . . . . *fig.* 5

Pottery :
— Askos . . . . *fig.* 484
— Bird rhyton . . . . *fig.* 483
— Bottle . . . . *fig.* 482
— Cup . . . . *fig.* 481
— Painted jug . . . . *fig.* 11, 14
— Painted sherds . . . . . . *fig.* 2, 9a-b, 412a-b
— Painted vases . *fig.* 6-8, 10, 12, 13, 334, 349, 411
— Vases with beak-spouts . . . *fig.* 416, 479, 480
Seal :
— Cylinder seal . . . . *fig.* 485, 486

SIDON — The principal city and seaport of ancient Phoenicia, situated on the Syrian coast between Beirut and Tyre, and the mainstay of Phoenician sea power until it was eclipsed by Tyre. Conquered by the Assyrians, it later came under Babylonian and Persian domination but was governed by its own kings. In Xerxes' expeditions against the Greeks (492-490 B.C.) the Sidonians supplied the best fleet. The city was burnt down by Artaxerxes III during a revolt against the Persians. Sidon was famed for its glassware. . . . . *p.* 350-352

Sculpture :
— Bull capital. . . . . *fig.* 448
— Sarcophagus of Alexander. . . . . . *fig.* 447
— Sarcophagus of the Satrap . . . . . *fig.* 446

SILENUS — Phrygian god, foster father of Bacchus. He possessed the gift of prophecy . . . . . *p.* 253

SINOPE — Black Sea port on the north coast of Asia Minor (present-day Turkey), said by ancient historians to have been the capital of the Cimmerians. *p.* 72

SIREN — Fabulous being, part woman, part bird, represented holding a lyre, who was supposed to lure sailors to destruction by her sweet singing. A goddess of music or a water sprite . . *p.* 297, 341

SITULA — Holy-water pail. . . *p.* 79, 80 *fig.* 107

SIYAVUSH — Legendary king whose exploits are sung by Firdausi in the *Shah-nama* (Book of Kings). He came from Iran to found the first dynasty of the ancient kingdom of Chorasmia, which suggests that the Iranians arrived on the Plateau by way of the Caucasus. . . . . *p.* 4

SOGDIANA — An ancient country between the Oxus (Amu Darya) and the Jaxartes (Syr Darya) which, under the Achaemenians, formed part of the 16th Satrapy. Chief town, Marakanda (present-day Samarkand). A prosperous kingdom from the early Christian era until the 8th century when it was overrun by the Arabs. Population of Iranian origin . . . . *p.* 140, 156

SOLDUZ — Iranian town south-west of the Caspian Sea. . . . . *p.* 24

SPARTA — City of ancient Greece, in the Peloponnese . . . . *p.* XII

SPHYRELATON — Hammered technique whereby a wooden statue was covered with thin strips of bronze (or some other metal), which were then riveted together. The best-known statuettes in this technique are those of Apollo and two attendant maidens from the Dreros temple in Crete . *p.* 173

SRAOSHA — Persian divinity, defender of the works of Ahuramazda, judge of the dead in association with Mithras and Rashnu. *p.* 44, 46-48, 52, 229, 297, 349 *fig.* 50, 51

STEATOPYGIA — Abnormal accumulation of fat in and around the buttocks . . . . . *p.* 35 *fig.* 32

STEREOBATE — The base of a plain wall . *p.* 135

STOCLET COLLECTION — Private collection in Brussels. The objects from it figuring in this volume belong to Madame Féron-Stoclet . . . . . *p.* 244

STRABO — Greek geographer and historian, born at Amasia in Cappadocia (kingdom of Pontus) about 58 B.C., died between 21 and 25 A.D. *p.* 319

SURDASH — Village in Iraqi Kurdistan near which lies the Kizkapan tomb. . . . . *p.* 88

SURKH DUM — Site in the plain of the Kuh-i-Dasht, in Luristan, with the remains of a temple. *p.* 42, 48, 52, 66, 70, 73, 91, 299, 343

SURYA — Sun god of Vedic mythology. . . . *p.* 70

SUSA — Chief town of Susiana, capital of the Elamite kingdom from the 3rd millennium B.C. on, and one of the four capitals of the Achaemenian Empire. The city was definitively abandoned in or about the 13th century A.D. Its ruins have been excavated by French expeditions from 1883 onward *p.* 20, 48, 59, 70, 77, 81, 90, 129, 135, 138-147, 156, 209, 214, 215, 222, 223, 224, 225, 229, 236, 243, 249, 250, 258, 260, 262, 264, 268, 283, 284, 289, 290, 318, 326, 333, 339, 348, 353, 355, 356, 357, 362

Architecture :
— Capital. . . . . *fig.* 186
— Palace and apadana . . . . *fig.* 187
— Plan of the palace. . . . . *fig.* 188

Glazed bricks :
— Frieze of archers. . . . . *fig.* 190
— Lion. . . . . *fig.* 193
— Lion-griffin. . . . . *fig.* 191
— Winged bull . . . . *fig.* 192
— Winged lion . . . . *fig.* 195

Pottery :
— Painted rhyton . . . . *fig.* 347, 348
— Painted sherd. . . . . *fig.* 351

Sculpture :
— Fertility goddess. . . . . *fig.* 433
— Statue of Darius. . . . . *fig.* 189
— Stairway relief. . . . . *fig.* 194

Various :
— Bronze lion. . . . . *fig.* 318
— Ear-rings. . . . . *fig.* 322
— Ivory carving. . . . . *fig.* 561, 562
— Silver cup . . . . *fig.* 545

SUSIANA — The modern province of Khuzistan, between Babylonia and Persis (Fars), in southwestern Iran, one of the leading provinces of the Achaemenian Empire. Before the coming of the Persians, Susiana was the centre of the Elamite kingdom. . . . . *p.* 2, 89, 144, 287, 289

SVOBODA (B.) — Czech Hellenist. . . . . *p.* 327

SYMPLEGMA — Interlocking: group of interlacing animals. . . . . *p.* 258

SYRIA — Country of Hither Asia lying south of the plateaux of Anatolia and Kurdistan. Conquered by the Persians under Cyrus (559-529 B.C.) and became the 5th Satrapy of the Achaemenian Empire, with Sidon as capital, under Darius (521-485 B.C.). Vast empire under Seleucus I (301-280 B.C.), spent its energies in futile conflicts and disintegrated. Made a Roman province, with Antioch as capital, by Pompey (63 B.C.): period of prosperity. Occupied by the Sassanians and freed itself from the foreign occupant, only to fall into the hands of the Arabs (A.D. 638) . . . *p.* 29, 130, 222, 284, 302, 306, 329

TAKHT-I-KAWADH, see TAKHT-I-KOBAD.

TAKHT-I-KOBAD — Hill in Bactria, on the right bank of the Oxus (Amu Darya), where the Oxus Treasure was discovered. . . . . *p.* 90, 250

TAKHT-I-MADAR-I-SULAIMAN (Throne of Solomon's Mother) — A man-made terrace some 40 feet high, backed against a hillside north of Pasargadae. Thought to have been built by Cambyses I.
p. 131 *fig.* 178

TAKHT-I-RUSTAM — Locality some 30 miles south of Teheran. . . . . *p.* 230

TAMAN — Peninsula of South Russia, between the Sea of Azov and the Black Sea . . . . . . *p.* 358

TAMGA — Ownership mark branded on the animals of their flocks by the nomads . . . . . *p.* 288, 290

TARQUINIA — Etruscan city (ancient Tarquinii) some 60 miles north-west of Rome, a few miles from the coast . . . . *fig.* 429

TARTESSUS — Ancient site on the south coast of Spain, on the Atlantic. . . . . *p.* 331

TASH TEPE — Locality in Atropatene (present-day Azerbaijan), south-east of Lake Urmia, with a rock inscription in the Urartian language. . . . *p.* 28

TEHERAN — Capital of Iran, situated on the edge of a sandy, sterile plain, overlooked by the Elburz mountains. *p.* XIV, XVII, I, 17, 18, 38, 55, 80, 91, 112, 116, 252, 263, 266, 290, 312, 321, 324, 341, 366

TEISHEBAINI, see KARMIR BLUR.

TEISPES — Founder of the Achaemenid dynasty (ruled 675-640 B.C.), son and successor of Achaemenes.
p. 129, 131, 268

TELEPHANES OF PHOCAEA — Greek bronze-founder and sculptor who worked at the court of Xerxes (early 5th century B.C.). . . . . . *p.* 347

TEMIR GORA — Locality in the Crimea, near Kerch. . . . . *p.* 304
— Harness pieces. . . . . *fig.* 366*b-c*

THANATOS — God of death in Greek mythology .
p. 338 *fig.* 426

THASOS — Aegean island, some 4 miles off the north-west coast of Macedonia. . . . . . . *p.* 351, 352
— Horse capital . . . . *fig.* 453

TIGRIS — One of the two great rivers of Mesopotamia. Rising in what is now eastern Turkey, it flows through Iraq (Mesopotamia) and joins with the Euphrates to form the Shatt el-Arab which empties into the Persian Gulf . . . . *p.* XII, XIV, 138, 357, 371

TIMBER-FRAME CULTURE — Bronze Age culture of South Russia (lower Volga, Don and Dnieper) characterized by burials in timber-frame pits.
p. 301, 307

TOBIADS — The son and grandson of Joseph who for twenty-two years (230-208 B.C.) was tax collector of Judaea in the time of the Egyptian domination. Joseph was the son of Tobiah and the son-in-law of Simeon the Righteous, high priest of Jerusalem (see Flavius Josephus, *Antiquities of the Jews*, XII. 4).
p. 335

TOPRAK-KALE — Stronghold with remains of royal Urartian buildings, near the Urartian capital of Tushpa (Lake Van). Second residence of the Urartian kings after 730 B.C. *p.* 108, 109, 296, 298, 299, 308, 309, 315
— Bronze plaque. . . . . *fig.* 354
— Cauldron lug . . . . *fig.* 355
— Frieze . . . . *fig.* 570
— Lion. . . . . *fig.* 141
— Sphinx. . . . . *fig.* 371
— Statuette with pectoral. . . . . *fig.* 370

TRANSCAUCASIA — The region south of the Caucasus mountains, between the Black Sea and the Caspian (Transcaucasien). *p.* 27, 28, 42, 88, 278, 279, 301, 302, 303, 305, 306, 307, 308, 329 *fig.* 358

TREBENISHCHEI — Site in Bulgaria where a pectoral of the 6th century B.C. was found. *p.* 310 *fig.* 375

TREBIZOND — Black Sea port on the north coast of Asia Minor (present-day Turkey), founded as a Greek colony by the Milesians in about the 8th century B.C. . . . . *p.* 331

TURANG TEPE — Prehistoric site in the province of Gurgan (eastern Iran). . . . . *fig.* I

TUSHPA — Capital of the kingdom of Urartu, on the south-east shore of Lake Van (south-eastern Turkey).
p. 296

UMBO — Centrepiece of a shield, sometimes adorned with the representation of a human or animal head. The goddess Athena had a Gorgon's head as the *umbo* of her shield. . . . *p.* 68, 100, 119, 321, 340 *fig.* 87-89, 430

UNTASH-GAL — Elamite king (13th century B.C.), builder of the Choga Zambil ziggurat. A bronze axe, adorned with a boar in electrum, has been found inscribed with his name . . . . *p.* 283

UR — Ancient Sumerian city of southern Mesopotamia (present-day Muqayyar), at the confluence of the Shatt-el-Hai with the Euphrates. Excavated from 1922 to 1934 by the Joint Expedition of the British Museum and the University Museum of Pennsylvania, led by C. (later Sir) Leonard Woolley. Royal tombs of the 3rd millennium B.C. and a large ziggurat were brought to light . . . . *p.* 307
— Bronze sarcophagus . . . . *fig.* 368

ZIWIYEH — Village near the town of Sakkiz, in Iranian Kurdistan, where in 1947 peasants discovered a magnificent treasure hoard in a Scythian royal tomb. *p.* 13, 29, 76, 96, 98, 99-125, 215, 237, 250, 255, 263, 266, 287, 302, 306, 307, 308, 309, 310, 315, 316, 317, 320, 321-324, 327, 329, 335, 338, 339, 341

Bronzes :

— Arrow-heads . . . . *fig.* 166
— Edge and plaque of sarcophagus. . . . *fig.* 369
— Lamp . . . . *fig.* 539
— Terminal of chariot shaft. . . . . . *fig.* 168
— Umbo . . . . *fig.* 162

Gold and silver :

— Belt-ends. . . . . *fig.* 144, 386
— Belt plaques. . . . . *fig.* 143, 146, 147
— Bracelets. . . . . *fig.* 145, 148, 150
— Bracteae. . . . . *fig.* 154, 532-537
— Cauldron handles . . . . . *fig.* 138, 139, 381
— Chains. . . . . *fig.* 151
— Chamfron . . . . *fig.* 167
— Chape. . . . . *fig.* 157
— Dish. . . . . *fig.* 142
— Drinking pipe. . . . . *fig.* 169
— Ear-rings. . . . . *fig.* 153
— Frontlet . . . . *fig.* 531
— Gauntlet. . . . . *fig.* 538
— Mounting of a seal. . . . . *fig.* 140
— Necklaces. . . . . *fig.* 152, 153
— Pectorals. . . . . . . *fig.* 137, 376, 377, 379
— Plaques . . . . *fig.* 378, 383, 527
— Rings . . . . *fig.* 529, 530
— Shield (fragment) . . . . *fig.* 163
— Sword hilt . . . . *fig.* 155
— Sword pommel . . . . *fig.* 158
— Sword sheath. . . . . *fig.* 156
— Torque (fragment). . . . . *fig.* 149

Ivory :

— Dagger handle . . . . *fig.* 161
— Plaques . . . . . *fig.* 134, 135, 524-526, 528

— Standing figure . . . . *fig.* 136
— Statuette. . . . . *fig.* 133
— Sword pommel . . . . *fig.* 155

Pottery :

— Jar . . . . *fig.* 398
— Lug of a pitcher. . . . . *fig.* 172
— Rhytons . . . . *fig.* 394-397
— Vases . . . . *fig.* 170, 171

Various :

— Iron daggers . . . . *fig.* 159, 160
— Harness piece. . . . . *fig.* 540
— Lion's head. . . . . *fig.* 392
— Marble mace-head. . . . . *fig.* 165
— Iron spear-head. . . . . *fig.* 164
— Wooden statuette . . . . *fig.* 173

ZOOMORPHIC JUNCTURE — Junction of forms of different animals, as when the tines of antlers are made to terminate in birds' heads. A distinctive feature of Scythian art, prevalent in Luristan. *p.* 45, 61, 317

ZOROASTER (ZARATHUSTRA) — Prophet and reformer of the Mazdaean religion. Date undetermined, but he is thought to have lived and taught in the 7th century B.C. He expounded the doctrine that Ahuramazda was the supreme god and the other gods but emanations of him, fulfilling his will. The conflict between Good and Evil was to end with the victory of the former. 'Good thoughts, good words, good deeds' (the triad of Zoroastrian ethics) were rewarded by an after-life in paradise. It was a sin to immolate the 'divine race.' Dead bodies must not be buried but exposed to the elements. *p.* 51, 227, 230

ZURVAN ('Infinite Time') — Primitive androgynous deity who gave birth to Ahuramazda and Ahriman, Good and Evil, Prince of Light and Prince of Darkness. This very ancient Iranian belief was incorporated in official Zoroastrianism under the Sassanians. Zurvan was a god of the celestial firmament and arbiter of destiny . . . . *p.* 51, 52, 71 *fig.* 64

BIBLIOGRAPHY

I. GENERAL

ALBRIGHT (W.F.). — FROM THE STONE AGE TO CHRISTIANITY, The Johns Hopkins Press, Baltimore, 1946.

BAHRAMI (M.). — SOME OBJECTS RECENTLY DISCOVERED IN IRAN, in BULLETIN OF THE IRANIAN INSTITUTE, Vol. VI, 1-4; Vol. VII, 1, pp. 71-77, New York, The Asia Institute, 1946.
— L'EXPOSITION D'ART IRANIEN A PARIS, in ARTIBUS ASIAE, Vol. XI, 1-2, pp. 13-22, Ascona, 1948.

BARTHOLD (W.). — IRAN (in Russian), Moscow-Leningrad, 1926.

BASCHMAKOFF (A.). — CINQUANTE SIÈCLES D'ÉVOLUTION TECHNIQUE AUTOUR DE LA MER NOIRE, Paris, Geuthner, 1937.

BERGHE (L. Van Den). — ARCHÉOLOGIE DE L'IRAN ANCIEN, Leiden, Brill, 1959.

BERGHE (L. Van Den) and MUSSCHE (H.F.). — BIBLIOGRAPHIE ANALYTIQUE DE L'ASSYRIOLOGIE ET DE L'ARCHÉOLOGIE DU PROCHE-ORIENT, Vol. I. L'ARCHÉOLOGIE, 1954-55, Leiden, Brill, 1956.

BITTEL (K.). — GRUNDZÜGE DER VOR- UND FRÜHGESCHICHTE KLEINASIENS, Tübingen, 1950.

BODE (Baron C.C. de). — TRAVELS IN LURISTAN AND ARABISTAN, London, 2 volumes, 1845.

BOSSERT (H.T.). — ALTANATOLIEN. KUNST UND HANDWERK IN KLEINASIEN VON DEN ANFÄNGEN BIS ZUM VÖLLIGEN AUFGEHEN IN DER GRIECHISCHEN KULTUR, Berlin, Ernst Wasmuth. 1942.
— ALTSYRIEN. KUNST UND HANDWERK IN CYPERN, SYRIEN, PALÄSTINA, TRANSJORDANIEN UND ARABIEN VON DEN ANFÄNGEN BIS ZUM VÖLLIGEN AUFGEHEN IN DER GRIECHISCH-RÖMISCHEN KULTUR, with the collaboration of R. Naumann, Tübingen, Ernst Wasmuth, 1952.

CHRISTENSEN (A.). — DIE IRANIER. KULTURGESCHICHTE DES ALTEN ORIENTS, in HANDBUCH DER ALTERTUMSWISSENSCHAFT, Vol. III, pp. 203-310, Munich, C.H. Becksche Verlagsbuchhandlung, 1933.

CONTENAU (G.). — LA DÉESSE NUE BABYLONIENNE, Paris, Geuthner, 1914.
— MANUEL D'ARCHÉOLOGIE ORIENTALE, Paris, Auguste Picard, 4 volumes, 1927-47.
— ARTS ET STYLES DE L'ASIE ANTÉRIEURE, Paris, collection "Arts, Styles et Techniques", Larousse, 1948.

CURZON (G.). — PERSIA AND THE PERSIAN QUESTION, London, 2 volumes, 1892.

DAREMBERG (C.) and SAGLIO (E.). — DICTIONNAIRE DES ANTIQUITÉS GRECQUES ET ROMAINES, Paris, Hachette, 10 volumes, 1877-1919.

DARMESTETER (J.). — LE ZEND-AVESTA, 3 volumes, Annales du Musée Guimet, Vol. XXI, XXII, XXIV. Paris, Leroux, 1892-93. Photographic reprint, Paris, Adrien-Maisonneuve, 1962.

DELAPORTE (L.). — See HUART.

DIEULAFOY (M.). — L'ART ANTIQUE DE LA PERSE. ACHÉMÉNIDES. PARTHES. SASSANIDES, Paris, Librairie centrale d'Architecture, 1884.
— L'ACROPOLE DE SUSE, D'APRÈS LES FOUILLES EXÉCUTÉES EN 1884, 1885, 1886, SOUS LES AUSPICES DU MUSÉE DU LOUVRE, Paris, Hachette, 1890.

DIEZ (E.). — IRANISCHE KUNST, Vienna, W. Andermann, 1944.

EBERT (M.). — REALLEXICON DER VORGESCHICHTE, Berlin, Walter de Gruyter, 15 volumes, 1924-32.

FALKE (Otto von). — KUNSTGESCHICHTE DER SEIDENWEBEREI, 4th edition, Tübingen, E. Wasmuth, 1936.

FLANDIN (E.) and COSTE (P.). — VOYAGE EN PERSE PENDANT LES ANNÉES 1840 ET 1842, Paris, Gide et Bandy, 6 volumes, 1843-54.

FORBES (R.J.). — METALLURGY IN ANTIQUITY, Leiden, Brill, 1950.

FRANKFORT (H.). — CYLINDER SEALS. A DOCUMENTARY ESSAY ON THE ART AND RELIGION OF THE ANCIENT NEAR EAST, London, Macmillan, 1939.
— THE ART AND ARCHITECTURE OF THE ANCIENT ORIENT. The Pelican History of Art, Harmondsworth, Penguin Books, 1954.

FURTWÄNGLER (A.). — DIE ANTIKEN GEMMEN, Berlin, 3 volumes, 1900.

GHIRSHMAN (R.). — L'IRAN, DES ORIGINES A L'ISLAM, Paris, Bibliothèque Historique, Payot, 1951. English edition: IRAN, FROM THE EARLIEST TIMES TO THE ISLAMIC CONQUEST, Pelican Archaeology Series, Penguin Books, Harmondsworth, 1954.
— French résumé of S. Tolstov, DREVNIY CHORESM, in ARTIBUS ASIAE, Vol. XVI, pp. 209-237 and 292-319, Ascona, 1953.

GODARD (A.). — IRAN. PIÈCES DU MUSÉE DE TÉHÉRAN, DU MUSÉE DU LOUVRE ET DE COLLECTIONS PARTICULIÈRES, Illustrated Catalogue, Musée Cernuschi, Paris, 1948.

GOOSSENS (G.). — L'ART DE L'ASIE ANTÉRIEURE DANS L'ANTIQUITÉ, Brussels, Collection Lebègue, L'Office de Publicité, 1948.

GROENEWEGEN-FRANKFORT (H.A.). — ARREST AND MOVEMENT. AN ESSAY ON SPACE AND TIME IN THE REPRESENTATIONAL ART OF THE ANCIENT NEAR EAST, London, Faber and Faber, 1951.

HANFMANN (G.M.A.). — THE BRONZE AGE IN THE NEAR EAST: A REVIEW ARTICLE, in AMERICAN JOURNAL OF ARCHAEOLOGY, Vol. 55, 1951, pp. 355-365, 1951-52.

HERZFELD (E.). — AM TOR VON ASIEN. FELDSDENKMALE AUS IRANS HELDENZEIT, Berlin, D. Reimer & E. Vohsen, 1920.
— ARCHAEOLOGICAL HISTORY OF IRAN. The Schweich Lectures of the British Academy, 1934. London, Oxford University Press, 1935.
— IRAN IN THE ANCIENT EAST, London & New York, Oxford University Press, 1941.

HUART (C.) and DELAPORTE (L.). — L'IRAN ANTIQUE. ELAM ET PERSE ET LA CIVILISATION IRANIENNE. L'Évolution de l'Humanité, Vol. XXIV, Paris, Albin Michel, 1943.

JACOBSTHAL (P.). — EARLY CELTIC ART. Oxford Monographs on Classical Archaeology, edited by J.D. Beazley & Paul Jacobsthal, Oxford, Clarendon Press, 1944.
— GREEK PINS AND THEIR CONNEXIONS WITH EUROPE AND ASIA. Oxford Monographs on Classical Archaeology, edited by J.D. Beazley & Paul Jacobsthal, Oxford, Clarendon Press, 1956.

KISSELEV (S.V.). — DREVNIYA ISTORIYA IOUJNOI SIBIRI (Ancient History of Southern Siberia), Academy of Sciences of the U.S.S.R., Moscow. French résumé by R. Ghirshman in ARTIBUS ASIAE, Vol. XIV, 1-2, pp. 169-189, Ascona, 1951.

LOFTUS (W.K.). — TRAVELS AND RESEARCHES IN CHALDEA AND SUSIANA, London, 1857.

MONGAIT (A.L.). — ARCHAEOLOGY IN THE U.S.S.R., translated from the Russian by M.W. Thompson, Penguin Books, Harmondsworth, 1961.

OSTEN (H.H. von der). — DIE WELT DER PERSER. Grosse Kulturen der Frühzeit, edited by Prof. Dr. H.T. Bossert, Stuttgart, G. Kippler-Verlag, 1956.

PERROT (G.) and CHIPIER (C.). — HISTOIRE DE L'ART DANS L'ANTIQUITÉ, Vol. II. LA CHALDÉE, L'ASSYRIE, LA PHÉNICIE, Paris, Hachette, 1883.

POPE (A. Upham) (editor). — A SURVEY OF PERSIAN ART FROM PREHISTORIC TIMES TO THE PRESENT, London & New York, Oxford University Press, 6 volumes, 1938.

POULSEN (F.). — DER ORIENT UND DIE FRÜHGRIECHISCHE KUNST, Leipzig, Teubner, 1912.

PRASEK (J.V.). — GESCHICHTE DER MEDER UND PERSER BIS ZUR MAKEDONISCHEN EROBERUNG, in HANDBÜCHER DER ALTEN GESCHICHTE, Gotha, Perthes, 1906.

RAWLINSON (G.). — THE FIVE GREAT MONARCHIES OF THE ANCIENT EASTERN WORLD OR THE HISTORY, GEOGRAPHY AND ANTIQUITIES OF CHALDEA, ASSYRIA, BABYLON, MEDIA AND PERSIA, London, John Murray, 1879.

R.L.V. — REALLEXIKON DER VORGESCHICHTE. Edited by Max Ebert, Berlin, Walter de Gruyter, 1924-32.

SARRE (F.) and HERZFELD (E.). — IRANISCHE FELSRELIEFS. AUFNAHMEN UND UNTERSUCHUNGEN VON DENKMÄLERN AUS ALT- UND MITTELPERSISCHER ZEIT, Berlin, E. Wasmuth, 1910.

SARRE (F.) — DIE KUNST DES ALTEN PERSIEN, Berlin, B. Cassierer, 1923.

SCHAEFFER (C.). — STRATIGRAPHIE COMPARÉE ET CHRONOLOGIE DE L'ASIE OCCIDENTALE (IIIe ET IIe MILLÉNAIRES). The Griffith Institute, Ashmolean Museum, Oxford. London, Oxford University Press, 1948.

SCHEFOLD (K.). — ORIENT, HELLAS UND ROM IN DER ARCHÄOLOGISCHEN FORSCHUNG SEIT 1939, Bern, Franke Verlag, 1949.

SCHMIDT (E.F.). — FLIGHTS OVER ANCIENT CITIES OF IRAN. Special Publication of the Oriental Institute of the University of Chicago, Chicago, The University of Chicago Press, 1940.

SINGER (C.), HOLMYARD (E.J.), HALL (A.R.) and WILLIAMS (T.I.) (editors). — HISTORY OF TECHNOLOGY, Vol. I, Clarendon Press, Oxford, 1954, and Vol. II, 1956.

SPEISER (W.). — VORDERASIATISCHE KUNST, Berlin, Safari-Verlag, 1952.

STEIN (Sir Aurel). — AN ARCHAEOLOGICAL TOUR IN ANCIENT PERSIS, in IRAQ, Vol. III, part 2, pp. 111-226, 1936.
— OLD ROUTES OF WESTERN IRAN, London, Macmillan, 1940.

STOCLET (A.). — COLLECTION ADOLPHE STOCLET. First Part, Vol. I. Edited by J.P. van Goidsenhoven, Brussels, 1956.

WABER (O.). — ALTORIENTALISCHE SIEGELBILDER, Leipzig, 2 volumes, text and plates, Heinrich, 1920.

WARD (W.H.). — THE SEAL CYLINDERS OF WESTERN ASIA, Washington, D.C. Carnegie Institution, 1910.

II. ARTICLES AND SPECIAL SUBJECTS

AKURGAL (E.). — PHRYGISCHE KUNST, Ankara, Institute of Archaeology, Ankara University, 1955.
— RECHERCHES FAITES A CYZIQUE ET A ERGILI, in ANATOLIA, Vol. I, pp. 15-24, Institute of Archaeology, Ankara University, 1956.
— URARTAISCHE KUNST, in ANATOLIA, Vol. IV, pp. 78, 114, 1962.

ALFOLDI (A.). — DER IRANISCHE WELTRIESE AUF ARCHÄOLOGISCHEN DENKMÄLERN, in SCHWEIZERISCHE GESELLSCHAFT FÜR URGESCHICHTE, Vol. XL, pp. 17-34, 1949-50.

ALTHEIM (F.) and STIEHL (R.). — SUPPLEMENTUM ARAMAICUM. ARAMÄISCHES AUS IRAN, Baden-Baden, Bruno Grimm, 1957.

AMANDRY (P.). — STATUETTE D'IVOIRE D'UN DOMPTEUR DE LION, DÉCOUVERTE A DELPHES, in SYRIA, Vol. XXIV, pp. 149-174, 1944-45.
— VAISSELLE D'ARGENT DE L'ÉPOQUE ACHÉMÉNIDE, in EN ATHENAIS, pp. 11-19, 1956.
— ORFÈVRERIE ACHÉMÉNIDE, in ANTIKE KUNST, Vol. I, No. 1, pp. 9-23, 1958.

ANDRAE (W.). — FARBIGE KERAMIK AUS ASSUR UND IHRE VORSTUFEN IN ALTASSYRISCHEN WANDMALEREIEN, Berlin, Scarabaeus-Verlag, 1923.
— NEUE FUNDE AUS SUSA, in ARCHÄOLOGISCHER ANZEIGER, Deutsches Archäologisches Institut, pp. 95-106, 1923-24.

ANDREAS and STOLZE (F.). — PERSEPOLIS, Berlin, 2 volumes, 1882.

AUBOYER (J.). — LES INFLUENCES ET LES RÉMINISCENCES ÉTRANGÈRES AU KONDO DU HORYUJI, Paris, Musée Guimet, 1951.

BARNETT (R.D.). — EARLY GREEK AND ORIENTAL IVORIES, in THE JOURNAL OF HELLENIC STUDIES, Vol. LXVIII, pp. 1-25, 1948.
— THE EXCAVATIONS OF THE BRITISH MUSEUM AT TOPRAK KALE NEAR VAN, in IRAQ, XII, Part I, pp. 1-43. The British School of Archaeology in Iraq, 1950.
— THE EXCAVATIONS OF THE BRITISH MUSEUM AT TOPRAK KALE, NEAR VAN. ADDENDA, in IRAQ, XVI, Part I, pp. 3-32. The British School of Archaeology in Iraq, 1954.
— THE TREASURE OF ZIWIYE, in IRAQ, Vol. XVIII, 2, pp. 111-116, 1956.
— ANCIENT ORIENTAL INFLUENCES ON ARCHAIC GREECE, in THE AEGEAN AND THE NEAR EAST, STUDIES PRESENTED TO HETTY GOLDMAN, pp. 212-238, New York, 1956.
— PERSEPOLIS, in IRAQ, Vol. XIX, Part I, pp. 55-57. The British School of Archaeology in Iraq, 1957.
— A CATALOGUE OF THE NIMRUD IVORIES WITH OTHER EXAMPLES OF ANCIENT NEAR EASTERN IVORIES, London, The Trustees of the British Museum, 1957.

BARNETT (R.D.) and WATSON (W.). — RUSSIAN EXCAVATIONS IN ARMENIA, in IRAQ, Vol. XIV, pp. 132-147, 1952.

BARNETT (R.D.) and GOCKE (N.). — THE FIND OF URARTIAN BRONZES AT ALTIN TEPE, NEAR ERZINCAN, in ANATOLIAN STUDIES, III, pp. 121-129, 1953.

BENVENISTE (E.). — THE PERSIAN RELIGION ACCORDING TO THE CHIEF GREEK TEXTS. University of Paris, Ratanbai Katrak Lectures, Paris, Geuthner, 1929.

BERGHE (L. Van Den). — DE STAND VAN DE ARCHAEOLOGISCHE ONDERZOEKINGEN IN IRAN, in JAARBERICHT EX ORIENTE LUX, No. 13, 1953-54, pp. 347-393. HET VOORAZIATISCH-EGYPTISCH GENOOTSCHAP, pp. 347-393, 1953-54.
— OPGRAVINGEN TE KHORWIN, EEN DER OUDSTE NECROPOLEN DER IRANIERS IN IRAN, in HANDELINGEN VAN HET EENENTWINTIGSTE VLAAMS FILOLOGENCONGRES, Louvain, April 12-14, 1955, pp. 117-121, 1955.

BIBEKOV (S.N.). — RANNETRIPOLSKOS POSELENIE LUKA-VRUBLEVETSKAYA NA DNESTRA (Luka-Vrublevetskaya on the Dniester. Site of the archaic period of Tripolie). Materiali i Issledovaniya po Arkheologuii S.S.S.R., No. 38, Moscow-Leningrad, 1953.

BITTEL (K.). — GRUNDZÜGE DER VOR- UND FRÜHGESCHICHTE KLEINASIENS, Tübingen, 1950.

BLINKENBERG (C.). — FIBULES GRECQUES ET ORIENTALES. Det Kgl. Danske Videnskabernes Selskab. Historiskfilologiske Meddelelser, XIII, 1, 1926.

BOROVKA (G.). — SCYTHIAN ART, Kai Khosru Monographs on Eastern Art, London, Ernst Benn Ltd., 1928.

BOSSERT (H.T.) and others. — KARATEPE KAZILARI (DIE AUSGRABUNGEN AUF DEM KARATEPE). Türk tarih kurumu Yayinlarindan V, Série No. 9, Ankara, 1950.

BOYCE (M.). — SOME REFLECTIONS ON ZURVANISM, in BULLETIN OF THE SCHOOL OF ORIENTAL AND AFRICAN STUDIES, Vol. XIX, 2, pp. 304-316, 1957.

BROWN (F.E.). — A RECENTLY DISCOVERED COMPOUND BOW, in SEMINARIUM KONDAKOVIANUM, Vol. IX, pp. 1-10, Prague, 1937.

BUSSAGLI (M.). — MOSTRA D'ARTE IRANICA (Catalogue of the exhibition of Iranian art in Rome), Milan, 1956.

CAMERON (G.). — HISTORY OF EARLY IRAN, Chicago, 1936.
— PERSEPOLIS TREASURY TABLETS, The University of Chicago, Oriental Institute Publications, Vol. LXV, Chicago, 1948.

CHARBONNEAUX (J.). — ANTIGONE LE BORGNE ET DÉMÉTRIUS POLIORCÈTE SONT-ILS FIGURÉS SUR LE SARCOPHAGE D'ALEXANDRE? in LA REVUE DES ARTS, No. 4, pp. 219-223, Paris, 1952.

CHILDE (V. Gordon). — THE FIRST WAGGONS AND CARTS FROM TIGRIS TO THE SEVERN, in PROCEEDINGS OF THE PREHISTORIC SOCIETY, 8, pp. 177-194, London, 1951.

CHRISTENSEN (A.). — ESSAI SUR LA DÉMONOLOGIE IRANIENNE, Det Kgl. Danske Videnskabernes Selskab. Historiskfilologiske Meddelelser, XXVII, 1, 1941.

CLEMENT (P.A.). — THREE EWERS FROM SIYALK IN PERSIA, in LOS ANGELES COUNTY MUSEUM, BULLETIN OF THE ART DIVISION, Vol. VI, No. 3, pp. 16-24, 1954.

CONTENAU (G.). — DEUXIÈME MISSION ARCHÉOLOGIQUE A SIDON, in SYRIA, IV, pp. 276 ff., 1923.

CONTENAU (G.) and GHIRSHMAN (R.). — FOUILLES DU TÉPÉ-GIYAN PRÈS DE NEHAVEND, 1931 ET 1932. Musée du Louvre. Département des Antiquités orientales. Série archéologique, Vol. III, Paris, Geuthner, 1935.

DALTON (O.M.). — THE TREASURE OF THE OXUS WITH OTHER EXAMPLES OF EARLY ORIENTAL METAL-WORK, 2nd edition, London, British Museum, 1926.

DEBEVOISE (N.C.). — ROCK RELIEFS OF ANCIENT IRAN, in JOURNAL OF NEAR EASTERN STUDIES, Vol. I, 1, pp. 76-104, 1942.

DEMARGNE (P.). — LE MAITRE DES ANIMAUX SUR UNE GEMME CRÉTOISE, in MÉLANGES SYRIENS OFFERTS A M. RENÉ DUSSAUD, Vol. I, pp. 121-127. Haut-Commissariat de la République française en Syrie et au Liban, Service des Antiquités, Bibliothèque archéologique et historique, Vol. XXX, Paris, Geuthner, 1939.
— LA CRÈTE DÉDALIQUE. ÉTUDES SUR LES ORIGINES D'UNE RENAISSANCE. Bibliothèque des Écoles françaises d'Athènes et de Rome, fascicule 164, Paris, E. de Boccard, 1947.

DEONNA (W.). — QUELQUES CONVENTIONS PRIMITIVES DE L'ART GREC, in REVUE DES ÉTUDES GRECQUES, Vol. XXIII, No. 105, pp. 379-401, 1910.
— ESSAI SUR LA GENÈSE DES MONSTRES DANS L'ART, in REVUE DES ÉTUDES GRECQUES, Vol. XXVIII, No. 128-129, pp. 288-349, 1915.

DIAKONOV (I.M.). — ASSIRO-VAVILONSKIYE ISTOTCHNIKI PO ISTORII URARTU (Assyro-Babylonian Sources for the History of Urartu), in VESTNIK DREVNEI ISTORII (Annals of Ancient History), fasc. 2-3-4, Moscow-Leningrad, 1951.
— POSLIEDNIÉ GODI TSARSTVA URARTU PO ASSIRO-VAVILONSKIM ISTOTCHNIKAN, in VESTNIK DREVNEI ISTORII, 1951, 2, pp. 29-39. (Last Years of the Kingdom of Urartu according to Assyro-Babylonian Sources, in Annals of Ancient History), Moscow-Leningrad, 1951.
— ISTORIA MEDII (History of Media). Academy of Sciences of the U.S.S.R. Institute of History and Philosophy, Academy of Sciences of the Soviet Republic of Azerbaijan, Moscow-Leningrad, 1956.

DIAKONOV (M.M.). — ARKHEOLOGUITCHESKIYE RABOTI B NI JNEM TECTHENII REKI KAFIRINGANA (KOBADIAN) (Archaeological Reports on the Lower Course of the River Kafiringan), in MATERIALI I ISSLEDOVANIYA PO ARKHEOLOGUII S.S.S.R. (Materials and Researches on the Archaeology of the U.S.S.R.), Vol. 37, 1953.
— TADJIKSKAYA ARKHEOLOGUITCHESKAYA EXPEDITZIYA (Tadzhik Archaeological Expedition), pp. 253-293. Academy of Sciences of the U.S.S.R., Moscow-Leningrad, 1953.

DRIVER (G.R.). — ARAMAIC DOCUMENTS OF THE FIFTH CENTURY B.C., Oxford, Clarendon Press, 1954.

DUNAND (M.). — SONDAGES ARCHÉOLOGIQUES A BOSTAN-ECH-CHEIKH, in SYRIA, Vol. VII, pp. 4-5, 1926.

DYSON (R.H.). — IRAN 1956, in THE UNIVERSITY MUSEUM BULLETIN, March, 1957, pp. 27-39, Philadelphia, University of Pennsylvania, 1957.

EDMONDS (C.J.). — A TOMB IN KURDISTAN, in IRAQ, I, pp. 183-192, 1934.

ERDMANN (K.). — DIE SASSANIDISCHEN JAGDSCHALEN. UNTERSUCHUNG ZUR ENTWICKLUNGSGESCHICHTE DER IRANISCHEN EDELMETALLKUNST UNTER DEN SASSANIDEN, in JAHRBUCH DER PREUSSISCHEN KUNSTSAMMLUNGEN, Vol. 75, pp. 193-232, Berlin, G. Grote, 1936.
— ZUR CHRONOLOGIE DER SASSANIDISCHEN KUNST, FORSCHUNGEN UND FORTSCHRITTE, XIII, p. 169, 1937.
— DAS IRANISCHE FEUERHEILIGTUM. II. Sendschrift der Deutschen Orient-Gesellschaft, Leipzig, J.C. Hinrich, 1947.
— DIE ALTÄRE VON NAQSH I RUSTEM, MITTEILUNGEN DER DEUTSCHEN ORIENT-GESELLSCHAFT, No. 81, pp. 6-15, 1949.
— LÜCKENFORSCHUNG IM IRANISCHEN KUNSTKREIS, in KUNST DES ORIENTS, Vol. I, pp. 20-56, 1950.
— GRIECHISCHE UND ACHAEMENIDISCHE PLASTIK (ZUM GEGENWÄRTIGEN STAND DER DISKUSSION), in FORSCHUNGEN UND FORTSCHRITTE, 26 Jahrg. Heft 11-12, pp. 150-153, 1950.
— Review of E. Schmidt, PERSEPOLIS I, 1953, in BIBLIOTHECA ORIENTALIS, Vol. XIII, 1-2, pp. 56-65, 1956.

FAJANS (S.). — RECENT RUSSIAN LITERATURE ON NEWLY FOUND MIDDLE EASTERN METAL VESSELS, in ARS ORIENTALIS, Vol. II, pp. 55-76, 1957.

FALKNER (M.). — DER SCHATZ VON ZIWIJE, in ARCHIV FÜR ORIENTFORSCHUNG, XVI, pp. 129-132, 1952-53.

FIRDAUSI. — LE LIVRE DES ROIS, French translation of the SHAH-NAMA by Julius von Mohl, Paris, Reinwald, 7 volumes, 1878.

FILOW (B.D.). — DIE ARCHAISCHE NECROPOLE VON TREBENISCHTE AM OCHRIDA-SEE, Berlin, W. de Gruyter, 1927.

FOSSING (P.). — DRINKING BOWL OF GLASS AND METAL FROM THE ACHAEMENIAN TIME, in BERYTUS, Vol. IV, pp. 121-129, 1937.

FRANKFORT (H.). — ACHAEMENIAN SCULPTURE, in AMERICAN JOURNAL OF ARCHAEOLOGY, Vol. I, 1, pp. 6-14, 1946.
— A PERSIAN GOLDSMITH'S TRIAL PIECE, in JOURNAL OF NEAR EASTERN STUDIES, Vol. IX, 2, pp. 111-112, Chicago, 1950.

GADD (C.J.). — THE FALL OF NINEVEH, THE NEWLY DISCOVERED BABYLONIAN CHRONICLE, No. 21.901 in the British Museum, London, 1923.
— ACHAEMENID SEALS. A. TYPES, in A SURVEY OF PERSIAN ART, Vol. I, pp. 383-388, London, New York, Oxford University Press, 1938.

GALLUS (S.) and HORVATH (T.). — UN PEUPLE CAVALIER PRÉSCYTHIQUE EN HONGRIE. Dissertationes Pannonicae, Series II, 9, Budapest, 2 volumes, text and plates, 1939.

GANSZYNIEC. — LABRYS, in PAULY'S REAL-ENCYCLOPÄDIE DER CLASSISCHEN ALTERTUMSWISSENSCHAFT, Vol. XII, 1, col. 286-307, Stuttgart, 1924.

GARDNER (P.). — THE COINS OF THE GREEK AND SCYTHIC KINGS OF BACTRIA AND INDIA IN THE BRITISH MUSEUM, London, 1886.

GERSHEVITCH (Y.). — SISSOO AT SUSA (O. PERS. YAKA = DALBERGIA SISSOO ROXB.), in THE BULLETIN OF THE SCHOOL OF ORIENTAL AND AFRICAN STUDIES, Vol. XIX, 2, pp. 317-320, 1957.

GETTENS (J.) and WARING (L.). — THE COMPOSITION OF SOME ANCIENT PERSIAN AND OTHER NEAR EASTERN SILVER OBJECTS, in ARS ORIENTALIS, Vol. II, pp. 83-90, 1957.

GHIRSHMAN (R.). — See also CONTENAU and GHIRSHMAN.
— NOTES SUR LES PEUPLES ET L'ART DE L'IRAN PRÉHISTORIQUE, in REVUE DES ARTS ASIATIQUES, Vol. X, fasc. 1, pp. 23-36, Paris, 1936.
— FOUILLES DE SIALK, PRÈS DE KASHAN, 1933, 1934, 1937, Vol. I. Musée du Louvre. Département des Antiquités orientales. Série archéologique, Vol. V, Paris, Geuthner, 1938.
— FOUILLES DE SIALK, PRÈS DE KASHAN, 1933, 1934, 1937, Vol. II. Musée du Louvre. Département des Antiquités orientales. Série archéologique, Vol. V, Paris, Geuthner, 1939.
— NOTES IRANIENNES. IV. LE TRÉSOR DE SAKKEZ, LES ORIGINES DE L'ART MÈDE ET LES BRONZES DU LURISTAN, in ARTIBUS ASIAE, Vol. XIII, 3, pp. 181-206, Ascona, 1950.
— MASJID-I SOLAIMAN. RÉSIDENCE DES PREMIERS ACHÉMÉNIDES, in SYRIA, XXVII, fasc. 3-4, pp. 205-220, 1950.
— French résumé of S.V. Kisselev, HISTOIRE ANCIENNE DE LA SIBÉRIE DU SUD, in ARTIBUS ASIAE, Vol. XIV, 1-2, pp. 169-189, Ascona, 1951.
— VILLAGE PERSE-ACHÉMÉNIDE. Mémoires de la mission archéologique en Iran, Vol. XXXVI. Mission de Susiane, Paris, Presses Universitaires de France, 1954.

— A PROPOS DE PERSÉPOLIS, in ARTIBUS ASIAE, Vol. XX, pp. 265 ff., 1957.
— A PROPOS DES ANNEAUX DESTINÉS A TENDRE LA CORDE DE L'ARC, in SYRIA, XXXV, pp. 61-72, 1958.

GINTERS (W.). — DAS SCHWERT DER SKYTHEN UND SARMATEN IN SÜDRUSSLAND. Vorgeschichtliche Forschungen, edited by E. Ebert. 2. Band, 1. Heft, Berlin, Walter de Gruyter, 1928.

GJERSTAD (E.), LINDOS (J.), SJOQVIST (E.) and WESTHOLM (A.). — THE SWEDISH CYPRUS EXPEDITION, Vol. III, Stockholm, 1937.

GODARD (A.). — LE TRÉSOR DE ZIWIYÉ (KURDISTAN), Haarlem, Service archéologique de l'Iran, 1950.

GOLDMAN (B.). — ACHAEMENIAN CAPES, in ARS ORIENTALIS, Vol. II, pp. 43-54, 1957.

GOOSSENS (G.). — L'HISTOIRE D'ASSYRIE DE CTÉSIAS, in L'ANTIQUITÉ CLASSIQUE, Vol. IX, pp. 29-30, 1940.
— ÉTRANGERS EN PERSE SOUS LES ACHÉMÉNIDES, in LA NOUVELLE CLIO, Vol. I, 1-2, pp. 32-44, 1949.
— L'ASSYRIE APRÈS L'EMPIRE, in RENCONTRE ASSYRIOLOGIQUE INTERNATIONALE 1952. Compte rendu, pp. 84-100, 1952.

GRABAR (A.). — LE THÈME RELIGIEUX DES FRESQUES DE LA SYNAGOGUE DE DOURA (245-256 APRÈS J.-C.), in REVUE DE L'HISTOIRE DES RELIGIONS, Vol. CXXIII Nos. 2-3, pp. 143-192; Vol. CXXIV, No. 1, pp. 1-35, 1941.

GRAKOV (B.N.) and MELIUKOVA (A.I.). — OB ETNITCHESKIKH I KULTURNIKH RAZLITCHIYAKH V STEPNIKH I LESOSTEPNIKH OBLASTIAKH EVROPEISKOI TCHASTI S.S.S.R. V SKIFSKOE VREMIA (On Cultural and Ethnic Differences in the Scythian Period in the Steppe Lands and Forest Steppes of European Russia), in VOPROSI SKIFO-SARMATSKOI ARKHEOLOGII (Questions of Scytho-Sarmatian Archæology), pp. 39-94, Moscow, 1952.

GROUSSET (R.). — LA CHINE ET SON ART, Paris, Plon, 1951.

GUMMEL (J.I.). — KURGAN N° 2 BLIZ KHANLARA, in KRATKIYE SOOBCHTENIYA O DOKLADAKH I POLEVIKH ISSLEDOVANIYAKH INSTITUTA ISTORII MATERIAL'NOÏ KULTURI (Barrow 2, near Khanlara, in Brief Communications of the Institute for the History of Material Culture), XXIV, pp. 55-58, 1949.

HAKEMI (A.) and RAD (M.). — CHARH VA NETIDJE KAVOCHHAYEH ELLNI HASSANLU (SOLDUZ) (Explanations and Results of the Scientific Researches at Hasanlu). GOZARECHHAYEH BASTANCHENASSI (Archæological Reports), Vol. I, pp. 1-103, Teheran 1950.

HALLER (A.). — DIE GRÄBER UND GRÜFTE VON ASSUR. Wissenschaftliche Veröffentlichungen der Deutschen Orient-Gesellschaft, Band 65, Berlin, Mann, 1954.

HAMPE (R.). — FRÜHE GRIECHISCHE SAGENBILDER IN BÖOTIEN. Deutsches Archaeologisches Institut, Athens, 1936.

HANCAR (F.). — HALSTATT-KAUKASUS, EIN BEITRAG ZUR KLÄRUNG DES KIMMERIER-PROBLEMS, in MITTEILUNGEN DER OESTERREICHISCHEN GESELLSCHAFT FÜR ANTHROPOLOGIE, ETHNOLOGIE UND PRÄHISTORIE, Vol. LXXIII-LXXVII, pp. 152-167, 1947.
— AUS DER PROBLEMATIK URARTU'S, in ARCHIV. ORIENTALNI, Vol. XVII, No. 1, pp. 298-309, 1949.
— DIE SKYTHEN ALS FORSCHUNGSPROBLEM, in REINECKE-FESTSCHRIFT, pp. 67-83, Mainz, 1950.
— DAS PFERD IN PRÄHISTORISCHER UND FRÜHER HISTORISCHER ZEIT. Wiener Beiträge zur Kulturgeschichte und Linguistik, XI. Institut für Völkerkunde der Universität Wien, Vienna-Munich, Herold, 1955.
— KULTURELEMENT PFERD: WERTUNG UND EINBAU, in SAECULUM, VII, 4. Jahrbuch für Universalgeschichte, Munich, 1956.

HANFMANN (G.M.A.). — FOUR URARTIAN BULLS' HEADS, in ANATOLIAN STUDIES. Journal of the British Institute of Archaeology at Ankara, Vol. VI, pp. 205-213, 1956.
— ETRUSKISCHE PLASTIK. DIE SAMMLUNG PARTHENON, Stuttgart, H.E. Günter, 1956.
— Review of Ulf Jantzen, GRIECHISCHE GREIFENKESSEL, in GNOMON, 1955, Band 29, pp. 241-248, 1957.

HARMATTA (J.). — LE PROBLÈME CIMMÉRIEN, in ARCHAEOLOGIAI ERTESITO, Series III, Vol. VII-IX, pp. 79-132. Budapest, 1946-1948.
— THE GOLDEN BOW OF THE HUNS, in ACTA ARCHAEOLOGICA ACADEMIAE SCIENTIARUM HUNGARICAE, pp. 107-151, Budapest, 1959.

HARPER (R.E.). — ASSYRIAN AND BABYLONIAN LETTERS, London, 1892.

HAUSSIG (H.W.). — THEOPHYLAKT'S EXKURS ÜBER DIE SKYTISCHEN VÖLKER, in BYZANTION, Vol. XXIII (1953), Brussels, 1954.

HEINE-GELDERN (R.). — NEW LIGHT ON THE ARYAN MIGRATION, in BULLETIN OF THE AMERICAN INSTITUTE FOR IRANIAN ART, Vol. V, pp. 7-16, New York, 1937.
— DAS TOCHARER PROBLEM UND DIE PONTISCHE WANDERUNG, in SAECULUM, Vol. II, pp. 225-255, Munich, 1951.
— THE COMING OF THE ARYANS AND THE END OF THE HARAPPA CIVILISATION, in MAN, Vol. LVI, October 1956, pp. 136-140, London, The Royal Anthropological Institute, 1956.

HEINRICH (E.). — SECHSTER VORLÄUFIGER BERICHT ÜBER DIE VON DER DEUTSCHEN FORSCHUNGSGEMEINSCHAFT IN URUK-WARKA UNTERNOMMENEN AUSGRABUNGEN, Berlin, 1935.

HERBIG. — SPHINX, in PAULY'S REAL-ENCYCLOPÄDIE DER CLASSISCHEN ALTERTUMSWISSENSCHAFT, III a 2, col. 1726 ff., Stuttgart, 1929.

HERZFELD (E.). — KHATTISCHE UND KHALDISCHE BRONZEN, in JANUS, Vol. I. FESTSCHRIFT ZU C. F. LEHMANN-HAUPT'S SECHZIGSTEM GEBURTSTAGE, pp. 145-157, Vienna and Leipzig, 1921.
— BERICHT ÜBER DIE AUSGRABUNGEN VON PASARGADAE, 1928, in ARCHAEOLOGISCHE MITTEILUNGEN AUS IRAN, I, p. 16, Berlin, Dietrich Reimer, 1929-30.
— ARIYARAMMA, KÖNIG DER KÖNIGE, in ARCHAEOLOGISCHE MITTEILUNGEN AUS IRAN, II, pp. 113-127, Berlin, Dietrich Reimer, 1930.
— ALTE PERSISCHE INSCHRIFTEN, Berlin, Dietrich Reimer, 1938.

HORVATH (T.). — See GALLUS (S.) and HORVATH (T.).

HOWE (T.P.). — THE ORIGIN AND FUNCTION OF THE GORGON-HEAD, in AMERICAN JOURNAL OF ARCHAEOLOGY, Vol. 58, No. 3, pp. 209-221, 1954.

HUMMEL (J.). — ZUR ARCHÄOLOGIE AZERBEIDZANS, in EURASIA SEPTENTRIONALIS ANTIQUA, VIII, pp. 211-234, 1933.

HUSING (G.). — DER ZAGROS UND SEINE VÖLKER, in DER ALTE ORIENT, Vol. IX, 3 and 4, Leipzig, 1908.
— VÖLKERSCHICHTEN IN IRAN, in MITTEILUNGEN DER ANTHROPOLOGISCHEN GESELLSCHAFT IN WIEN, Band XXXXVI, pp. 199-250, 1916.
— VORGESCHICHTE UND WANDERUNGEN DER PARSAWA, in MITTEILUNGEN DER ANTHROPOLOGISCHEN GESELLSCHAFT IN WIEN, Vol. LX, pp. 246 ff., 1930.

ILIFFE (J.H.). — A TELL FAR'A TOMB GROUP RECONSIDERED. SILVER VESSELS OF THE PERSIAN PERIOD, in THE QUARTERLY OF THE DEPARTMENT OF ANTIQUITIES IN PALESTINE, Vol. IV, No. 4, pp. 182-186, Jerusalem, 1935.

JACOBSTHAL (P.). — THE DATE OF THE EPHESIAN FOUNDATION-DEPOSIT, in JOURNAL OF HELLENIC STUDIES, Vol. LXXI, pp. 85-95, 1951.

JANTZEN (U.). — GRIECHISCHE GREIFENKESSEL, Deutsches Archäologisches Institut, Berlin, Mann, 1955.

JETTMAR (K.). — THE ALTAI BEFORE THE TURKS, in THE MUSEUM OF FAR EASTERN ANTIQUITIES, Bulletin No. 25, pp. 135-223, Stockholm, 1951.
— ARCHÄOLOGISCHE SPUREN VON INDOGERMANEN IN ZENTRALASIEN, in PAIDEUMA, Band V, December 1952, Heft 5, pp. 236-254, 1952.
— MONGOLIDE SCHÄDEL IN DER FRÜHBRONZEZEIT MITTEL- UND NORDEUROPAS? in ARCHIV FÜR VÖLKERKUNDE, Vol. IX, pp. 8-20, Vienna, 1954.
— ZUR WANDERUNG DER IRANIER, in DIE WIENER SCHULE DER VÖLKERKUNDE, FESTSCHRIFT ZUM 25-JÄHRIGEN BESTAND 1929-1954, pp. 327-348, Vienna, 1955.

JOHNS (C.H.W.). — ASSYRIAN DEEDS AND DOCUMENTS, I, 1898.

KALITINSKIY (A.). — ON THE HISTORY OF THE FIBULA IN THE CAUCASUS (in Russian), in RECUEIL KONDAKOV, pp. 39-64, Prague, 1926.
— ON SOME FIBULA FORMS IN SOUTH RUSSIA (in Russian), in SEMINARIUM KONDAKOVIANUM, I, pp. 191-211, Prague, 1927.

KANTOR (H.J.). — SYRO-PALESTINIAN IVORIES, in JOURNAL OF NEAR EASTERN STUDIES, Vol. XV, No. 3, July 1956, pp. 153-174, 1956.
— ACHAEMENID JEWELRY IN THE ORIENTAL INSTITUTE, Oriental Institute Museum Notes, 8. JOURNAL OF NEAR EASTERN STUDIES, Vol. XVI, 1, pp. 1-23, 1957.
— GOLD WORK AND ORNAMENTS FROM IRAN, in THE CINCINNATI ART MUSEUM BULLETIN, Vol. V, No. 2, October 1957, pp. 9-20, 1957.
— A FRAGMENT OF A GOLD APPLIQUE FROM ZIWIYE AND SOME REMARKS ON THE ARTISTIC TRADITIONS OF ARMENIA AND IRAN DURING THE EARLY FIRST MILLENNIUM B.C., in JOURNAL OF NEAR EASTERN STUDIES, Vol. XIX (January), pp. 3 ff., 1960.

KARO (G.). — ORIENT UND HELLAS IN ARCHAISCHER ZEIT, in MITTEILUNGEN DES DEUTSCHEN ARCHÄOLOGISCHEN INSTITUTS, ATHENISCHE ABTEILUNG, Band XXXXV, pp. 106-156, 1920.

KENT (R.G.). — OLD PERSIAN GRAMMAR, TEXTS, LEXICON, New Haven, American Oriental Society, 1950.

KING (L.W.). — BRONZE RELIEFS FROM THE GATES OF SHALMANESER KING OF ASSYRIA, B.C. 860-825, London, 1915.

KNUDTRON (J.A.). — DIE GEBETE AN DEN SONNENGOTT FÜR STAAT UND KÖNIGLICHES HAUS AUS DER ZEIT ASARHADDONS UND ASSURBANIPALS, Leipzig, 1893.

KOLDEWEY (R.) and WETZEL (F.). — DIE KÖNIGSBURGEN VON BABYLON. I. TEIL. DIE SÜDBURG, Wissenschaftliche Veröffentlichungen der Deutschen Orient-Gesellschaft, Vol. LIV, 1931.

KONDAKOFF (N.). — See TOLSTOI and KONDAKOFF.

KÖNIG (F.W.). — DER BURGBAU ZU SUSA NACH DEN BAUBERICHTEN DES KÖNIGS DAREIOS I, MITTEILUNGEN DER VORDERASIATISCH-ÄGYPTISCHEN GESELLSCHAFT, XXXV, 1, Berlin, 1930.
— ÄLTESTE GESCHICHTE DER MEDER UND PERSER, in DER ALTE ORIENT, Band 33, Heft 3-4, Leipzig, Hinrich, 1934.
— RELIEF UND INSCHRIFT DES KÖNIGS DAREIOS I. AM FELSEN VON BAGISTAN, Leiden, Brill, 1938.
— DIE GÖTTERWELT ARMENIENS ZUR ZEIT DER CHALDER-DYNASTIE (9.-7. JAHRHUNDERT V. CHR.), ARCHIV FÜR VÖLKERKUNDE, Vol. VIII, pp. 142-171, 1953.
— GESELLSCHAFTLICHE VERHÄLTNISSE ARMENIENS ZUR ZEIT DER CHALDER-DYNASTIE (9. BIS 7. JAHRHUNDERT V. CHR.), ARCHIV FÜR VÖLKERKUNDE, IX, pp. 21-65, 1954.

— HANDBUCH DER CHALDISCHEN INSCHRIFTEN, Teil I. Archiv für Orientforschung, edited by Ernst Weidner, Beiheft 8. Graz, 1955.
— VORCHRISTLICHES ARMENIEN, Studien zur armenischen Geschichte, VII, Mechitaristen-Buchdruckerei, Vienna, 1955.
— HANDBUCH DER CHALDISCHEN INSCHRIFTEN, Teil II, Archiv für Orientforschung, edited by Ernst Weidner, Beiheft 8, Graz, 1957.

KRAIKER (W.). — AIGINA. DIE VASEN DES 10. BIS 7. JAHRHUNDERTS V. CHRIST, Deutsches Archäologisches Institut, Berlin, Mann, 1951.

KRUPNOV (E.I.). — O POKHODAKH SKIFOV TCHEREZ KAVKAZ (On the Scythian Campaigns in the Caucasus), in VOPROSI SKIFO-SARMATSKOI ARKHEOLOGUII (Questions of Scytho-Sarmatian Archaeology), pp. 186-194, Academy of Sciences of the U.S.S.R., 1952.

KUFTIN (B.A.). — ARKHEOLOGUITCHESKIE RASKOTPI V TRIALETI (Archaeological Excavations at Trialeti), Vol. I, Tiflis, 1941.

KUNZE (E.). — KRETISCHE BRONZERELIEFS, Sächsisches Forschungsinstitut in Leipzigs Forschungsinstitut für klassische Philologie und Archäologie, Stuttgart, two volumes, text and plates, 1931.
— OLYMPISCHE FORSCHUNGEN, Band II, ARCHAISCHE SCHILDBÄNDER, Deutsches Archäologisches Institut, Berlin, Walter de Gruyter, 1950.
— VERKANNTER ORIENTALISCHER KESSELSCHMUCK AUS ARGIVISCHEN HERAION, in FESTSCHRIFT REINECKE, pp. 96-101, Mainz, 1950.

LANDSBERGER (B.). — SAM'AL. STUDIEN ZUR ENTDECKUNG DER RUINENSTÄTTE KARATEPE, Erste Lieferung, Veröffentlichungen der türkischen historischen Gesellschaft, VII, Series No. 16, Ankara, 1948.

LAROCHE (E.). — L'INSCRIPTION HITTITE D'ALEP, in SYRIA, XXXIII, pp. 131-141, 1956.

LAWRENCE (A.W.). — THE ACROPOLIS AND PERSEPOLIS, in THE JOURNAL OF HELLENIC STUDIES, Vol. LXXI, pp. 110-119, 1951.

LAYARD (A.H.). — A SECOND SERIES OF THE MONUMENTS OF NINEVEH, London, 1853.

LEHMANN-HAUPT (C.F.). — ARMENIEN EINST UND JETZT. REISEN UND FORSCHUNGEN, Berlin, Behr's Verlag. Two volumes in three parts, 1910-23.
— KIMMERIER, in PAULY'S REAL-ENCYCLOPÄDIE DER CLASSISCHEN ALTERTUMSWISSENSCHAFT, Vol. XI, 1, col. 397-434, 1921.

LESKY. — SPHINX, in PAULY'S REAL-ENCYCLOPÄDIE DER CLASSISCHEN ALTERTUMSWISSENSCHAFT, Vol. III a, 2, col. 1803 ff., Stuttgart, 1929.

LUSCHEY (H.). — DIE PHIALE, Bleicherode am Harz, Carl Nieft, 1939.

MALLOWAN (M.E.L.). — THE EXCAVATIONS AT TELL CHAGAR BAZAR AND AN ARCHAEOLOGICAL SURVEY OF THE HABUR REGION, 1934-1935, in IRAQ, Vol. III, Part I. British School of Archaeology in Iraq, 1937.
— WHITE-PAINTED SUBARTU POTTERY, in MÉLANGES SYRIENS OFFERTS A M. RENÉ DUSSAUD, Vol. II, pp. 887-894, Paris, Geuthner, 1939.
— EXCAVATIONS AT BRAK AND CHAGAR BAZAR, in IRAQ, Vol. IX, Part I, pp. 1-87, 1947.
— TWENTY-FIVE YEARS OF MESOPOTAMIAN DISCOVERY, To Commemorate the Silver Jubilee of the British School of Archaeology in Iraq, London, 1956.

MALTEN (L.). — DAS PFERD IM TOTENGLAUBEN, in JAHRBUCH DES KAISERLICHEN DEUTSCHEN ARCHÄOLOGISCHEN INSTITUTS, Band XXIX, pp. 179-255, 1914.
— BELLEROPHONTES, in JAHRBUCH DES DEUTSCHEN ARCHÄOLOGISCHEN INSTITUTS, XXX, pp. 121-160, 1925.

MANCEVIC (A.). — O SKIFSKIKH POIASAKH (On Scythian Belts), in SOVIETSKAYA ARKHEOLOGUIYA (Soviet Archaeology), VII, pp. 19-30, 1941. With a résumé in French.

MARINATOS (S.). — FUNDE UND FORSCHUNGEN AUF KRETA, in JAHRBUCH DES DEUTSCHEN ARCHÄOLOGISCHEN INSTITUTS, Vol. XLVIII, pp. 304-308, 1938.

MASSON (M.E.). — NOVIE DANNIE PO DREVNEI ISTORII MERVA (New Data on the Ancient History of Merv), in VESTNIK DREVNEI ISTORII (Annals of Ancient History), 4, pp. 89-101, 1951.

MASSON (V.M.). — PAMIATNIKI KULTURI ARKHAITCHESKOGO DAHISTANA V IOUGO-ZAPADNOÏ TURKMENII (Monuments of the Cultures of Archaic Daghestan in South-western Turkmenia), in TRUDI IOUJNOTURKMENISTANSKOI ARKHEOLOGUICHESKOI COMPLEKSNOI EXPEDITZII (Reports of the Joint Archaeological Expedition to South Turkmenistan), Vol. VII, pp. 385-458. Academy of Sciences of the S.S.R. of Turkmenia, Ashkhabad, 1956.

MATZ (F.) — GESCHICHTE DER GRIECHISCHEN KUNST. DIE GEOMETRISCHE UND DIE FRÜHARCHAISCHE FORM, Frankfurt am Main, Klostermann, 2 volumes, text and plates, 1950.

MAXIMOVA (M.). — LES VASES PLASTIQUES DANS L'ANTIQUITÉ, Paris, Geuthner, 1937.
— GRIECHISCH-PERSISCHE KLEINKUNST IN KLEINASIEN NACH DEN PERSERKRIEGEN, in ARCHAEOLOGISCHER ANZEIGER, III-IV, pp. 647-678, 1928.
— SEREBRIANNOYE ZERKALO IZ KELERMESA (Silver Mirror from Kelermes), in SOVIETSKAYA ARKHEOLOGUIYA (Soviet Archaeology), Vol. XXI, pp. 281-305, 1954.

MAXWELL-HYSLOP (R.). — DAGGERS AND SWORDS IN WESTERN ASIA, in IRAQ, Vol. VIII, pp. 1-65, 1946.
— URARTIAN BRONZES IN ETRUSCAN TOMBS, in IRAQ, Vol. XVIII, Part 2, pp. 150-167, 1956.

— NOTES ON SOME DISTINCTIVE TYPES OF BRONZES FROM POPULONIA, ETRURIA, in PROCEEDINGS OF THE PREHISTORIC SOCIETY, Vol. XXII, pp. 126-142, 1956.

MELIKISHVILI (G.A.). — URARTSKIYE KLINOOBRAZNIE NADPISI (Urartian Cuneiform Inscriptions), in VESTNIK DREVNEI ISTORII (Annals of Ancient History), Nos. 1, 2, 3, 4, 1953. No. 1, 1954.
— NAÏRI-URARTU, Academy of Sciences of the Georgian Soviet Republic, Tiflis, 1954.

MELIUKOVA (A.I.). — See GRAKOV and MELIUKOVA.

MENDEL (G.). — CATALOGUE DES SCULPTURES GRECQUES, ROMAINES ET BYZANTINES, Constantinople, Musées impériaux ottomans, Vol. III, 1914.

MINNS (E.H.). — SCYTHIANS AND GREEKS. A SURVEY OF ANCIENT HISTORY AND ARCHAEOLOGY ON THE NORTH COAST OF THE EUXINE FROM THE DANUBE TO THE CAUCASUS, Cambridge, University Press, 1913.
— THE ART OF THE NORTHERN NOMADS. Annual Lecture on Aspects of Art, London, Henriette Hertz Trust, British Academy, 1942.

MOORTGAT (A.). — HELLAS UND DIE KUNST DER ACHAEMENIDEN, Mitteilungen der Altorientalischen Gesellschaft, II, 1, Leipzig, 1926.
— DIE BILDENDE KUNST DES ALTEN ORIENTS UND DIE BERGVÖLKER, 1932.
— See also M. F. VON OPPENHEIM.

MORGAN (J. de). — MISSION SCIENTIFIQUE EN PERSE. RECHERCHES ARCHÉOLOGIQUES, Vol. IV, 1, Paris, Leroux, 1891.
— DÉCOUVERTE D'UNE SÉPULTURE ACHÉMÉNIDE A SUSE, MÉMOIRES DE LA DÉLÉGATION EN PERSE, Vol. VIII. Recherches archéologiques, pp. 29-58, Paris, Leroux, 1905.

MOSTAFAVI (M.T.). — HAGMATANÈ ASAR-É TARIKHI HAMADAN (Historical Monuments of Hamadan), Teheran, 1953.

MUHLESTEIN (H.). — DIE KUNST DER ETRUSKER, Berlin, Frankfurter Verlags-Anstalt, 1929.

MULLER (V.). — FRÜHE PLASTIK IN GRIECHENLAND UND VORDERASIEN, Augsburg, 1929.

NAUMANN (R.). — ARCHITEKTUR KLEINASIENS VON IHREN ANFÄNGEN BIS ZUM ENDE DER HETHITISCHEN ZEIT, Deutsches Archäologisches Institut, Tübingen, E. Wasmuth, 1955.

NOTH (M.). — HISTOIRE D'ISRAEL, Paris, Payot, 1954.

NYBERG (H.S.). — DIE RELIGIONEN DES ALTEN IRAN. Mitteilungen der Vorderasiatisch-Aegyptischen Gesellschaft, 43, Leipzig, Hinrich, 1938.

OGANESIAN (K.L.). — KARMIR-BLUR IV. ARKHITECTURA TEISHEBAINI (Architecture of Teishebaini), Academy of Sciences of the Armenian Soviet Republic, Erivan, 1955.

OLMSTEAD (A.T.). — HISTORY OF THE PERSIAN EMPIRE (ACHAEMENID PERIOD), Chicago, The University of Chicago Press, 1948.

OPITZ (D.). — See OPPENHEIM, M. F. VON.

OPPENHEIM (M.F. von). — TELL HALAF. Dritter Band : Die Bildwerke unter Verwendung der Bildbeschreibungen von Dietrich Opitz, bearbeitet und herausgegeben von Anton Moortgat, Berlin, Walter de Gruyter, 1955.

OPPENHEIMER (A.L.). — THE GOLDEN GARMENTS OF THE GODS, in JOURNAL OF NEAR EASTERN STUDIES, Vol. VIII, 3, pp. 172-193, 1949.

OUCHAKOV (P.). — K POKHODAM URARTIYZEF V ZAKAVKAZIÉ V IX I VII VV. DO N. E. (The Campaigns of the Urartians in Transcaucasia), in VESTNIK DREVNEI ISTORII (Annals of Ancient History), 1946, 2, pp. 31-44.

PALLOTTINO (M.). — L'ART DES ÉTRUSQUES, Collection Atlantis, Paris, Braun & Cie, 1955. English edition: ART OF THE ETRUSCANS, London, Thames and Hudson.
— ART ET CIVILISATION DES ÉTRUSQUES, Musée du Louvre, Exhibition Catalogue, October-December, Editions des Musées nationaux, 1955.
— GLI SCAVI DI KARMIR-BLUR IN ARMENIA E IL PROBLEMA DELLE CONNESSIONI TRA L'URARTU, LA GRECIA E L'ETRURIA, in ARCHEOLOGIA CLASSICA, REVISTA DELL'ISTITUTO DI ARCHEOLOGIA DELL'UNIVERSITA DI ROMA, Vol. VII, fasc. 2, pp. 109-123, Rome, 1955.

PAPER (H.H.). — Review of Kemal Balkan, KASSITENSTUDIEN. I. DIE SPRACHE DER KASSITEN, New Haven, 1954, in JOURNAL OF NEAR EASTERN STUDIES, Vol. XV, 4, October 1956, pp. 251-254, 1956.

PAYNE (H.). — NECROCORINTHIA. A STUDY OF CORINTHIAN ART IN THE ARCHAIC PERIOD, Oxford, Clarendon Press, 1931.

PAYNE (H.) and others. — PERACHORA. THE SANCTUARIES OF HERA AKRAIA AND LIMENIA. ARCHITECTURE, BRONZES, TERRACOTTAS, Oxford 1940.

PFUHL (E.). — MALEREI UND ZEICHNUNG DER GRIECHEN, Munich, 1923. English edition: MASTERPIECES OF GREEK DRAWING AND PAINTING, translated by J. D. Beazley, London, 1926; reissued 1955.

PICARD (C.). — OBSERVATIONS SUR LA SOCIÉTÉ DES POSEIDONIASTES DE BERYTON ET SUR SON HISTOIRE, in BULLETIN DE CORRESPONDANCE HELLÉNIQUE, Vol. XLIV, 1920, pp. 263-311.
— DE L'INCENDIE DE L'ARTEMISION D'ÉPHÈSE AU SAC DES PALAIS DE PERSÉPOLIS, in ACADÉMIE DES INSCRIPTIONS ET BELLES-LETTRES, Comptes rendus des séances de l'année 1956, January-March, pp. 81-99, 1956.
— L'IVOIRE ARCHAÏQUE DES DEUX DÉESSES, in MONUMENTS ET MÉMOIRES. FONDATION EUGÈNE PIOT, Vol. XLVIII, 2, pp. 9-28, 1956.

PIJOAN (J.). — In Cossio-Pijoan, SUMMA ARTIS, HISTORIA GENERAL DEL ARTE, Vol. II, ARTE DEL ASIA OCCIDENTAL, Bilbao, 1931.

PILLET (M.). — LE PALAIS DE DARIUS I A SUSE, Paris, 1914.

PIOTROVSKY (B.). — URARTU. DREVNEICHEE GOSOUDARSTVO ZAKAVKAZIYA (Urartu, the Oldest State of Transcaucasia), Leningrad, 1939.
— URARTU I ZAKAVKAKIÉ. Kratkie soobchteniya o dokladakh i polevikh issledovaniyakh Instituta Istorii Material'noï Kulturi (Urartu and Transcaucasia. Brief Communications concerning the Field Work, Institute for the History of Material Culture), Vol. III, 1940.
— ISTORIYA I KULTURA URARTU (History and Culture of Urartu), Erivan, 1944.
— ARKHEOLOGUIYA ZAKAVKAZIA S DREVNEICHIKH VREMEN DO I TYSIATCHILETIYA DC NACHEI ERI (Archaeology of Transcaucasia from the Earliest Times to the 1st Millennium B.C.), Leningrad, 1949.
— KARMIR-BLUR. I. 1939-49 (excavation report, in Russian), Academy of Sciences of the Armenian S.S.R., Erivan, 1950.
— KARMIR-BLUR. II. 1949-50 (excavation report, in Russian), Academy of Sciences of the Armenian S.S.R., Erivan, 1952.
— SKIFI I DREVNIY VOSTOK, in SOVIETSKAYA ARKHEOLOGUIYA (The Scythians of the Ancient East, in Soviet Archaeology), Vol. XIX, pp. 140-158, 1954.
— KARMIR-BLUR. III. 1951-53 (excavation report, in Russian), Academy of Sciences of the Armenian S.S.R., Erivan, 1955.
— RAZVITIYE SKOTOVODSTVA V DREVNEICHE ZAKAVKAZIÉ (Development of Stock-breeding in Ancient Transcaucasia), in SOVIETSKAYA ARKHEOLOGUIYA (Soviet Archaeology), XXIII, pp. 1-15, 1955.
— VANSKOE TSARSTVO (Kingdom of Van), Moscow, 1959.
— ISKOUSSTVO URARTU VIII-VI V. V. DO N. E. (Art of Urartu), Leningrad, 1962.

POSENER (G.). — LA PREMIÈRE DOMINATION PERSE EN ÉGYPTE. RECUEIL D'INSCRIPTIONS HIÉROGLYPHIQUES. Bibliothèque d'études, publiée sous la direction de M. Jouguet, directeur de l'Institut français d'archéologie orientale, 1936.

PRZEWORSKI (S.). — ALTORIENTALISCHE ALTERTÜMER IN SKANDINAVISCHEN SAMMLUNGEN, in EURASIA SEPTENTRIONALIS ANTIQUA, Vol. X, pp. 73-128, Helsinki, 1936.

RAD (M.). — See HAKEMI and RAD.

RAWLINSON (G.). — HISTORY OF HERODOTUS, London, J. Murray, 4 volumes, 1879.

REINACH (S.). — ANTIQUITÉS DU BOSPHORE CIMMÉRIEN (1854). Réédité avec un commentaire nouveau et un index général des comptes rendus, Paris, Firmin-Didot, 1892.

REUTHER (D.). — DIE AUSGRABUNGEN DER DEUTSCHEN KTESIPHON-EXPEDITION IM WINTER 1928-1929, Staatliche Museen in Berlin, Islamische Kunstabteilung, 1930.

413

RICHTER (G.M.A.). — GREEK, ETRUSCAN AND ROMAN BRONZES, New York, The Metropolitan Museum of Art, 1915.
— ANIMALS IN GREEK SCULPTURE, London, 1930.
— GREEKS IN PERSIA, in AMERICAN JOURNAL OF ARCHAEOLOGY, Vol. L, No. 1, pp. 15-30, 1946.
— ARCHAIC GREEK ART, New York, Oxford University Press, 1949.
— THE LATE ACHAEMENIAN OR GRECO-PERSIAN GEMS, in HISPERIA, SUPPLEMENT VIII : COMMEMORATIVE STUDIES IN HONOR OF THEODORE LESLIE SHEAR, pp. 291-298. American School of Classical Studies at Athens, 1949.
— GREEK SUBJECTS ON GRECO-PERSIAN SEAL STONES, in ARCHAEOLOGICA ORIENTALIS IN MEMORIAM ERNST HERZFELD, pp, 189-194, New York, G. C. Miles Editor, Locust Valley, 1952.

ROBINSON (E.S.G.). — A SILVERSMITH'S HOARD FROM MESOPOTAMIA, in IRAQ, Vol. XIII, 1, pp. 44-51, 1950.
— COINS FROM THE EPHESIAN ARTEMISION RECONSIDERED, in THE JOURNAL OF HELLENIC STUDIES, Vol. LXXI, pp. 156-167, 1951.

ROES (A.). — GREEK GEOMETRIC ART : ITS SYMBOLISM AND ITS ORIGIN, Oxford, 1933.
— UN MOTIF IRANIEN : LES PROTOMES DOUBLES, in REVUE DES ÉTUDES ANCIENNES, Vol. XXXVII, No. 3, pp. 289-300, 1935.
— NEW LIGHT ON THE GRYLLI, in THE JOURNAL OF HELLENIC STUDIES, Vol. LIV, pp. 232-235, 1935.
— L'ANIMAL AU SIGNE SOLAIRE, in REVUE ARCHÉOLOGIQUE, VIe Série, Vol. XII, pp. 153-182, 1938.
— THE GOAT AND THE HORSE IN THE CULT OF HITHER ASIA, in STUDIA VARIA CAROLO GUILIELMO VOLLGRAFF A DISCIPULIS OBLATA (Studia Vollgraff), pp. 99-138, Amsterdam, North-Holland Publishing Company, 1948.
— THE ACHAEMENID ROBE, in BIBLIOTHECA ORIENTALIS, Vol. VIII, pp. 137-141, 1951.
— ACHAEMENID INFLUENCE UPON EGYPTIAN AND NOMAD ART, in ARTIBUS ASIAE, XV, 1-2, pp. 17-30. Ascona, 1952.

ROSTOVTZEFF (M.). — IRANIANS AND GREEKS IN SOUTH RUSSIA, Oxford, Clarendon Press, 1922.
— LE CENTRE DE L'ASIE, LA RUSSIE, LA CHINE ET LE STYLE ANIMALIER, in SKYTHIKA I, pp. 31-48, SEMINARIUM KONDAKOVIANUM, Prague, 1929.
— SKYTHIEN UND DER BOSPORUS, Band I (the only one published). KRITISCHE ÜBERSICHT DER SCHRIFTLICHEN UND ARCHÄOLOGISCHEN QUELLEN, Berlin, Hans Schoetz & Co., 1931.

RUDENKO (S.I.) and RUDENKO (N.M.). — ISKOUSSTVO SKIFOV ALTAÏA (The Art of the Scythians of the Altai), Moscow, 1949.

RUDENKO (S.I.). — KULTURA NASSELENIYA GORNOGO ALTAÏA V SKIFSKOYE VREMIA (Culture of the Mountain Peoples of the Altai in the Scythian Period), Academy of Sciences of the U.S.S.R., Moscow-Leningrad, 1953.

RUMPF (A.). — MALEREI UND ZEICHNUNG, in HANDBUCH DER ARCHÄOLOGIE IM RAHMEN DES HANDBUCHS DER ALTERTUMSWISSENSCHAFT, Sechste Lieferung, Begründet von Walter Otto, fortgeführt von Reinhard Herbig, Munich, C. H. Beck'sche Verlagsbuchhandlung, 1953.

SAFLUND (G.). — THE SWEDISH EXCAVATIONS AT LABRANDA, 1953, in TÜRK ARKEOLOJI DERGSI, Vol. VI, 1, pp. 3-4, Ankara, 1956.

SALMONY (A.). — SINO-SIBERIAN ART IN THE COLLECTION OF C. T. LOO, Paris, C.T. Loo, 1933.
— EINE CHINESISCHE SCHMUCKFORM UND IHRE VERBREITUNG IN ASIEN, in EURASIA SEPTENTRIONALIS ANTIQUA, Vol. IX, MINNS VOLUME, pp. 321-335, Helsinki, 1934.

SCHEFOLD (K.). — DER SKYTHISCHE TIERSTIL IN SÜDRUSSLAND, in EURASIA SEPTENTRIONALIS ANTIQUA, Vol. XII, pp. 3-78, Helsinki, 1938.
— DIE IRANISCHE KUNST DER PONTUSLÄNDER, in HANDBUCH DER ARCHÄOLOGIE IM RAHMEN DES HANDBUCHS DER ALTERTUMSWISSENSCHAFT, pp. 423-454, Munich, C. H. Beck'sche Verlagsbuchhandlung, 1954.

SCHEIL (R.P.V.). — INSCRIPTIONS DES ACHÉMÉNIDES A SUSE, in MÉMOIRES DE LA MISSION ARCHÉOLOGIQUE DE PERSE, Vol. XXI, Paris, 1929.

SCHMIDT (E.). — GRIECHEN IN BABYLON UND DAS WEITERLEBEN IHRER KULTUR, in ARCHÄOLOGISCHER ANZEIGER, col. 786-844 and fig. 7-11, 1941.

SCHMIDT (E.F.). — THE SECOND HOLMES EXPEDITION TO LURISTAN, in BULLETIN OF THE AMERICAN INSTITUTE FOR IRANIAN ART AND ARCHAEOLOGY, Vol. V, pp. 205-216, New York, 1937.
— THE TREASURY OF PERSEPOLIS AND OTHER DISCOVERIES IN THE HOMELAND OF THE ACHAEMENIANS, in ORIENTAL INSTITUTE COMMUNICATIONS, No. 21, Chicago, The Oriental Institute of the University of Chicago, 1939.
— PERSEPOLIS. I. STRUCTURES — RELIEFS — INSCRIPTIONS, The University of Chicago Oriental Institute Publications, Vol. LXVIII, Chicago, 1953.
— PERSEPOLIS. II. CONTENTS OF THE TREASURY AND OTHER DISCOVERIES, The University of Chicago Oriental Institute Publications, Vol. LXIX, Chicago, 1957.

SCHOPPA (H.). — DIE DARSTELLUNG DER PERSER IN DER GRIECHISCHEN KUNST BIS ZUM BEGINN DES HELLENISMUS, Dissertation, Heidelberg, 1933.

SEGALL (B.). — THE ARTS AND KING NABONIDUS, in AMERICAN JOURNAL OF ARCHAEOLOGY, Vol. LIX, 4, pp. 315-318, 1955.

SEYRIG (H.). — CACHETS ACHÉMÉNIDES, in ARCHAEOLOGICA ORIENTALIS IN MEMORIAM ERNST HERZFELD, pp. 195-202, New York, G. C. Miles, Locust Valley, 1952.

SMIRNOV (J.I.). — VOSTOTCHNOE SEREBRO (Oriental Silverware), St Petersburg, 1909.
— DER SCHATZ VON AKHALGORI, Aus dem Nachlass von Georg Tschubinaschvili herausgegeben, Verlag des Georgischen Museums, Tiflis, 1934.

SMITH (A.H.). — A CATALOGUE OF SCULPTURE IN THE DEPARTMENT OF GREEK AND ROMAN ANTIQUITIES, London, British Museum, Vol. I, 1892.
— THE NEREID MONUMENT AND LATER LYCIAN SCULPTURES IN THE BRITISH MUSEUM, Catalogue of Sculptures in the Department of Greek and Roman Antiquities, Vol. II, Part IV, London, 1900.

SMITH (S.). — THE GREEK TRADE AT AL MINA, in THE ANTIQUARIES' JOURNAL, Vol. XXI, pp. 87-112, 1942.

STARR (R.F.S.). — NUZI, Cambridge, Harvard University Press, Vol. I, text; Vol. II, plates, 1939.

STIEHL (R.). — See ALTHEIM and STIEHL.

SULIMIRSKI (J.). — SCYTHIAN ANTIQUITIES IN WESTERN ASIA, in ARTIBUS ASIAE, Vol. XVII, pp. 282-318, Ascona, 1954.

SVOBODA (B.). — ZUR GESCHICHTE DES RHYTONS, in B. Svoboda and D. Concev, NEUE DENKMÄLER ANTIKER TOREUTIK, Prague, 1956.

TALBOT RICE (T.) — THE SCYTHIANS, London, Thames and Hudson, 1957.

TALLGREEN (A.M.). — ZUR WESTSIBIRISCHEN GRUPPE DER SCHAMANISTISCHEN FIGUREN, in SEMINARIUM KONDAKOVIANUM, Vol. IV, pp. 39-46, Prague, 1931.

THIERSH. — PRO SAMOTHRAKE, Vienna-Leipzig, Holder, Pichler & Tempsky, 1930.

THUREAU-DANGIN (F.). — UNE RELATION DE LA HUITIÈME CAMPAGNE DE SARGON (714 AV. J.-C.), Paris, Musée du Louvre, Département des antiquités orientales, 1912.

TOLSTOI (Count I.) and KONDAKOFF (N.). — ROUSSKIYA DREVNOSTI V PAMIATNIKAKH ISKOUSSTVA. II. St Petersburg. (Russian Antiquities in the Art Monuments), 1889.

TOLSTOV (S.). — DREVNIY CHOREZM (Ancient Chorasmia), Moscow, 1948. See French résumé by R. Ghirshman, in ARTIBUS ASIAE, XVI, pp. 209-237 and 292-319, Ascona, 1948.
— KHOREZMSKAYA ARKHEOLOGO-ETNOGRAFITCHESKAYA EXPEDITZIA AKADEMII NAOUK S. S. S. R. 1950 G. (Archaeological and Ethnographic Expedition of the Academy of Sciences of the U.S.S.R. in Chorasmia in 1950), in SOVIETSKAYA ARKHEOLOGUIYA (Soviet Archaeology), Vol. XVIII, pp. 301-325, 1953.

TREVER (C.). — NOVYE SASANIDSKIYE BLIOUDA ERMITAJA (New Sassanian Dishes in the Hermitage), Moscow, Leningrad, 1937.

TRITSCH (F.J.). — THE HARPY TOMB AT XANTHOS, in THE JOURNAL OF HELLENIC STUDIES, Vol. LXII, pp. 39-50, 1942.

TURIN (V.O.). — SOTZIAL'NOE POLOGENIE KUR-TAS (Social Position of the Kur-tas), in VESTNIK DREVNEI ISTORII (Annals of Ancient History), pp. 21-39, 1951.

VALLOIS (R.). — L'ARCHITECTURE HELLÉNIQUE ET HELLÉNISTIQUE A DÉLOS, Paris, 1944.

VERNADSKY (G.). — VASES DE BRONZE GRECS DANS UNE TOMBE ÉTRUSQUE DU VIIᵉ SIÈCLE, in MONUMENTS ET MÉMOIRES. FONDATION EUGÈNE PIOT, Vol. XLVIII, fasc. 2, pp. 25-53, 1950.

VITT (B.O.). — LOCHADI PAZYRYKSKIKH KOURGANOV (The Horses of the Pazyryk Barrows), in SOVIETSKAYA ARKHEOLOGUIYA (Soviet Archaeology), Vol. XVI, pp. 163-205, 1952.

VOSHCHININA (A.V.). — O SVIAZIAKH PRIOURALIA S VOSTOKOM (Links between the Ural Region and the East), in SOVIETSKAYA ARKHEOLOGUIYA (Soviet Archaeology), Vol. XVII, pp. 183-210, 1953.

WALDHAUER (O.). — SKYTISCHE KUNST, in PANTHEON, Band XI, pp. 29-35, 1900.

WARING (L.). — See GETTENS and WARING.

WATSON (W.). — See BARNETT and WATSON.

WEIDNER (E.). — WEISSE PFERDE IM ALTEN ORIENT, BIBLIOTHECA ORIENTALIS, Vol. IX, pp. 157-159, Leiden, 1952.

WESENDONK (O.G. von). — DAS PROBLEM DER ALTPERSISCHEN KUNST, in LITTERAE ORIENTALIS, Heft 42, April 1930, pp. 1-9, Leipzig, 1930.
— ZUR ÄLTESTEN PERSISCHEN GESCHICHTE, in LITTERAE ORIENTALIS, Heft 56, October 1933, pp. 1-4, Leipzig, 1933.

WETZEL (F.). — See KOLDEWEY and WETZEL.

WIEDENGREN (G.). — HOCHGOTTGLAUBE IM ALTEN IRAN, University of Uppsala, 1938.

WIESENER (J.). — FRÜHZEITLICHE GRIECHISCHE BRONZEN UND IHRE AUSWÄRTIGEN BEZIEHUNGEN, in ARCHÄOLOGISCHER ANZEIGER, pp. 313-332, 1939.
— KIMMERIER UND SKYTHEN IM LICHTE NEUER INDOGERMANENFORSCHUNG, in FORSCHUNGEN UND FORTSCHRITTE, 10, pp. 214-217, 1943.

WIKANDER (S.). — FEUERPRIESTER IN KLEINASIEN UND IRAN, Lund, C. K. Gleerup, 1946.

WILKINSON (C.K.). — SOME NEW CONTACTS WITH NIMRUD AND ASSYRIA, in THE METROPOLITAN MUSEUM OF ART BULLETIN, April 1952, pp. 233-240, New York, 1952.
— ASSYRIAN AND PERSIAN ART, in THE METROPOLITAN MUSEUM OF ART BULLETIN, March 1955, pp. 213-224, New York, 1955.

WISEMAN (D.J.). — CHRONICLES OF CHALDEAN KINGS (626-556 B.C.) IN THE BRITISH MUSEUM, London, The Trustees of the British Museum, 1956.

WOOLLEY (Sir L.). — A NORTH SYRIAN CEMETERY OF THE PERSIAN PERIOD, in ANNALS OF ARCHAEOLOGY AND ANTHROPOLOGY ISSUED BY THE LIVERPOOL INSTITUTE OF ARCHAEOLOGY, Vol. VII, 1914-16.
— ALALAKH, AN ACCOUNT OF THE EXCAVATIONS AT TELL ATCHANA IN THE HATAY, 1937-49, Oxford, The Society of Antiquaries, 1955.
— EXCAVATIONS NEAR ANTIOCH IN 1936, in ANTIQUARIES' JOURNAL, Vol. XVII, pp. 1-15, 1957.
— EXCAVATIONS AT AL MINA SUEIDIA, in THE JOURNAL OF HELLENIC STUDIES, Vol. LVIII, pp. 1-30, 1958.

WURZ (E. and R.). — DIE ENTSTEHUNG DER SÄULEN-
BASEN DES ALTERTUMS UNTER BERÜCKSICHTI-
GUNG VERWANDTER KAPITELLE, in ZEITSCHRIFT
FÜR GESCHICHTE DER ARCHITEKTUR, Beiheft 15,
pp. 42-47 : La Perse, Heidelberg, 1925.

YALOURIS (N.). — ATHENA ALS HERRIN DER PFERDE,
in MUSEUM HELVETICUM, Vol. VII, fasc. 1-2,
pp. 19-101, Basel, 1950.

YESSEN (A.A.). — RANNIE SVIAZI PRIOURALIYA S
IRANOM (Early Relations between the Ural
Region and Iran), in SOVIETSKAYA ARKHEO-
LOGUIYA (Soviet Archaeology), XVI, pp. 206-
231, 1952.
— NEKOTORIE PAMIATNIKI VIII-VII VV. DE N. E.
NA SEVERNOM KAVKAZÉ (Some Monuments
of the 8th-7th Century B.C. in the Northern
Caucasus), in VOPROSI SKIFOSARMATSKOI
ARKHEOLOGUII (Questions of Scytho-Sarma-
tian Archaeology), pp. 112-131, Moscow, 1952.
— K VOPROSOU O PAMIATNIKAKH VIII-VII VV.
DO N.E. NA IOUGUÉ EVROPEISKOÏ TCHASTI

S.S.S.R. (On the Monuments of the 8th-
7th Century B.C. in the Southern Part of
European Russia), in SOVIETSKAYA ARCHEOLO-
GUIYA (Soviet Archaeology), XVIII, pp. 49-
110, 1953.

YETTS (W.P.). — THE HORSE, A FACTOR IN EARLY
CHINESE HISTORY, in EURASIA SEPTENTRIONALIS
ANTIQUA, IX, Minns Volume, pp. 231-255,
Helsinki, 1934.

YOUNG (R.S.). — THE CAMPAIGN OF 1955 AT GOR-
DION : PRELIMINARY REPORT, in AMERICAN
JOURNAL OF ARCHAEOLOGY, Vol. LX, pp. 249-
266, 1956.

YOYOTTE (J.). — LA PROVENANCE DU CYLINDRE DE
DARIUS (B.M. 89.132), in REVUE D'ASSYRIOLOGIE
ET D'ARCHÉOLOGIE ORIENTALE, XLVI, 3,
pp. 165-167, 1952.

ZAEHNER (R.C.). — ZURVAN, A ZOROASTRIAN DILEMMA,
Oxford, Clarendon Press, 1955.

III. LURISTAN BRONZES

ACKERMANN (P.). — A LURISTAN ILLUSTRATION OF
A SUNRISE CEREMONY, in THE CINCINNATI ART
MUSEUM BULLETIN, Vol. V, No. 2, October
1957, pp. 3-6, 1957.

AGA OGLU. — OLD POTTERY AND BRONZES FROM
PERSIA, in BULLETIN OF THE DETROIT INSTITUTE
OF ARTS, Vol. XII, pp. 85 ff., 1931.

ARNE (T.J.). — LURISTAN AND THE WEST, in EURASIA
SEPTENTRIONALIS ANTIQUA, Vol. IX, pp. 279
ff., Helsinki, 1934.
— KEULENKÖPFE, SZEPTER UND HANDGRIFFE
VON LURISTAN, in PRUSSIA, Vol. XXXIII,
pp. 15-20, 11 figures, 1939.

ASHTON (L.). — THE PERSIAN EXHIBITION IN 1931,
VI : EARLY METAL WORK, in BURLINGTON
MAGAZINE, Vol. LVIII, pp. 34-35, 1931.

BAUMGARTNER (W.). — ZWEI NEUE LURISTAN-
BRONZEN, in ARCHIV FÜR ORIENTFORSCHUNG,
Vol. XII, pp. 57-59, 1937-1939.

BOHL (E.M.T.). — DE TIJDSBEPALING DER 'BRONZEN'
UIT DE LURISTAN, in JAARBERICHT EX ORIENTE
LUX, Vol. IX, pp. 193-197, 1944.

BUHL (M.L.). — RECENTLY ACQUIRED IRANIAN ANTI-
QUITIES IN THE DANISH NATIONAL MUSEUM,
in ACTA ARCHAEOLOGICA, Vol. XXI, pp. 183-
210, 1950.

BUSCHOR (E.). — EINE LURISTAN-KANNE AUS SAMOS,
in FORSCHUNGEN UND FORTSCHRITTE, I, May
1932, No. 13, p. 161 and fig. 2.

CABRIOL (A.). — BRONZES PRÉHISTORIQUES DE PERSE,
in BULLETIN DE LA SOCIÉTÉ PRÉHISTORIQUE
FRANÇAISE, Vol. XXIX, 1932.

CONTENAU (G.). — LES BRONZES DU LURISTAN, in
GENAVA, Vol. XI, pp. 43-48, 1933.

DESH (C.H.). — METALLURGICAL ANALYSES OF THE
BRONZES OF LURISTAN, in A. Upham Pope
(editor), A SURVEY OF PERSIAN ART, I, p. 278,
1938.

DEONNA (W.). — BRONZES DU LURISTAN, in GENAVA,
Vol. X, pp. 84-98, 1932.

DIMAND (M.S.). — IRANIAN BRONZES, in BULLETIN
OF THE METROPOLITAN MUSEUM OF ART,
Vol. XXVI, pp. 48-50, New York, 1931.

DUMEZIL (G.). — DIEUX CASSITES ET DIEUX VÉDIQUES,
A propos d'un bronze du Luristan, in REVUE
HITTITE ET ASIANIQUE, Vol. X, fasc. 52,
pp. 18-37, 1 pl., 1950.

DUSSAUD (R.). — HACHES A DOUILLE DU TYPE ASIA-
TIQUE, in SYRIA, Vol. XI, pp. 245-271, 1930.
— PASSE-GUIDES DU LURISTAN, in SYRIA,
Vol. XIII, pp. 227 ff., 1932.
— CEINTURE EN BRONZE DU LURISTAN AVEC
SCÈNE DE CHASSE, in SYRIA, Vol. XV, pp. 185-
199; 2 pl. and 8 fig., 1934.
— TYPES AND HISTORY OF THE BRONZES OF
LURISTAN, in A. Upham Pope (editor), A
SURVEY OF PERSIAN ART, I, pp. 254-277, 1938.
— ANCIENS BRONZES DU LURISTAN ET CULTES
IRANIENS, in SYRIA, Vol. XXVI, fasc. 3-4,
pp. 196-229, 2 pl. 14 fig., 1949.

FORRER (R.). — SIX BRONZES PRÉHISTORIQUES DU
LURISTAN, in BULLETIN DE LA SOCIÉTÉ PRÉHIS-
TORIQUE DE FRANCE, Vol. XXII, pp. 191 ff.,
1932.

GADD (C.J.). — LURISTAN BRONZES, in BRITISH MUSEUM QUARTERLY, Vol. V, pp. 109-110, 1930.
— MORE LURISTAN BRONZES, in BRITISH MUSEUM QUARTERLY, Vol. VI, pp. 79-80, 1931.
— BRONZES FROM NORTH-WEST PERSIA, in BRITISH MUSEUM QUARTERLY, Vol. VII, pp. 44-45, 1932.
— THREE LURISTAN BRONZES, in BRITISH MUSEUM QUARTERLY, Vol. IX, pp. 94-95, 1934.
— A BRONZE HANDLE FROM IRAN, in BRITISH MUSEUM QUARTERLY, Vol. XIII, pp. 16-17, 1939.
— THE RAPHAEL BEQUEST, Egyptian and West-Asiatic Antiquities, in BRITISH MUSEUM QUARTERLY, Vol. XV, pp. 57-60, 1941-50.
— LURISTAN BRONZES FROM THE COLLECTION OF FRANK SAVERY, in TRANSACTIONS OF THE ORIENTAL CERAMIC SOCIETY, Vol. XIX, pp. 33-36, 1942-43.

GHIRSHMAN (R.). — LE DIEU ZURVAN SUR LES BRONZES DU LURISTAN, in ARTIBUS ASIAE, Vol. XXI, pp. 37 ff., 1958.

GODARD (A.). — LES BRONZES DU LURISTAN, in ARS ASIATICA, Vol. XVII, Paris, Van Oest, 1931.
— BRONZES DU LURISTAN, ATHÄRE IRÄN, Vol. III, pp. 233-263, 1938.

GODARD (A. and Y.). — BRONZES DU LURISTAN. Collection E. Graeffe. Exhibition Catalogue, The Hague, edited by L. J. C. Boucher, 1954.

GOOSSENS (G.). — BRONZEN UIT LOERISTAN, Brussels, Koninklijke Musea voor Kunst en Geschiedenis, 1956.

HANCAR (F.). — KAUKASUS-LURISTAN, in EURASIA SEPTENTRIONALIS ANTIQUA, Vol. IX, pp. 47-112, Helsinki, 1935.
— THE EURASIAN ANIMAL STYLE AND THE ALTAÏ COMPLEX, in ARTIBUS ASIAE, Vol. XV, pp. 171-194, 1952.

HOLLIS (H.C.). — A LURISTAN BRONZE, in BULLETIN OF THE CLEVELAND MUSEUM OF ART, 1951, pp. 191-192.

HUDSON (B.M.). — LURISTAN BRONZES, in BULLETIN OF THE CITY ART MUSEUM OF SAINT LOUIS, Vol. XVII, pp. 12-14, 1932

LANCASTER (C.). — LURISTAN BRONZES, THEIR STYLE AND SYMBOLISM, in ARCHAEOLOGY, Vol. V (1952), pp. 94-99.

LANGDON (S.). — SOME INSCRIPTIONS ON THE BRONZES OF LURISTAN, in A. Upham Pope (editor), A SURVEY OF PERSIAN ART, I, pp. 279-285, 1938.

LEGRAIN (L.). — A COLLECTION OF BRONZES FROM LURISTAN, in UNIVERSITY MUSEUM BULLETIN, Vol. II, pp. 194 ff., Philadelphia, 1931.
— LURISTAN BRONZES IN THE UNIVERSITY MUSEUM, 20 pages and 25 plates, Philadelphia, 1934.

MAXWELL-HYSLOP (K.). — NOTE ON A LURISTAN AXE IN THE OTAGE MUSEUM, NEW ZEALAND, in IRAQ, Vol. XII, p. 52, 1950.

MEEK (T.J.). — BRONZE SWORDS FROM LURISTAN, in BULLETIN OF THE AMERICAN SCHOOL OF ORIENTAL RESEARCH, Vol. LXXIV, pp. 7-11, 1939.

MICHELET (J.C.). — LURISTAN BRONZES, in BULLETIN OF THE ART INSTITUTE OF CHICAGO, Vol. XXV, p. 104, 1931.

MINORSKY (V.). — THE LURISTAN BRONZES, in APOLLO, Vol. XIII, pp. 141-142, 1931.

MOORTGAT (A.). — ALTIRANISCHES TON- UND BRONZEGERÄT, in BERICHTE DER BERLINER MUSEEN, Vol. LII, pp. 70-73, 1900.
— BRONZEGERÄT AUS LURISTAN, 15 pages, Berlin, 1932.

NAUMANN (F.K.). — UNTERSUCHUNG EINES EISERNEN LURISTANISCHEN KURZSCHWERTES, in ARCHIV FÜR DAS EISENHÜTTENWESEN, XXVIII (1957), Heft 9, pp. 575-581, 1957.

POPE (A.Upham). — In ILLUSTRATED LONDON NEWS, 8. 6. 1929, pp. 982-983; 6. 9. 1930, pp. 388-391; 418; 13. 9. 1930, p. 444; 17. 1. 1931, p. 89; 22. 10. 1932, pp. 613-615; 29. 10. 1932, pp. 666-667; 6. 5. 1939, pp. 790-791; 31. 12. 1932, pp. 1054 ff.
— LURISTAN BRONZES IN THE BOSTON MUSEUM OF FINE ARTS, in CAHIERS D'ART, 1931.
— DATED LURISTAN BRONZES, in BULLETIN OF THE AMERICAN INSTITUTE FOR PERSIAN ART AND ARCHAEOLOGY, Vol. III, pp. 19-20, 1934.
— A NOTE ON SOME POTTERY FROM THE HOLMES LURISTAN EXPEDITION OF THE INSTITUTE, in BULLETIN OF THE AMERICAN INSTITUTE FOR IRANIAN ART AND ARCHAEOLOGY, Vol. IV, fasc. 3, pp. 120-125, 1936.

POTRATZ (H.). — DIE LURISTAN-BRONZEN DES STAATLICHEN MUSEUMS FÜR VOR- UND FRÜHGESCHICHTE IN BERLIN, in PRAEHISTORISCHE ZEITSCHRIFT, Vol. XXX-XXXI, pp. 169-198, 1940.
— DIE LURISTANISCHEN PFERDEGEBISSE, in PRAEHISTORISCHE ZEITSCHRIFT, Vol. XXXII-XXXIII, pp. 169-234, 1941-42.
— LURISTANFUNDE AUS DEM MAINZER ZENTRALMUSEUM, in IPEK, pp. 33-62, 1941-42.
— SCHEIBENKOPFNADELN AUS LURISTAN, in ARCHIV FÜR ORIENTFORSCHUNG, Vol. XV, pp. 38-51, 1945-51.
— DAS KAMPFMOTIV IN DER LURISTANKUNST, in ORIENTALIS, Vol. XXI, pp. 13-36, 1952.
— DIE STANGEN-AUFSÄTZE IN DER LURISTANKUNST, in JAHRBUCH FÜR KLEINASIATISCHE FORSCHUNGEN, Vol. III, 1, Ankara, 1953.
— BÄR UND HASE IN DER BILDKUNST DES ALTEN LURISTAN, ARCHIV FÜR ORIENTFORSCHUNG, Vol. XVII, pp. 121-128, 1954-55.
— DIE LURISTAN-BRONZEN DES MUSEUMS FÜR KUNST UND GEWERBE IN HAMBURG, in ZEITSCHRIFT FÜR ASSYRIOLOGIE, N. F. 17 (51), pp. 180-224, 1955.

PRZEWORSKI (S.). — LURISTAN BRONZES IN THE COLLECTION OF FRANK SAVERY, in ARCHAEOLOGIA, 88, pp. 229-269, 1940.

REXROTH (F.). — BRONZEN AUS LURISTAN, in OSTASIATISCHE ZEITSCHRIFT. Vol. VIII, 1932.

ROES (A.). — DE BRONZEN VAN LURISTAN, in JAAR-BERICHT EX ORIENTE LUX, Vol. VII, pp. 477-488, 1940.

ROSTOVTZEFF (M.). — SOME REMARKS ON THE LURISTAN BRONZES, in IPEK, Vol. VII, pp. 45-56, 1931.

SARRE (F.). — ALTPERSISCHE STANDARTE AUS LURIS-TAN, in ARCHIV FÜR ORIENTFORSCHUNG, Vol. XIV, p. 152, 1942.

SCHAEFFER (C.). — STRATIGRAPHIE COMPARÉE ET CHRONOLOGIE DE L'ASIE OCCIDENTALE, pp. 477-495, Oxford, 1948.

SCHEFOLD (K.). — BRONZES OF LURISTAN, in EURASIA SEPTENTRIONALIS ANTIQUA, Vol. XII, pp. 67-68, 1938.

SMITH (S.). — REIN-RING FROM LURISTAN, in BRITISH MUSEUM QUARTERLY, Vol. VI (1931), pp. 32-33, 1931.
— TWO LURISTAN BRONZES FROM SOUTHERN ARABIA, in ARCHAEOLOGICA ORIENTALIS IN MEMORIAM ERNST HERZFELD, Locust Valley-New York, G. C. Miles, 1952.

SPELEERS (L.). — NOS BRONZES PERSES, in BULLETIN DES MUSÉES ROYAUX D'ART ET D'HISTOIRE DE BRUXELLES, pp. 56-63; pp. 77-90, 1931.
— NOS NOUVEAUX BRONZES PERSES, in BULLE-TIN DES MUSÉES ROYAUX D'ART ET D'HISTOIRE DE BRUXELLES, pp. 56-71; 93-104; 115-119, 1932.
— UNE ÉPÉE EN FER DU LURISTAN, in BULLE-TIN DES MUSÉES ROYAUX D'ART ET D'HISTOIRE DE BRUXELLES, p. 111, 1933.

— BRONZES PERSES, in BULLETIN DES MUSÉES ROYAUX D'ART ET D'HISTOIRE DE BRUXELLES, pp. 42-43, 1934.
— UNE APPLIQUE DE MEUBLE, LURISTAN, in BULLETIN DES MUSÉES ROYAUX D'ART ET D'HISTOIRE DE BRUXELLES, pp. 83-89, 1939.
— NOS DERNIERS BRONZES IRANIENS, in BULLE-TIN DES MUSÉES ROYAUX D'ART ET D'HISTOIRE DE BRUXELLES, pp. 81-87, 1942.
— LA DONATION S. CORBIAU, in BULLETIN DES MUSÉES ROYAUX D'ART ET D'HISTOIRE DE BRUXELLES, 1946, pp. 1-15; 1947, pp. 41-47.

STARK (F.). — THE BRONZES OF LURISTAN, in GEOGRA-PHICAL JOURNAL, Vol. LXXX, pp. 498 ff., 1932.
— THE VALLEYS OF THE ASSASSINS, London, 1934.
— LURISTAN, in JOURNAL OF THE ROYAL ASIATIC SOCIETY, pp. 241-251, 1935.

VAN WIJNGAARDEN. — DE LOERISTANBRONZES IN HET RIJKSMUSEUM VAN OUDHEDEN, in SUP-PLEMENT OP NIEUWE REEKS XXXV VAN DE OUDHEIDKUNDIGE MEDEDELINGER VAN HET RIJKSMUSEUM VAN OUDHEDEN, 29 pages, 68 figures, Leiden, 1954.

WEIDNER (E.F.). — AUSGRABUNGEN IN LURISTAN, in ARCHIV FÜR ORIENTFORSCHUNG, Vol. VIII, pp. 255-260, 1932-35.

YETTS (W.F.). — CHINESE CONTACTS WITH LURISTAN BRONZES, in BURLINGTON MAGAZINE, Vol. LIX, pp. 76-81, 1931.

LIST OF ILLUSTRATIONS

20. *Protohistoric Art. Khurvin (50 miles north-west of Teheran). Warrior Figurine. 9th-8th centuries B.C. Private Collection, Teheran. Bronze, height* 2⁷/₈ *inches. (Photo Dr. A. Razavi)*
Probably a pendant worn round the neck.

21. *Protohistoric Art. Khurvin (50 miles north-west of Teheran). Pendants. 9th-8th centuries B.C. Private Collection, Teheran. Bronze, height* ⁷/₈ *of an inch to* 1³/₄ *inches. (Photo Dr. A. Razavi)*

22. *Protohistoric Art. Khurvin (50 miles north-west of Teheran). Belt. 9th-8th centuries B.C. Private Collection, Teheran. Bronze, length* 25⁵/₈ *inches, width* 3¹/₈ *inches. (Photo Dr. A. Razavi)*

23. *Protohistoric Art. Khurvin (50 miles north-west of Teheran). Mirror with Handle in the form of a Caryatid Figurine. 9th-8th centuries B.C. Private Collection, Teheran. Bronze, height* 10¹/₄ *inches, diameter of disk* 5⁷/₈ *inches. (Photo Dr. A. Razavi)*

24. *Protohistoric Art. Hasanlu (Azerbaijan). Kernos. 9th-8th centuries B.C. Archaeological Museum, Teheran. Red earthenware, height* 6¹/₂ *inches. (Museum Photo)*
Vessel composed of three communicating cups joined together by figurines of a bird and a man.

25. *Protohistoric Art. Hasanlu (Azerbaijan). Libation Vase. 9th-8th centuries B.C. Archaeological Museum, Teheran. Black earthenware, height 9 inches. (Museum Photo)*
Animal on the pouring lip and quadruped in relief on the body.

26. *Protohistoric Art. Luristan. Vessel in the form of a Human Figure holding a Ritual Vase. 8th-7th centuries B.C. Private Collection. Earthenware, height c. 8 inches. (After* GODARD, *1938, fig.* 152)

27a. *Protohistoric Art. Hasanlu (Azerbaijan). Ear-ring of Clustered Drops. 9th-8th centuries B.C. Archaeological Museum, Teheran. Gold, height* 2⁵/₈ *inches. (Museum Photo, Rostamy)*

27b. *Protohistoric Art. Hasanlu (Azerbaijan). Necklace. 9th-8th centuries B.C. Archaeological Museum, Teheran. Gold and white stones. (Photo Dr. A. Razavi)*

27c. *Protohistoric Art. Hasanlu (Azerbaijan). Necklace. 9th-8th centuries B.C. Archaeological Museum, Teheran. Gold and stones, length* 17³/₄ *inches. (Photo Dr. A. Razavi)*

28. *Protohistoric Art. Hasanlu (?) (Azerbaijan). Crouching Lion. 9th-8th centuries B.C. From the Jacques Coiffard Collection, acquired by the Louvre, 1958 (AO* 20472). *Bronze, height* 2¹/₈ *inches, length* 3³/₄ *inches. (Photo Istituto Italiano per il Medio ed Estremo Oriente)*
Hitherto regarded as a Luristan bronze, but here assigned to the workshops of the Hasanlu region.

29. *Protohistoric Art. Hasanlu (Azerbaijan). Crouching Lion. 9th-8th centuries B.C. Archaeological Museum, Teheran. Bronze and iron, length 4 inches. (Photo Dr. A. Razavi)*

30. *Protohistoric Art. Hasanlu (Azerbaijan). Large Bowl adorned with Religious Scenes, detail. 9th-8th centuries B.C. Archaeological Museum, Teheran. Solid gold, height* 8¹/₈ *inches, width* 11 *inches, weight* 945 *grammes. (Photo Draeger)*

31. *Protohistoric Art. Hasanlu (Azerbaijan). Large Bowl adorned with Religious Scenes, detail. 9th-8th centuries B.C. Archaeological Museum, Teheran. Solid gold, height* 8¹/₈ *inches, width* 11 *inches, weight* 945 *grammes. (Photo Draeger)*

32. *Protohistoric Art. Amlash (south-west of the Caspian Sea). Statuette of the Steatopygous Type. 9th-8th centuries B.C. Private Collection, Paris. Terracotta, height* 18⁷/₈ *inches, width* 5⁷/₈ *inches. (Collection Photo)*

33. *Protohistoric Art. Amlash (south-west of the Caspian Sea). Statuette of a Warrior armed with a Dagger. 9th-8th centuries B.C. Private Collection, Teheran. Bronze, height* 3⁵/₈ *inches, width* 1¹/₂ *inches. (Photo Hadi)*

34. *Protohistoric Art. Amlash (south-west of the Caspian Sea). Rhyton in the form of a Humped Ox. 9th-8th centuries B.C. Private Collection, Teheran. Red terracotta, height* 10³/₈ *inches, length* 12³/₄ *inches. (Photo Vahe)*

35. *Protohistoric Art. Amlash (south-west of the Caspian Sea). Horse Rhyton. 9th-8th centuries B.C. Private Collection, Teheran. Red terracotta, height 6 inches, length* 6³/₄ *inches. (Photo Vahe)*
Forelock indicated on the horse's head, neck of the vessel on the rump, outlet on the breast.

36. *Protohistoric Art. Amlash (south-west of the Caspian Sea). Large Goblet. 9th-8th centuries B.C. Private Collection, New York. Gold, height* 8¹/₄ *inches, diameter of mouth* 3³/₄ *inches, weight* 235 *grammes. (Photo Draeger)*
Designs in relief: winged lion attacking a goat (upper register) and stags separated by rosettes (lower register).

37. *Protohistoric Art. Amlash (south-west of the Caspian Sea). Cup with Handle and Stem, adorned with Rams. 9th-8th centuries B.C. Private Collection, Teheran. Silver, height* 4³/₄ *inches, diameter* 6¹/₈ *inches, weight* 560 *grammes. (Photo Draeger)*

38. *Protohistoric Art. Amlash (south-west of the Caspian Sea). Cup with Handle, adorned with a Hunting Scene. 9th-8th centuries B.C. Private Collection, New York. Silver, height* 4⁷/₈ *inches, diameter* 6⁷/₈ *inches. (Photo Draeger)*

39. *Protohistoric Art. Amlash (south-west of the Caspian Sea). Statuette of Horse and Rider. 9th-8th centuries B.C. Private Collection, Teheran. Bronze, height* 2¹/₂ *inches, length* 2¹/₂ *inches. (Photo Hadi)*

40. *Protohistoric Art. Amlash (south-west of the Caspian Sea). Statuette of a Humped Ox. 9th-8th centuries B.C. Private Collection, Teheran. Bronze, height 2 inches, length* 2³/₄ *inches. (Photo Hadi)*

41. *Protohistoric Art. Amlash (south-west of the Caspian Sea). Statuette of a Stag. 9th-8th centuries B.C. William Rockhill Nelson Gallery of Art, Atkins Museum of Fine Arts, Kansas City. Bronze, height* 10 *inches, length* 7³/₈ *inches. (Museum Photo)*

42. *Protohistoric Art. Amlash (south-west of the Caspian Sea). Statuette of a Boar. 9th-8th centuries B.C. Private Collection, Teheran. Bronze, height* 1⁵/₈ *inches, length* 2¹/₂ *inches. Belly of the animal hollowed out. (Photo Hadi)*

43. *Protohistoric Art. Amlash (south-west of the Caspian Sea). Statuette of a Unicorn. 9th-8th centuries B.C. Private Collection, Teheran. Bronze, height* 2⁷/₈ *inches, length* 2¹/₂ *inches. Belly of the animal hollowed out. (Photo Hadi)*

44. *Protohistoric Art. Amlash (south-west of the Caspian Sea)*. Recumbent Ibex forming part of a Horse's Trappings. *9th-8th centuries B.C. Private Collection, Teheran. Bronze, height 1 inch, length 1³/₈ inches. (Photo Hadi)*
Knob, in the Scythian style, fastened at the point where two cross-straps meet.

45. *Protohistoric Art. Amlash (south-west of the Caspian Sea)*. Sword Hilt in the form of a Nude Goddess, with Confronted Horses on the Pommel. *9th-8th centuries B.C. Private Collection, Teheran. Bronze, length 19⁷/₈ inches, width 2¹/₂ inches. (Collection Photo)*

46. *Protohistoric Art. Amlash (south-west of the Caspian Sea)*. Mace-head adorned with Three Human Faces. *9th-8th centuries B.C. Archaeological Museum, Teheran. Bronze, height 3³/₈ inches. (Museum Photo)*

47. *Protohistoric Art. Amlash (south-west of the Caspian Sea)*. Stag Rhyton. *9th-8th centuries B.C. Private Collection, Teheran. Maroon terracotta, height 8¹/₄ inches, length 8⁵/₈ inches. (Photo Vahe)*

48. *Protohistoric Art. Amlash (south-west of the Caspian Sea)*. Statuette of a Woman pressing her Hands against her Belly. *9th-8th centuries B.C. Private Collection, Teheran. Yellow terracotta, height 6¹/₈ inches, width 3³/₈ inches. (Photo Vahe)*

49. *Art of Luristan*. Statuette of a Nude Goddess holding her Breasts with her Hands, with an Ibex on her Head. *8th-7th centuries B.C. Private Collection, Teheran. Bronze, height 9⁵/₈ inches, width 3¹/₈ inches. (Photo Draeger)*

50. *Art of Luristan*. Idol: The God Sraosha (?) gripping two long-necked Animals with gaping Jaws, detail. *8th-7th centuries B.C. Private Collection, New York. Bronze, height 6¹/₄ inches. (Photo Istituto Italiano per il Medio ed Estremo Oriente)*

51. *Art of Luristan*. Idol: The God Sraosha (?), flanked by two Cocks, gripping two long-necked Animals. *8th-7th centuries B.C. Musées Royaux d'Art et d'Histoire, Brussels. Bronze, height 14¹/₈ inches. (Photo A.C.L., Brussels)*

52. *Art of Luristan*. Votive Idol, detail: One of two Confronted Animals with Long Necks and Gaping Jaws. *8th-7th centuries B.C. Museum of Fine Arts, Boston. Bronze, height 6¹/₄ inches. (Photo Istituto Italiano per il Medio ed Estremo Oriente)*

53. *Art of Luristan*. Idol with Confronted Animals. Zoomorphic Composition, detail. *8th-7th centuries B.C. From the Jacques Coiffard Collection, acquired by the Louvre, 1958 (AO 20490). Bronze, height 5¹/₂ inches, width 2¹/₄ inches. (Photo Istituto Italiano per il Medio ed Estremo Oriente)*

54. *Art of Luristan*. Pinhead with the Goddess Ashi (?) protecting Two Pairs of Ibexes and Gazelles. *8th-7th centuries B.C. Private Collection, Teheran. Bronze, length 6¹/₄ inches. (Photo Dr. A. Razavi)*

55. *Art of Luristan*. Idol with a God (Mithras?) seated between Two Horse Protomes. *8th-7th centuries B.C. Private Collection, Paris. Bronze. (Collection Photo)*

56. *Art of Luristan*. Statuette of a Goddess, flanked by Two Cocks' Heads, holding her Bare Breasts. *8th-7th centuries B.C. Private Collection, Paris. Bronze, height 4¹/₄ inches. (Collection Photo)*

57. *Art of Luristan*. Round Pinhead. *8th-7th centuries B.C. Private Collection, Paris. Bronze. (Collection Photo)*

58. *Art of Luristan*. Round Pinhead with the Head of a Goddess. *8th-7th centuries B.C. Private Collection, Paris. Bronze, height 10³/₄ inches, diameter 5 inches. (Photo Istituto Italiano per il Medio ed Estremo Oriente)*

59. *Art of Luristan*. Rectangular Pinhead, detail: Goddess holding her Breasts. *8th-7th centuries B.C. Private Collection, Paris. Bronze. (Collection Photo)*

60. *Art of Luristan*. Round Pinhead, detail: Head of the Goddess Ashi (?). *8th-7th centuries B.C. Bronze, diameter 6¹/₈ inches. (Photo Istituto Italiano per il Medio ed Estremo Oriente)*

61. *Art of Luristan*. Round Pinhead, detail: The Goddess Ashi (?) flanked by her Animal Attributes. *8th-7th centuries B.C. Graeffe Collection, Musées Royaux d'Art et d'Histoire, Brussels. Bronze, height 8⁵/₈ inches, diameter 4 inches. (Photo A.C.L., Brussels)*

62. *Art of Luristan*. Round Pinhead, detail: Head of the Goddess Ashi (?) surmounted by Two Lions with a Single Head. *8th-7th centuries B.C. Private Collection, Paris. Bronze, diameter 4¹/₂ inches. (Collection Photo)*

63. *Art of Luristan*. Fragment of a Round Pinhead, detail: The God Zurvan giving Birth to the Twins Ahuramazda and Ahriman. *8th-7th centuries B.C. Private Collection, New York. Bronze, diameter 6¹/₈ inches. (Photo Istituto Italiano per il Medio ed Estremo Oriente)*

64. *Art of Luristan*. Plaque showing the God Zurvan giving Birth to the Twins Ahuramazda and Ahriman. *8th-7th centuries B.C. Cincinnati Art Museum. Chased silver, height 4⁵/₈ inches, length 10¹/₈ inches. (Photo Draeger)*

65. *Art of Luristan*. Worshipper Statuette. *8th-7th centuries B.C. Private Collection, New York. Bronze, height 3¹/₈ inches. (Photo Istituto Italiano per il Medio ed Estremo Oriente)*

66. *Art of Luristan*. Worshipper Statuette, in the attitude of offering. *8th-7th centuries B.C. Private Collection, Paris. Bronze. (Collection Photo)*

67. *Art of Luristan*. Worshipper Statuette. *8th-7th centuries B.C. Private Collection, Teheran. Bronze, height 2 inches. (Photo Hadi)*

68. *Art of Luristan*. Statuette of the Patron Goddess of an Unknown City. *8th-7th centuries B.C. Archaeological Museum, Teheran. Bronze, height 15 inches. (Museum Photo)*

69. *Art of Luristan*. Statuette of a Couple with a Child, on Horseback. *8th-7th centuries B.C. Private Collection, Teheran. Bronze, height 1⁵/₈ inches, length 1³/₈ inches. (Photo Dr. A. Razavi)*

70. *Art of Luristan*. Ibex. *8th-7th centuries B.C. Private Collection, New York. Cast bronze, height 4 inches. (Collection Photo)*

71. *Art of Luristan.* Gazelle. *8th-7th centuries B.C. Musées Royaux d'Art et d'Histoire, Brussels. Hammered bronze, riveted together, height* 2³/₄ *inches.* (*Photo A.C.L., Brussels*)

72. *Art of Luristan.* Bit with Two Horse Protomes. *8th-7th centuries B.C. Musées Royaux d'Art et d'Histoire, Brussels. Bronze, length* 4 *inches.* (*Photo A.C.L., Brussels*)

73. *Art of Luristan.* Bit in the form of Chariot and Driver. *8th-7th centuries B.C. Louvre, Paris (AO 18848), acquired 1936. Bronze, length* 4¹/₄ *inches.* (*Museum Photo*)

74. *Art of Luristan.* Bit in the form of a Hybrid Creature with Two Horned Human Heads, its Body ending in the Head of a long-necked Animal. *8th-7th centuries B.C. British Museum, London. Bronze, height* 3³/₄ *inches.* (*Museum Photo*)

75. *Art of Luristan.* Bit with Beribboned Winged Doe suckling a Fawn. *8th-7th centuries B.C. Private Collection, Teheran. Bronze, height* 8¹/₄ *inches, width* 6¹/₄ *inches.* (*Photo Draeger*)

76. *Art of Luristan.* Clapper-hanger, composed of Two Naked Goddesses pressing a Breast and holding a Motif in the form of a Hut. *8th-7th centuries B.C. Private Collection, Teheran. Bronze, height* 4 *inches, width* 4¹/₂ *inches.* (*Photo Draeger*)

77. *Art of Luristan.* Rein-ring surmounted by Four Movable Horses. *8th-7th centuries B.C. Private Collection, Teheran. Bronze, height* 6¹/₄ *inches, width* 5⁷/₈ *inches.* (*Photo Draeger*)
The horses' eyes were originally inlaid.

78. *Art of Luristan.* Rein-ring surmounted by a Worshipper between Two Animals. *8th-7th centuries B.C. Teheran Art Market. Bronze, height* 13 *inches, diameter* 4³/₈ *inches.* (*Photo Audrain*)

79. *Art of Luristan.* Axe (Simulacrum), the Blade issuing from an Animal's Jaws. On the socket, Two Pairs of Confronted Sphinxes. *8th-7th centuries B.C. Private Collection, Teheran. Bronze, length* 9¹/₂ *inches.* (*Photo Draeger*)

80. *Art of Luristan.* Axe Blade. In relief on the blade, Mounted Horse with a Fish-tail. *8th-7th centuries B.C. Private Collection, New York. Bronze, height* 8⁵/₈ *inches.* (*Photo Istituto Italiano per il Medio ed Estremo Oriente*)

81. *Art of Luristan.* Axe Blade with Two Rows of Spikes on the Socket. In relief on the blade, an Archer drawing his Bow. *8th-7th centuries B.C. Private Collection, Paris. Bronze, length* 10 *inches.* (*Collection Photo*)
The cutting edge is at right angles to the handle.

82. *Art of Luristan.* Axe Blade. On the socket, a Row of Spikes and a Vulture's Head. In relief on the blade, a Figure holding a Fish in his Arms. *8th-7th centuries B.C. Archaeological Museum, Teheran. Bronze, length* 7⁷/₈ *inches.* (*Photo Istituto Italiano per il Medio ed Estremo Oriente*)

83. *Art of Luristan.* Dagger Haft with a Semicircular Pommel and Animal Designs in Relief. *8th-7th centuries B.C. British Museum, London. Silver.* (*Museum Photo*)

84. *Art of Luristan.* Handle of a Whetstone in the form of an Animal. *8th-7th centuries B.C. Musées Royaux d'Art et d'Histoire, Brussels. Bronze, length* 4 *inches.* (*Museum Photo*)

85. *Art of Luristan.* Handle of a Whetstone with an Ibex Protome. *8th-7th centuries B.C. Private Collection, Paris. Bronze.* (*Photo Istituto Italiano per il Medio ed Estremo Oriente*)

86. *Art of Luristan.* Handle of a Whetstone. *8th-7th centuries B.C. Seattle Art Museum. Bronze, length* 7 *inches.* (*Photo Istituto Italiano per il Medio ed Estremo Oriente*)

87. *Art of Luristan.* Centrepiece of a Shield adorned with a Mask. *8th-7th centuries B.C. Musées Royaux d'Art et d'Histoire, Brussels. Bronze, diameter* 5¹/₄ *inches.* (*Photo A.C.L., Brussels*)
The eyes were originally filled with a black and white enamel paste.

88. *Art of Luristan.* Loop Handle of a Shield (?) adorned with Reliefs. *8th-7th centuries B.C. Private Collection, Paris. Bronze, height* 4 *inches.* (*Collection Photo*)

89. *Art of Luristan.* Centrepiece of a Shield adorned with a Mask. *8th-7th centuries B.C. Musées Royaux d'Art et d'Histoire, Brussels. Bronze, diameter* 4¹/₈ *inches.* (*Photo A. Dingjan*)

90. *Art of Luristan.* Centrepiece of a Shield adorned with a Mask and Scenes in Relief. *8th-7th centuries B.C. Private Collection, Basel. Bronze, diameter* 8¹/₄ *inches.* (*Photo Draeger*)

91. *Art of Luristan.* Sheathing Plaque of a Quiver, with Reliefs on Superimposed Registers. *8th-7th centuries B.C. Metropolitan Museum of Art, New York. Bronze.* (*Museum Photo*)

92. *Art of Luristan.* Belt adorned with Figures and Scenes of Sacrifice. *8th-7th centuries B.C. Private Collection, Brussels. Gold, length* 17³/₄ *inches, width* 2³/₈ *inches.* (*Photo Draeger*)

93. Detail of No. 92. (*Photo Draeger*)

94. *Art of Luristan.* Bracelet with Confronted Animals. *8th-7th centuries B.C. Archaeological Museum, Teheran. Bronze, diameter* 2³/₄ *inches.* (*Photo Istituto Italiano per il Medio ed Estremo Oriente*)

95. *Art of Luristan.* Frontlet adorned with Animals. *8th-7th centuries B.C. Private Collection, New York. Silver, length* 7¹/₂ *inches.* (*Photo Istituto Italiano per il Medio ed Estremo Oriente*)
Compare these designs with those of certain Greek vase paintings, in which animals with two or four paws are also represented in side view.

96. *Art of Luristan.* Round Pinhead with a Figure wearing the Median Headdress. *8th-7th centuries B.C. Private Collection. Bronze, height* 5¹/₂ *inches.* (*After W. SPEISER, 1952, Pl. 100*)

97. *Art of Luristan.* Round Votive Pinhead with a Genius seated on a Panther (?). *8th-7th centuries B.C. Musées Royaux d'Art et d'Histoire, Brussels. Bronze, diameter* 4 *inches.* (*Photo A.C.L., Brussels*)

98. *Art of Luristan.* Fragment of a Pin with Birds and Geometric Designs. *8th-7th centuries B.C. Teheran Art Market. Silver, length* 1⁵/₈ *inches.* (*Photo Audrain*)

99. *Art of Luristan.* Votive Pinhead in the form of a Bactrian Camel. *8th-7th centuries B.C. Bronze, length of the animal* 1³/₈ *inches.* (*After GODARD, 1938, fig. 159*)

100. *Art of Luristan.* Mirror with a Lion Protome at each end of the Handle. *8th-7th centuries B.C. Musées Royaux d'Art et d'Histoire, Brussels. Bronze, diameter* 30 ¹/₈ *inches. (Photo A.C.L., Brussels)*

101. *Art of Luristan.* Mirror Handle in the form of a Nude Caryatid Figurine. *8th-7th centuries B.C. Louvre, Paris (AO* 20181*), anonymous gift,* 1954. *Bronze, height* 10 ³/₄ *inches, length* 6 ¹/₄ *inches. (Photo Roman Ghirshman)*

102. *Art of Luristan.* Vase with Basket Handle. *8th-7th centuries B.C. Private Collection. Earthenware, height 7 inches. (Collection Photo)*
Pottery made in imitation of a bronze vessel.

103. *Art of Luristan.* Spherical Vase with a Handle in the form of Two Confronted Ibexes, detail. *8th-7th centuries B.C. Cincinnati Art Museum. Bronze, height* 12 ¹/₈ *inches, width* 5 ³/₄ *inches. (Museum Photo)*
On the body of the vase, winged ibexes.

104. *Achaemenian Art.* Vase Handle: Ibex standing on its Hind Legs in an Heraldic Pose. Greek Workmanship. *4th century B.C. Berlin Museum. Gilt silver, height* 10 ³/₄ *inches. (Photo A.C. Cooper)*
The other handle of the same vase is in the Louvre. Cf. *The Arts of Assyria* (American edition) or *Nineveh and Babylon* (English edition), Pl. 254 and p. 374 (where Samsun or Armenia are proposed as the place of origin).

105. *Art of Luristan.* Boar's Head Rhyton. *8th-7th centuries B.C. Teheran Art Market. Bronze, height* 4 ¹/₄ *inches. (Photo Audrain)*

106. *Art of Luristan.* Vase with Animal Designs on the Neck. *8th-7th centuries B.C. Teheran Art Market. Bronze, height* 3 ¹/₂ *inches, diameter of mouth* 2 ¹/₄ *inches. (Photo Audrain)*
The neck is divided into metopes and decorated with reliefs of animals.

107. *Art of Luristan.* Situla with Animals in Relief. *8th-7th centuries B.C. Archaeological Museum, Teheran. Bronze, height* 6 ¹/₄ *inches. (Photo Istituto Italiano per il Medio ed Estremo Oriente)*

108. *Art of Luristan.* Painted Vase in the form of a Figure holding a Goblet. *8th-7th centuries B.C. Private Collection, Rome. Painted earthenware. (Photo M. Sakamoto)*

109. *Median Art.* Oxus Treasure *(Bactria).* Plaque with the Figure of a Man holding a Barsom. *7th-6th centuries B.C. British Museum, London. Gold, height* 5 ⁷/₈ *inches. (Museum Photo)*
This plaque is the only example of repoussé work found in the Oxus Treasure, the other pieces, more summary in execution, being engraved with the burin.

110. *Assyrian Art.* The Median Town of Kishesim in north-west Iran, after an Assyrian Bas-relief. *8th century B.C. (After R. GHIRSHMAN,* 1951, *fig.* 34, *p.* 71*)*

111. *Median Art.* Dukkan-i-Daud *(Kurdistan).* Rock Tomb. *7th-6th centuries B.C. In situ. (After VON DER OSTEN,* 1956, *Pl.* 39*)*

112. *Median Art.* Dukkan-i-Daud *(Kurdistan).* Rock Tomb, detail: Figure holding a Barsom. *7th-6th centuries B.C. In situ. Bas-relief on the rock face. (After SARRE and HERZFELD,* 1910, *fig.* 21*)*
Detail of No. 111.

113. *Median Art.* Farhad-u-Shirin, near Sehna *(Kurdistan).* Rock Tomb. On the façade, Winged Disk (symbol of Ahuramazda). Plan and Cross-section. *7th-6th centuries B.C. In situ. (After E. HERZFELD,* 1920, *fig.* 4*)*

114. *Median Art.* Fakhrika, south of Lake Urmia, near Tash Tepe *(Azerbaijan).* Rock Tomb, showing Façade, with Plan and Cross-section. *7th-6th centuries B.C. In situ. (After E. HERZFELD,* 1920, *fig.* 5*)*

115. *Medo-Scythian Art.* Kizkapan, near Surdash *(Iraqi Kurdistan).* Rock Tomb, showing the Decoration of the Façade. *Second half of 7th - first half of 6th century B.C. In situ. Rock face hollowed out and carved. (Reconstruction after C.J. EDMONDS,* 1934*)*
Engaged columns supporting the porch roof, with symbolic disks and, above the door, a scene showing two figures holding a bow on either side of a fire altar.

116. *Medo-Scythian Art.* Kizkapan, near Surdash *(Iraqi Kurdistan).* Entrance of the Rock Tomb. *Second half of 7th - first half of 6th century B.C. In situ. Rock face hollowed out and carved. (After C.J. EDMONDS, Iraq, I, Pl. XXIV, p.* 184*)*
For the decoration, cf. No. 115. The porch roof, supported by engaged columns, is carved in imitation of timber-work.

117. *Medo-Cimmerian Art.* Sakavand or Deh-i-Nau *(Kurdistan).* Rock Tomb. *7th-6th centuries B.C. In situ. Rock face hollowed out and carved. (After SARRE and HERZFELD,* 1910, *p.* 63, *fig.* 22*)*
A funerary niche where the dead man's bones were deposited. Over the opening, a relief representing two figures before two fire altars.

118. *Median Art.* Oxus Treasure *(Bactria).* Scabbard adorned with a Hunting Scene. *7th-6th centuries B.C. British Museum, London. Wrought gold, length* 10 ⁷/₈ *inches. (Museum Photo)*

119. *Urartian Art.* Karmir Blur *(Transcaucasia).* Helmet of King Sarduris. *Mid-8th century B.C. Chased bronze. Erivan Museum. (After PIOTROVSKY,* 1950, *fig.* 40a*)*
Found in 1950 in excavations conducted by B. Piotrovsky. On the front of the helmet, two superimposed registers with winged gods beside sacred trees. On either side, lion-headed snakes.

120a-g. *Median Art.* Oxus Treasure *(Bactria).* Votive Plaques. *7th-6th centuries B.C. British Museum, London. Gold engraved with a burin; height of the plaque with a half-length figure holding a* barsom, 9 *inches. (Museum Photo)*
The Oxus Treasure contained several dozen of these plaques deposited in a temple by the faithful in token of personal requests addressed to the divinity.

121a-c. *Median Art.* Oxus Treasure *(Bactria).* Votive Plaques. *7th-6th centuries B.C. British Museum, London. Gold engraved with a burin. (Museum Photo)*
Two of the plaques show human figures, one with a spear, the other with a *barsom*. The figure of the horse (like that of the camel in the previous plate) was presumably an offering made to the patron goddess of flocks.

122. *Median Art.* Hamadan *(Media).* Jug with long Beak-Spout and Stirrup Handle. *8th-7th centuries B.C. Louvre, Paris (AO* 7005-7008*). Bronze; ornament, height* 3 ¹/₂ *inches; handles and studs (7 fragments), height* 1 ¹/₂ *inches. Reconstruction. (After a drawing by* Louis LE BRETON*)*
Excavations of the French expedition of Virolleaud and Fossey (1913).

123. *Achaemenian Art. Persepolis (Fars).* Metal Vase carried by a Median. *5th century B.C. Bas-relief on the east stairway of the Apadana, detail. In situ. (Photo Antonello Perissinotto)*
This bas-relief represents a vase made of metal, of the same type as the one illustrated in No. 122.

124. *Median Art. Hamadan (Media).* Ibexes. *8th-7th centuries B.C. Cabinet des Médailles, Bibliothèque Nationale, Paris, gift of Charles Virolleaud, 1913. Bronze, height* $1^1/_2$ *to* $1^3/_4$ *inches, length* $3/4$ *of an inch to 1 inch. (Photo Bibliothèque Nationale)*

125. *Median Art (?). Hamadan (?) (Media).* Bowl with Double Ibex Protomes mounted on the Handles. *7th-6th centuries B.C. Cincinnati Art Museum. Gold, height* $4^3/_4$ *inches, width* $3^1/_4$ *inches including the handles. (Museum Photo)*
Neck adorned with palmettes, shoulder with winged lions passant, body with flutings.

126. *Art of Luristan.* Two-headed Animal with Soldered Horns. *8th-7th centuries B.C. Private Collection, Teheran. Bronze, width* $1^3/_8$ *inches. (Photo Roman Ghirshman)*

127. *Median Art. Kalar Dasht (Mazandaran).* Cup adorned with Three Lions. *8th-7th centuries B.C. Archaeological Museum, Teheran. Gold, height* $4^7/_8$ *inches, diameter* $4^1/_2$ *inches, weight 238 grammes. (Photo Draeger)*
Bodies of the lions in repoussé, heads in the round.

128. *Median Art. Kalar Dasht (Mazandaran).* Animal Rhyton. *8th-7th centuries B.C. Archaeological Museum, Teheran. Red terracotta, length* $11^1/_2$ *inches. (Photo Istituto Italiano per il Medio ed Estremo Oriente)*

129. *Median Art. Kalar Dasht (Mazandaran).* Dagger adorned with a Circle in Relief. *8th-7th centuries B.C. Archaeological Museum, Teheran. Gold, length 15 inches. (Photo G. Franceschi)*

130. Map showing the Area of Scythian Expansion, from the 8th to the 3rd century B.C.

131. *Protohistoric Art. Hasanlu (Azerbaijan).* Grave with Horse Sacrifices. *8th century B.C. (After M. RAD)*

132a-b. *Scythian Art. Kostromskaya Stanitza (Kuban).* Scythian Barrow: (a) Section, (b) Plan. *6th century B.C. (After* T. TALBOT RICE, The Scythians, Thames and Hudson, 1957, figs. 22 and 23, pp. 102-3)

133. *Urartian Art (?). Ziwiyeh, east of Sakkiz (Kurdistan).* Statuette of a Bearded Standing Figure with Arms drawn across the Stomach. *Late 7th century B.C. Archaeological Museum, Teheran. Ivory inlaid with polychrome glass paste, height* $4^1/_2$ *inches, width* $1^1/_4$ *inches. (Photo Dr. A. Razavi)*

134. *Assyrian Art. Ziwiyeh, east of Sakkiz (Kurdistan).* Plaque with Hunting Scene. *7th century B.C. Private Collection. Ivory, length* $3^1/_2$ *inches, ornament in relief for a piece of furniture. (Photo Dr. A. Razavi)*

135. *Median Art (?). Ziwiyeh, east of Sakkiz (Kurdistan).* Plaque with the Meeting of Two Princes (lower register) and a Scene of Sacrifice (upper register). *Late 7th century B.C. Archaeological Museum, Teheran. Ivory, length 7 inches, width 4 inches. Fragment of a plaque decorating a box. (Photo Dr. A. Razavi)*

136. *Local Art. Ziwiyeh, east of Sakkiz (Kurdistan).* Standing Figure in profile with Arms drawn across the Stomach. *Late 7th century B.C. Archaeological Museum, Teheran. Ivory, height 4 inches. Ornament for a piece of furniture. (Photo Dr. A. Razavi)*

137. *Composite Art with Scythian and Irano-Urartian Elements. Ziwiyeh, east of Sakkiz (Kurdistan).* Pectoral. *Late 7th century B.C. Archaeological Museum, Teheran. Gold, overall length 13 inches, width in the centre* $5^1/_4$ *inches, weight 275 grammes. (Photo Draeger)*
Ornamentation in two registers showing two processions of hybrid beings moving towards a tree of life flanked by two pairs of animals. At each end, a Scythian feline and a hare. In the borders, pine-cones.

138. *Urartian Art. Ziwiyeh, east of Sakkiz (Kurdistan).* Cauldron Handle in the form of a Griffin Protome. *Late 7th century B.C. Archaeological Museum, Teheran. Gold, height* $3^1/_8$ *inches, width* $2^1/_8$ *inches, weight 59 grammes. (Photo Draeger)*

139. *Urartian Art. Ziwiyeh, east of Sakkiz (Kurdistan).* Cauldron Handle in the form of a Lion Protome. *Late 7th century B.C. Archaeological Museum, Teheran. Gold, height* $2^3/_8$ *inches, width* $2^3/_4$ *inches, weight 58 grammes. (Photo Draeger)*

140. *Urartian Art. Ziwiyeh, east of Sakkiz (Kurdistan).* Mounting of a Cylinder Seal. *Late 7th century B.C. Archaeological Museum, Teheran. Gold, diameter* $1/_2$ *inch. (Photo Dr. A. Razavi)*
The cylinder has disappeared. The two parts of the mounting are brought together and the seal is shown in front view.

141. *Urartian Art. Toprak-kale, capital of Urartu, on the shore of Lake Van in eastern Asia Minor.* Lion's Head forming part of a Throne. *8th-7th centuries B.C. British Museum, London. Bronze. (Museum Photo)*

142. *Composite Art with Scythian and Irano-Urartian Elements. Ziwiyeh, east of Sakkiz (Kurdistan).* Large Dish. *Late 7th century B.C. Archaeological Museum, Teheran. Silver with gold inlays, diameter* $14^3/_4$ *inches, weight 2,092 grammes. (Photo Draeger)*
Incised with ten concentric circles illustrating various subjects, with a rosette in the centre.

143. *Scytho-Urartian Art. Ziwiyeh, east of Sakkiz (Kurdistan).* Belt Plaque (?). *Late 7th century B.C. Archaeological Museum, Teheran. Gold, length* $11^3/_4$ *inches, width* $6^1/_4$ *inches, weight 447 grammes. (Photo Draeger)*
Twenty-three pieces fitted together. Decorated with ogee arches at the tip of which are lions' heads seen from above. In the field are stags and ibexes.

144. *Irano-Urartian Art. Ziwiyeh, east of Sakkiz (Kurdistan).* Butt-end of a Belt in the form of a Lion's Head. *Late 7th century B.C. Private Collection, Teheran. Gold originally inlaid, length* $7/_8$ *of an inch, width 1 inch. (Photo Roger Parry)*

145a-b. *Urartian Art. Ziwiyeh, east of Sakkiz (Kurdistan).* Bracelet broadening out in the centre to form a triangular surface with a pair of crouching lion cubs on each side. At each end, a lion's head, one of them movable, fastened with a pin. *Late 7th century B.C. Archaeological Museum, Teheran. Gold, diameter* $3^5/_8$ *inches, width* $2^1/_2$ *inches, weight 254 grammes. (Photo Draeger)*

146. *Composite Art. Ziwiyeh, east of Sakkiz (Kurdistan).*
Belt Plaque (?) with Lions standing on Ogee Arches
tipped with Palmettes. *Late 7th century B.C. Private
Collection, Lucerne, and University Museum, Philadelphia.
Gold, height 2^{11}/$_{16}$ inches, width 2^1/$_4$ inches; height 2^3/$_4$ inches,
width 2^1/$_4$ inches. Two fragments reassembled. (Photo
Draeger)*

147a. *Composite Art. Ziwiyeh, east of Sakkiz (Kurdistan).*
Belt Plaque (?) decorated with Felines and Birds' Heads.
*Late 7th century B.C. University Museum, Philadelphia.
Gold inlaid with coloured glass paste, length* 6^1/$_8$ *inches.
(Photo Draeger)*
A fragment of a similar plaque is in a private collection
in New York.

147b. Detail of No. 147a. *(Photo Draeger)*

148. *Scythian Art. Ziwiyeh, east of Sakkiz (Kurdistan).*
Bracelet with a Moufflon's Head at each End. *Late
7th century B.C. Private Collection, Teheran. Gold, diameter*
3^1/$_8$ *inches, length of the heads* ^{13}/$_{16}$ *of an inch. (Photo Audrain)*

149. *Scythian Art. Ziwiyeh, east of Sakkiz (Kurdistan).*
Fragment of a Torque adorned with Moufflons' Heads.
*Late 7th century B.C. Archaeological Museum, Teheran. Gold.
(Photo Dr. A. Razavi)*

150. *Scythian Art. Ziwiyeh, east of Sakkiz (Kurdistan).*
Bracelet with an Animal's Head at each End. *Late
7th century B.C. University Museum, Philadelphia. Gold,
diameter* 2^3/$_4$ *inches. (Museum Photo)*

151. *Scythian Art. Ziwiyeh, east of Sakkiz (Kurdistan).*
Two chains of three ropes each, held together by sliding
rings decorated with graining, and ending in a network
of interwoven strands to which tiny bells are attached.
*Late 7th century B.C. Archaeological Museum, Teheran. Gold,
length of large chain* 58^3/$_4$ *inches, end of the chain* 8^3/$_4$ *inches.
(Photo Dr. A. Razavi)*

152. *Local Art. Ziwiyeh, east of Sakkiz (Kurdistan).*
Necklace decorated with Graining and Animals' Heads.
*Late 7th century B.C. Private Collection, Teheran. Gold,
length of one element* ^{7}/$_8$ *of an inch. (Photo Roman Ghirshman)*

153a-b. *Local Art. Ziwiyeh, east of Sakkiz (Kurdistan).*
Necklace and Ear-rings. *Late 7th century B.C. Archaeological Museum, Teheran. Gold, length of the necklace* 18^1/$_2$
inches, diameter of an ear-ring 1 *inch. (Photo Dr. A. Razavi)*

154. *Local Art. Ziwiyeh, east of Sakkiz (Kurdistan).*
Bractea in the form of a Recumbent Ibex. *Late 7th century
B.C. Archaeological Museum, Teheran. Gold, length* ^{3}/$_4$ *of an
inch, width* ^{3}/$_4$ *of an inch, weight 2 grammes. (Photo Dr. A.
Razavi)*

Such ornaments as this, regarded as having 'protective' virtues, were sewn on to garments.

155. *Composite Art. Ziwiyeh, east of Sakkiz (Kurdistan).*
Sword Hilt with Two Confronted Lions' Heads spitting
out the Blade. On the pommel, Lotus Flowers and a
Coiling Animal. *Late 7th century B.C. Archaeological
Museum, Teheran. Gold pommel with ivory lions' heads,
length* 3^1/$_8$ *inches. (Photo Dr. A. Razavi)*
For the animal on the pommel, cf. No. 158.

156. *Scythian Art. Ziwiyeh, east of Sakkiz (Kurdistan).*
Fragment of a Sword Sheath adorned with Superimposed Rows of Gazelles' Heads. *Late 7th century B.C.
Archaeological Museum, Teheran. Gold, width at the top*
2 *inches, width at the bottom* 1^3/$_4$ *inches, length* 17^7/$_8$ *inches,
weight 247 grammes. (Photo Dr. A. Razavi)*

157. *Scythian Art. Ziwiyeh, east of Sakkiz (Kurdistan).*
Chape adorned with Two Scythian Felines Confronted.
*Late 7th century B.C. Archaeological Museum, Teheran. Gold,
length* 1^3/$_8$ *inches, width* 1^1/$_4$ *inches, weight 77 grammes.
(Photo Roman Ghirshman)*

158. *Scythian Art. Ziwiyeh, east of Sakkiz (Kurdistan).*
Sword Pommel adorned with an Animal coiling round
an Ornamental Pattern. *Late 7th century B.C. Ernest
Erickson Foundation, New York. Gold, diameter* 1 ^{5}/$_8$ *inches.
(Photo Roman Ghirshman)*

159. *Median Art. Ziwiyeh, east of Sakkiz (Kurdistan).*
Dagger. *Late 7th century B.C. Archaeological Museum,
Teheran. Iron blade with limestone handle overlaid with
silver foil, length* 9^1/$_2$ *inches. (Photo Dr. A. Razavi)*

160. *Local Art. Ziwiyeh, east of Sakkiz (Kurdistan).*
Dagger. *Late 7th century B.C. Archaeological Museum,
Teheran. Iron blade, bone handle lined inside with thin bronze
leaf, silver pommel, length* 11^3/$_8$ *inches. (Photo Dr. A. Razavi)*

161. *Assyrian Art (?). Ziwiyeh, east of Sakkiz (Kurdistan).*
Dagger Handle with Animal Figures. *Late 7th century
B.C. Archaeological Museum, Teheran. Ivory, length*
3^3/$_4$ *inches. (Photo Dr. A. Razavi)*

162. *Local Art. Ziwiyeh, east of Sakkiz (Kurdistan).*
Centrepiece (umbo) of a Shield. *Late 7th century B.C.
Archaeological Museum, Teheran. Gilt bronze, diameter*
2^5/$_8$ *inches. (Photo Dr. A. Razavi)*

163. *Local Art. Ziwiyeh, east of Sakkiz (Kurdistan).*
Fragment of a Shield engraved with a Palmette. *Late
7th century B.C. Archaeological Museum, Teheran. Silver
chased and engraved, length* 5^1/$_8$ *inches. (Photo Dr. A. Razavi)*

164. *Scythian Art (?). Ziwiyeh, east of Sakkiz (Kurdistan).*
Ceremonial Mace, pear-shaped, adorned with Two
Birds' Heads. *Late 7th century B.C. Archaeological Museum,
Teheran. White marble, height* 2^3/$_8$ *inches, width 3 inches.
(Photo Dr. A. Razavi)*

165a-b. *Scythian Art. Ziwiyeh, east of Sakkiz (Kurdistan).*
Two Arrowheads. *Late 7th century B.C. Private Collection,
Teheran. Bronze and bone. (Photo Roman Ghirshman)*

166. *Local Art. Ziwiyeh, east of Sakkiz (Kurdistan).*
Spearhead. *Late 7th century B.C. Archaeological Museum,
Teheran. Iron, length 26 inches. (Photo Dr. A. Razavi)*

167. *Irano-Urartian Art. Ziwiyeh, east of Sakkiz (Kurdistan).* Chamfron adorned with a Bounding Lion
between Two Stylized Trees. *Late 7th century B.C.
Archaeological Museum, Teheran. Engraved silver, length*
12^3/$_8$ *inches, width* 5^1/$_4$ *inches, weight 174 grammes. Holes
on the sides for fastening. (Photo Draeger)*

168. *Urartian Art (?). Ziwiyeh, east of Sakkiz (Kurdistan).* Terminal of a Chariot Shaft, in the form of a
Horse's Head. *Late 7th century B.C. Archaeological Museum,
Teheran. Bronze, height* 6^3/$_4$ *inches, length of the neck*
9^1/$_2$ *inches. (Photo Dr. A. Razavi)*

169. *Urartian Art (?)*. *Ziwiyeh, east of Sakkiz (Kurdistan)*. Drinking-pipe ending in a Heifer's Head. *Late 7th century B.C. Private Collection, Teheran. Silver, length of pipe 4³/₄ inches, length of head ¹/₂ an inch. (Photo Roger Parry)*

170. *Medo-Scythian Art*. *Ziwiyeh, east of Sakkiz (Kurdistan)*. Vase with Vertical Spout, the Body incised with Triangles. *Late 7th century B.C. Archaeological Museum, Teheran. Dark yellow terracotta well burnished, height 5¹/₄ inches. (Photo Istituto Italiano per il Medio ed Estremo Oriente)*

171. *Medo-Scythian Art*. *Ziwiyeh, east of Sakkiz (Kurdistan)*. Vase with Beak-Spout. *Late 7th century B.C. Archaeological Museum, Teheran. Polished yellow terracotta, height 2¹/₂ inches. (Photo Dr. A. Razavi)*

172. *Scytho-Urartian Art*. *Ziwiyeh, east of Sakkiz (Kurdistan)*. Lug of a Pitcher in the form of a Recumbent Feline. *Late 7th century B.C. Private Collection, Teheran. Yellow terracotta, inner side painted red, length 1⁵/₈ inches, width 1³/₈ inches. (Photo Dr. A. Razavi)*

173. *Local Art*. *Ziwiyeh, east of Sakkiz (Kurdistan)*. Statuette of a Man in Nomad Costume. *Late 7th century B.C. Archaeological Museum, Teheran. Wood, height 5⁷/₈ inches, width 1⁵/₈ inches. (Photo Dr. A. Razavi)* The statuette, whose face, probably of ivory or stone, has disappeared, must have been covered with thin gold leaf.

174. *Achaemenian Art*. *Pasargadae (Fars)*. Bas-Relief with a Winged Genius in Elamite Costume. *6th century B.C. In situ. Stone, height 9 feet. (Photo Roman Ghirshman)* Bas-Relief decorating a gate. In the early nineteenth century the following inscription was still visible above the figure: 'I Cyrus, the King, the Achaemenid (built this).'

175. *Achaemenian Art*. *Pasargadae (Fars)*. Lion's Head. *6th century B.C. In situ. Stone. (After E. Herzfeld, Iran in the Ancient East, New York, 1941, Pl. XXXIX)*

176. *Achaemenian Art*. *Masjid-i-Sulaiman, 30 miles southeast of Shushtar (Khuzistan)*. Stairway of the Man-made Terrace backed against the Mountain. *7th century B.C. In situ (to the east). Stone, 82 feet wide. (Photo Dr. Lockhart)*

177. *Achaemenian Art*. *Masjid-i-Sulaiman, 30 miles southeast of Shushtar (Khuzistan)*. Plan of the Terrace. *7th century B.C. (After R. Ghirshman, Syria, XXVII, 1950, p. 208, fig. 2)*

178. *Achaemenian Art*. *Pasargadae (Fars)*. Terrace called Takht-i-Madar-i-Sulaiman, or 'Throne of Solomon's Mother.' *6th century B.C. In situ (to the north). Courses of large stones in rustic work with grooved joints. Height, 35 feet. (Photo Van den Berghe)*

179. *Achaemenian Art*. *Pasargadae (Fars)*. Bas-Relief with Cyrus and an Attendant. *6th century B.C. In situ. Stone. (After E. Herzfeld, 1929-30, Pl. III)*

180. *Achaemenian Art*. *Da-u-Dukhtar, in the Kuh-i-Unari (Fars)*. Façade of a Rock Tomb. *7th-6th centuries B.C. (between 640 and 560). In situ. Hewn in the rock face, at a height of 1000 feet. (After Sir Aurel Stein, 1940, fig. 14)* Tomb of one of the earlier Persian kings, perhaps Cambyses I.

181. *Achaemenian Art*. *Pasargadae (Fars)*. Reconstruction of the Audience Hall. *6th century B.C. (After E. Herzfeld, 1941, Pl. XLIII)*

182. *Achaemenian Art*. *Pasargadae (Fars)*. Plan of the Reception Hall. *6th century B.C. (After Ali Hakemi, Iranian Archaeological Service)*

183. *Achaemenian Art*. *Pasargadae (Fars)*. Two Stepped Fire Altars. *6th century B.C. In situ (1100 yards west of Palace P). Large blocks of stone. (Photo Van den Berghe)*

184. *Achaemenian Art*. *Pasargadae (Fars)*. Vestiges of the Fire Temple. *6th century B.C. In situ. Ashlar. (Photo Roman Ghirshman)*

185. *Achaemenian Art*. *Pasargadae (Fars)*. Tomb of Cyrus II (559-529). *6th century B.C. In situ (southern extremity of the site). Carefully trimmed blocks of white limestone; overall height 35 feet; height of the base 17 feet. (Photo Roman Ghirshman)*

186. *Achaemenian Art*. *Susa (Khuzistan)*. Detail of a Bull Capital. *Late 6th century B.C. Restored under Artaxerxes II (404-358). Louvre, Paris. Stone, height 7 feet 7 inches, width 12 feet 3 inches. (Photo Tel-Vigneau)* Capital of one of the columns supporting the roof of the Apadana.

187. *Susa (Khuzistan)*. Aerial View of the Palace and the Apadana. *(Photo Hunting Aerosurveys Ltd, London)*

188. *Achaemenian Art*. *Susa (Khuzistan)*. Plan of the Palace. *6th century B.C. (After R. de Mecquenem, completed by the results of recent excavations of the Apadana. Cf. A. Upham Pope, A Survey of Persian Art, I, fig. 75)*

189. *Achaemenian Art*. *Susa (Khuzistan)*. Fragment of the Statue of Darius the Great. *Late 6th - early 5th century B.C. Louvre, Paris. Stone, originally about 10 feet high. (Photo Serge Maire)*

190. *Achaemenian Art*. *Susa (Khuzistan)*. Frieze of Archers of the Royal Guard from the Palace of Darius. *5th century B.C. Louvre, Paris. Glazed bricks; height of the panels 6 feet, width 26³/₄ inches; height of the bricks 3³/₈ inches, width 13³/₈ inches. (Photo Draeger)*

191. *Achaemenian Art*. *Susa (Khuzistan)*. Lion-Griffin from the Palace of Darius. *5th century B.C. Louvre, Paris. Glazed bricks; height of the panels 54 inches, width 13 feet 9 inches; height of the bricks 3³/₈ inches, width 13³/₈ inches. (Photo Draeger)*

192. *Achaemenian Art*. *Susa (Khuzistan)*. Winged Bull from the Palace of Darius. *5th century B.C. Louvre, Paris. Glazed bricks, height 5 feet 4 inches, length 6 feet 4 inches. (Photo Draeger)*

193. *Achaemenian Art*. *Susa (Khuzistan)*. Lion Passant from the Palace of Darius. *5th century B.C. Louvre, Paris. Glazed bricks, length 8 feet 3 inches. (Photo Draeger)*

194. *Achaemenian Art*. *Susa (Khuzistan)*. Stairway Relief from the Small Palace: Servant carrying a Dish. *5th century B.C. Archaeological Museum, Teheran. Stone, fragment of a bas-relief. (After R. de Mecquenem, Mémoires, Vol. XXX, Pl. VI, fig. 5)*

195. *Achaemenian Art*. *Susa (Khuzistan)*. Winged Lion from the Small Palace. *5th century B.C. Archaeological Museum, Teheran. Stone, height 17¹/₄ inches, width 16³/₄ inches. (Photo Dr. A. Razavi)*

196. *Greek Art. Rome, Villa Palombara.* Young Woman with a Dove. *Last quarter of the 6th century B.C. Museo del Palazzo dei Conservatori, Rome. Marble funerary stele, height 68 inches.* (*After* André MALRAUX, Des bas-reliefs aux grottes sacrées, *Ill. 142, notice by* Jean CHARBONNEAUX, *p. 476*)

197. *Greek Art. Delphi. Siphnian Treasury, North Frieze.* Battle of the Giants: A Lion harnessed to Dionysos' Chariot attacking a Fleeing Giant. *Mid or late 6th century B.C. Delphi Museum. Marble, height 25 inches.* (*Photo Friedrich Hewicker*)

198. *Persepolis (Fars).* Aerial View of the Terrace. (*Photo Aerial Survey, Oriental Institute, Chicago*)

199. *Persepolis (Fars).* Aerial View. (*Photo Vahé*)

200. *Achaemenian Art. Persepolis (Fars).* Stairway to the Terrace, first flight to the left. *Late 6th century B.C. (reign of Darius I, about 518). In situ. Stone, width 23 feet. 58 steps to the lower ramp.* (*Photo Lucien Hervé*)

201. *Achaemenian Art. Persepolis (Fars).* Stairway to the Terrace, first flight to the right. *Late 6th century B.C. (reign of Darius I, about 518). In situ. Stone, width 23 feet. 58 steps to the lower ramp.* (*Photo Lucien Hervé*)

202. *Achaemenian Art. Persepolis (Fars).* Monumental Stairway to the Terrace, opposite the Gate-House of Xerxes I. *Late 6th century. In situ. Stone, width 23 feet. 106 steps. Two divergent flights running parallel to the retaining wall.* (*Photo Lucien Hervé*)

203. *Achaemenian Art. Persepolis (Fars).* Gate-House of Xerxes I. *Reign of Xerxes I, 485-465. In situ. Stone, height of the three monumental doorways 36 feet.* (*Photo Lucien Hervé*)
Gate-house composed of a square hall with four columns (two of them extant), pierced by three monumental doorways opening to the east, west and south.

204. *Achaemenian Art. Persepolis (Fars).* View of the Hypostyle Halls of the Royal Treasury. *5th century B.C. In situ. Remains of stone column bases.* (*Photo Lucien Hervé*)
View showing part of the terrace cleared by Dr Erich Schmidt from 1935 to 1939.

205. *Achaemenian Art. Persepolis (Fars).* Royal Treasury, with Column Bases indicating the Position of the Hypostyle Halls. *5th century B.C. In situ. Remains of stone column bases.* (*Photo Lucien Hervé*)
Part of the terrace cleared by Dr Erich Schmidt from 1935 to 1939.

206. *Achaemenian Art. Persepolis (Fars).* Royal Treasury. In the foreground, Hall of a Hundred Columns. Behind, Hall of Ninety-nine Columns or Temporary Throne Hall of Darius. *5th century B.C. (reigns of Darius I and Xerxes I). In situ. Remains of stone column bases.* (*Photo Lucien Hervé*)
Part of the terrace cleared by Dr Erich Schmidt from 1935 to 1939.

207. *Achaemenian Art. Persepolis (Fars).* Monumental Entrance of the Gate-House of Xerxes I, with Human-headed Bulls. *5th century B.C. In situ. Stone, height 36 feet.* (*Photo Georges Bourdelon-Noel Ballif*)

208. *Achaemenian Art. Persepolis (Fars).* Foundation Plaque of Darius buried under the Apadana. *Late 6th century B.C. Archaeological Museum, Teheran. Gold, height 12³/₄ inches, width 13 inches, weight 4,998 kilogrammes.* (*Photo Bourdelon*)
Found in a stone box, together with a silver plaque. Inscription in three languages, ten lines in Old Persian, seven in Babylonian, eight in Elamite, reading as follows. 'Darius the Great King, King of Kings, King of the Countries, son of Hystaspes the Achaemenid. Saith Darius the King: This is the kingdom which I possess from the land of the Sakas on this side of Sogdiana as far as Kush, from India to Sardis. Over this Ahuramazda has granted me dominion, he who is great above all the Gods. May Ahuramazda protect me and my Royal House.'

209. *Achaemenian Art. Persepolis (Fars).* Stairway Relief of the Tripylon: Median Nobles. *6th-5th centuries B.C. In situ. Stone bas-reliefs.* (*Photo The Oriental Institute, University of Chicago, after* E.F. SCHMIDT, 1953, *Pl. 72 A*)

210. *Achaemenian Art. Persepolis (Fars).* Gate-House of Xerxes: Winged Human-headed Bull of the East Doorway. *5th century B.C. In situ. Stone.* (*Photo The Oriental Institute, University of Chicago*)

211. *Achaemenian Art. Persepolis (Fars).* East Stairway of the Apadana. *6th-5th centuries B.C. In situ. Stone, decorated with bas-reliefs.* (*Photo The Oriental Institute, University of Chicago, after* E.F. SCHMIDT, 1953, *Pl. 19*)

212. *Achaemenian Art. Persepolis (Fars).* Gate-House of Xerxes: Human-headed Bulls flanking the 'Gate of All Countries.' *5th century B.C. In situ. Stone, height of the bulls 18 feet.* (*Photo Georges Bourdelon-Noel Ballif*)

213. *Achaemenian Art. Persepolis (Fars).* Human-headed Bull, detail of a Capital. *5th century B.C. Oriental Institute, University of Chicago. Stone.* (*Museum Photo*)

214. *Achaemenian Art. Persepolis (Fars).* Entrance Stairway of the Tripylon. *6th-5th centuries B.C. In situ. Stone, decorated with reliefs.* (*Photo The Oriental Institute, University of Chicago*)

215. *Achaemenian Art. Persepolis (Fars).* Persian Dignitary with a Lotus Flower, detail. Inner Wall, Right Wing of the Entrance Stairway of the Tripylon. *6th-5th centuries B.C. In situ. Stone.* (*Photo Georges Bourdelon-Noël Ballif*)

216. *Achaemenian Art. Persepolis (Fars).* Three Registers of Bas-Reliefs above the East Stairway of the Apadana: Susians, Armenians and Persian Guards. *6th-5th centuries B.C. In situ. Stone.* (*Photo Lucien Hervé*)

217. *Achaemenian Art. Persepolis (Fars).* East Stairway of the Apadana, detail: Persian Guards. *6th-5th centuries B.C. In situ. Stone. West side of the outer flight of steps, north wing of east stairway.* (*Photo Antonello Perissinotto*)

218. *Achaemenian Art. Persepolis (Fars).* East Stairway of the Apadana, detail: Susian Guards. *6th-5th centuries B.C. In situ. Stone. West side of the outer flight of steps, north wing of east stairway.* (*Photo Antonello Perissinotto*)

219. *Achaemenian Art. Persepolis (Fars).* East Stairway of the Apadana, detail: Persian Guard. *6th-5th centuries B.C. In situ. Stone.* (*Photo Antonello Perissinotto*)

220. *Achaemenian Art. Persepolis (Fars).* East Stairway of the Apadana, detail: Syrians or Lydians. *6th-5th centuries B.C. In situ. Stone. Right part, lower register, near the steps. (Photo Antonello Perissinotto)*

221. *Achaemenian Art. Persepolis (Fars).* East Stairway of the Apadana, detail: A Babylonian. *6th-5th centuries B.C. In situ. Stone. Right part, middle register, left side. (Photo Antonello Perissinotto)*

222. *Achaemenian Art. Persepolis (Fars).* East Stairway of the Apadana, detail: An Armenian (?). *6th-5th centuries B.C. In situ. Stone. Right part, middle register, to the left near the steps. (Photo Antonello Perissinotto)*

223. *Achaemenian Art. Persepolis (Fars).* East Stairway of the Apadana, detail: Delegation of Babylonians. *6th-5th centuries B.C. In situ. Stone. Right part, middle register, left side. (Photo Antonello Perissinotto)*

224. *Achaemenian Art. Persepolis (Fars).* East Stairway of the Apadana, detail: A Syrian or Lydian. *6th-5th centuries B.C. In situ. Stone. Right part, lower register, far left. (Photo Antonello Perissinotto)*

225. *Achaemenian Art. Persepolis (Fars).* East Stairway of the Apadana, detail: A Syrian or Lydian. *6th-5th centuries B.C. In situ. Stone. Right part, lower register, to the left. (Photo Antonello Perissinotto)*

226. *Achaemenian Art. Persepolis (Fars).* East Stairway of the Apadana, detail: Head of a Persian Dignitary. *6th-5th centuries B.C. In situ. Stone. Lower register, west side of the outer flight of steps, north wing. (Photo Antonello Perissinotto)*

227. *Achaemenian Art. Persepolis (Fars).* East Stairway of the Apadana, detail: Head of a Median Dignitary. *6th-5th centuries B.C. In situ. Stone, overall height of figure 35 1/2 inches. (After A. Upham* Pope, *1938, IV, Pl. 90) Lower register, west side of the outer flight of steps, north wing, near the inscribed panel. (Photo Antonello Perissinotto)*

228. *Achaemenian Art. Persepolis (Fars).* East Stairway of the Apadana, detail: Representatives of Various Countries. *6th-5th centuries B.C. In situ. Stone. (Photo Lucien Hervé)*

229. *Achaemenian Art. Persepolis (Fars).* North Façade of the Apadana Stairway, detail: Representatives of Various Countries. *6th-5th centuries B.C. In situ. Stone. (Photo Lucien Hervé)*

230. *Achaemenian Art. Persepolis (Fars).* East Stairway of the Apadana, detail: Head of a Bactrian. *6th-5th centuries B.C. In situ. Stone. (Photo Antonello Perissinotto)*

231. *Achaemenian Art. Persepolis (Fars).* East Stairway of the Apadana, detail: A Chorasmian. *6th-5th centuries B.C. In situ. Stone. (Photo Antonello Perissinotto)*

232. *Achaemenian Art. Persepolis (Fars).* East Stairway of the Apadana, detail: An Usher leading forward a Chorasmian. *6th-5th centuries B.C. In situ. Stone. (Photo Antonello Perissinotto)*

233. *Achaemenian Art. Persepolis (Fars).* Tripylon Door: Darius I beneath a Sunshade. *6th-5th centuries B.C. In situ. Stone. (Photo Lucien Hervé)*

234. *Achaemenian Art. Persepolis (Fars).* South Stairway of the Tripylon. *6th-5th centuries B.C. In situ. Stone. (Photo The Oriental Institute, University of Chicago, after E.F.* Schmidt, *1953, Pl. 82)*

235. *Achaemenian Art. Persepolis (Fars).* Tripylon Stairway, detail: Persian Dignitaries. *6th-5th centuries B.C. In situ. Stone. East wing of the stairway. (Photo Antonello Perissinotto)*

236. *Achaemenian Art. Persepolis (Fars).* Tripylon Stairway, detail: Persian and Median Guards. *6th-5th centuries B.C. In situ. Stone. West side of west wing. (Photo Antonello Perissinotto)*

237. *Achaemenian Art. Persepolis (Fars).* Tripylon Stairway, detail: Head of a Median Guard. *6th-5th centuries B.C. In situ. Stone. East side of east wing. (Photo Antonello Perissinotto)*

238. *Achaemenian Art. Persepolis (Fars).* Tripylon Stairway, detail: Head of a Persian Guard. *6th-5th centuries B.C. In situ. Stone. Central façade of the stairway. (Photo Antonello Perissinotto)*

239. *Achaemenian Art. Persepolis (Fars).* Fragment of a Bas-Relief in front of the Palace of Darius: Servants. *6th-5th centuries B.C. In situ. Stone. (Photo Georges Bourdelon-Noël Ballif)*

240. *Achaemenian Art. Persepolis (Fars).* Stairway Reliefs of the Palace of Darius: Servants. In the foreground, Lion and Bull Fighting. *6th-5th centuries B.C. In situ. Stone. (Photo Georges Bourdelon-Noël Ballif)*

241. *Achaemenian Art. Persepolis (Fars).* Door Jamb of the Palace of Darius: Servant. *6th-5th centuries B.C. In situ. Stone. (Photo Lucien Hervé)*

242. *Achaemenian Art. Persepolis (Fars).* Palace of Darius: Two Guards. *6th-5th centuries B.C. In situ. Stone. West entrance, north door jamb. (Photo Georges Bourdelon-Noël Ballif)*

243. *Achaemenian Art. Persepolis (Fars).* Palace of Darius: Servant. *6th-5th centuries B.C. In situ. Stone, height of figure 5 feet 5 inches. South jamb of the west door of Room 12. (After E.F.* Schmidt, *1953, Pl. 149). (Photo Georges Bourdelon-Noël Ballif)*

244. *Achaemenian Art. Persepolis (Fars).* West Stairway of the Palace of Xerxes, detail: Two Servants. *5th century B.C. In situ. Stone. East side, parapet of the north flight of steps. (Photo Antonello Perissinotto)*

245. *Achaemenian Art. Persepolis (Fars).* West Stairway of the Palace of Xerxes, detail: Servants. *5th century B.C. In situ. Stone. Right-hand flight of steps. (Photo Antonello Perissinotto)*

246. *Achaemenian Art. Persepolis (Fars).* East Door of the Tripylon: The Crown Prince Xerxes standing behind Darius seated on a Throne upheld by the 28 Nations. Above, the Great God Ahuramazda. *6th-5th centuries B.C. In situ. Stone. (Photo The Oriental Institute, University of Chicago, after E.F.* Schmidt, *1953, Pl. 79)*

247. *Achaemenian Art. Persepolis (Fars).* East Door of the Tripylon, detail: Ahuramazda. *6th-5th centuries B.C. In situ. Stone. (Photo The Oriental Institute, University of Chicago, after E.F.* Schmidt, *1953, Pl. 78)*

248. *Achaemenian Art. Persepolis (Fars)*. South Door of the Hall of a Hundred Columns: Artaxerxes I enthroned, borne by his Subject Peoples, disposed in Three Rows. Above, Winged Symbol of the God Ahuramazda. *5th century B.C. In situ. Stone. (Photo The Oriental Institute, University of Chicago, after E.F.* SCHMIDT, 1953, *Pl.* 107*)*

249. *Achaemenian Art. Persepolis (Fars)*. South Door of the Hall of a Hundred Columns, detail: Bearers of the Royal Throne. *5th century B.C. In situ. Stone. (Photo Lucien Hervé)*

250. *Achaemenian Art. Persepolis (Fars)*. West Door of the Hall of a Hundred Columns, detail: 'Royal Hero' subduing a Composite Animal. *5th century B.C. In situ. Stone. (Photo The Oriental Institute, University of Chicago)*

251. *Achaemenian Art. Persepolis (Fars)*. Door of the Hall of a Hundred Columns: 'Royal Hero' grappling with a Griffin. *5th century B.C. In situ. Stone. (After* E. HERZFELD, 1941, *Pl. LXV)*

252. *Achaemenian Art. Persepolis (Fars)*. Door of the Hall of a Hundred Columns: 'Royal Hero' grappling with a Lion. *5th century B.C. In situ. Stone. (After* E. HERZFELD, 1941, *Pl. LXVI)*

253. *Achaemenian Art. Persepolis (Fars)*. Door of the Hall of a Hundred Columns: 'Royal Hero' grappling with a Bull. *5th century B.C. In situ. Stone. (After* E. HERZFELD, 1941, *Pl. LXVI)*

254. *Achaemenian Art. Persepolis (Fars)*. North Door of the Hall of a Hundred Columns: Royal Audience. *5th century B.C. In situ. Stone. (Photo The Oriental Institute, University of Chicago)*

255. *Achaemenian Art. Persepolis (Fars)*. South Bas-Relief on the Portico of the Treasury: Darius giving Audience before Two Fire Altars, with the Usher who introduces the Delegations. *6th-5th centuries B.C. Archaeological Museum, Teheran. Stone, length 20 feet. (Photo The Oriental Institute, University of Chicago)*

256. *Achaemenian Art. Persepolis (Fars)*. General Plan of the Terrace. *(After the survey of Ali* HAKEMI *of the Iranian Archaeological Service)*

257. *Achaemenian Art. Persepolis (Fars)*. Unidentified Ruins sometimes attributed to Artaxerxes III (358-338). Stairway Relief: Servants. *4th century B.C. In situ. Stone. (Photo Lucien Hervé)*

258. *Achaemenian Art. Persepolis (Fars)*. Unidentified Ruins sometimes attributed to Artaxerxes III (358-338). In the foreground, Stairway Reliefs, fragment: Servants. *4th century B.C. In situ. Stone. (Photo Lucien Hervé)*

259. *Achaemenian Art. Persepolis (Fars)*. Unidentified Ruins sometimes attributed to Artaxerxes III (358-338). Reliefs: Tribute Bearers. *4th century B.C. In situ. Stone. (Photo Lucien Hervé)*

260. *Achaemenian Art. Persepolis (Fars)*. Unidentified Ruins sometimes attributed to Artaxerxes III (358-338). Relief: Lion attacking a Bull. *4th century B.C. In situ. Stone. (Photo Lucien Hervé)*

261. *Achaemenian Art. Persepolis (Fars)*. Reconstructed Column with Complete Capital. *5th century B.C. Archaeological Museum, Teheran. Stone. (Photo Dr. A. Razavi)*

262. *Achaemenian Art. Persepolis (Fars)*. North Column of the Gate-House of Xerxes I. *5th century B.C. In situ. Stone. (Photo Lucien Hervé).*

263. *Achaemenian Art. Persepolis (Fars)*. Columns. *6th-5th centuries B.C. (Drawing after E.* HERZFELD, 1941, *Pl. LVIII)*

264. *Achaemenian Art. Persepolis (Fars)*. Capital with Bull Protomes. *5th century B.C. In situ. Discovered in 1947 north of the Hall of a Hundred Columns. Stone, length 10 feet 10 inches, from one head to the other. (Photo Georges Bourdelon-Noël Ballif)*

265. *Achaemenian Art. Persepolis (Fars)*. East Portico of the Apadana: Lion on a Capital. *5th century B.C. Archaeological Museum, Teheran. Stone. (Photo Dr A. Razavi)*

266. *Achaemenian Art. Persepolis (Fars)*. Hall of a Hundred Columns: Bull on a Capital. *5th century B.C. Nelson Gallery of Art, Kansas City. Stone. (Museum Photo)*

267. *Achaemenian Art. Persepolis (Fars)*. Capital with Griffin Protomes, detail. *5th-4th centuries B.C. In situ. Stone. (Photo Lucien Hervé)*

268. *Achaemenian Art. Persepolis (Fars)*. Capital with Two Lion Protomes, detail. In the background, Gate-House of Xerxes I. *5th century B.C. In situ. Stone. (Photo Georges Bourdelon-Noël Ballif)*

269. *Achaemenian Art. Persepolis (Fars)*. Lion discovered in 1951. *5th-4th centuries B.C. Archaeological Museum, Teheran. Lapis lazuli paste, height $6^3/_4$ inches, length 4 inches. (Photo Istituto Italiano per il Medio ed Estremo Oriente)*

270. *Achaemenian Art. Persepolis (Fars)*. Tripylon: Human-headed Capital, detail. *5th century B.C. Archaeological Museum, Teheran. Stone, carved in the round and painted. (Photo Lucien Hervé)*

271. *Achaemenian Art. Persepolis (Fars)*. East Stairway of the Apadana: A Persian Guard, detail showing drapery. *6th-5th centuries B.C. In situ. Stone. (Photo Antonello Perissinotto)*

272. *Greek Art. Persepolis (Fars)*. Statue of Penelope, found in the Treasury in 1938. *Second half of 5th century B.C. Archaeological Museum, Teheran. Marble. (Museum Photo, Rostamy)*

273. *Achaemenian Art. Jin Jin, 4 miles west of Fahlian (Fars)*. Column Base with Flower Designs. *5th-4th centuries B.C. In situ. Stone, diameter $47^1/_4$ inches. (Photo Van den Berghe)*
Vestige of a royal pavilion which served as a relay station on the road from Susa to Persepolis.

274. *Achaemenian Art. Babylon (Mesopotamia)*. Plan of an Achaemenian Building. *5th-4th centuries B.C. (After E. F.* SCHMIDT, 1941, *fig.* 9-11*)*

275. *Achaemenian Art. Naqsh-i-Rustam (Fars).* Royal Achaemenian Rock Tombs and Sassanian Bas-Reliefs. *6th-5th centuries B.C. (tombs) and 3rd-4th centuries A.D. (reliefs). In situ, carved in the rock face of the Kuh-i-Husain. (Photo Ernst Herzfeld)*

276. *Sassanian Art. Naqsh-i-Rustam (Fars).* Fire Altars. *3rd-6th centuries A.D. In situ, carved in the rock. Height 61 and 69 inches; width of cavity in which the fire burned, 15 3/4 inches. (Photo Roman Ghirshman)*

277. *Achaemenian Art. Naqsh-i-Rustam (Fars).* Fire Temple called 'Ka'ba-i-Zardusht.' *6th-5th centuries B.C. In situ. Light-coloured limestone masonry with blind windows in black stone. Height 36 feet, width 23 feet, inner chamber measuring 17 feet 4 inches by 12 feet 4 inches. (Photo Roman Ghirshman)*

278. *Achaemenian Art. Bisutun, 20 miles east of Kermanshah (Kurdistan).* Bas-Relief of Darius I, detail: The God Ahuramazda. *6th century B.C. In situ. Rock carving. (Photo G. Cameron)*

279. *Achaemenian Art. Naqsh-i-Rustam (Fars).* Tomb of Darius the Great. *6th-5th centuries B.C. In situ, carved in the rock face of the Kuh-i-Husain. (Photo The Oriental Institute, University of Chicago)*

280. *Achaemenian Art. Persepolis (Fars).* Tomb of Artaxerxes II or III. *4th century B.C. In situ, carved in the rock face of the Kuh-i-Rahmat. (Photo Lucien Hervé)*

281. *Persepolis (Fars).* View of the Plain from within the Tomb of Artaxerxes II or III. *(Photo Lucien Hervé)*

282. *Achaemenian Art. Bisutun (Kurdistan).* View of the Bisutun Rock. *Wash Drawing by Sir Robert Ker Porter, 1818. British Museum, London. (Museum Photo)*

283. *Achaemenian Art. Bisutun (Kurdistan).* Rock Relief glorifying Darius's Victory over the Upstart Kings. *6th century B.C. In situ, carved in the rock face. (Photo Georges Bourdelon-Noël Ballif)*

284. *Achaemenian Art. Bisutun (Kurdistan).* Head of Darius the Great in side view, detail of No. 283. *6th century B.C. In situ. (Photo G. Cameron)*

285. *Achaemenian Art. Persepolis (Fars).* Bas-Relief on the Inner Side of a Door of the Hall of a Hundred Columns: Monster with a Scorpion Dart, detail. *5th century B.C. In situ. Stone. (Photo Georges Bourdelon-Noël Ballif)*

286. *Achaemenian Art. Persepolis (Fars).* Pillar of One of the Doors of the Hall of a Hundred Columns: Detail of the Baldachin with Rows of Lions and Bulls between Palmettes. *5th century B.C. In situ. Stone. (Photo Georges Bourdelon-Noël Ballif)*

287. *Achaemenian Art. Persepolis (Fars).* Stairway Relief of the Tripylon, detail: Tip of a Guard's Scabbard. *5th century B.C. In situ. Stone. (Photo Antonello Perissinotto)*

288. *Achaemenian Art. Persepolis (Fars).* Stairway Relief of the Tripylon, detail: Tip of a Guard's Scabbard. *5th century B.C. In situ. Stone. (Photo Antonello Perissinotto)*

289. *Achaemenian Art. Persepolis (Fars).* Treasury Relief of Darius giving Audience, detail: Dagger of a Dignitary in the Third Row behind the King. *6th-5th centuries B.C. Length of the dagger 19 inches. (Photo Georges Bourdelon-Noël Ballif)*
Cf. No. 255.

290. *Achaemenian Art. Hamadan (?).* Rhyton with Winged Lion. Rim of the Vase adorned with Lotus Buds and Flowers. *5th century B.C. Archaeological Museum, Teheran. Gold, height 8 5/8 inches, width 7 inches, weight 1897 grammes. (Photo Draeger)*

291. *Achaemenian Art (Ionian workmanship?). Persepolis (Fars).* Stand in the form of Three Lions. *6th-5th centuries B.C. Archaeological Museum, Teheran. Bronze, height 11 inches, width 15 3/8 inches. (Museum Photo, Rostamy)*

292. *Achaemenian Art.* Head of a Prince. *5th century B.C. Private Collection, Brussels. Limestone, height 2 3/4 inches. (Collection Photo)*

293. *Achaemenian Art. Memphis (Egypt).* Man's Head. *5th-4th centuries B.C. Louvre, Paris. Stone. (Photo Maurice Chuzeville)*

294. *Achaemenian Art. Persepolis (Fars).* Head of a King with Crenellated Crown. *5th-4th centuries B.C. Archaeological Museum, Teheran. Lapis lazuli paste, height 2 1/2 inches, width 2 3/8 inches. (Photo Draeger)*

295. *Achaemenian Art.* Bust of a Median holding a Lion Cub. *5th-4th centuries B.C. Cleveland Museum of Art. Lapis lazuli, height 7 1/2 inches, width 6 1/4 inches. (Museum Photo)*

296. *Median or Achaemenian Art. Oxus Treasure (Bactria).* Statuette of a Donor. *6th century B.C. British Museum, London. Silver, height 2 1/4 inches. (Museum Photo)*

297. *Art of Luristan.* Statuette of a Woman in a Long Dress. *7th-6th centuries B.C. Private Collection, Teheran. Bronze, height 3 1/2 inches, width 1 inch. (Photo Draeger)*
The statuette is hollow and was fitted on to a support. The figure is making the gesture of the Venus Pudica.

298. *Achaemenian Art. Oxus Treasure (Bactria).* Statuette of a High Bactrian (?) Dignitary. *5th-4th centuries B.C. British Museum, London. Gold, height 2 1/8 inches. (Museum Photo)*

299. *Achaemenian Art. Oxus Treasure (Bactria).* Small Plaque representing an Achaemenian King in Profile. *5th-4th centuries B.C. British Museum, London. Gold, height 2 3/8 inches. (Museum Photo)*

300. *Achaemenian Art. Oxus Treasure (Bactria).* Head of a Beardless Man. *6th-4th centuries B.C. British Museum, London. Gold, height 4 1/2 inches, originally adorned with ear-rings. (Museum Photo)*

301. *Achaemenian Art. Oxus Treasure (Bactria).* Chariot with Driver and Another Figure, drawn by Four Horses. *6th-4th centuries B.C. British Museum, London. Gold. (Museum Photo)*

302a. *Achaemenian Art. Oxus Treasure (Bactria).* Bracelet. *6th-4th centuries B.C. British Museum, London. Gold, diameter 4 3/4 inches. Cloisonné decoration originally inset with stones. (Museum Photo)*

302b. *Achaemenian Art. Oxus Treasure (Bactria).* Vase Handle in the form of an Ibex. *5th century B.C. British Museum, London. Silver, length 8¹/₄ inches. (Museum Photo)*

302c. *Achaemenian Art. Oxus Treasure (Bactria).* Deer. *5th century B.C. British Museum, London. Gold, height 2¹/₂ inches. (Museum Photo)*

303. *Achaemenian Art.* Basin supported by Eight Lion Protomes. *6th-5th centuries B.C. Private Collection, New York. Limestone, diameter 26⁵/₈ inches. (After the catalogue of the Iran Exhibition, Paris, 1961-62, No. 633, Pl. LXX)*

304. *Achaemenian Art.* Corrugated Vase supported by Three Ibex Protomes. *5th-4th centuries B.C. Private Collection, Geneva. Stone, height 24 inches. (After the catalogue of the Iran Exhibition, Paris, 1961-62, No. 660, Pl. LXXII)*

305. *Achaemenian Art.* Ibex. *5th-4th centuries B.C. Private Collection, New York. Black limestone, height 13¹/₂ inches, length at the base 14³/₄ inches. (Collection Photo)*

306. *Achaemenian Art. Hamadan (?).* Rhyton with Winged Lion. *5th century B.C. Metropolitan Museum of Art, New York. Gold, height 6³/₄ inches. (Museum Photo)*

307. *Achaemenian Art.* Fluted Amphora-Rhyton with Two Ibex Handles. *Late 6th-4th centuries B.C. Private Collection, Paris. Silver gilt, height (with handles) 14¹/₄ inches, width 9³/₄ inches. Two outlets at the bottom. (Photo Draeger)*

308. *Achaemenian Art.* Ovoid Fluted Jug with Ibex Handles. *6th-5th centuries B.C. Archaeological Museum, Teheran. Silver, height 8¹/₄ inches, width 4³/₄ inches, weight 1360 grammes. (Photo Draeger)*

309. *Achaemenian Art. Hamadan (?).* Bowl with Trilingual Inscription in Xerxes' Name. *5th century B.C. Archaeological Museum, Teheran. Gold, height 4¹/₂ inches, width 8 inches, weight 1407 grammes. (Museum Photo)*

310. *Achaemenian Art. Hamadan (?).* Bowl with Trilingual Inscription in Darius's Name. *5th century B.C. Private Collection, Geneva. Gold, diameter 9¹/₄ inches, weight 1800 grammes. (Photo Draeger)*

311. *Achaemenian Art.* Dish with Winged Bull in the Centre. *5th-4th centuries B.C. Private Collection, New York. Silver, diameter 13³/₄ inches. (Photo Draeger)*

312. *Achaemenian Art.* Dish with Two Ibexes in the Centre. *5th century B.C. Private Collection, Geneva. Gold, diameter 13 inches, weight 2050 grammes. (Photo Draeger)*

313. *Achaemenian Art.* Large Dish with Lion attacking Bull in the Centre. *5th-4th centuries B.C. Private Collection, Teheran. Chased silver, height 2³/₈ inches, diameter 16³/₈ inches, diameter of central disk 8 inches, weight 2390 grammes. (Photo Draeger)*
The same subject occurs in the Persepolis bas-reliefs.

314. *Achaemenian Art. Persepolis (Fars).* Cup with Twelve Swans' Heads and a Trilingual Inscription in Xerxes' Name. *5th century B.C. Archaeological Museum, Teheran. Granite, height 5⁷/₈ inches. (Photo Dr. A. Razavi)*

315. *Achaemenian Art.* Iranian Horseman. *6th-4th centuries B.C. British Museum, London. Bronze. (Museum Photo)*

316. *Achaemenian Art (Ionian workmanship?). Persepolis (Fars).* Applied Ornament: Two Harnessed Horses Galloping. *5th-4th centuries B.C. Archaeological Museum, Teheran. Bronze, length 10¹/₄ inches. (Museum Photo, Rostamy)*

317. *Achaemenian Art. Hamadan (?).* Applied Ornament: Bactrian Camel at the Flying Gallop. *5th-4th centuries B.C. Private Collection, New York. Gold, length 3³/₈ inches. (Photo Musée Cernuschi)*

318. *Achaemenian Art. Susa (Khuzistan).* Crouching Lion. *5th-4th centuries B.C. Louvre, Paris (Sb 2718). Bronze, length 20⁷/₈ inches, height 11³/₄ inches. (Museum Photo)*

319. *Achaemenian Art.* Ring with Engraved Bezel: Winged Human-headed Bull. *5th-4th centuries B.C. Private Collection, Paris. Gold, diameter ³/₈ of an inch. (Collection Photo)*

320. *Achaemenian Art. Hamadan (?).* Bractea in the form of a Horned Animal. *5th-4th centuries B.C. Archaeological Museum, Teheran. Gold, diameter 2¹/₄ inches, weight 9 grammes. (Museum Photo, Rostamy)*

321. *Achaemenian Art.* Bracelet ending in Two Lions' Heads. *6th-4th centuries B.C. Louvre, Paris (AO 1463). Gold, height 2¹/₂ inches, length 3¹/₈ inches. (Archives Photographiques)*

322. *Achaemenian Art. Susa (Khuzistan).* Ear-rings. *4th century B.C. Louvre, Paris (Sb 2764 and 2765). Gold and cloisonné enamel, outer diameter 1³/₄ inches, thickness 3.2 millimetres. (Archives Photographiques)*

323. *Achaemenian Art.* Ear-ring. On each side, A Bes holding Two Ibexes by the Horns. *5th-4th centuries B.C. Louvre, Paris (AO 3171). Gold, height 2 inches, diameter 2¹/₈ inches. (Museum Photo)*

324. *Achaemenian Art.* Ear-ring adorned with a Head in the Centre. *4th century B.C. Private Collection, Teheran. Gold, height 2³/₈ inches. (Photo Dr. A. Razavi)*

325. *Achaemenian Art. Akhalgori (Caucasus).* Braid Ornament. *4th century B.C. Tiflis Museum. Gold, height 5¹/₈ inches. (After SMIRNOV, 1934, Pl. III)*

326. *Achaemenian Art. Hamadan.* Belt Buckle with Two-Headed Lion. *6th-4th centuries B.C. Private Collection, New York. Gold, height 1¹/₂ inches. (Photo Gérard Franceschi)*

327. *Achaemenian Art. Hamadan (?).* Plaque with Two Horned Winged Lions Confronted. *6th-5th centuries B.C. Metropolitan Museum of Art, New York, Rogers Fund. Gold, height 5¹/₄ inches, width 3³/₈ inches, weight 105 grammes. (Museum Photo)*

328. *Achaemenian Art. Hamadan (?).* Sword Hilt. On the pommel, Two Lions' Heads. On the guard, Two Ibex Heads. *5th century B.C. Archaeological Museum, Teheran. Gold, length 16¹/₄ inches, width 4¹/₈ inches, weight 817 grammes. (Photo Draeger)*

329. *Achaemenian Art.* Cylinder Seal of Darius: The King in his Chariot hunting Lions, with Trilingual Inscription. *About 500 B.C. British Museum, London (No. 89132, acquired in Egypt). (Museum Photo)*

330. *Achaemenian Art.* Cylinder Seal: King before a Fire Altar, with Ahuramazda hovering in the Air. *6th-4th centuries B.C. Bibliothèque Nationale, Paris. (Photo Serge Maire)*

331. *Achaemenian Art.* Cylinder Seal: Medes and Scythians Fighting. *6th-4th centuries B.C. Bibliothèque Nationale, Paris. (Photo Serge Maire)*

332. *Achaemenian Art.* Cylinder Seal: King hunting Lions with Bow and Arrow. *6th-4th centuries B.C. Kunsthistorisches Museum, Vienna. (Photo Porada-Noll)*

333. *Achaemenian Art.* Amphora with Horse Protomes on the Handles. *5th-4th centuries B.C. Private Collection, Basel. Silver, height 6¼ inches, width 6⅛ inches. (Photo Draeger)*

334. *Protohistoric Art. Tepe Sialk, Cemetery B.* Painted Vase with a Long Beak-Spout, detail: Warrior-Hunter. *10th-9th centuries B.C. Private Collection, Lucerne. Painted terracotta. (Photo J. Koch)*
Cf. No. 7.

335. *Protohistoric Art. Hasanlu (Azerbaijan).* Detail of a Kernos: Figure holding a Vase with a Beak-Spout. *9th-8th centuries B.C. Archaeological Museum, Teheran. Red terracotta. (Photo Dr. A. Razavi)*
Cf. No. 24.

336. *Caucasus and South Russia.* Different Types of Horse Bits: (1) Georgia, (2) Kislovodsk (Caucasus), (3) Kiev Region, (4) Rostov. *8th-7th centuries B.C. Bronze. (After* YESSEN, *1953, fig. 2)*

337. *Caucasus and South Russia.* Different Types of Psalia. *8th-7th centuries B.C. From the Museums of* (1) *Novocherkassk,* (2) *Maikop,* (3) *Rostov on the Don,* (4 and 5) *Leningrad (Hermitage),* (6) *Voronezh,* (7) *Novocherkassk,* (8) *Kiev. Bronze. (After* YESSEN, *1953, fig. 3)*

338. *Protohistoric Art. Hasanlu (Azerbaijan).* Broken and Twisted Bit, with Stirrup-shaped Rings. *8th century B.C. Archaeological Museum, Teheran. Bronze, length 8¾ inches. (Photo Dr. A. Razavi)*

339. *Protohistoric Art. Hasanlu (Azerbaijan).* Broken Bit. *9th-8th centuries B.C. Archaeological Museum, Teheran. Bronze, length 10⅝ inches. (Photo Dr. A. Razavi)*

340. *Akkadian Art. Luristan Tomb (Zagros Mountains).* Bowl with a Four-Line Cuneiform Inscription in the name of Naram-Sin, King of Akkad (24th century *B.C.*). *Private Collection, Teheran. Bronze, height 3⅛ inches, diameter 5¼ inches. (Photo Draeger)*

341. *Elamite Art. Luristan Tomb (Zagros Mountains).* Votive Axe with the name of King Shilhak-Inshushinak. *12th century B.C. Private Collection, Teheran. Bronze, length 9 inches. (Photo Hadi)*

342. *Elamite Art. Temple of Choga Zambil, near Susa.* Votive Axe with a Boar on the Socket. Blade inscribed with the name of Untash-Gal. *Mid-13th century B.C. Louvre, Paris. Bronze blade with boar in electrum, length 4¾ inches. (Museum Photo)*

343a-b. *Babylonian Art. Luristan Tombs (Zagros Mountains).* Daggers inscribed with the names of Babylonian Kings. *Late second millennium B.C. British Museum, London. Bronze. (Museum Photo)*

344. *Babylonian Art. Luristan Tomb (Zagros Mountains).* Dagger with Two-Line Inscription on both sides in the name of Adad-shum-usur, son of Kashtiliash, King of Babylon (13th century *B.C.?*). *Private Collection, Teheran. Bronze, length 12⅜ inches, width 1½ inches. (Photo Draeger)*

345. *Protohistoric Art. Maku (Azerbaijan).* Painted Rhyton in the form of a Horse. *8th century B.C. Archaeological Museum, Teheran. Buff-yellow terracotta with red and black designs, height 8 inches, length 11¾ inches. (Photo Gérard Franceschi)*

346. *Protohistoric Art. Maku (Azerbaijan).* Development of the Saddle-Cloth on the Horse Rhyton: Birds and Animals on a flower-patterned Ground. *8th century B.C. Archaeological Museum, Teheran. (After the drawing by G. Haeny)*
Detail of No. 345.

347. *Protohistoric Art. Susa (Khuzistan).* Painted Rhyton in the form of a Horse. *7th century B.C. Archaeological Museum, Teheran. Buff-coloured terracotta with purplish-red designs, height 9 inches, length 11⅜ inches. (Expedition Photo)*

348. *Protohistoric Art. Susa (Khuzistan).* Development of the Saddle-Cloth on the Horse Rhyton: Boars and Birds. *7th century B.C. Archaeological Museum, Teheran. (After the drawing by Mme T. Ghirshman)*
Detail of No. 347.

349. *Protohistoric Art. Tepe Sialk, Cemetery B.* Vase with Long Beak-Spout, decorated with Confronted Animals and Geometric Designs. *10th-9th centuries B.C. Archaeological Museum, Teheran. Painted pottery. (After the drawing by A.P. Hardy)*

350. *Protohistoric Art. Hasanlu (Azerbaijan).* Phalera with Winged Horse in Relief. *8th century B.C. Archaeological Museum, Teheran. Bronze, diameter 6¼ inches. (Museum Photo, Rostamy)*

351. *Protohistoric Art. Susa (Khuzistan).* Fragment of Painted Pottery with Plant and Animal Designs. *7th century B.C. Archaeological Museum, Teheran. (Expedition Photo)*

352. *Urartian Art. Vetulonia (Etruria), Tomba dei Lebeti.* Cauldron Handle, detail: Bearded Head with Two Faces. *8th-7th centuries B.C. Museo Archeologico, Florence. Bronze. (Photo Scala)*

353. *Urartian Workmanship (?). Luristan (?).* Cauldron Handle in the form of a Winged Bird, with Ring. *8th-7th centuries B.C. Archaeological Museum, Teheran. Bronze, height 6⅛ inches, length 7½ inches. (Photo Dr. A. Razavi)*

354. *Urartian Art. Toprak-kale (Armenia).* Plaque representing a Urartian Building. *8th-7th centuries B.C. British Museum, London. Bronze. (Museum Photo)*

355. *Urartian Art. Toprak-kale (Armenia).* Cauldron Lug in the form of a Bull's Head. *8th-7th centuries B.C. British Museum, London. Bronze. (Museum Photo)*

356a. *Urartian Art. Vetulonia (Etruria), Tomba dei Lebeti.* Cauldron Handle in the form of a Winged, Two-faced, Half-length Figure (outer side). *8th-7th centuries B.C. Museo Archeologico, Florence. Bronze. (Photo Scala)*
Cf. No. 352 and No. 356b.

356b. *Urartian Art. Vetulonia (Etruria), Tomba dei Lebeti.* Cauldron Handle in the form of a Winged, Two-faced, Half-length Figure (inner side). *8th-7th centuries B.C. Museo Archeologico, Florence. Bronze. (Photo Scala)*
Cf. No. 352 and No. 356a.

357. *Urartian Art (?).* Lamp Stand: Statuette of a Woman on a Tripod ending in Birds' Heads. *8th-7th centuries B.C. Erlangen Museum. Bronze, height 9³/₄ inches. (After* FRANKFORT, *1954, Pl.* 117*)*

358. *Urartian Art (?). Transcaucasia.* Seated Goddess, in front view, between Two Horse Protomes. *8th-7th centuries B.C. British Museum, London. Bronze. (Museum Photo)*

359. *Urartian Art (?).* Warrior Figurine. *8th-7th centuries B.C. Louvre, Paris. Bronze, height 3³/₄ inches. (Photo Draeger)*

360. *Urartian Art (?).* Statuette of a Prince wearing a Gold Pectoral. *8th-7th centuries B.C. Museum of Fine Arts, Boston. Amber and gold, height 9¹/₂ inches. (Museum Photo)*

361. *Urartian Art. Van (Armenia).* Cauldron Handle with Two Winged 'Sirens.' *8th-7th centuries B.C. Private Collection, Paris. Bronze. (After* MAXWELL-HYSLOP, *1956, Pl. XXVI)*

362. *Scythian Art. Kelermes (Kuban).* Applied Ornament in the form of a Lioness (?). *6th century B.C. Hermitage, Leningrad. Chased gold with amber and enamel inlays, length c. 12 inches. (Museum Photo)*

363. *Scythian Art. Kostromskaya Stanitza (Kuban).* Gorytus Ornament with Stags. *6th century B.C. Hermitage, Leningrad. Gold. (After* BOROVKA, *1928, Pl. 2)*

364. *Scythian Art. Kelermes (Kuban).* Iron Sword with Gold Scabbard. *6th century B.C. Hermitage, Leningrad. Iron and gold. (Museum Photo)*

365. *Scythian Art. Kelermes (Kuban).* Gold-plated Iron Axe. *6th century B.C. Hermitage, Leningrad. Iron and gold. (Museum Photo)*

366a. *Scythian Art. Kelermes (Kuban).* Mirror. *6th century B.C. Hermitage, Leningrad. Silver gilt. (Museum Photo)*

366b-c. *Scythian Art. Temir Gora, near Kerch (Crimea).* Harness Pieces. *7th century B.C. Hermitage, Leningrad. Bone carvings. (Museum Photo)*

367. Map of the Kingdom of Urartu.

368. *Neo-Babylonian Art. Ur (Mesopotamia).* Sarcophagus. *7th century B.C. British Museum, London. Bronze. (Museum Photo)*

369a. *Assyrian Art (?). Ziwiyeh, east of Sakkiz (Kurdistan).* Edge of a Sarcophagus with Engraved Design. *7th century B.C. Metropolitan Museum of Art, New York. Bronze. (Museum Photo)*

369b. *Assyrian Art (?). Ziwiyeh, east of Sakkiz (Kurdistan).* Plaque of a Sarcophagus with Engraved Design: Ibex standing on a Marguerite. *7th century B.C. Metropolitan Museum of Art, New York. Bronze, length 26³/₄ inches, width 3⁵/₈ inches. (Museum Photo)*

370. *Toprak-kale (Armenia).* Statuette of a Figure wearing a Pectoral. *8th-7th centuries B.C. Staatliche Museen, Berlin. Bronze, height 14³/₄ inches. (Museum Photo)*

371. *Urartian Art. Toprak-kale (Armenia).* Sphinx forming part of a Throne. *8th-7th centuries B.C. British Museum, London. Bronze. (Museum Photo)*

372. *Protohistoric Art. Hasanlu (Azerbaijan).* Plaque with Stag's Head in Relief. *8th century B.C. Archaeological Museum, Teheran. Bronze. (Museum Photo, Rostamy)*

373. *Etruscan Art. Regolini-Galassi Tomb, Caere (Etruria).* Pectoral with Designs on Eighteen Registers. *8th-7th centuries B.C. Museo Gregoriano, Rome. Gold. (After* MUHLESTEIN, *1929, Pl. 56)*

374. *Scythian Art. Dalboki (Bulgaria).* Pectoral with Animal and Geometric Designs. *5th century B.C. Ashmolean Museum, Oxford. Gold. (Museum Photo)*

375. *Thracian Art. Trebenishchei (Bulgaria).* Pectoral. *Third quarter of the 6th century B.C. Sofia Museum. Gold. (After* JACOBSTHAL, *1956, fig. 302)*

376. *Composite Art of Western Asia. Ziwiyeh, east of Sakkiz (Kurdistan).* Pectoral. *Late 7th century B.C. Archaeological Museum, Teheran. Gold, height and width 13 inches, weight 275 grammes. (Museum Photo, Rostamy, and Photos Dr. A. Razavi)*
Cf. No. 137.

377. *Composite Art of Western Asia. Ziwiyeh, east of Sakkiz (Kurdistan).* Fragmentary Pectoral (?) with Processions of Hybrid Beings moving towards Sacred Trees. *Late 7th century B.C. (A) Archaeological Museum, Teheran. (B) Metropolitan Museum of Art, New York, Dick Fund, 1954. Gold, 9 fragments (Teheran), weight 55 grammes; 3 registers (New York), width 5¹/₄ inches, length 10⁷/₈ inches. (Photos Draeger and Metropolitan Museum)*
Reconstruction of the pectoral.

378. *Composite Art of Western Asia. Ziwiyeh, east of Sakkiz (Kurdistan).* Plaques of a Shoulder Piece (?) with Processions of Hybrid Animals. *Late 7th century B.C. Private Collection, New York. Gold. (Photos Roman Ghirshman and Draeger)*
Reconstruction of the work as a whole.

379. *Composite Art of Western Asia. Ziwiyeh, east of Sakkiz (Kurdistan).* Fragments of a Pectoral (?) with Processions of Hybrid Animals moving towards Sacred Trees. *Late 7th century B.C. Private Collection, New York; Royal Ontario Museum, Toronto; Cincinnati Art Museum, and Private Collections, New York. Gold, length 10⁷/₈ inches, height 11¹/₂ inches. (Photo Draeger)*
Reconstruction of the work as a whole.

380a. *Scythian Art. Mount Beshtau (Caucasus).* Half-moon Shaped Pectoral. *8th-7th centuries B.C. Piatigorsk Museum. Bronze. (After* YESSEN, *1952, fig. 13)*

380b. *Art of Luristan.* Pectoral adorned with Concentric Circles with a Human Face in the Centre. *8th-7th centuries B.C. Private Collection, Teheran. Bronze, width 9 inches. (Photo Draeger)*

381. *Urartian Art. Ziwiyeh (Kurdistan).* Cauldron Lugs in the form of Griffin and Lion Protomes. *Late 7th century B.C. Archaeological Museum, Teheran. Gold griffin, height* 3 $^1/_8$ *inches, width* 2 $^1/_2$ *inches, weight* 59 *grammes; gold lion, height* 2 $^3/_8$ *inches, width* 2 $^3/_4$ *inches, weight* 57 *grammes. (Photo Draeger)*

382. *Urartian Art. Palestrina (ancient Praeneste, in Latium), Barberini Tomb.* Cauldron with Lion and Griffin Protomes. *8th–7th centuries B.C. Villa Giulia, Rome. Bronze. (After* MUHLESTEIN, *1929, Pl. 100)*

383. *Art of North-western Iran. Ziwiyeh (Kurdistan).* Plaque with a Tree of Life and Two Confronted Lions with a Single Head. *Late 7th century B.C. Metropolitan Museum of Art, New York, Pulitzer Bequest Fund, 1954. Gold, height* 8 $^5/_8$ *inches, width* 5 *and* 6 *inches, weight* 198 *grammes. (Museum Photo)*

384. *Art of Luristan. Luristan Tomb (Zagros Mountains).* Round Pinhead with Mask of the Goddess Ashi (?) surmounted by Two Lions with a Single Head. *8th–7th centuries B.C. Private Collection, Paris. Bronze, diameter* 4 $^1/_2$ *inches. (Collection Photo)* Cf. No. 62.

385. *Art of Luristan. Luristan Tomb (Zagros Mountains).* Idol with Confronted Animals. Zoomorphic Composition, detail. *8th–7th centuries B.C. Louvre, Paris (AO 20490), acquired* 1958 *from the Coiffard Collection. (Museum Photo)* Cf. No. 53.

386. *Scythian Art. Ziwiyeh (Kurdistan).* Belt-end (?) with Felines and Birds' Heads, detail. *Late 7th century B.C. University Museum, Philadelphia. Gold, length* 3 *inches, width* 1 *inch. (Museum Photo)*

387. *Median Art. Oxus Treasure (Bactria).* Scabbard, detail: Hunting with Bow and Arrow. *7th–6th centuries B.C. British Museum, London. Gold. (Museum Photo)* Cf. No. 118.

388. *Art of Luristan. Luristan Tomb (Zagros Mountains).* Belt, detail: Hunting with Bow and Arrow. *8th–7th centuries B.C. Louvre, Paris (AO 17267). Bronze, length* 20 *inches. (Photo Tel-Vigneau)*

389. *Art of Luristan. Luristan Tomb (Zagros Mountains).* Archers' Rings for bending their Bows. *8th–7th centuries B.C. Archaeological Museum, Teheran, and Private Collection, Teheran. (Photo Roman Ghirshman)*

390. Types of Bows: (A) Assyrian, (B) from Yrzi, (C) from Turkestan (later Middle Ages), (D) Scythian, (E) Sassanian. *(After* F.E. BROWN, *1937, fig. 1 and fig. 3)*

391. *Art of Luristan. Luristan Tomb (Zagros Mountains).* Vase in the form of a Human Figure holding a Vase. *8th–7th centuries B.C. Private Collection, Teheran. Common earthenware, height c.* 8 *inches. (After* GODARD, *1938, fig. 182)*

392. *Scythian Art (?). Ziwiyeh (Kurdistan).* Lion's Head. Centrepiece of a Votive Shield or Lug of a Vase (?). *Late 7th century B.C. Private Collection, Paris. Yellow terracotta (hollow), moulded and burnished. Height* 2 *inches. (Photo Dr. A. Razavi)*

393. *Greek Art. Prinias (Crete).* Lion's Head from a Votive Shield. *Late Geometric style. Private Collection, Berlin. Painted terracotta, length* 3 $^5/_8$ *inches. (After* KUNZE, *1931, Pl. 52a)*

394. *Iranian Art. Ziwiyeh (Kurdistan).* Rhyton in the form of a Duck. *Late 7th century B.C. Archaeological Museum, Teheran. Glazed terracotta, yellow, white and black, with traces of green. Height* 10 *inches, length* 13 $^3/_8$ *inches. (Photo Istituto Italiano per il Medio ed Estremo Oriente)*

395. *Iranian Art. Ziwiyeh (Kurdistan).* Rhyton with Saiga's Head. *Late 7th century B.C. Archaeological Museum, Teheran. Polychrome glazed terracotta, height* 8 $^5/_8$ *inches, length* 13 $^3/_8$ *inches. (Museum Photo, Rostamy)*

396. *Iranian Art. Ziwiyeh (Kurdistan).* Rhyton with Saiga's Head. *Late 7th century B.C. Archaeological Museum, Teheran. Glazed terracotta, length* 6 $^1/_2$ *inches. (Photo Dr. A. Razavi)*

397. *Iranian Art. Ziwiyeh (Kurdistan).* Rhyton with Moufflon's Head. *Late 7th century B.C. Archaeological Museum, Teheran. Glazed terracotta, diameter* 6 $^7/_8$ *inches, length* 11 *inches. Damaged. (Museum Photo, Rostamy)*

398. *Assyrian Art. Ziwiyeh (Kurdistan).* Small Jar. On the shoulder, Ibexes flanking a Star. Above them, Designs running up to the Neck. *7th century B.C. Archaeological Museum, Teheran. Glazed terracotta, green, blue and maroon. Height* 14 $^1/_2$ *inches, diameter of mouth* 4 $^1/_4$ *inches. (Photo Istituto Italiano per il Medio ed Estremo Oriente)*

399. *Iranian Art. North-western Iran.* Gazelle's Head Rhyton. Engraved Design between the Horns: Sacred Tree flanked by Ibexes with Birds on the Branches. *8th–7th centuries B.C. Private Collection, Teheran. Bronze, height* 5 $^7/_8$ *inches, diameter* 4 $^1/_8$ *inches. (Photo Hadi)* The eyes and eyebrows were originally inlaid.

400. *Iranian Art. Luristan Tomb (Zagros Mountains).* Ear-ring with Gazelle's Head. *8th–7th centuries B.C. Private Collection, Teheran. Gold, height* 1 *inch. (Photo Hadi)*

401. *Local Art. North-western Iran.* Lion's Head Rhyton. *7th century B.C. Art Market, Teheran. Bronze, height* 5 $^7/_8$ *inches. (Photo Dr A. Razavi)*

402. *Median Art. Kalar Dasht.* Rhyton in the form of an Animal's Horn, ending in the Head of a Gazelle (?). *7th–6th centuries B.C. Archaeological Museum, Teheran. Red terracotta, length* 12 $^1/_4$ *inches. (Museum Photo, Rostamy)*

403. *Assyrian Art.* Bas-Relief representing a Banquet. The figures are holding up goblets in the form of animal-head rhytons, which are thus proved to have been in use in Assyria as early as the 8th century B.C. *(After* G. RAWLINSON, *1879, I, p. 580)*

404. *Iranian Art. North-western Iran.* Gazelle's Head Rhyton. *8th–7th centuries B.C. Private Collection, Teheran. Bronze, height* 5 $^7/_8$ *inches, diameter* 4 $^1/_8$ *inches. (Photo Draeger)* Detail of No. 399.

405. *Etruscan Art. Chiusi (Etruria).* Jug with a Woman's Head. *Mid-6th century B.C. (?). Antiquarium, Berlin. Black terracotta, height 8⁵/₄ inches. (After the catalogue of the Etruscan Exhibition, Louvre, 1955, fig. 6, No. 47)*

406a. *Iranian Art of Luristan. Island of Samos.* Vase with Long Beak-Spout. *8th-7th centuries B.C. Samos Museum. Bronze. (After MAXWELL-HYSLOP, 1956, Pl. XXXIV, fig. 4)*

406b. *Iranian Art of Luristan. Kephalia, near Knossos (Crete).* Pendant. *8th-7th centuries B.C. Archaeological Museum, Heraklion. Bronze. (After MARINATOS, 1938, fig. 16)*

407. *Greek Art.* Boeotian Fibula engraved with Human Figures. *Late 8th century B.C. Late Geometric style. Private Collection, Philadelphia. Silver. (After HAMPE, 1936, Pl. 8, No. 135)*

408. *Greek Art.* Fibula engraved with Animal Designs. *Late 8th century B.C. Late Geometric style. Antiquarium, Munich. Silver. (After HAMPE, 1936, Pl. 8, No. 103)*

409. *Greek Art.* Attic Bowl with Pyrrhic Scenes. *Late 8th century B.C. National Museum, Copenhagen. Terracotta. (Museum Photo)*

410. *Greek Art. Thebes (Boeotia).* Painted Amphora, detail. *About 700 B.C. National Museum, Athens. Painted pottery. (After HAMPE, 1936, Pl. 17, No. 1)*

411a. *Protohistoric Iranian Art. Tepe Sialk, Cemetery B.* Libation Vase. *10th-9th centuries B.C. Archaeological Museum, Teheran. Painted pottery. (Photo Roman Ghirshman)*
Introduction of clear spaces (necklets, belts) in the animal's body.

411b. *Protohistoric Iranian Art. Tepe Sialk, Cemetery B.* Libation Vase. *10th-9th centuries B.C. Archaeological Museum, Teheran. Painted pottery. (Expedition Photo)*
Fixture of the painted design: animals on the lower part of the body of the vase, with geometric patterns running up to the neck.

412a-b. *Protohistoric Iranian Art. Tepe Sialk, Cemetery B.* Potsherds with Dancing Warriors and Rider on a Winged Horse. *10th-9th centuries B.C. (A) Louvre, Paris (AO 19471). (B) Archaeological Museum, Teheran. (After the drawings in colour by A.P. Hardy)*

413. *Greek Art. Aegina.* Potsherd with Two Stags Fighting. *Late 8th century B.C. Painted pottery, height 2³/₄ inches. (After KRAIKER, 1951, Pl. 10, 182)*

414. *Art of Luristan. Luristan Tomb (Zagros Mountains).* Situla with Grazing Stag. *8th-7th centuries B.C. Art Market, Teheran. Bronze. (After GODARD, 1938, fig. 180)*

415. *Greek Art under Oriental Influence. Analatos (Greece).* Painted Hydria. On the body, Antithetic Group of Lions with Raised Forepaw and Grazing Stags. *Before 720 B.C. National Museum, Athens. Painted pottery, height 20³/₄ inches. (After F. MATZ, 1950, Pl. 190)*

416. *Protohistoric Iranian Art. Tepe Sialk, Cemetery B.* Vase with Long Beak-Spout. On the body, Roaring Lion with Raised Forepaw. *10th-9th centuries B.C. Private Collection, Lucerne. Yellow terracotta with purplish red designs. Height 7¹/₂ inches, length (with spout) 11³/₄ inches. (Collection Photo)*

417. *Greek Art. Aphrati (Crete).* Pyxis with Scroll Designs ending in Animals' Heads. *Second quarter of 7th century B.C. Painted pottery. (After F. MATZ, 1950, Pl. 165a)*

418. *Art of Luristan. Luristan Tomb (Zagros Mountains).* Helmet with Scroll Designs. *8th-7th centuries B.C. Private Collection, Teheran. Bronze, height 11³/₄ inches, diameter 8¹/₄ inches. Designs in repoussé. (Photo Draeger)*

419. *Greek Art. Aphrati (Crete).* Cauldron with Griffin Lugs. *660-640 B.C. Painted terracotta, height 8¹/₄ inches. (After F. MATZ, 1950, Pl. 165b, p. 259)*

420. *Greek Art. Olympia.* Disk with Woman's Face. *Late 7th century B.C. Berlin Museum. Bronze. (After F. MATZ, 1950, Pl. 93a)*

421. *Art of Luristan. Luristan Tomb (Zagros Mountains).* Round Pinhead with the Mask of a Goddess. *8th-7th centuries B.C. Private Collection, Paris. Bronze, height 10⁷/₈ inches, diameter 5¹/₈ inches. (Photo Istituto Italiano per il Medio ed Estremo Oriente)*

422. *Greek Art. Olympia.* Band of a Shield with Mythological Scenes. *Last third of the 7th century B.C. Olympia Museum. Bronze. (After KUNZE, 1950, Pl. 73, type V)*

423. *Art of Luristan. Luristan Tomb (Zagros Mountains).* Sheathing Plaque of a Quiver with Designs on Four Registers. (1) Hunter in a Chariot. (2) Two Figures grappling with a Lion. (3) Two Lions attacking an Ibex. (4) Banquet Scene, placed on a Crouching Lion. *8th-7th centuries B.C. Private Collection, Paris. Bronze, length 23¹/₂ inches, width 5¹/₂ inches. (Collection Photo)*

424. *Greek Art.* Painted Vase with Winged Demon carrying off the Dead. *Berlin Museum. Painted pottery. (After MALTEN, 1914, fig. 28)*

425. *Greco-Persian Art. Xanthos (Lycia).* Harpy Tomb, north side: Offering Scene between Symmetrical Harpies. *About 500 B.C. British Museum, London. Height 40 inches. (Museum Photo)*

426. *Greek Art.* Painted Lekythos with Thanatos carrying off a Dead Man. *British Museum, London. (After MALTEN, 1914, fig. 36)*

427. *Greek Art. Kamiros (Rhodes).* Cauldron Handle in the form of a Griffin. *7th-6th centuries B.C. British Museum, London. Bronze, height 9 inches. (Museum Photo)*

428. *Iranian Art (?). Susa (Khuzistan).* Griffin's Head. *8th-7th centuries B.C. Louvre, Paris (Sb 2890). Bronze, height 2³/₄ inches. (Photo Draeger)*

429. *Etruscan Art. Tarquinia (Etruria).* Centrepiece of a Votive Shield: Head of Achelous. *Antiquarium, Berlin. Bronze. (After MUHLESTEIN, 1919, fig. 145)*

430. *Art of Luristan.* Centrepiece of a Small Round Votive Shield: Human Face. *8th-7th centuries B.C. Art Market, Teheran. Bronze, diameter of shield 11³/₄ inches. (Photo Vahé)*

431. *Greek Art.* Detail of a Painted Cup: Gorgon's Head. *About 600 B.C. British Museum, London. Painted pottery. (After F. MATZ, 1950, Pl. 231a) (Museum Photo)*

432. *Greek Art. Idaean Cave (Crete).* Design on a Shield: Lion Hunt, anticipating the theme of the 'Parthian Arrow.' *7th-6th centuries B.C. Archaeological Museum, Heraklion. Bronze. (After* KUNZE, *1931, Beilage* 1)

433. *Greco-Parthian Art. Susa (Khuzistan).* Fertility Goddess. *2nd-1st centuries B.C. Louvre, Paris (Sb* 3800*). Terracotta, height* 7⁷/₈ *inches, width* 6⁵/₈ *inches (Museum Photo)*

434. *Etruscan Art. Marsiliana d'Albegna (Etruria).* Statuette of a Naked Goddess squeezing a Breast with one hand and catching the Milk with a Bowl held in the Other. *7th-6th centuries B.C. (?). Museo Archeologico, Florence. Ivory. (After* MUHLESTEIN, *1929, fig.* 50)

435. *Protohistoric Iranian Art. Luristan Tomb (Zagros Mountains).* Bracelet with Animal Designs. *8th-7th centuries B.C. Louvre, Paris (AO* 20136*). Gold, height* 3³/₄ *inches. (Museum Photo)*

436. *Etruscan Art.* Belt Buckle adorned with a Human Head and Two Lions' Heads. *7th-6th centuries B.C. Museo Archeologico, Florence. Bronze. (Museum Photo)*

437. *Etruscan Art. Vetulonia (Etruria).* Bracelet adorned with Heads. *7th-6th centuries B.C. Museo Archeologico, Florence. Gold. (After* MUHLESTEIN, *1929, fig.* 85)

438. *Scythian Art. Pazyryk (Altai).* Bridle Ornament in the form of a Stag. *4th-3rd centuries B.C. Hermitage, Leningrad. Wood and leather, length* 4 *inches. (Photo A. Boulgakov)*

439. *Scythian Art. Pazyryk (Altai).* Saddle Ornament: Tiger attacking an Elk. *4th-3rd centuries B.C. Hermitage, Leningrad. Leather, length* 13 *inches. (Photo A. Boulgakov)*

440. *Greco-Persian Art. Eregli (Dascylion), Asia Minor.* Bas-Relief with Scene of Sacrifice. *Late* 5th *century B.C. Archaeological Museum, Istanbul. Height* 26³/₈ *inches. (Museum Photo)*

441. *Greco-Persian Art. Eregli (Dascylion), Asia Minor.* Bas-Relief with Procession of Mounted Women. *Late* 5th *century B.C. Archaeological Museum, Istanbul. (Museum Photo)*

442. *Greco-Persian Art. Çavuch Köi, near Panderma (Asia Minor).* Funerary Stele with Hunting and Banquet Scenes. *Late* 4th *century B.C. Archaeological Museum, Istanbul (No.* 1054*). White marble, height* 42¹/₂ *inches, length* 27 *inches, thickness* 4¹/₂ *inches. (Museum Photo)*

443. *Achaemenian Art. Persepolis (Fars).* Bas-Relief from the Treasury: Royal Audience, detail. *6th-5th centuries B.C. Archaeological Museum, Teheran. (Museum Photo)*

444. *Greco-Persian Art. Xanthos (Lycia).* Harpy Tomb: Servant offering a Cock to the Governor seated on his Throne. *About* 500 *B.C. British Museum, London. (Museum Photo)*

445. *Greco-Persian Art. Xanthos (Lycia).* Funerary Bas-Relief: Persian Personage riding in a Chariot to his Last Resting Place. *About* 470 *B.C. British Museum, London. (Museum Photo)*

446. *Greco-Persian Art. Cemetery of Sidon (Phoenicia).* Sarcophagus of the Satrap: Dead Man led to his Last Resting Place, with Hunting Scene evoking his Exploits in his Lifetime. *Mid-4th century B.C. Archaeological Museum, Istanbul. Height* 57 *inches, length* 112 *inches. (Photo Bildarchiv Foto, Marburg)*

447. *Greco-Persian Art. Royal Cemetery of Sidon (Phoenicia).* Sarcophagus of Alexander: Hunters slaying a Panther. *4th century B.C. Archaeological Museum, Istanbul. Polychrome marble, length of sarcophagus* 10 *feet* 5 *inches, width* 5 *feet* 6 *inches, height* 4 *feet* 1 *inch. (Photo Alinari)*

448. *Achaemenian Art. Sidon (Phoenicia).* Capital with Two Bull Protomes. *5th-4th centuries B.C. Beirut Museum. (Museum Photo)*

449. *Hellenistic Art. Delos, House of the Trident.* Capital with Bull Protomes. *2nd century B.C. (Photo École Française d'Athènes)*

450. *Hellenistic Art. Delos, Sanctuary of the Bulls.* Capital with Bull Protomes. *(Photo École Française d'Athènes)*

451. *Hellenistic Art. Delos, House B.* Capitals with Bull Protomes. *(Photo École Française d'Athènes)*

452. *Hellenistic Art. Delos, Portico of Antigonus.* Bull Capital. *Second half of* 3rd *century B.C. (Photo École Française d'Athènes)*

453. *Hellenistic Art. Island of Thasos.* Capital in the form of a Winged Horse. *(Photo École Française d'Athènes)*

454. *Greco-Persian Art. Salamis (Cyprus).* Capital from the Palace of Evagoras I (411-374 B.C.): Caryatids between Bull Protomes. *4th century B.C. British Museum, London. (Museum Photo)*

455. *Hellenistic Art. Paphos (Cyprus), Sanctuary of Aphrodite.* Pinhead in the form of a Capital with Ram Protomes. *3rd century B.C. British Museum, London. Gold-plated bronze. (After* JACOBSTHAL, *1956, fig.* 314)

456. *Greco-Persian Art. Labranda (Asia Minor).* Sphinx. *4th century B.C. (After* VON DER OSTEN, *1956, Pl.* 67) Decorated the antae of a building on the upper terrace of the sacred enclosure of the city, famous for the cult of Zeus Labrandeus.

457. *Achaemenian Art.* Head of a Prince. *5th century B.C. Private Collection, Brussels. Limestone, height* 2³/₄ *inches. (Collection Photo)*

458. *Greco-Persian Art (?). Sarnath (India).* Lion Capital from a Pillar of Asoka (242-236 B.C.). *National Museum, New Delhi. Polished sandstone, height* 8 *feet. (After* BACHHOFER, *Pl.* 5)

459. *Indian Art. Amaravati (India).* Pilaster with Winged Lions. *3rd century A.D. Musée Guimet, Paris. Stone. (Museum Photo)*

460. *Indian Art. Begram-Kapici (Afghanistan).* Carved Ivory Panel. *1st-2nd centuries A.D. Kabul Museum. Ivory. (Photo Délégation Archéologique Française en Afghanistan)*

461. *Indian Art. Mathura (India).* Capital with Addorsed Animals. *1st century A.D. Mathura Museum. Sandstone, height* 19³/₄ *inches. (After* VON DER OSTEN, *1956, Pl.* 112)

462. *Achaemenian Art. Seven Brothers Barrow (Kuban).* Rhyton with a Winged Ibex Protome. *5th century B.C. Hermitage, Leningrad. Silver, length* 19³/₄ *inches. (After* SMIRNOV, 1909, *fig.* 15*)*

463. *Scythian Art. Chertomlyk (South Russia).* Sword Hilt. On the pommel, Two Heifers' Heads. On the haft, Mounted Hunters pursuing Gazelles. *First half of the 4th century B.C. Hermitage, Leningrad. Gold hilt of an iron sword. (Museum Photo)*

464. *Median Art. Oxus Treasure (Bactria).* Sword Sheath with Scenes of a Royal Hunt with Spear and Bow. *7th-6th centuries B.C. British Museum, London. Gold, length* 10⁷/₈ *inches. (Museum Photo)*

465. *Greco-Scythian Art. Karagodenashk (South Russia).* Rhyton with an Investiture Scene. *4th-3rd centuries B.C. Hermitage, Leningrad. Silver. (After* ROSTOVTZEFF, 1931-32, *Pl.* LVIIa*)*

466. *Persian Art. Pazyryk (Altai).* Carpet adorned with Rows of Four-Pointed Stars in the Centre and Two Processions in the Borders. *4th-3rd centuries B.C. Hermitage, Leningrad. Wool,* 74¹/₂ *by* 78³/₄ *inches. (Museum Photo)*

467. *Persian Art. Pazyryk (Altai).* Detail of a Carpet: Horseman with Border of Griffins. *4th-3rd centuries B.C. Hermitage, Leningrad. Wool, detail* 5⁷/₈ *by* 4¹/₄ *inches. (Photo A. Boulgakov)*

468. *Persian Art. Pazyryk (Altai).* Detail of a Wall Hanging: Women before an Altar. *4th-3rd centuries B.C. Hermitage, Leningrad. Wool, detail about* 5 *by* 2¹/₂ *inches. (Photo A. Boulgakov)*

469. *Persian Art. Pazyryk (Altai).* Detail of a Wall Hanging: Frieze of Lions Passant. *4th-3rd centuries B.C. Hermitage, Leningrad. Wool. (After* RUDENKO, 1953, *fig.* 191*)*

470. *Persian Art. Pazyryk (Altai).* Applied Ornaments on a Felt Carpet: Lions' Heads with Ruffled Manes. *4th-3rd centuries B.C. Hermitage, Leningrad. Leather Cutouts. (Museum Photo)*

471. *Persian Art. Pazyryk (Altai).* Saddle-Cloth. *4th-3rd centuries B.C. Hermitage, Leningrad. Felt with painted leather cut-outs. (Museum Photo)*

472. *Scythian Art. Pazyryk (Altai).* Saddle-Cloth, detail: Griffin attacking an Ibex. *4th-3rd centuries B.C. Hermitage, Leningrad. Felt, detail about* 17 *inches square. (Photo A. Boulgakov)*

473a. *Art of the Nomads. Pazyryk (Altai).* Harness Ornament with a Human Face. *4th-3rd centuries B.C. Hermitage, Leningrad. Painted leather. (Museum Photo)*

473b. *Art of the Nomads. Pazyryk (Altai).* Harness Pendant with a Human Face. *4th-3rd centuries B.C. Hermitage, Leningrad. Wood carving. (Museum Photo)*

473c. *Art of the Nomads. Pazyryk (Altai).* Horse's Head surmounted by the Mask of an Elk. *4th-3rd centuries B.C. Hermitage, Leningrad. Felt, leather, copper and gold. (Museum Photo)*

473d. *Art of the Nomads. Pazyryk (Altai).* Arrow Shaft. *4th-3rd centuries B.C. Hermitage, Leningrad. Painted wood. (After* RUDENKO, 1953, *Pl.* 119*)*
Design similar to that on the wooden columns of the Treasury at Persepolis.

474. *Scythian Art. Pazyryk (Altai).* Stag's Head in the Jaws of a Griffin. *4th-3rd centuries B.C. Hermitage, Leningrad. Wood and leather, height* 10¹/₂ *inches. (Photo A. Boulgakov)*

475. *Scythian Art. Pazyryk (Altai).* Tattooings on the Body of a Chieftain buried in Barrow 2. *4th-3rd centuries B.C. Hermitage, Leningrad. (After* RUDENKO, 1953, *Pl.* 80-81*)*
Designs deriving from animal forms.

476. *Iranian Art of Luristan.* Two Male Statuettes with Tattooings on the Body. *8th-7th centuries B.C. Art Market, Teheran. Bronze, height* 5¹/₂ *inches. (Photo Roman Ghirshman)*

477. *Scythian Art. Pazyryk (Altai).* Tattooings on the Right Arm of the Chieftain buried in Barrow 2: Fantastic Animal, detail. *4th-3rd centuries B.C. Hermitage, Leningrad. Size of detail,* 9¹/₂ *by* 7 *inches. (Photo A. Boulgakov)*

478. *Achaemenian Art. Hamadan (?).* Dish with a Flying Eagle in the Centre. On the edge, Small, Olive-shaped Bosses. *5th-4th centuries B.C. Private Collection, New York. Gold, height* 1¹/₂ *inches, diameter* 12¹/₄ *inches, weight* 1870 *grammes. (Photo Rostamy)*

479. *Protohistoric Art. Tepe Sialk, Cemetery B.* Vase with a Long Beak-Spout. *10th-9th centuries B.C. Louvre, Paris (AO* 17912*). Bronze, height* 6⁷/₈ *inches. (Photo Archives d'Art et d'Histoire)*

480. *Protohistoric Art. Tepe Sialk, Cemetery B.* Vase with Long Beak-Spout, painted with Geometric and Animal Designs. Above the spout, Horse Protome. *10th-9th centuries B.C. Private Collection, Lucerne. Painted terracotta, height* 6⁷/₈ *inches, length* 15⁷/₈ *inches. (Collection Photo)*

481-482. *Protohistoric Art. Tepe Sialk, Cemetery B.* Cup and Bottle with Geometric Designs. *10th-9th centuries B.C. Archaeological Museum, Teheran. Painted terracotta; height of cup* 2³/₈ *inches, diameter* 3³/₈ *inches; height of bottle* 6¹/₈ *inches. (Expedition Photo)*

483. *Protohistoric Art. Tepe Sialk, Cemetery B.* Bird Rhyton. *10th-9th centuries B.C. Louvre, Paris. Painted terracotta, height* 4¹/₂ *inches, width* 4¹/₄ *inches. (Photo Roman Ghirshman)*

484. *Protohistoric Art. Tepe Sialk, Cemetery B.* Vase in the form of an Askos. *10th-9th centuries B.C. Archaeological Museum, Teheran. Painted terracotta, height* 3¹/₈ *inches, length* 4¹/₄ *inches, width* 2³/₄ *inches. (Photo Roman Ghirshman)*

485-486. *Protohistoric Art. Tepe Sialk, Cemetery B.* Cylinder Seals: Horseman fighting a Dragon and Animals Fighting. *10th-9th centuries B.C. Archaeological Museum, Teheran and Louvre, Paris. Green stone, height* 1¹/₁₆ *inches and* ¹⁵/₁₆ *of an inch (Photo Roman Ghirshman)*

487. *Protohistoric Art. Khurvin (50 miles north-west of Teheran).* Vase in the form of a Shoe. *9th-8th centuries B.C. Private Collection, Paris. Terracotta, length* 3 1/2 *inches, width* 1 1/2 *inches. (Photo Dr. A. Razavi)*

488. *Protohistoric Art. Khurvin (50 miles north-west of Teheran).* Ear-rings. *9th-8th centuries B.C. Private Collection, Teheran. Gold, diameter* 1 1/8 *inches. (Photo Dr. A. Razavi)*

489. *Protohistoric Art. Khurvin (50 miles north-west of Teheran).* Pin with Sheath. *9th-8th centuries B.C. Private Collection, Teheran. Bronze pin with gold sheath, length* 3 5/8 *inches. (Photo Dr. A. Razavi)*

490. *Protohistoric Art. Luristan Tomb (Zagros Mountains).* Round Pinhead. *8th-7th centuries B.C. Art Market, Teheran. Bronze, diameter 6 inches. (Photo Roman Ghirshman)*

491. *Protohistoric Art. Luristan Tomb (Zagros Mountains).* Round Pinhead. *8th-7th centuries B.C. Louvre, Paris, formerly Coiffard Collection. Bronze, diameter* 3 3/4 *inches. (Photo Istituto Italiano per il Medio ed Estremo Oriente)*

492. *Protohistoric Art. Luristan Tomb (Zagros Mountains).* Stamp Seal in the form of a Seated Figure. *8th-7th centuries B.C. Private Collection, Teheran. Bronze, height* 1 1/4 *inches. (Photo Dr. A. Razavi)*

493. *Protohistoric Art. Luristan Tomb (Zagros Mountains).* Tool with Kneeling Figure. *8th-7th centuries B.C. Private Collection, Teheran. Bronze, height* 4 1/8 *inches. (Photo Dr. A. Razavi)*

494-495. *Protohistoric Art. Luristan Tomb (Zagros Mountains).* Two Figurines of Mourners. *8th-7th centuries B.C. Private Collection, Teheran. Bronze, height 2 inches and* 2 1/8 *inches. (Photo Hadi)*

496. *Protohistoric Art. Luristan Tomb (Zagros Mountains).* Pendant with Two Animal Protomes. *8th-7th centuries B.C. Private Collection, Paris. Bronze, length* 3 1/2 *inches. (Collection Photo)*

497. *Protohistoric Art. Luristan Tomb (Zagros Mountains).* Votive Bit. *8th-7th centuries B.C. Louvre, Paris, formerly Coiffard Collection. Bronze, height 7 inches. (Photo Istituto Italiano per il Medio ed Estremo Oriente)*

498. *Protohistoric Art. Luristan Tomb (Zagros Mountains).* Votive Bit. *8th-7th centuries B.C. Art Market, Teheran. Bronze, length* 4 3/4 *inches. (Photo Roman Ghirshman)*

499. *Protohistoric Art. Luristan Tomb (Zagros Mountains).* Votive Bit. *8th-7th centuries B.C. Musée du Cinquantenaire, Brussels. Bronze, height 4 inches. (Photo A.C.L., Brussels)*

500. *Protohistoric Art. Luristan Tomb (Zagros Mountains).* Votive Bit. *8th-7th centuries B.C., possibly early 6th. Private Collection, Paris. Bronze, height* 2 5/8 *inches. (Collection Photo)*

501. *Protohistoric Art. Luristan Tomb (Zagros Mountains).* Bell in the form of a Pomegranate. *8th-7th centuries B.C. Louvre, Paris. Bronze, height* 3 1/4 *inches. (Museum Photo)*

502. *Protohistoric Art. Luristan Tomb (Zagros Mountains).* Harness Piece (?). *8th-7th centuries B.C. Private Collection, New York. Bronze, height* 5 7/8 *inches. (Collection Photo)*

503. *Protohistoric Art. Luristan Tomb (Zagros Mountains).* Votive Axe. *8th-7th centuries B.C. University Museum of Philadelphia. Bronze, length* 8 1/4 *inches. (Photo Istituto Italiano per il Medio ed Estremo Oriente)*

504. *Protohistoric Art. Luristan Tomb (Zagros Mountains).* Votive Axe. *8th-7th centuries B.C. Private Collection, Teheran. Bronze, length* 7 3/4 *inches. (Photo Dr. A. Razavi)*

505. *Protohistoric Art. Luristan Tomb (Zagros Mountains).* Halberd Axe. *8th-7th centuries B.C. Private Collection, Paris. Bronze, length* 6 3/4 *inches. (Photo Istituto Italiano per il Medio ed Estremo Oriente)*

506. *Protohistoric Art. Luristan Tomb (Zagros Mountains).* Fenestrate Axe. *8th-7th centuries B.C. Private Collection, Paris. Bronze, length* 3 7/3 *inches. (Collection Photo)*

507. *Protohistoric Art. Luristan Tomb (Zagros Mountains).* Sword. *8th-7th centuries B.C. Private Collection, Teheran. Iron, length* 16 3/8 *inches. (Photo Dr. A. Razavi)*

508-509. *Protohistoric Art. Luristan Tomb (Zagros Mountains).* Human Head and Crouching Lion, details of No. 507. *8th-7th centuries B.C. Private Collection, Teheran. (Photo Dr. A. Razavi)*

510. *Protohistoric Art. Luristan Tomb (Zagros Mountains).* Belt Buckle. *8th-7th centuries B.C. Private Collection, Paris. Bronze with iron inlays, height* 8 1/2 *inches, width* 1 3/4 *inches. (Photo Dr. A. Razavi)*
Probably came originally from the Koban cemeteries in the Caucasus, but was found in a Luristan tomb.

511. *Protohistoric Art. Luristan Tomb (Zagros Mountains).* Diadem. *8th-7th centuries B.C. Museum of Fine Arts, Boston. Bronze. (Museum Photo)*

512. *Protohistoric Art. Luristan Tomb (Zagros Mountains).* Round Pinhead. *8th-7th centuries B.C. Louvre, Paris, formerly in the Coiffard Collection. Bronze, diameter* 4 1/4 *inches. (Photo Musée Cernuschi)*
Design composed of three lions, *membra disjecta* and demi-palmettes.

513. *Protohistoric Art. Luristan Tomb (Zagros Mountains).* Pinhead. *8th-7th centuries B.C. Private Collection, Teheran. Bronze, length* 2 3/8 *inches. (Photo Dr. A. Razavi)*

514. *Protohistoric Art. Luristan Tomb (Zagros Mountains).* Fibula. *8th-7th centuries B.C. Archaeological Museum, Teheran. Bronze, length 2 inches. (Museum Photo, Rostamy)*

515. *Protohistoric Art. Luristan Tomb (Zagros Mountains).* Animal-shaped Fibula. *8th-7th centuries B.C. Private Collection, Teheran. Bronze, length* 1 5/8 *inches. (Photo Dr. A. Razavi)*

516. *Protohistoric Art. Luristan Tomb (Zagros Mountains).* Vase with Long Beak-Spout. *8th-7th centuries B.C. Louvre, Paris (AO 14957). Painted terracotta. (Museum Photo)*

517. *Protohistoric Art. Luristan Tomb (Zagros Mountains).* Bottle with Lugs. *8th-7th centuries B.C. Private Collection, Teheran. Opaque glass, height* 4 1/4 *inches. (Photo Hadi)*

518. *Medo-Scythian Art. Kizkapan, near Surdash (Iraqi Kurdistan).* Rock Tomb. Right-hand capital and ceiling carved in imitation of timber-work. *Second half of 7th - first half of 6th century B.C. In situ. Rock face hollowed out and carved. (After C.J. EDMONDS, 1934, Pl. XXIII, fig. c)*

519. *Protohistoric Art. Luristan Tomb (Zagros Mountains).* Small Incised Plaque with a Worshipper. *8th-7th centuries B.C. Private Collection, Teheran. Bronze, height* ³/₄ *of an inch. (Photo Marc Foucault)*

520. *Protohistoric Art. Luristan Tomb (Zagros Mountains).* Small Incised Plaque with a Worshipper. *8th-7th centuries B.C. Private Collection, Teheran. Bronze, height 1 inch. (Photo Marc Foucault)*

521. *Protohistoric Art. Luristan Tomb (Zagros Mountains).* Small Incised Plaque with a Worshipper. *8th-7th centuries B.C. Private Collection, Teheran. Gold, height* ³/₄ *of an inch. (Photo Marc Foucault)*
The worshipper is holding a *barsom.*

522. *Protohistoric Art. Luristan Tomb (Zagros Mountains).* Vase with Long Beak-Spout and Lug in the form of a Winged Figure. *8th-7th centuries B.C. Louvre, Paris. Bronze, height* 10¹/₄ *inches. (Photo Archives d'Art et d'Histoire)*

523. Detail of No. 522. *(Photo Archives d'Art et d'Histoire)*

524. *Assyrian Art. Ziwiyeh, east of Sakkiz (Kurdistan).* Plaques with Hunting Scenes. *7th century B.C. Archaeological Museum, Teheran. Ivory carvings, height* 5³/₈ *inches, width* 3³/₈ *inches. (Photo Dr. A. Razavi)*

525. *Assyrian Art. Ziwiyeh, east of Sakkiz (Kurdistan).* Plaque with Hunting Scene. *7th century B.C. Metropolitan Museum, New York. Ivory carving, height* 6¹/₄ *inches, width* 2¹/₄ *inches. (Museum Photo)*

526. *Assyrian Art. Ziwiyeh, east of Sakkiz (Kurdistan).* Plaque with Three Registers. *7th century B.C. Archaeological Museum, Teheran. Ivory carving, height 6 inches. (Photo Dr. A. Razavi)*

527. *Assyrian Art (?). Ziwiyeh, east of Sakkiz (Kurdistan).* Plaque with Two Registers. *7th century B.C. Private Collection, Paris. Chased gold, height* 3¹/₄ *inches, width* 1⁷/₈ *inches. (Photo Roger Parry)*

528. *Urartian Art (?). Ziwiyeh, east of Sakkiz (Kurdistan).* Plaque representing a Winged Genius and an Ibex. *7th century B.C. Private Collection, Paris. Ivory inlaid with polychrome glass paste, height* 7¹/₄ *inches, width* 2¹/₈ *inches. (Photo Roger Parry)*

529-530. *Local Art. Ziwiyeh, east of Sakkiz (Kurdistan).* Rings. *Late 7th century B.C. Archaeological Museum, Teheran. Gold, width* 1¹/₈ *inches. (Photo Dr. A. Razavi)*

531. *Urartian Art (?). Ziwiyeh, east of Sakkiz (Kurdistan).* Frontlet adorned with Rosettes. *Late 7th century B.C. Archaeological Museum, Teheran. Gold inlaid with glass paste, length* 22¹/₂ *inches, width* ¹/₂ *inch. (Photo Dr. A. Razavi)*

532-537. *Local Art (?). Ziwiyeh, east of Sakkiz (Kurdistan).* Bracteae of Various Shapes. *Late 7th century B.C. Archaeological Museum, Teheran. Embossed gold, length* ⁵/₈ *of an inch. (Photo Dr. A. Razavi)*

538. *Local Art (?). Ziwiyeh, east of Sakkiz (Kurdistan).* Gauntlet with Rings. *Late 7th century B.C. Archaeological Museum, Teheran. Gold, width* 4³/₄ *inches. (Photo Dr. A. Razavi)*

539. *Local Art (?). Ziwiyeh, east of Sakkiz (Kurdistan).* Lamp (?) in the form of a Water-skin. *Late 7th century B.C. Archaeological Museum, Teheran. Bronze, height* 2¹/₂ *inches. (Photo Dr. A. Razavi)*

540. *Scythian Art. Ziwiyeh, east of Sakkiz (Kurdistan).* Harness Piece in the form of a Boar's Tusk. *Late 7th century B.C. Private Collection, Paris. Bone carving, length 2 inches. (Photo Roger Parry)*

541. *Achaemenian Art. Oxus Treasure (Bactria).* Openwork Bractea. *6th-5th centuries B.C. British Museum, London. Chased gold, diameter 2 inches. (Museum Photo)*

542. *Achaemenian Art. Oxus Treasure (Bactria).* Centrepiece of a Shield adorned with Hunting Scenes. *6th-5th centuries B.C. British Museum, London. Silver gilt, diameter* 3³/₄ *inches. (Museum Photo)*

543. *Achaemenian Art. Oxus Treasure (Bactria).* Disk adorned with an Eagle with Outspread Wings. *6th-4th centuries B.C. British Museum, London. Gold, diameter* 3⁷/₈ *inches. (Museum Photo)*

544. *Achaemenian Art. Kazbek (Caucasus).* Cup adorned with Swans. *About 500 B.C. Historical Museum, Moscow. Silver, diameter* 7¹/₄ *inches. (After J.I. SMIRNOV, 1909, fig. 13)*

545. *Achaemenian Art. Susa.* Cup adorned with Lanceolate Designs, with a Rosette in the Centre. *4th century B.C. Louvre, Paris. Silver, height* 1⁵/₈ *inches, diameter* 11¹/₈ *inches. (Photo Serge Maire)*

546. *Assyrian Art. Persepolis.* Bowl with Lion-shaped Lugs and a Cuneiform Inscription in the name of King Assurbanipal. *7th century B.C. Archaeological Museum, Teheran. Granite, height* 3⁷/₈ *inches. (Photo Dr. A. Razavi)*

547. *Achaemenian Art. Ephesus (Asia Minor).* Cup with Lanceolate Designs. *6th-5th centuries B.C. British Museum, London. Cut glass, diameter* 6⁵/₈ *inches. (Museum Photo)*

548-549. *Achaemenian Art. Hamadan (?).* Bracteae in the form of Lions Passant. *5th-4th centuries B.C. Archaeological Museum, Teheran. Gold originally inlaid, length 1 inch. (Photo Dr. A. Razavi)*

550. *Achaemenian Art. Hamadan (?).* Openwork Bractea with Two Lions in an Antithetical Pose. *5th-4th centuries B.C. Archaeological Museum, Teheran. Embossed gold, diameter* 1³/₈ *inches. (Museum Photo, Rostamy)*

551-552. *Achaemenian Art. Hamadan (?).* Bracteae in the form of Boars' Heads. *5th-4th centuries B.C. Archaeological Museum, Teheran. Chased gold, length* ³/₄ *of an inch. (Museum Photo, Rostamy)*

553-554. *Achaemenian Art. Hamadan (?).* Bracteae in the form of Roaring Lions' Heads. *5th-4th centuries B.C. Archaeological Museum, Teheran. Chased gold, length* ³/₄ *of an inch. (Museum Photo, Rostamy)*

555. *Achaemenian Art. Hamadan (?).* Bractea representing a Horned, Winged Lion enclosed in a Braided Circle. *5th-4th centuries B.C. Oriental Institute, Chicago. Chased gold, height* 1⁵/₈ *inches. (Museum Photo)*

556. *Achaemenian Art. Hamadan (?).* Pendant with Two Crossed Lions in an Octagonal Frame. *5th-4th centuries B.C. Archaeological Museum, Teheran. Chased gold, height 2 inches. (Museum Photo, Rostamy)*

557. *Achaemenian Art. Hamadan (?)*. Bractea representing Ahuramazda (?) enclosed in a Circle. *6th-4th centuries B.C. Archaeological Museum, Teheran. Chased gold, diameter* 1 ⁵/₈ inches. *(Museum Photo, Rostamy)*

558. *Achaemenian Art. Sardis (Asia Minor)*. Bractea representing Ahuramazda surrounded by Five Wings. *6th century B.C. Archaeological Museum, Istanbul. Chased gold, height* 2 ¹/₈ inches. *(After H.T. Bossert, 1942, fig. 175)*

559. *Achaemenian Art. Akhalgori (Caucasus)*. Ear-ring adorned with Graining. *4th century B.C. Tiflis Museum. Gold, diameter* 2 inches. *(After Smirnov, 1934, Pl. III)*

560. *Achaemenian Art. Hamadan (?)*. Necklace composed of cask-shaped elements and rings covered with graining, to which horned lions' heads are soldered. *5th-4th centuries B.C. Oriental Institute, Chicago. Gold, height of the heads 8 millimetres. (Museum Photo)*

561-562. *Achaemenian Art. Susa (from the 'Keep')*. Two Fragments of a Comb, adorned with a Winged Bull and a Winged Human-headed Bull. *5th-4th centuries B.C. Archaeological Museum, Teheran. Ivory carving, height* 3 ¹/₈ inches. *(Photo R. de Mecquenem)*
The wings of the bulls end in birds' heads.

563. *Achaemenian Art.* Cylinder Seal representing a King standing on a Lion and holding a Bow and Three Arrows. *5th-4th centuries B.C. Private Collection, Teheran. Chalcedony. (Photo Hadi)*

564. *Greco-Persian Art. Dascylion (Asia Minor)*. Stamp Seal representing a Battle Scene. *5th-4th centuries B.C. Museum of Ankara University. Clay. (After E. Akurgal, 1956, Pl. XII, 2)*

565. *Greco-Persian Art.* Stamp Seal representing a Combat between a Persian Horseman and a Greek Warrior. *5th-4th centuries B.C. Private Collection. Chalcedony. (After H. Seyrig, 1952, Pl. XXXI, 1)*

566. *Greco-Persian Art.* Stamp Seal representing a Boar at the Flying Gallop. *5th-4th centuries B.C. Metropolitan Museum, New York. Chalcedony. (After G. Richter, 1949, Pl. XXXV, 1)*

567. *Achaemenian Art.* Daric of Darius III (?). *4th century B.C. Private Collection, Teheran. Gold, diameter* ⁵/₈ *of an inch. (Photo Hadi)*

568. *Urartian Art. Vetulonia (Etruria), Tomba dei Lebeti.* Cauldron Handle. *8th-7th centuries B.C. Museo Archeologico, Florence (No. 9619). Engraved bronze. (Museum Photo)*

569. *Protohistoric Art. Luristan Tomb (Zagros Mountains)*. Couple seated on Two Horse Protomes. *8th-7th centuries B.C. Private Collection, Teheran. Bronze, height* 2 ¹/₂ inches, length 2 ³/₄ inches. *(Collection Photo)*

570. *Urartian Art. Toprak-kale (Armenia)*. Fragment of a Frieze of Ogee Arches. *8th-7th centuries B.C. Engraved marble. (After R.D. Barnett, 1950, fig. 15)*

571. *Urartian Art. Zakim, Kars region (Armenia)*. Belt with Animals and Archers enclosed in Ogee Arches. *7th century B.C. Engraved bronze. (After M. Ebert, R.L.V., Vol. XIII, Pl. 34a)*

572. *Urartian Art. Gusci, near Lake Urmia*. Belt with Animals and Rosettes. *7th century B.C. Metropolitan Museum, New York (No. 52.123). Bronze chased and engraved. (Museum Photo)*

573-579. *Scythian and Transcaucasian Art.* The 'Sacred Tree' as represented on Scythian and Transcaucasian Objects. *8th-7th centuries B.C. (After B.B. Piotrovsky, 1950, fig. 57)*

580. *Greek Art.* Jug with Handle. *Last quarter of the 7th century B.C. Vatican Museum, Rome. Painted terracotta,* 10 ⁵/₈ inches. *(After F. Matz, 1950, Pl. 146c)*
Two registers of animals, bipeds and quadrupeds.

581. *Greek Art. Arkadhes (Crete)*. Bowl with Handle and a Design representing Two Animals with a Single Head. *7th century B.C. Painted terracotta. (After R.D. Barnett, 1956, Pl. XXI, fig. 3)*

582. *Greek Art. Syracuse (Sicily)*. Detail of a Vase Painting representing Two Harpies with a Single Head. *640-625 B.C. Painted terracotta. (After H. Payne, 1931, Pl. 52, fig. 12)*

583. *Greek Art. Cumae (Italy)*. Aryballos with Designs on Three Registers. *Late 8th - early 7th century B.C. Museo Nazionale, Naples. Painted terracotta, height* 2 ³/₈ inches. *(After F. Matz, 1950, Pl. 143d)*

584. *Greek Art. Temple of Hera, Argos*. Bottom of a Pyxis. *7th century B.C. Painted terracotta. (After A. Rumpf, 1953, Pl. 3, 2)*

585. *Etruscan Art. Caere (Italy)*. Centrepiece of a Shield showing Three Lions around a Rosette. *7th century B.C. Museo Gregoriano, Rome. Chased bronze. (After H. Muhlestein, 1929, fig. 121)*

586. Map of Prehistoric and Protohistoric Persia (5th to first half of 1st millennium B.C.).

587. Map of Persia in the Median Period (8th to 6th century B.C.).

588. Map of Persia in the Achaemenian Period (6th to 4th century (B.C.).

589. Map of the Iranian Plateau shwing Proto-Iranian, Median and Achaemenian Sites.

590. Map of Proto-Iranian, Median and Achaemenian Persia in the Ancient World.

We would like to thank especially all the private collectors who have permitted us to show in this book significant works of art from their collections.

Jean-Luc HERMAN and Marie-Hélène MARTIN have collaborated with Roger PARRY in the design of this book. Drawings are by Marie-Hélène MARTIN. Maps by Jacques PERSON.

MAPS

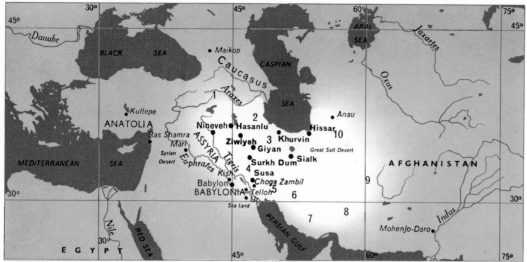

1 - URARTU
2 - MANNAI
3 - MEDIA
4 - LURISTAN
5 - ELAM
6 - PARSUMASH
7 - ANSHAN
8 - PARSA
9 - SEISTAN
10 - KHORASAN

586 - PREHISTORIC AND PROTOHISTORIC PERSIA (5th MILL. TO FIRST HALF OF 1st MILL. B.C.)

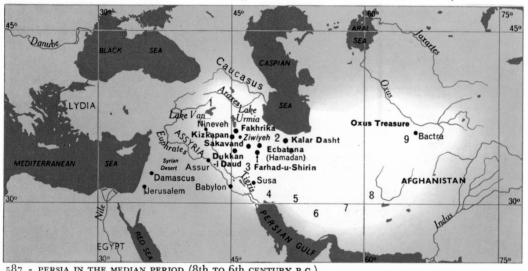

1 - URARTU
2 - MEDIA
3 - LURISTAN
4 - ELAM
5 - PARSUMASH
6 - ANSHAN
7 - PARSA
8 - SEISTAN
9 - BACTRIA

587 - PERSIA IN THE MEDIAN PERIOD (8th TO 6th CENTURY B.C.)

1 - PHRYGIA [DASCYLION]
2 - MYSIA 3 - LYDIA
4 - IONIA 5 - CARIA
6 - CILICIA 7 - LYCIA
8 - SEA PEOPLES
[CYPRUS, PHOENICIA,
SYRIA, PALESTINE]
9 - CAPPADOCIA
10 - COLCHIS
11 - ARMENIA
12 - ASSYRIA 13 - MEDIA
14 - PERSIA 15 - GEDROSIA
16 - ARACHOSIA
17 - MARGIANA
18 - CHORASMIA AND SOGDIANA
19 - BACTRIA
20 - INDIA [GANDHARA]

588 - PERSIA IN THE ACHAEMENIAN PERIOD (6th TO 4th CENTURY B.C.)

589 - THE IRANIAN PLATEAU: PROTO-IRANIAN, MEDIAN AND ACHAEMENIAN SITES

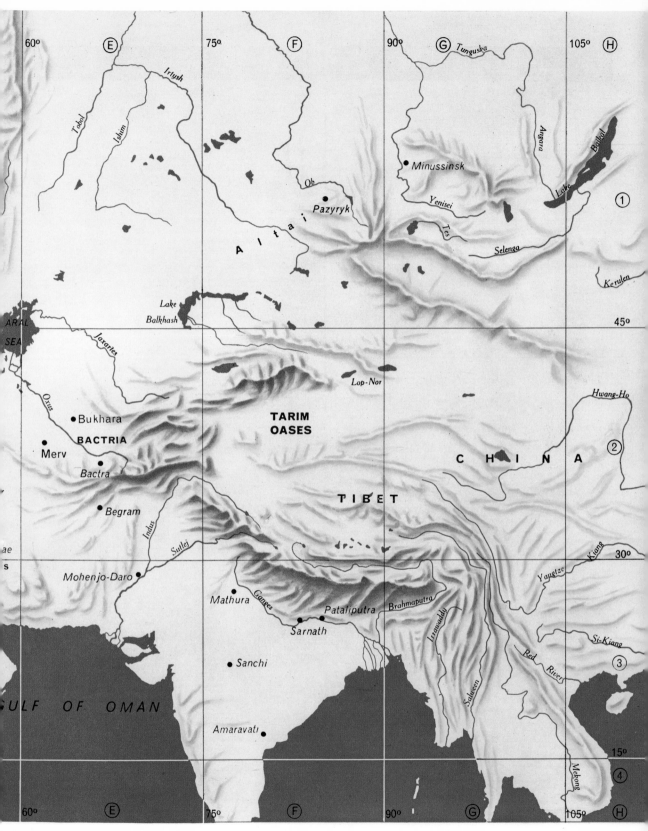

THIS, THE FIFTH VOLUME OF 'THE ARTS OF MANKIND' SERIES, EDITED BY ANDRÉ MALRAUX AND GEORGES SALLES, HAS BEEN PRODUCED UNDER THE SUPERVISION OF ALBERT BEURET, EDITOR-IN-CHARGE OF THE SERIES. THE BOOK WAS DESIGNED BY ROGER PARRY, THE TEXT AND PLATES IN BLACK AND WHITE WERE PRINTED BY L'IMPRIMERIE GEORGES LANG, PARIS; PLATES IN GREY, BISTRE AND COLOUR BY L'IMPRIMERIE DRAEGER, MONTROUGE. DESIGNED BY MASSIN, THE BINDING WAS EXECUTED BY BABOUOT, GENTILLY.

PRINTED IN FRANCE